The MacIntyre Reader

The MacIntyre Reader

Edited by Kelvin Knight

University of Notre Dame Press
Notre Dame, Indiana

Published in the U.S.A. in 1998 by
University of Notre Dame Press
Notre Dame, IN 46556
All Rights Reserved

Copyright © this collection Polity Press 1998

Published in Great Britain in 1998 by Polity Press
in association with Blackwell Publishers Ltd.

Library of Congress Cataloging-in-Publication Data

MacIntyre, Alasdair C.
    [Selections. 1998]
    The MacIntyre reader / edited by Kelvin Knight
        p.   cm.
    Includes bibliographical references and index.
    ISBN 0-268-01436-1 (alk. paper). — ISBN 0-268-01437-X (pbk. :
alk. paper)
    1. Philosophy and social sciences. 2. Aristotle. 3. Ethics.
I. Knight, Kelvin. II. Title.
    B1647.M121M33   1998
192—dc21   98-24229
                                                           CIP

Typeset in 10 on 11 pt Times New Roman
by Ace Filmsetting Ltd, Frome, Somerset
Printed in Great Britain by TJ International, Padstow, Cornwall

This book is printed on acid-free paper.

Contents

Acknowledgements and Sources

This book has benefited from the publishing expertise of David Held, Ann Bone and Richard Purslow, from the advice of John Horton, Paul Lancaster, Alasdair MacIntyre, Tolis Malakos, Seiriol Morgan, John O'Neill and Alex Reynolds, from criticisms of papers I have presented at the London School of Economics, Leeds University, Nuffield College, Oxford, the Political Studies Association and the Socialist Philosophy Group, and from criticisms of lectures I have delivered at the University of North London. My greatest thanks go to Samantha Ashenden for her encouragement, for commenting on several drafts of the introduction, and for hauling me off to Scotland at what I naively thought was the end of the task.

MacIntyre's texts are reprinted almost entirely as originally published except for the correction of typographical errors, some minor changes in punctuation and the standardization of referencing. Full references are given in the Bibliography. In the extracts from *After Virtue* and *Whose Justice? Which Rationality?* an ellipsis of three dots indicates that one or more words have been omitted, an ellipsis of four dots indicates that one or more sentences have been omitted, and an ellipsis of four dots on a separate line indicates that one or more paragraphs have been omitted between passages. In obtaining material for the Guide to Further Reading I have enlisted the help of innumerable librarians. I thank them all, and especially Megan Redmond for arranging interlibrary loans. Although I have waded through a mass of commentary on MacIntyre, only a fraction of which is listed, I cannot claim to have consulted everything that might have proven noteworthy. I apologize for all errors in editorial matters, including those of omission.

The author and publishers are grateful for permission to reproduce the following works of Alasdair MacIntyre and interviews with him:

'Notes from the Moral Wilderness', first published in *The New Reasoner*, nos 7 and 8, 1958–9, reproduced by permission of New Left Review, London.

'Social Science Methodology as the Ideology of Bureaucratic Authority', first published in Maria J. Falco, ed., *Through the Looking Glass: Epistemology and the Conduct of Enquiry,* University Press of America, 1979, reproduced by permission of the author.

'The Claims of *After Virtue*', first published in *Analyse & Kritik*, vol. 6, no. 1, 1984, reproduced by permission of Westdeutscher Verlag, Wiesbaden.

Extracts from *After Virtue: A Study in Moral Theory* (originally 1981), revised edition © 1984 by Alasdair MacIntyre, published by University of Notre Dame Press, Notre Dame, 1984, and Duckworth, London, 1985. By permission of the author and publishers.

'Précis of *Whose Justice? Which Rationality?*', first published in *Philosophy and Phenomenological Research*, vol. 51, no. 1, 1991, by permission of the publishers.

Extracts from *Whose Justice? Which Rationality?*, © 1988 by Alasdair MacIntyre, published by University of Notre Dame Press, Notre Dame, and Duckworth, London, 1988 by Alasdair MacIntyre, published by University of Notre Dame Press, Notre Dame, and Duckworth, London, 1988. By permission of the author and publishers.

'Practical Rationalities as Forms of Social Structure', first published in *Irish Philosophical Journal*, vol. 4, no. 1, 1987, by permission of Dr Bernard Cullen.

'Plain Persons and Moral Philosophy: Rules, Virtues and Goods', first published in *American Catholic Philosophical Quarterly*, vol. 66, Winter 1992, reproduced by permission of the American Catholic Philosophical Association.

First Principles, Final Ends and Contemporary Philosophical Issues, first published as the annual Aquinas Lecture, 1990, reproduced by permission of Marquette University Press.

'Moral Relativism, Truth and Justification', first published in Luke Gormally, ed., *Moral Truth and Moral Tradition: Essays in Honour of Peter Geach and Elizabeth Anscombe*, Four Courts Press, Blackrock, County Dublin, 1994, reproduced by permission of the author and publisher.

'The *Theses on Feuerbach*: A Road Not Taken', first published in Carol C. Gould and Robert S. Cohen, eds, *Artifacts, Representations, and Social Practice: Essays for Marx Wartofsky*, Kluwer Academic Publishers, 1994, by permission of the author and publisher.

'Politics, Philosophy and the Common Good', first published in Italian in *Studi Perugini*, no. 3, 1997, a special issue on the thought of Alasdair MacIntyre, published for the first time in English by permission of the author and Studi Perugini, Perugia.

Interview with Giovanna Borradori, originally published in Italian in 1991 and first published in English as 'Nietzsche or Aristotle?', in Giovanna Borradori, ed., *The American Philosopher: Conversations with Quine, Davidson, Putnam, Nozick, Danto, Rorty, Cavell, MacIntyre, and Kuhn*, University of Chicago Press, 1994. Reproduced by permission of University of Chicago Press.

Interview conducted postally for *Cogito* by Gordon Reddiford and William Watts Miller, first published in *Cogito*, vol. 5, no. 2, 1991. Reproduced by permission of Cogito.

Introduction

Revolutionary *or* communitarian, ethical *and* sociological: the most evident characteristic of Alasdair MacIntyre's work is its provocativeness. Unfortunately, the controversy that it has provoked is often ill-informed. MacIntyre's critique of 'the Enlightenment project' may be well known but his own Aristotelian project is not. This is unfortunate because his rejection of the Enlightenment's separation of reason and morality from practice and tradition is given point by the way in which he effects their recombination. The full significance of MacIntyre's demolition job in *After Virtue* is only comprehensible in the light of his construction, in subsequent essays, of the premises of an alternative.

This *Reader* collects some of MacIntyre's most important work in order to make his project fully comprehensible. Although it is entitled a 'reader', I edit it as someone unimpressed by that genre. It does not, except for the extracts from *After Virtue* and *Whose Justice? Which Rationality?*, consist of snippets but of entire arguments. MacIntyre speaks, not the editor. Nor does it include much of MacIntyre's early work. The reason for this omission is that, while MacIntyre's ideas have changed considerably over the years, his central concerns have remained the same. His early work reveals how his ideas developed but his later and self-consciously Aristotelian work reveals those ideas in their most powerful and illuminating form. If his early work raised important questions, his later work provides important answers. The aims of the *Reader* are, therefore, first to present MacIntyre's central arguments, secondly to make available some of his most important but least known work and, only thirdly, to trace the development of his ideas. This last aim is the primary reason for including two interviews and the opening paper. It is also the reason for this introduction. The remainder of this introduction is arranged into six parts, corresponding to the arrangement of MacIntyre's works below.

Part I: Establishing the Project

Only one very early paper is included, to indicate the origin of MacIntyre's project. Written when he was twenty-nine, and already author of books on Marx and Freud (see Further Reading), 'Notes from the Moral Wilderness' was one of the most widely respected papers of the pre-1968 New Left in Britain. Formerly a member of the Communist Party, MacIntyre had left before the shocks of 1956: Khrushchev's revelations about Stalin, and the Red Army's crushing of the Hungarian uprising. Differentiating Stalinism from Marxism, MacIntyre first joined a dogmatically Trotskyist group. Then, after being expelled with other semi-syndicalists who objected to the deceit of 'entryism' in the Labour Party, he joined another, less dogmatic one. Throughout this period he attempted to maintain both a commitment to Leninist forms of revolutionary organization and links to those who abandoned the Communist Party in 1956 to create such vehicles for a New Left as the *New Reasoner*. He was, however, to become increasingly disillusioned with all forms of Marxist politics, his resignation as an editor of *International Socialism* being announced in 1968, just in time to avoid association with the posturing of the second and final wave of the New Left.

'Notes from the Moral Wilderness' was a contribution to a debate, initiated by E. P. Thompson in the first issue of the *New Reasoner*, on 'socialist humanism'. The debate was joined by Charles Taylor, Harry Hanson and others, who suggested the culpability of Marxism for Stalinism and the desirability of freeing humanism from socialism. MacIntyre entered the lists in defence of Marx and Lenin. As he told fellow Trotskyists, the New Left were right in observing 'that capitalism tends to corrupt our whole cultural and social life' but wrong to claim 'that it is possible to build community under capitalism'. The conclusion that he then drew, the 'thesis which Marxists must consistently develop in discussions on the New Left', was 'that the only way to overcome the corruption of our culture is through the achievement of working-class power' ('The "New Left" ', pp. 99–100).

What is striking about 'Notes from the Moral Wilderness' is not the dogmatism that this stricture suggests but, on the contrary, the candour with which its author admitted the problems for his project of elaborating a genuinely 'Marxist alternative to liberal morality' (below, p. 36). If this alternative could not be the 'means–ends model of morality' of Stalinism, what could it be? It would have to take the form of a 'general theory of society' that combined morality with history, values with facts. This theory would have to avoid the arbitrariness of individual choice by providing a common moral image for society on the basis of Marx's revision of Hegel's account of human nature. MacIntyre attempted to elaborate such a theory but admitted a lack of clarity as to how this might be done that suggests, in retrospect, that the task was impossible and that neither Marx nor Hegel provide self-sustainable foundations

upon which one might construct a thoroughgoing alternative to liberalism. Only later was MacIntyre to accept that there is no Marxist concept
of human nature capable of informing an alternative to liberals' variously
individualist moralities. Then, as now, he wanted to combine 'an assertion of moral absolutes' with 'an assertion of desire and of history', but
then, unlike now, he also seemed to believe that history was on his side,
that morality and desire, 'ought' and 'is', 'Man' and 'men' might be
definitively combined in a communist millennium.

The second half of the paper prefigures aspects of *After Virtue*. MacIntyre
compared the unintelligibility of modern morality to that of 'primitive
taboos' in which 'the rules still have point, but men have forgotten what
their point is'. He noted, all too briefly, Aquinas's combination of 'an
Aristotelian view of desire with a Christian view of the moral law', liberals' later separation of desire from rules and, following that separation,
Nietzsche's rejection of the constraint of social rules upon individual
desire now that the point of those rules, in teleological reasoning, had
been forgotten. Already the outline of MacIntyre's critique of liberal
morality was apparent. What was not yet apparent, even to MacIntyre,
was any solid ground from which to advance that critique.

Critics of 'Notes from the Moral Wilderness' fastened on an illustra-
tion of MacIntyre's Marxist morality, that of viewing 'with equal contempt those [Stalinists] who failed to protest at Nagy's murder [after a
secret trial of this leader of the Hungarian revolt] and those [liberals] who
jump to protest at the late Cuban trials' in which Castro's enemies were
condemned to death (below, p. 48). What they criticized was the arbitrariness with which MacIntyre dismissed their own liberal claims in favour of a third, ostensibly Marxist, position. MacIntyre claimed history
as his warrant for that position, yet history only appears as such a basis
once one has chosen to adopt Marx's materialist conception of it. How
might such circularity be justified?

As yet, MacIntyre had no answer. Nor had he any answer when he
wrote his celebrated *A Short History of Ethics*. Here, again, he traced the
historical development of moral concepts, but no longer posed Marxism
as their culmination. He did, though, still invoke Marx in the book's
conclusion. Marx, he noted, envisaged a form of society in which individuals agree on ends and, therefore, on rules, virtues and what is meant
by 'good'. Such a society had existed, MacIntyre suggested, in classical
Greece but, as it exists no more, 'moralizing can no longer play a genuine
role in settling social differences' (*A Short History of Ethics*, 1967, pp.
267–8). Whereas others who had also been influenced by the later
Wittgenstein spoke of separate cultures having incommensurable and even
mutually unintelligible forms of life, MacIntyre perceived such forms of
life coexisting within the culture of the contemporary West.

> We live with the inheritance of not only one, but of a number of well-
> integrated moralities. . . . It follows that we are liable to find two kinds

of people in our society: those who speak from within one of these surviving moralities, and those who stand outside all of them. Between the adherents of rival moralities and between the adherents of one morality and the adherents of none there exists no court of appeal, no impersonal neutral standard. For those who speak from within a given morality, the connection between fact and valuation is established in virtue of the meanings of the words they use. To those who speak from without, those who speak from within appear merely to be uttering imperatives which express their own liking and their private choices. The controversy between emotivism and prescriptivism on the one hand and their critics on the other thus expresses the fundamental moral situation of our own society. (*A Short History of Ethics*, p. 266)

MacIntyre is here making a truth-claim about the social and historical form of morality, not about its content. Morality is about how people live together, about society and therefore history, not about hypothetically presocial individuals. The problem we now face, in the absence of either an agreed morality or of an 'impersonal neutral standard', would appear to be one that can only be solved by 'private choice': 'Each of us . . . has to choose both with whom we wish to be morally bound and by what ends, rules and virtues we wish to be guided' (*A Short History of Ethics*, p. 268). This solution need not appear incompatible with Marxism (at least if Sartre is regarded as a Marxist) but nor does it derive from Marxism; Marxism is simply posed as one perspective, the one which MacIntyre happens to have chosen for himself. Such adherence to one given morality, any morality, is, as the only alternative to 'social solipsism', what 'I must adopt . . . if I am to have any social relationships' (*A Short History of Ethics*, p. 268). MacIntyre here seems to acknowledge that he is trapped not only in the moral relativism of 'our own society' but also in an existential priority of individual choice, a priority of 'I' to 'we' as he had put it in 'Notes from the Moral Wilderness'. He still appeared far from escaping the fundamental arbitrariness of individual choice and moral relativism to which, nevertheless, he remained profoundly opposed.

Part II: Combining Social Science with Moral Theory

Over twenty years after writing 'Notes from the Moral Wilderness' MacIntyre referred back to it in prefacing *After Virtue*. 'Embodied in this book', he explained, is his conclusion

that Marxism's moral defects and failures arise from the extent to which it, like liberal individualism, embodies the *ethos* of the distinctively modern and modernizing world, and that nothing less than a rejection of a large part of that ethos will provide us with a rationally and morally defensible standpoint from which to judge and to act – and in terms of which to evaluate various rival and heterogeneous moral schemes which compete for our allegiance. (*After Virtue*, 2nd edn, 1985, p. x)

He continues to hold to this position, noting recently that 'those who make the conquest of state power their aim are always in the end conquered by it and, in becoming the instruments of the state, themselves become in time the instruments of one of the several versions of modern capitalism' (*Marxism and Christianity*, 2nd edn, 1995, p. xv). Under capitalism what should be regarded as means instead come to be institutionalized as ends in themselves.

This is true not only of capital but also of political power. 'All power tends to coopt and absolute power coopts absolutely,' as MacIntyre put it in *After Virtue*. Marxists failed to understand this, blithely predicting that under their rule the state would 'wither away'. It was not a Marxist but the greatest sociological opponent of socialism, Max Weber, who analysed the characteristically modern form of impersonal rationality institutionalized by capitalism and by bureaucracy, the form of amorally goal-orientated, instrumental or 'means-ends' reasoning excoriated by MacIntyre in 'Notes from the Moral Wilderness'. Socialists, seeking to promote the rational administration of society, would simply further this process of bureaucratic modernization and instrumental rationalization. 'As Marxists organize and move toward power they always do and have become Weberians in substance ... for in our culture we know of no organized movement towards power which is not bureaucratic and managerial in mode and we know of no justifications for authority' other than those couched in terms of instrumental effectiveness (*After Virtue*, p. 109).

In one of his first papers after emigration to the United States in 1970 MacIntyre attacked the 'epistemological self-righteousness' that would-be revolutionaries share with the ' "bourgeois" ' social scientists they criticize. Both claim a knowledge superior to that of 'ordinary agents' and thereby adhere to 'the ideology of expertise [that] embodies a claim to privilege with respect to power' ('Ideology, Social Science, and Revolution', pp. 322, 340, 342). MacIntyre rejected that ideology. As he was to put it in *After Virtue*:

What if effectiveness were a quality widely imputed to managers and bureaucrats both by themselves and others, but in fact a quality which rarely exists apart from this imputation? .... It is specifically and only managerial and bureaucratic expertise that I am going to put in question. And the conclusion to which I shall finally move is that such expertise does indeed turn out to be one more moral fiction, because the kind of knowledge which would be required to sustain it does not exist. But what would it be like if social control were indeed a masquerade? Consider the following possibility: that what we are oppressed by is not power, but impotence; that one key reason why the presidents of large corporations do not, as some radical critics believe, control the United

States is that they do not even succeed in controlling their own corporations. (*After Virtue*, p. 75)

MacIntyre was less concerned here with attacking Stalinist state capitalists, whose 'totalitarian project' he already considered likely to be defeated by more flexible versions of capitalism (*After Virtue*, p. 106), than
with attacking pretensions to a 'value-free' or neutral social science. The
power of managers is legitimated by imputations of effectiveness, as the
epigoni who follow Weber in organization studies well recognize. These
Weberians explain and justify such imputations by describing managerial
techniques as expressions of an instrumental form of reasoning that is
concerned with finding the most efficient means by which to achieve
given ends but unconcerned about the substance of those ends. They
claim that this is the form of rationality capable of delivering the goods,
assuming, as they do, that we already know what the goods are. The
increasing dominance of such instrumental rationality is, on these Weberian
accounts, what is most distinctive about the ethos of the modern and
modernizing world. And, to this extent, these accounts are accurate. That
is to say, a central characteristic of modernity is indeed the dominance of
the belief that rationality is properly understood as instrumental and,
because actions are informed by beliefs, that belief really is effective (even
though it is not effective in the way that thousands of MBAs and management students are taught that it is).

For MacIntyre, none of this entails that the belief is right. Whereas
social scientists and managers claim that their form of reasoning is superior to that of ordinary people, MacIntyre denies this, arguing instead for
a kind of reasoning that combines facts with values and means with ends.
The dominance of instrumental reason is, we might say, ideological, in
that it obscures the significance of means for ends, of practice for theory,
of production for producers, and of conceptual contestability and social
conflict for all of these.

To characterize Weberianism as ideological is not to imply that we
should seek some more 'positive' and predictive form of knowledge, which
MacIntyre considered unattainable (largely for reasons now commonly
advanced in terms of 'risk' or 'chaos'). What we should do is 'discover
the distortions of ideology first of all in ourselves and learn to live with
them, at the same time that we learn, through self-conscious awareness,
to avoid being their victims' ('Ideology, Social Science, and Revolution',
p. 337). By the time he wrote 'Social Science Methodology as the Ideology of Bureaucratic Authority' it was no longer simply to awareness of
oneself that MacIntyre appealed in opposing the ideology of managerial
expertise but to an Aristotelian understanding of work, to workers' resistance informed by that understanding, and to an awareness of 'tradition' as always resistant to managerial rationality. He had by now
abandoned his original aim of elaborating 'a new approach to moral
issues' (below, p. 31) and instead aimed to revive and revise an approach

far older than that of liberalism itself. He had also abandoned his original plan for his work in the 1970s, which had 'been to write two quite independent books: one on the fate of morality in the modern world, another on the philosophy of the social sciences. But the argument of each book turned out to require the argument of the other' ('Moral Rationality, Tradition, and Aristotle', p. 447). At last MacIntyre, by combining his historical sociology with Aristotelian ethics, could discern an intellectually compelling way to avoid the epistemological self-righteousness shared by the followers of Enlightenment philosophers, of Marx, and of Weber.

MacIntyre argued in *After Virtue* that Weberianism's articulation of the modern ethos is complemented by that of what he called emotivism. The term emotivism is usually used to denote the doctrine, inspired by Hume and enunciated in mid-twentieth century by logical positivists, that moral statements are neither true nor false but express only the subjective feelings or attitudes of their speaker. For positivists, statements about facts are objectively meaningful because empirically verifiable, but statements about values are not. More generally, this distinction between facts and values, between 'is' and 'ought' statements, is one of the elemental distinctions drawn by many 'analytic' (typically Anglo-American) philosophers, and perhaps the most important one. It is a distinction to which MacIntyre has always been opposed. MacIntyre, therefore, did not claim that emotivism is true. Perhaps perplexingly, nor did he claim that emotivism is straightforwardly false. Rather, he claimed that it accurately describes an increasingly prevalent belief about moral claims. Like Weberianism, it apprehends an aspect of contemporary reality. As with the idea of rationality as instrumental, it postulates a reality in which ends are presumed to be subjective and beyond the reach of reason. Emotivists infer that moral stipulations, in so far as they are susceptible of explanation, must be regarded as instrumental to the subjective goals of the stipulators. Therefore emotivists, like Weberians, fail to distinguish 'between manipulative and non-manipulative social relations' (below, p. 73). The ways in which we pursue our goals cannot but profoundly affect, and be affected by, others. In the absence of agreement with others upon common goals we must, therefore, either sacrifice our ends or manipulate others as means to them. Not only does emotivism accurately describe a current reality but it also describes what necessarily obtains in a society the institutions of which are organized in accordance with an instrumental conception of rationality.

Emotivists are, nevertheless, on MacIntyre's account, cruder than Weberians (or, at least, than Weber) in that they extrapolate from an apprehension of modernity certain postulates that they claim are universally and necessarily valid. In this, at least, their reasoning resembles that of the seminal figures of the Enlightenment. Enlightenment thinkers considered their common project to be an epistemological one, a search of individuals' senses and faculties for new and indubitable foundations upon which to construct a comprehensive framework for objective knowledge. Unlike latter-day social scientists, most Enlightenment philosophers intended those premises to provide for moral knowledge. Kant, in responding to Hume, propounded the influential idea that empirical knowledge and moral imperatives have separate bases. MacIntyre agrees with Kant, in opposition to Hume, that 'ought' implies 'can' (and that 'passions' ought to be subordinated to reason). But he opposes both Kant and Hume in arguing that 'ought' derives from 'is'. And, in further opposition to analytic philosophy, he argues that not individuated actions but social practices are the real stuff of ethics.

What united Hume, Kant and others in a single project was, for MacIntyre, their agreement that the prerequisite for enlightenment was the rejection of their Aristotelian heritage. A central part of what they thereby rejected was a syllogistic way of justifying the rules of morality on the bases not only of an apprehension of 'man-as-he-happens-to-be' but also of 'human-nature-as-it-could-be-if-it-realized-its-*telos*' (below, p. 77). In so doing, claims MacIntyre, they rejected the only way of coherently moving from an apprehension of what is to an apprehension of what ought to be. Only when apprehended as the only means by which to move from one's present self to one's *telos*, to one's true good in society with others, can it be concluded that the rules of morality are categorical. What followed from Enlightenment philosophers' rejection of teleology was their interminable disagreement about how the rules of morality might be justified, insoluble problems in the proposals of each being identified by others. It is these problems, and that interminability, that make clear the failure of the Enlightenment's aim of justifying the rules of morality. Following this failure people understandably concluded that, though what constitutes knowledge might be ascertained with regard to natural science, this is not possible in ethics or politics.

After Virtue concludes in a chapter entitled 'After Virtue: Nietzsche *or* Aristotle, Trotsky *and* St Benedict' (see below). Before Weber and before emotivism it was Nietzsche who first and most compellingly argued that the Enlightenment's project of justifying the rules of morality had failed, proposing that this problem be solved by rejecting those rules and replacing them with the will to power of the *Übermensch*. MacIntyre endorsed Nietzsche's critique of the Enlightenment but argued that the critique does not work against Aristotle's teleological justification of those rules and of the virtues. MacIntyre therefore also opposes Nietzsche's proposed solution. Instead, MacIntyre cited Trotsky and St Benedict as exemplars of what Aristotle called friendship. Both the advocate of party-led world revolution and the advocate of communal retreat exemplified the virtues necessary for the cooperative pursuit of shared goals. Such political friendship is necessary for pursuit of a shared and reasoned good under the hostile conditions of the post-Enlightenment dark ages.

If we return to the passages quoted above from *A Short History of*

Ethics it may appear that what MacIntyre presented there was a radically criterionless choice between alternatives. As he was to observe later (below, p. 261), that book 'should perhaps have ended by giving Nietzsche the final word' rather than in existential angst. However, a criterion of sorts can be perceived even there. What MacIntyre then identified as imperative was making a choice between alternative forms of life so as to avoid 'solipsism' and have 'social relationships'. What a consistent Nietzscheanism entails, MacIntyre now emphasized in *After Virtue*, is precisely the eschewal of relationships, as exemplified by the lonely character of Nietzsche himself (below, pp. 95–7; whereas MacIntyre wrote of the unpopularity of 'an intelligent Nietzschean', there are presently plenty of fashionably inconsistent ones). It would seem that the reason why MacIntyre never allowed Nietzsche the final word, even when he could find no answer to Nietzsche's perspectivism, is that the presuppositions of Nietzscheanism exclude any conception of society other than as mutual struggle. It is, MacIntyre now claimed, 'the tradition of the virtues' that sustains social relations.

MacIntyre was well aware that he had not yet laid sufficient bases from which to refute Nietzsche, a task he put off until later. More immediately, he tried to improve the Aristotelian tradition of the virtues by refuting some basic elements of Aristotle's own philosophy. 'Philosophy', MacIntyre claimed, 'necessarily has a sociological, or as Aristotle would have said, political starting-point' (*After Virtue*, p. 148). Yet Aristotle himself did not quite claim this. On the contrary, as MacIntyre acknowledged, 'in Aristotle's account [the concept of a virtue] is secondary to that of *the good life for man* conceived as the *telos* of human action' (below, p. 82). This is what MacIntyre famously rejected in *After Virtue* as 'Aristotle's metaphysical biology' (below, pp. 80, 89; in the first edition of *After Virtue* he also rejected 'any teleology in nature'), suggesting that what Aristotle said about human nature had proven as partial as what he said about piscine nature. No doubt this rejection was prompted in part by MacIntyre's own previous failure to derive an ethics from either Hegel's or Marx's account of human nature. In part, also, he rejected Aristotle's 'ahistorical' conception of the nature of political animals (which was the original source for those later and more egalitarian accounts) because Aristotle's exclusion from that nature of women, slaves and craftsmen is clearly, in historical retrospect, a failure of Aristotle's reasoning to overcome his culturally specific presuppositions (*After Virtue*, p. 159). And, in part, MacIntyre rejected it because its positing of a unitary *telos* for the sake of which all lesser goods are pursued is incompatible with his own sociological or political idea of a tragic conflict between different kinds of good. He described this idea as Heraclitean or Sophoclean, although these terms might well be replaced by 'Nietzschean', and, in any case, Isaiah Berlin and others had more recently made the idea a liberal commonplace. This post-Enlightenment qualification of Aristotle helped prevent MacIntyre from drawing any more than his notoriously 'provisional conclusion' that 'the good life for man is the life spent in seeking for the good life for man' (below, p. 91).

MacIntyre's major difference from Aristotle in *After Virtue* was his attempt to elaborate wholly sociological and non-metaphysical premises or first principles for philosophy. In this respect MacIntyre remained something of a Marxist. He rejected Aristotle's metaphysics largely because he thought it afforded no way of apprehending the kind of radical social and ideological conflict that he, like Marx, considered pervasive in modern society. He presented the logic of his argument as proceeding from entirely sociological premises. 'A moral philosophy . . . characteristically presupposes a sociology' (below, p. 73). Virtue ethics, unlike emotivism, cannot presuppose a positive or value-neutral sociology but nor can it any longer simply take its presuppositions from the surrounding culture. What it requires is a historically informed but somehow teleological sociology, and this is what MacIntyre produced. What the concept of a virtue is secondary to on his account is not a metaphysical biology but a 'logical development' of three stages in which 'each later stage presupposes the earlier, but not *vice versa*'. The foundational concept is that of a practice, followed by that of 'the narrative order of a single human life' (which should be spent seeking for its social, non-metaphysical good) and, thirdly, 'a moral tradition' (below, p. 82). The idea of a social practice (partially inspired by Wittgenstein) therefore served as the basic supposition or, more accurately, the first principle of the argument of *After Virtue*.

What defines each of the numerous examples of a practice cited by MacIntyre is a particular goal or good internal to it and common to its practitioners. In pursuing this internal good, practitioners are able to achieve excellence of character, or virtue. To be virtuous is to emulate the rules of morality rather than simply obey them because one is commanded to do so. Practices are the schools of the virtues. Justice, courage and truthfulness are cultivated through participation in practices, as practitioners come to find in a practice something beyond themselves that may be valued for its own sake rather than as a mere means to satisfy their more immediate and selfish desires. Practitioners recognize that they can only achieve such an internal good by doing what is required to emulate the standards of excellence already established within the practice. (That individuals' transformation through subordinating themselves to standards of excellence internal to practices is itself partially constitutive of the moral good of practices led MacIntyre to later rename the 'internal goods' of practices 'goods of excellence'.) They also recognize that such goods are goods not only for themselves but also for other practitioners and for the wider society, not least because they comprise its moral structure and shared way of life and because their pursuit is what produces moral, intellectual and technological progress. Anything that does not promote justice, courage and truthfulness within individuals, and anything that does not aim in this and other ways to promote the common good of society, is not properly regarded as a practice.

Not all goods are internal to practices. MacIntyre called (and calls) money, power and (again following Weber) status goods external to practices, instrumental goods, or goods of effectiveness. These, he emphasized, 'genuinely are goods' (below, p. 89) although they are not properly regarded as goods in themselves but only as means to further ends. They are external to practices in the sense that they may be used in pursuit of goods that are internal to practices, or in acquiring more of the same, or in satisfying immediate needs or desires. They are also external to practices in the sense that they may be acquired through participation in any practice or in none. They are zero-sum rather than common goods; not goals that may be shared but things that one individual can only possess to the exclusion of others. Nor do they correspond to excellences of character, their acquisition more likely to be impeded than assisted by such virtues as justice and truthfulness. They are the currency of what MacIntyre calls institutions.

MacIntyre's distinction between practices and institutions is what makes his sociology of practices more rigorously analytical than that of any other theorist, and also more value-laden and political. Institutions are necessary for the organization and sustenance of practices. However, these indispensable institutions constantly threaten to corrupt practices and demoralize practitioners, to subordinate pursuit of internal goods to that of external goods. This is the case with the present domination of practices by the characteristically modern institutions that are bureaucratic nation-states, organized for the sake of monopolizing and exercising coercive power, and capitalist corporations, organized for the sake of profit. To act effectively in a society it is necessary to adopt that society's ethos or presuppositions. Therefore the most effective kinds of people in modern society are those such as managers who characteristically attempt to affect the actions of others by manipulation rather than by rational argument. Such characters presume that ends are necessarily subjective, given, and beyond the reach of reason and that this warrants them exercising power over others. MacIntyre disagrees, contending that institutions ought to be organized for the sake of practices and practices for the sake of goods of excellence. For example, a university should be organized for the sake of enquiry and enquiry for the sake of truth, not profit. Unfortunately, it is now the tail that wags the dog.

Part III: Establishing a Tradition of Practical Rationality

As MacIntyre had anticipated, his explicit posing of a choice of Nietzsche *or* Aristotle and his implied criterion for making that choice intrigued many but persuaded few. Most critics alleged that he was once again facing that arbitrariness of individual choice which he had always resisted but which seems implicated in the very consideration of apparently incommensurable alternatives. What he still appeared to be confronted by was the characteristically post-Enlightenment problem of relativism.

The first text in part III is MacIntyre's précis of the argument of *Whose Justice? Which Rationality?*, a book which, as he announced in the post-script to the second edition of *After Virtue*, he wrote as the latter's sequel. However, like *After Virtue*, this later book encapsulated a lot of rethinking. In writing on 'what rationality is' and, separately, on 'different and incompatible conceptions of justice', MacIntyre came to realize that those 'conceptions of justice are characteristically closely linked to different and incompatible conceptions of practical rationality'. As with the development of *After Virtue*, so with that of its sequel, 'what had been originally conceived of as two distinct tasks became one' (*Whose Justice? Which Rationality?*, p. ix). I suggest, however, that this task may itself be understood in two stages, even though such simplification cannot but do violence to MacIntyre's philosophy. The second stage comprises his controversial metatheory or second-order theory of theory, his account of philosophy in terms of rival conceptual schemes and of these in terms of their histories. The texts in part IV all pertain to this second stage. The remaining texts in part III pertain instead to a prior stage comprising a substantive or first-order theory of practices and practical rationality. They therefore elaborate further upon the sociological premises of the ethical argument of *After Virtue*.

In elaborating upon the argument of *After Virtue* MacIntyre was to recharacterize the tradition of which his project forms a part, referring to it not just as the tradition of the virtues but also as a socially embodied tradition and as a tradition of practical rationality. For MacIntyre, practical rationality guides individual action but it derives from the practices that structure society. Practical rationality comprises the rationalities of particular practices and of individuals as practitioners. As such, it opposes the ideology of expertise that seeks to replace direct relations between practitioners with hierarchical administration and to replace reasoning with routine.

MacIntyre poses Aristotelianism less as *a* tradition of practical rationality than as *the* tradition of practical rationality, as the tradition that articulates the kind of teleological reasoning exemplified by those who act in pursuit of goods of excellence internal to social practices. To pursue a good of excellence is to cultivate the virtues by subordinating oneself and one's relations with others to the kind of teleological reasoning that is internal (and in that sense relative) to a particular social practice. It is only by participating in a particular practice and emulating the highest standards achieved within it that one can learn, as an apprentice learns, how to exercise sound judgment with regard to what is the best or most perfected example of a good yet achieved. It is only by becoming proficient in such judgment that one might be able to exceed previously established standards and advance the kind of reasoning that is internal to the practice and, thereby, the kind of knowledge to which that reasoning gives rise. To reason better about how to build a house is to advance knowledge about how houses can best be built. The rules of practices are made to be broken, but only by those who have become so proficient in practical reason that they know better than those who previously framed the rules. This is how such practices as building or chess or physics progress.

As *the* tradition of such practical rationality Aristotelianism 'may be socially embodied in times and places where Aristotle himself receives no acknowledgement', such as among not only Trotskyists but even Chinese communists and others in non-Western cultures. Aristotelianism, it transpires, is not only a philosophical but also a 'social tradition' (below, p. 133). In *Whose Justice? Which Rationality?*, as in *After Virtue*, MacIntyre begins his historical account of this tradition (as he had his *Short History* of Western ethics before) by exploring the ethos of the kind of society that preceded Aristotle, as described by Homer. In such a 'heroic' and 'prephilosophical' society one is conscious of oneself in terms of one's role and conscious of what one ought to do in terms of the requirements of that role. One's social relations are structured by one's role and by the respective roles of others, each of whom is required to act in the way appropriate to their particular role. To fail to act in such a way is to act wrongly and unjustly, to derange the social order. Aristotelianism developed as a philosophical tradition following the supersession of this society by the classical *polis*. People's proper performance of their roles continued to be a condition of social order but social change was accompanied by scrutiny of what had previously been the unquestioned presuppositions of action. Socrates elevated such questioning into a search for truth, leading Plato to universalize ideas that Aristotle turned into the essential goals of natural kinds.

To be human is to act rationally in society with others. This involves identifying a good to be pursued, identifying the action most likely to secure that good under present conditions, and therefore acting accordingly. This was described by Aristotle in his syllogistic account of the general form of practical reasoning. To act justly is to give everyone and everything its due. Action is to be undertaken for the sake of some good, lesser goods being pursued for the sake of greater goods, the greatest good being that of the good life. Four implications of this are especially noteworthy. First, both ends and means are subject to reason. Secondly, reasoning about means cannot be merely instrumental because reason and action are themselves partially constitutive of that for which they are undertaken. Thirdly, practical reasoning necessarily results in action. Finally, rationality can be articulated in ways that are no longer simply cultural and conventional but also philosophical and critical.

Aristotelianism is faced by other, incompatible and rival conceptions of practical rationality in modern Western culture. That which MacIntyre gives most attention to in *Whose Justice? Which Rationality?* and in 'Practical Rationalities as Forms of Social Structure' was best articulated by Hume. In Hume's schema it is only means that are subject to reason, ends being given by natural passions. As ends are fully prior to and separate from means, means stand in a merely instrumental relation to ends. Social order is sustained, and the passions and the choice of means to their satisfaction is constrained, not by reason but by the 'artificial virtues' or, in other words, by habit and convention. Hume thereby reduces practical rationality to instrumental rationality, giving theoretical expression to the institutions of eighteenth-century aristocratic English society and (together with Adam Smith) legitimating these as the historically evolved effect of human nature.

MacIntyre also takes care to differentiate a third conception of practical rationality, that of contemporary liberalism. This conception of practical rationality differs from Hume's in that ends are no longer considered to arise from natural passions but are considered as entirely subjective preferences. No longer is choice of ends and means constrained by common convention and by laws which properly formalize such convention, but only by the enforcement of laws that are supposed to comprise a neutral ground upon which individuals can bargain with one another. (At this point MacIntyre makes the familiar charge against liberals that such procedures, far from being neutral as between rival conceptions of the good life, presuppose and enforce the form of practical reasoning that he here describes.) Contemporary liberals' form of practical reasoning differs from those of both Hume and Aristotle in that its execution does not require the execution of any action as its corollary. MacIntyre hereby consigns to liberalism affirmation of the idea of tragic conflict; because the liberal self is simultaneously subject to a range of different desires, those desires must themselves be ranked according to preference so that pursuit of some ends is necessarily undertaken at the expense of others. Contemporary liberalism therefore legitimates not only manipulation but also passivity.

Both Humean and contemporary liberals prioritize and promote goods of effectiveness over goods of excellence. Both consider that goods of effectiveness must be good, as these are means to a plurality of other ends, whereas the value of what Aristotelians regard as goods of excellence is contingent upon (for Humeans) passion and convention or (for contemporary liberals) individual preference. Both Humean and contemporary liberals regard money, power and status as susceptible to rational evaluation but anything postulated as a final end to be beyond the scope of reason. Both articulate the presuppositions of a social order that found early institutional embodiment in a legally regulated market and was then increasingly reinforced by bureaucratic organization. Their socially embodied tradition had much earlier philosophical expression (by Thucydides, Isocrates and others) within the classical *polis*, in rivalry to Aristotelianism, but had found those conditions far less propitious. However, now that what may be crudely described as this tradition of instrumental rationality is dominant, it is likely that it will further subordinate Aristotelian forms of rational practice in the future. The breakdown of liberal ideas of market, legal and bureaucratic neutrality is likely to be taken to warrant ever more explicit expressions of the will to power. In this way, instrumental rationality will have been legitimated initially by a conception of it as embodied in social convention, then by a conception of it as embodied only in the preferences of asocial individuals, and finally by a conception of it as surpassing and subordinating social relations altogether. In each of these conceptions, instrumental rationality is undifferentiated from practical rationality. MacIntyre, in contrast, conceives practical rationality as neither merely conventional nor merely subjective but as reasoning about practice, about what should be done in society with others.

In 'Plain Persons and Moral Philosophy' the thrust of MacIntyre's argument remains 'at the level of practice', at which 'the ability to judge and to act in accordance with the precepts of the natural law, the ability to acquire an increasing set of dispositions to act virtuously, and the ability to judge rightly about goods are all exercised as aspects of one and the same complex ability, the ability to engage in sound practical reasoning' (below, p. 150). People are naturally endowed with such an ability. This ability may be reflectively strengthened by Aristotelianism but may be negated by the effects of institutional domination legitimated by rival conceptions of rationality. An Aristotelian's answer to the question 'whose rationality?' is 'that of plain persons'. The practical form of reasoning articulated by MacIntyre's Aristotelianism is that of those whom Nietzsche dismissed as 'the herd'.

The moral disorder of our emotivist culture and the institutionalized dominance of instrumental rationality do not, it now seems, prevent us from engaging in an Aristotelian form of practical reasoning. On the contrary, our everyday engagement in social practices impels us to so reason. MacIntyre has not thereby reneged on his previous condemnations of either liberalism or its capitalist embodiments, or on what he said in *After Virtue* about the incoherence of contemporary moral reasoning, or yet on what he said there about Nietzscheanism as the heir of liberalism. What he has done is develop his account of practices into a conception of the social embodiment of Aristotelian rationality that suggests that it is more robust than he previously suggested. What he has reneged on is his previous dismissal of Aristotle's metaphysical conception of human nature, now locating such a nature within a 'teleologically ordered . . . theistic universe' (below, p. 152). No longer are the foundations of his first-order theory merely sociological. Practices are simultaneously ineliminable constituents of various forms of social order and necessary consequences of our political, or social and rational, nature. The conflict between practical rationality and instrumental rationality, and between their respective social embodiments, is therefore set to continue.

Part IV: Challenging Contemporary Philosophy

It is not MacIntyre's substantive theory of practical rationality but what
I have crudely differentiated as his second-order theory of theory that has
preoccupied his numerous critics within academic philosophy over the
past decade (see Guide to Further Reading). Most of these critics have
regarded MacIntyre as being primarily concerned with elaborating both
a history of philosophy and a theory of knowledge in terms of rival
traditions. MacIntyre anticipated such misunderstanding of *Whose Justice? Which Rationality?*, attempting to pre-empt it at the beginning of the
book's concluding chapter: 'it is important to remind ourselves that the
discussion of the nature of tradition-constituted and tradition-constitutive enquiry has been undertaken not for its own sake but in order to
arrive, so far as is possible, at a true account of justice and of practical
rationality' (*Whose Justice? Which Rationality?*, p. 389; see also below, p.
105).

It would be inaccurate to say that MacIntyre's critics have wholly
disregarded his substantive account of practical rationality. Rather they
have usually understood that account in terms of his second-order theory.
So, when MacIntyre reiterates that 'philosophical theories give organized
expression to concepts and theories already embodied in forms of practice and types of community' (*Whose Justice? Which Rationality?*, p. 390),
his critics have often inferred that he is claiming that all claims to truth
are relative to cultural particularity. Those who continue to pursue the
Enlightenment's aims accuse MacIntyre of relativism and of arbitrariness, of falsely asserting that the truth of any claim is relative to one of a
number of incommensurable conceptual schemes and of then incon-
sistently asserting the superiority of one such scheme over its rivals.
Nietzscheans accuse him of inconsistency on other grounds, agreeing with
his genealogical critique of the Enlightenment project, and sometimes
also with what they take to be his perspectivist positing of rivals to it, but
attacking his agreement with its proponents that one should pursue something more than a merely perspectival truth.

MacIntyre resists both charges. He is right to do so, given that those
who level them have understood his substantive social and ethical theory
in terms of his metatheory, even though the latter is necessarily incomplete unless understood in terms of the former. MacIntyre is well aware
that his metatheory cannot comprise a solution to the problem of competing paradigms any more than, say, Kuhn's metatheory of scientific
revolutions can resolve any disputes in natural science. All that MacIntyre's
second-order theory can establish is that what may be called the problem
of relativism or of perspectivism is in principle soluble, a claim already
implicit in his first-order theory. Only a substantive theory might, according to MacIntyre's metatheory of traditions, solve the problem by demonstrating its superiority over its rivals.

MacIntyre summarizes his metatheory in his account of 'the rationality of traditions' (below, pp. 159–70; see also pp. 216–20). Conceptual schemes are never without presuppositions. These presuppositions are themselves rational in that they have developed over time through trial, error and correction. Therefore, although they are presuppositions of reasoning, they are also susceptible to scrutiny *in extremis*. The point at which pre-suppositions are necessarily brought into question is when the tradition that they inform is confronted by some critically important and un-avoidable problem that it cannot solve. If, at this point, protagonists of another tradition are able to explain to those confronted by this episte-mological crisis why it has arisen, how their own presuppositions prevent them from overcoming it, and how the conceptual resources of the sec-ond tradition enable it to be overcome without confronting any other insurmountable problem, then it would be rational, on their own terms, for those in crisis to abandon their previous tradition and to instead adopt the alternative.

MacIntyre no longer conceives rival perspectives as being the kind of things that he suggested they are in *A Short History of Ethics*, things to which one might freely choose to adhere or not. Rather, individuals' reasoning is necessarily practised within some tradition of reasoning and upon some set of presuppositions. Therefore reasoning within the post-Enlightenment world cannot be as fragmentary as he suggested in *After Virtue*. We do not live after the fragmentation of tradition *per se* but after the displacement from dominance of one socially embodied tradition by another.

In acknowledging rivalry between traditions MacIntyre might appear to be adopting perspectivism, albeit in a revised form according to which the rational superiority of one perspective over another is sometimes ascertainable. 'Progress in rationality is achieved only from a point of view' (below, p. 118), MacIntyre agrees. As in *After Virtue*, so also since, he endorses the Nietzschean critique of the Enlightenment project. How-ever, in 'Moral Relativism, Truth and Justification' especially, MacIntyre clearly differentiates truth from 'rational justification [which] can only be internal . . . and relative to . . . each particular standpoint' (below, p. 203). Truth, in contrast, is not relative to a standpoint but is the *telos*, the final end, of all versions of veritable enquiry, so that 'progress in enquiry consists in transcending the limitations of such particular and partial standpoints in a movement towards truth' (below, p. 207).

What MacIntyre endorses in Nietzscheanism is not its perspectivism but its genealogical mode of excavating the origins, unmasking the pre-suppositions and subverting the arguments of rival traditions. MacIntyre used this tool in *After Virtue* for the unNietzschean 'ends' (below, pp. 172, 196) of demonstrating where moral philosophy went wrong, how Enlightenment philosophers had the unintended effect of subverting plain persons' use of moral language, and how and why Nietzsche's perspect-ivist and impersonally voluntarist project issued from this failure of the epistemologically and ethically individualist project of the Enlightenment. MacIntyre seeks to subvert the Nietzschean project by tracing it back to an erroneous inference. Nietzscheans have inferred from liberals' failure to agree on first principles that the very idea of foundations for understanding should be rejected and that claims to knowledge should therefore be understood as expressions of the will to power. Nietzscheans assert that one can do no more than assert, which is tantamount to the illogical claim to know that one cannot know. 'A radical sceptic is', as MacIntyre puts it, 'an epistemologist with entirely negative findings' (below, p. 176).

MacIntyre's assessment of perspectivism as a socially embodied theory resembles his assessment of emotivism and Weberianism. Like the latter, it rightly describes an important aspect of the modern condition but wrongly (and, in the case of perspectivism, paradoxically) extrapolates from this to claim a necessary truth. It simply does not follow from the present failure to identify the truth of some matter that such truth is permanently unattainable. Nor does the present inability of any one perspective to prove its rational superiority over its rivals entail that no such demonstration could ever be possible.

Liberals, in becoming increasingly aware of theirs as one tradition amongst others, have already gone a considerable way towards conceding Nietzscheans' perspectivist claims. Aware of the interminability of their mutual disagreements, liberals increasingly propound an irreducible 'fact of pluralism' as a justification for their failure to answer those questions posed by the Enlightenment. The final end to which liberalism appears to be moving is no more than an agreement to permanently disagree. And it is this end which constitutes the starting point for Nietzscheanism.

MacIntyre does not claim that Aristotelianism is yet in a position to prove its superiority over its rivals. The substantive claim that he does make in his metatheory is that those rivals are, but do not sufficiently understand themselves to be, temporally and teleologically ordered practices. As a philosophical tradition whose protagonists are aware of it as such, Aristotelianism is, on MacIntyre's account, itself a teleologically ordered practice, 'the craft of crafts' (see especially *Three Rival Versions of Moral Enquiry: Encyclopaedia, Genealogy, and Tradition*). The *telos* of this practice is truth. 'Achieved understanding is the *theoretical* goal of the *practical* activity of enquiry' (below, p. 183). MacIntyre's conception of first principles, like his conception of morality, differs from that of liberals in being teleological. Truth is not something that can be encapsulated in some epistemological theory but is the final end of enquiry, giving point to the theorization of schemes of rational justification. This is the first principle of the Aristotelian tradition of enquiry and, as such, the most satisfaction that MacIntyre will give to those academic philosophers who have demanded of him yet another epistemological theory. MacIntyre is well aware of 'the fate of all philosophies which give priority to epistemological questions: the indefinite multiplication of disagreement' (*Three Rival Versions of Moral Enquiry*, p. 75).

I have already referred to one way in which MacIntyre has significantly recharacterized his own standpoint since *After Virtue*. A second and more obvious way is in specifying it as Thomistic Aristotelianism. He had not previously claimed that Aristotle had said the last word on anything. What he had affirmed was, first, that Aristotle's teleological form of reasoning was capable of coherently answering the questions raised by Aristotle's predecessors and, secondly, that Aristotle's reasoning about ethics still remains the best so far. Now, in *Whose Justice? Which Rationality?*, he affirms instead that Aquinas's treatment of rationality and of ethics is superior to that of Aristotle (below, pp. 156–7). This superiority was achieved by building upon and revising Aristotle's arguments but it was also achieved by building upon arguments from elsewhere, from the Christian tradition and particularly from Augustine. In coherently combining the two major traditions of philosophical enquiry that then existed in Europe, Aquinas produced an account of rationality and of justice that is superior to that of any of his predecessors, and also to that of any one of his successors, or so MacIntyre claims. MacIntyre also claims that the full significance of Aquinas's achievement was lost even on most Thomists (below, p. 158). MacIntyre intends his metatheory to clarify the importance of that achievement, both historically and as the highest standard of dialectical enquiry that has yet been achieved. It this standard that philosophers should now emulate.

In becoming a Thomist MacIntyre has become a thoroughgoing realist, conceiving the *telos* of enquiry as perfected understanding, as the adequacy of an intellect to its object. Such knowledge is pursued and constructed in cooperative and ongoing practices of enquiry. This was understood by Plato in building upon the work of Socrates, by Aristotle in amending Plato, by Aquinas in combining two traditions, and by many in the tradition of Thomistic Aristotelianism. It is also understood by almost any practising scientist. But it is denied in one way by liberal epistemologists and in another by Nietzschean perspectivists.

In becoming a Thomist MacIntyre has also became more of an Aristotelian. MacIntyre's substantive theory of practical rationality and his metatheory of the rationality of traditions are both constructed upon Aristotelian first principles. Or rather, in elaborating these theories MacIntyre has come to understand what had previously been his own inadequately scrutinized presuppositions, enabling him to coherently ground his theories in the premises of the Aristotelian tradition. MacIntyre's substantive theory draws upon Marx, Weber, Wittgenstein and others in developing an account of social conflict. His complementary metatheory draws upon a range of similarly unAristotelian and unThomistic sources to develop an account of philosophical rivalry. Yet both theories are consistent with the premises of Aristotelianism. This coherence is demonstrated by the way in which elaboration of these theories has led MacIntyre

to accept those very principles. For example, MacIntyre now acknowledges that reasoning about the highest good permits deduction about the
proper ordering of lesser goods and, therefore, permits people to avoid
what would otherwise appear to be tragic choices between incommensurable goods. Aristotelians should still ask 'what is this for?' in seeking
knowledge of the world but should now also ask the historical and, as it
turns out, metatheoretical question 'why do others no longer ask that
question of themselves and of their conditions?' Whereas MacIntyre long
ago noted 'an interesting similarity in philosophical style between Marxists and neo-Thomists, which springs from their sharing the same type of
self-imposed isolation' ('On Not Misrepresenting Philosophy', p. 72), he
now criticizes neo-Thomists not for their isolation but for their attempts
to make of Thomism a post-Enlightenment epistemology. Rather than
participate in such capitulation MacIntyre returns to Thomistic Aristotelianism's own first principles in the hope of defeating its rivals, attempting
'to identify the limitations and to integrate the strengths and successes of
each rival into its overall structure' (below, p. 158).

Part V: Challenging Contemporary Politics

The most absurd consequence of MacIntyre's critics' misconstrual of his
substantive social theory in terms of his metatheory must be the occa-
sional claim that he is a political conservative. Those who prioritize
tradition are conservatives; MacIntyre prioritizes tradition: therefore
MacIntyre is a conservative. Or so the reasoning goes.

This reasoning is mistaken. Like Aristotle, MacIntyre considers people
to be essentially political beings. His first principles and his final ends are,
accordingly, political. Politics is itself a teleologically ordered practice
but one concerned with the proper ordering of all other practices within
a community. As such, it is a form of enquiry regarding the purpose of all
practice. Just as MacIntyre poses Aristotle's *Posterior Analytics* as 'an
account of what it is or would be to possess, to have already achieved, a
perfected science' (below, p. 182), so he may be taken as posing parts of
Aristotle's *Politics* and *Ethics* as an account of what it would be to have
constructed an ideal *polis*. For MacIntyre, this is the kind of political
institution that best suits the nature of human beings – not just of ancient
Greek slave-owning men, for the good of whom the Athenian *polis* was
organized, but of all people. In such a polity what is now considered
private would be treated as ultimately political, goods of effectiveness
being systematically subordinated to goods of excellence. Productive,
domestic and other practices would be ordered for the sake of their internal goods and those internal goods would be ordered for the sake of what
was rationally agreed to be the common and highest good for human
beings. The practice of reasoning towards, and of implementing, such
agreement would be that of politics. It would therefore be an essential

task of politics to combine the different conceptions of the good life that are engendered within different practices.

This is not a conservative conception of politics. On the contrary, it is a revolutionary conception. MacIntyre has always held that conflict rather than community must be the starting point for any Aristotelian politics within capitalism. He has also opposed 'communitarianism' ever since its identification in the mid-1980s, arguing that bureaucratic nation-states are wholly incompatible with a politics of the common good. 'Politics, Philosophy and the Common Good' is only the most recent and synoptic elaboration of these arguments.

Liberalism, having originally challenged the authority of tradition in the name of a universalizing Reason, has now itself been transformed into a tradition. It is a tradition of reasoning that legitimates the institutions of state and capitalism and, in turn, is sustained by them. It is not Aristotelians but liberals who seek to conserve the dominance of those institutions, arguing, within the constraints of liberal democracy, only about what is their preferable balance. Rawls's Kantianism and Rorty's pragmatism stand between Hayek's Humean promotion of the market and Taylor's Hegelian promotion of the state. MacIntyre stands outside of this interminable debate, rejecting bureaucratic states, corporations and parties alike, well aware that 'the incoherences of the principles embodied in the social and political *status quo*' that are revealed by the debate do nothing to bring 'about its downfall' (below, p. 226). Now realizing that we do not live after the fragmentation of tradition *per se* but after the displacement from dominance of one socially embodied tradition by another, he acknowledges that exposing the incoherence of liberal ethics and social science does little to undermine the substantial control that capitalists, managers, politicians and bureaucrats really do exercise over the practices of plain persons.

That Aristotelianism is so radically at odds with modern politics is something that may not be immediately apparent. Indeed, much of modern political thought may be considered an attempt to infuse institutions with Aristotelian ideals. Our use of the term politics itself bears witness to the efforts of Renaissance humanists to emulate the classical *polis* in the organization of their own city states. When Ferguson and other members of the Scottish Enlightenment explained the tragic conflict between wealth and virtue as the necessary outcome of separating the republic from the private and economic sphere, Hegel responded by theorizing a hierarchy in which unity was once again achieved by the state officiating over the market and households. Leo XIII and other neo-Thomists followed by developing a corporatist politics for the Catholic Church and for Christian democracy, whilst neo-Hegelians even shifted the mainstream of liberalism in a similar, social democratic direction. All of this has greatly affected the appearance and legitimation of politics, not least in integrating workers' organizations into the political system. But modern society is so vast, so conflictual and so saturated with instrumental reasoning that no substantive agreement about the common good is possible, notwithstanding any amount of academic moralizing, political rhetoric or bureaucratic administration. And that is why MacIntyre dismisses all high-minded discussion of contemporary politics in terms of community or a common good.

MacIntyre originally took from Marx the critique of any attempt to practise a politics of the common good in the capitalist present. He now rejects Marx as having himself been too utopian in imagining that capitalism makes available the material conditions under which such a politics will be practised in a post-revolutionary future. MacIntyre's political aspiration is no more the eschatological one of Marx than it is the institutionally progressive one of Hegel. Teleology is, for MacIntyre, essential to human nature and practice but not to any overarching process in human history. What intelligible process there has been in modern history was more acutely articulated by Weber than by Hegel or Marx. Where Marx goes beyond Weber, and beyond Nietzscheans and emotivists, is in refusing to extrapolate from a description of the modern world to an assertion that there can be no alternative. Marx's fault is the opposite one of asserting that an alternative to capitalism's negation of human nature is not only possible but inevitable. MacIntyre accepts that there is a contradiction between human nature and the nature of capitalism, between the need of capital to accumulate and the need of human beings to fulfil their potential, but he denies that Marx's proletariat has any more chance of negating capitalism's negation of human nature than does Hegel's bureaucracy. Unlike Marx, who saw alienation being overcome by a revolutionary act of the most alienated, MacIntyre has long taken no comfort from the further expansion of capitalist rationality. The alienation of workers in the cause of accumulating goods of effectiveness prevents them from developing their ability to engage in sound practical reasoning. Denial to workers of responsibility for their own work denies them the opportunity to develop themselves through that work. Workers who understand their social situation only in terms of trying 'to secure a greater share than their competitors of such goods as power, security, autonomy – and money' thereby render 'themselves manageable and to this extent defeatable by others' (below, p. 55). Marx was, for MacIntyre, not nearly radical enough in his understanding of social conflict, of the ideological obfuscation of that conflict, and of the demoralizing effects of capitalism.

The terminal crisis suffered by Marxism is the most dramatic example of one tradition being defeated by another, liberalism. MacIntyre had foreseen this failure by the end of the 1960s, after having himself failed to make out of Marxism an ethics capable of answering its liberal critics. If there is an adequate alternative to liberal ideas and capitalist institutions, Marxism's 'socialization' of production by the state is not it. Nevertheless, much in Marx's critique of commodity fetishism and of alienation and exploitation, and much in his labour theory of value, might now be detached from other aspects of Marxism and combined instead with a more philosophically radical critique of capitalism and liberalism. Marx erred, according to MacIntyre, in failing to complete his critique of the presuppositions of capitalism by scrutinizing his own and by elaborating a coherent alternative. Without any first principles of their own, later Marxists opposed but were also unable to escape the ethos of the modern world. Their failure to solve this dilemma was to have disastrous consequences. In 'The *Theses on Feuerbach*: A Road Not Taken' MacIntyre also relates his mature political theory to Thompson's socialist exploration of the autonomous agency, practical rationality and self-making of the pre-proletarian working class. But perhaps MacIntyre has not returned so far to his political roots as to repeat the quote from Tawney's *Religion and the Rise of Capitalism* with which he prefaced his first book: 'The true descendant of the doctrines of Aquinas is the labour theory of value. The last of the Schoolmen was Karl Marx' (*Marxism: An Interpretation*, p. 3).

MacIntyre's politics may now, to an extent, be described in terms of resistance. The idea of a politics of resistance is familiar to many Nietzscheans. For them it involves resistance to domination of one's will by others and asserting oneself in the *agon* that is society. For MacIntyre it involves something else. What is to be resisted is injustice. Capitalism is to be understood as a society which is structured by institutional manipulation of people in pursuit of goods of effectiveness. Therefore, given the Aristotelian conception of justice as the virtue of treating people as they deserve, capitalism is to be understood as structurally unjust. MacIntyre's politics of resistance is one of collective action in defence of practices against institutional domination and corruption. The substantial control that capitalists, managers, politicians and bureaucrats exercise over practices does not preclude plain persons from resisting their institutionalized will to power. What I have described as MacIntyre's substantive theory of practical rationality maintains that social order of any kind depends upon practices, that practices have goods and rationalities internal to them, and therefore that the kind of rationality that he identifies with Aristotelianism is ineliminable. Practitioners will always have grounds for collective defence of shared goods and for resistance to managerial manipulation. The greater the scope of practitioners for organizing the allocation of goods of effectiveness, the greater their ability to cultivate practical rationality and virtue in their practices, in their characters and their communities. Such scope and ability may remain considerable in the kind of remote farming and fishing community that MacIntyre knew in his youth. Presumably he has these in mind in advocating 'a politics of self-defence for all those local societies that aspire to achieve some relatively self-sufficient and independent form of participatory practice-based community' (*Marxism and Christianity*, p. xxvi). But there is scope for resistance even within factories, workshops, studios, laboratories, hospitals, schools and other institutions. And it is now only in such discrete communities of practice, and in familial and bipartisan relations, rather than in more integrated communities of locality, that most people have the opportunity to cultivate virtue and practical reasoning.

MacIntyre's politics is, in ambition, much more than a politics of resistance. Understood as a practice itself, politics involves creating and sustaining communities in which people can practise cooperative reasoning about common goals so that their other other practices can be rationally related to one another. It is through political activity in coordinating practices, as well as through theoretical enquiry, that rationalities internal to practices may be articulated into something greater. For all its patriarchal and other fundamental faults, the Athenian *polis* displayed such an ordering of society for the common and highest good. And just as its conditions constrained Aristotle's consciousness, so too do our conditions constrain ours. We therefore cannot yet say how it might be possible to realize Aquinas's 'conception of order, that of the order of a community directed toward its common good through the discharge of those functions necessary for the achievement of that good' ('Natural Law as Subversive', p. 74). What can be said is that although exposing incoherence in a rival tradition is insufficient to bring about the downfall of that rival's institutional embodiments, it is a precondition of so doing. This is why MacIntyre practises philosophy.

Part VI: Reflecting on the Project

By the time that MacIntyre had elaborated the argument of *First Principles, Final Ends and Contemporary Philosophical Issues* he was prepared to reflect upon his project for the public record. He had previously exposed himself to interview only once, in 1970, shortly before he left Britain to settle in the US. What is most striking about MacIntyre then is his perspectival agnosticism, a quality absent from the two later interviews that are included below.

These two interviews speak, for the most part, for themselves. Nevertheless, MacIntyre's claim that his philosophy is both 'theistic' and 'as secular in its content as any other' might be considered paradoxical (below, p. 266). When young, MacIntyre trained to be a Presbyterian minister. For a time he tried to combine Christian faith with his political commitments and his sociological and historical understanding of religion, exploring Karl Barth's fideistic and antinomian standpoint as a particular form of life. Faith lost out. *After Virtue* was the result of a long period of reflection upon how morality might best be justified apart from faith. This aspect of his argument has convinced some notable theorists but not MacIntyre himself. Reflection upon the inadequacies of the argument's premises has led him back to faith, albeit not the Protestant faith of his youth but a faith confirmed by the metaphysical reasoning of the Thomist tradition and sustained by the institution of the Roman

Catholic Church. This, he has concluded, is the most rigorous way to respond to Nietzsche's attempt to kill off the popular belief in truth by proclaiming the death of God. Given this theistic underpinning of his philosophy, it would appear that MacIntyre must be making more of a claim about the theistic presuppositions of others' philosophies than about the secularity of his own.

MacIntyre's sociological and historical understanding of liberalism has led him to deny the legitimacy of the modern age. 'The liberal tradition', which MacIntyre has always opposed (below, p. 32), rests upon something rather like fideistic and antinomian presuppositions, which now go unscrutinized by its protagonists. 'Here I stand, I can do no other' (below, p. 35), announced Luther, striking a stridently individualist pose premised upon an adaption of the Augustinian idea of will and Thomist idea of conscience. This pose was later adopted by Kant and, later again, by that peculiarly ascetic Nietzschean, Weber. It expressed for Luther and Kant a certainty other and greater than the certainties that plain persons derived from traditional kinds of authority and reasoning. For Luther this certainty could be based only on faith in divine command and calling and was unaffected by temporal acts or vocational roles. For Kant such certainty provided bases for an alternative and superior kind of practical reasoning oriented to individual acts in isolation from social practices. By the time of Weber, the categorical imperatives of conscience remained but appeared alien to reason. After the death of God a disenchanted, demoralized world affords no basis for an ethic of responsibility other than individual will. Either duty or power can, it seems, be willed as an end in itself. This separation of facts about the world from meaningful values which individuals might enunciate within it can be traced back (as Weber himself did) to the Reformation's separations of individual from society and of faith from reason, continued as these were in capitalism's bifurcation of market and state and the Enlightenment's bifurcation of science and metaphysics. This is the genealogy of the separation of social science from moral philosophy, a history that enables social scientists to be untroubled in their presuppositions by the administration of Auschwitz and moral philosophers to be untroubled in theirs by the alienation of workers.

MacIntyre's substantive theory of practical rationality challenges the presuppositions of social scientists and of moral philosophers alike. His metatheory explains what is involved in making this challenge. Aristotelianism is, he claims accordingly, 'not only the best theory so far, but the best theory so far about what makes a particular theory the best one' (below, p. 264). Both theories presuppose what MacIntyre now says about truth. It has always been his most basic presupposition that there is a real world which we experience through our senses, about which we might discover more through rational enquiry, and about which we can know and pursue truth. In recent years this has changed from an unscrutinized presupposition into an explicit premise and object of rigorous enquiry.

This change is the latest and perhaps highest stage in the ongoing process by which MacIntyre has sought to 'discover the distortions of ideology' in his own thought so as 'to avoid being their victim'.

MacIntyre's metatheory concerns how to go about scrutinizing the presuppositions of a rival standpoint. In so doing, an Aristotelian has to adopt, as a 'second first language', the idiom of that rival. In that rival idiom, the differences between the two standpoints are characterized differently from the way in which one would characterize them as an Aristotelian. Aristotelians should learn to do this because adopting that rival's idiom is the only way in which to discover how that rival might be shown to be inadequate to the task of making sense of reality in its own terms. How, though, should an Aristotelian characterize the differences between Aristotelianism and its rivals in Aristotelian terms? The immediate answer must be in terms of tradition, but what are those terms?

'Debate and conflict as to the best forms of practice have to be debate and conflict between rival institutions and not merely between rival theories' ('The Privatization of Good', p. 344). Practices are the real bases of any social order and are bound to subsist irrespective of the traditions they support, however much they are corrupted by those traditions. Rivalry between traditions within a single culture, such as occurs in the contemporary West, will therefore involve rivalry between different institutions and between different ways of organizing practices. It will also involve rivalry between different philosophical practices. But it will not involve much more in the way of rivalry between practices. On MacIntyre's account, mistakes in theory may be exposed by and are significant because of their consequences in practice. Liberalism's mistake in regarding 'individuals as distinct and apart from their social relationships is a mistake of theory, but not only a theoretical mistake. It is a mistake embodied in institutionalized social life. And it is therefore a mistake which cannot be corrected merely by better theoretical analysis' (below, pp. 228–9). It is not a mistake that can be corrected by Nietzscheanism. Although Nietzscheanism, in the form of 'postmodernism', has received a mighty boost from the death of Marxism, its radicalism is entirely theoretical and not at all institutional. Rather than challenge capitalist institutions it accepts them as expressions of an ineluctable process of modernization which it interprets, in turn, as the principal expression of the impersonal will to power. It appeals to 'charisma' or 'difference' but obscures institutions' corruption of practices by collapsing practice into discourse, knowledge into power and truth into rhetoric. Therefore, although Nietzscheanism represents a break from the liberal tradition of theoretical enquiry, that break reinforces capitalism by further reducing the purchase of theoretical analysis upon institutionalized social life.

Whereas MacIntyre's metatheory posits a number of traditions in philosophical contention, his substantive theory paints a simpler picture from an expressly Aristotelian perspective. In this picture the Aristotelian rationality of practices confronts a succession of rationalizations of the subordination of moral excellence to institutional effectiveness. This picture illustrates MacIntyre's underlying sense of tradition, the sense in which he can describe Aristotelianism as the tradition 'of tradition'. Aristotelianism is the tradition that is intentionally ordered by its protagonists as a tradition; teleologically, as a metapractice of philosophical enquiry into and political pursuit of *the* true and *the* good. MacIntyre is by now the most self-conscious of those protagonists, attempting to muster and mobilize the tradition in order to challenge both Nietzschean theory and capitalist practice. If conflict as to the best way of organizing society has to include conflict between rival institutions, then Aristotelianism is as yet in no position to challenge its instrumentalist rivals. Nevertheless, MacIntyre clearly believes that Thomistic Aristotelian theory stands on solid foundations. He also clearly believes that a strength of self-conscious tradition is that arguments elaborated within it are less those of an individual theorist than of a cooperative project. This is why he concludes recent papers with appeals to others for further work to be done.

Kelvin Knight

PART I

Establishing the Project

'Notes from the Moral Wilderness'

Part 1

A position which we are all tempted into is that of moral critic of Stalinism. One point to begin thinking about socialism from is that of dissatisfaction with this figure. This dissatisfaction may force us into a rereading of the Marxism which such a critic rejects. What I want to ask is whether our dissatisfaction with the moral critic and a contemporary rereading of Marxism may not together suggest a new approach to moral issues. It is worth mentioning that this is what I want to do, because this is so much a question to which I still lack an answer that even as a question what follows may seem too tortuous and indefinite. Moreover I cannot even say with certainty from what standpoint I ask this question. And this, I suspect, is not merely a matter of my own private confusions. The various characters who walk through these pages, the Stalinist, the moral critic, the Revisionist and so on, if they succeed in being more than lay figures do so not just because they are present in the real world, but also because they represent moments in the consciousness of all of us, masks that we each wear or have worn at some time or other. The need to overcome and transcend their limitations and mistakes, their 'false consciousness' in moral matters, is the need to find a way out of our own wilderness.

I

Don Quixote long ago paid the penalty for wrongly imagining that knight errantry was compatible with all economic forms of society. (K. Marx)

The ex-Communist turned moral critic of Communism is often a figure of genuine pathos. He confronts the Stalinist with attitudes that in many ways deserve our respect – and yet there is something acutely disquieting about him. I am not speaking now, of course, of those who exchange the doctrines of Stalinism for those of the Labour Party leadership, the

Congress for Cultural Freedom or the *Catholic Herald*. They have their reward. I mean those whose self-written epitaph runs shortly, 'I could remain no longer in the Party without forfeiting my moral and intellectual self-respect; so I got out' (A. H. Hanson, 'An Open Letter to Edward Thompson', p. 79). They repudiate Stalinist crimes in the name of moral principle; but the fragility of their appeal to moral principle lies in the apparently arbitrary nature of that appeal. Whence come these standards by which Stalinism is judged and found wanting and why should they have authority over us? What disturbs me in the character of these moral critics of Stalinism is not just their inability to answer this question. It is that this inability seems to me to arise from a picture of their own situation, a picture profoundly influential among ex-Communists, which is at the root of much contemporary self-deception.

What is this picture? It is a picture of independence regained, of a newly won power to speak with a voice of one's own, instead of being merely a gramophone for the Stalinist bureaucracy. What this picture conceals from those whose minds and imaginations it informs is the extent to which they have merely exchanged a conscious dependence for an unconscious. The form of their appeal to moral principle is largely the outcome of the pressures upon them both of Stalinism and of the moral liberalism of the West, pressures which produce a surprisingly similar effect. So far as Stalinism is concerned, it provides a pattern which the moral critic simply inverts. The Stalinist identifies what is morally right with what is actually going to be the outcome of historical development. History is for him a sphere in which objective laws operate, laws of such a kind that the role of the individual human being is predetermined for him by his historical situation. The individual can accept his part and play it out more or less willingly; but he cannot rewrite the play. One is nothing in history but an actor and even one's moral judgments on historical events are only part of the action. The 'ought' of principle is swallowed up in the 'is' of history. By contrast the moral critic puts himself outside history as a spectator. He invokes his principles as valid independently of the course of historical events. Every issue is to be judged on its moral merits. The 'ought' of principle is completely external to the 'is' of history. For the Stalinist the actual course of history is the horizon of morality; that which belongs to the future is progressive and is made into a necessary truth. For the moral critic the question of the course of history, of what is actually happening, and the question of what ought to happen are totally independent questions.

So far I have represented the moral critic's standpoint as a kind of photographic negative of Stalinism. And this would not in any case be surprising since the typical critic of this kind is an ex-Stalinist. But the hold of this pattern on the mind is enormously strengthened by the fact that it is the pattern of the liberal morality which prevails in our society. For it is of the essence of the liberal tradition that morality is taken to be autonomous. What this means can be made clear by considering it first at a fairly sophisticated level. In the philosophical textbooks it is the doctrine that moral principles can have no non-moral basis. Our judgments on specific moral issues may be supported by the invocation of more general principles. But in the end our most general and ultimate principles, because they are that in terms of which all else is justified, stand beyond any rational justification. In particular, they cannot be justified by any appeal to facts, historical or otherwise. This isolation of the moral from the factual is presented as a necessary and ineluctable truth of logic. The argument here is that all valid argument is argument in which the premises entail the conclusion; and the concept of entailment can be sufficiently explained for our present purpose by saying that one set of propositions entails another proposition or set of propositions, if and only if nothing is asserted in the latter which was not already implicitly or explicitly asserted in the former. And since clearly in going from factual to moral assertions one is not merely repeating oneself, factual assertions cannot entail moral assertions. But, as entailment is accepted as the only form of valid argument, it follows that moral assertions cannot be backed up rationally at all by factual or any other non-moral assertions. And this has as its central consequence the view that on ultimate questions of morality we cannot argue, we can only choose. And our choice is necessarily arbitrary in the sense that we cannot give reasons for choosing one way rather than another; for to do this we should have to have a criterion in moral matters more ultimate than our ultimate criterion. And this is nonsensical.

About this doctrine we may note two things. First, it is remarkable how much it has in common with Sartrian existentialism. Those philosophical journalists who lament the lack of relationship between British analytical philosophers and Continental metaphysicians might take heart from seeing how the moral philosophy of both can breed the notion of unconditional and arbitrary choice as a, if not the, crucial feature of the individual's moral life. In both there is a picture of the individual standing before the historical events of his time, able to pass judgment on them exactly as he pleases. His values are for him to choose; the facts in no way constrain him. And we can see at once how this dovetails with and reinforces the negation of Stalinism. Secondly, leaving aside the question of whether this view of morality is correct or not, we can see how strikingly it corresponds to the actual moral condition of many people in our society. For them their moral principles are completely isolated from the facts of their existence and they simply accept one set of principles rather than another in arbitrary fashion. They affirm this or that 'ought'; but their morality has no basis. I am not speaking here of the morality of intellectuals which might be thought (albeit wrongly) to reflect the philosophical currents; I am speaking of the largely inarticulate whose moral discourse nevertheless provides the standard and normal usage in our society.

There are then some grounds for a suspicion that the moral critics of

Stalinism may have done no more than exchange one dominant pattern of thought for another; but the new pattern gives them the illusion of moral independence. Yet the very nature of their new morality must make their answer to the question which I originally posed seem extraordinarily thin and unconvincing even to them. Why do the moral standards by which Stalinism is found wanting have authority over us? Simply because we choose that they should. The individual confronting the facts with his values condemns. But he can only condemn in the name of his own choice. The isolation which his mode of moral thinking imposes on the critic can tempt him in two directions. There is the pressure, usually much exaggerated by those who write about it, to exchange the participation in a Stalinist party for some other equally intense form of group membership. But there is also the pressure, far less often noticed, to accept the role of the isolated moral hero, who utters in the name of no one but himself. Ex-Stalinists who pride themselves on having become hard-headed realists seem to be peculiarly prone to this form of romanticism. They are the moral Quixotes of the age.

The value of their Quixotry varies of course with the circumstances in which they proclaim it. The reassertion of moral standards by the individual voice has been one of the ferments of Eastern European revisionism. But, because of the way in which it is done, this reassertion too often leaves the gulf between morality and history, between value and fact as wide as ever. Kolakowski and others like him stress the amorality of the historical process on the one hand and the moral responsibility of the individual in history on the other. And this leaves us with the moral critic as a spectator, the categorical imperatives which he proclaims having no genuine relationship to his view of history. One cannot revive the moral content within Marxism by simply taking a Stalinist view of historical development and adding liberal morality to it. But however one may disagree with Kolakowski's theoretical position, the kind of integrity involved in reasserting moral principles in the Polish situation is entirely admirable. To speak against the stream in this way means that, even if the morality in question seems somehow irrational and arbitrary, in the protest which sustains it it can find its justification. But to assert this position in the West is to flow with the stream. It is merely to conform.

The pressures towards conformism, moral and otherwise, do not need re-emphasising. And it ought to be said for the moral critic of Stalinism that he is usually also the moral critic of Suez, Cyprus, and the H-Bomb. At least he delivers his censures impartially. Yet even here I want to put a question mark against his attitudes. For the Western social pattern has a role all ready for the radical moral critic to play. It is accepted that there should be minorities of protest on particular issues. And it is even a reinforcement for the dominant picture of morality that the moral critic should exhibit himself choosing his values of protest. For they remain *his* values, his private values. There is no set of common, public standards to which he can appeal, no shared moral image for his society by means of which he can make his case. And if he chooses his values in the spirit of *Hier steh' ich, ich kann nicht anders*, is it not equally open to his opponents to do the same? It is this that seems to be the cause of the deep suspicion of and muddle over moral arguments among the leaders of the Campaign for Nuclear Disarmament. Thus the isolation of the moral from the factual, the emphasis on choice, the arbitrariness introduced into moral matters, all these play into the hands of the defenders of the established order. The moral critic, especially the ex-Stalinist moral critic, pays the penalties of both self-deception and ineffectiveness for imagining that moral knight errantry is compatible with being morally effective in our form of society.

The argument as I have presented it so far is highly schematic. It could be reinforced at many points. And in concluding this stage of the argument it is perhaps worth noticing one of them very briefly. Just as the ex-Stalinist critic of Communism reflects both the negation of Stalinism and the dominant temper of Western liberalism in his moral attitudes, so also with his approach to matters of fact. The Stalinist approaches the historical developments of our time with a tightly organized general theory; the ex-Stalinist repudiates theory. But what he means by 'theory' he tends to take over from the Stalinist. And in his repudiation of general theories he falls in with the prevailing empiricism of our society. I want to follow through this pattern, not for its own sake, but for the further light it may throw on contemporary thinking about morality.

What the Stalinist thinks that he possesses, what the empiricist critic thinks to be logically impossible, is a blueprint of the social clockwork. For Stalinist theory the laws which govern social development are treated as if they have a character closely similar to that of the laws which govern the behaviour of a mechanical system. In Sartre's novel *La Mort dans l'âme* (translated as *Iron in the Soul*), a member of the French CP in 1940 is made to say:

'it is *conceivable* that the Politburo might founder in the depths of stupidity: by the same token, it is *conceivable* that the roof of this hut might fall on your head, but that doesn't mean you spend your time keeping a wary eye on the ceiling. You may say, of course, if you feel like it, that your hopes are founded on God, or that you have confidence in the architect – but any reply of that kind would be mere words. You know perfectly well that there are certain natural laws, and that it is the way of buildings to stay standing when they have been built in conformity with those laws. Why, then, should I spend my time wondering about the policy of the USSR, and why should you raise the question of my confidence in Stalin? I have complete confidence in him, *and* in Molotov, *and* in Zhdanov – as much confidence as you have in the solidity of these walls. In other words, I know that history has its laws, and that, in virtue of those laws, an identity of interest binds the country of the workers and the European proletariat.'

When Popper attacks historicism, it is essentially this doctrine that historical development is governed by laws and that its future course is therefore predictable which he is concerned to undermine. Equally this is what Stalin defends. But in the definition of what is at issue Stalin and Popper shake hands. The Marxism that Stalin presents is recognisably the Marxism that Popper also presents. And it is this same conception of theory which is evident throughout the contemporary anti-theoretical empiricism that is fashionable in the West both in academic and in political circles. Its relevance to the present topic is solely that it provides the straitjacket within which it is possible to confine and misrepresent the Marxist alternative to liberal morality. If it were the case that Marxism was a system in which the clockwork of society was laid bare, then it would be true that 'the *essence* of the Marxist ethic . . . is its *futurism*' (Hanson, pp. 80–1). For it would be true that the only effective way of remedying the evils of class-society would be to manipulate into existence the classless society; the blueprint of a mechanical system will tell us which levers we must pull to transform the system. And we pull the levers to contrive some new state of the system. The counterpart to a mechanical theory of society is a means–ends morality. But so too the counterpart to a rejection of a mechanical theory may be a very similar sort of morality. How can this be so?

'We have no general theory; we approach each issue on its merits. We can remedy this or that detail of the social set-up; it would be Utopian to hope for more. History eludes theory; it just happens. And the theorists and even the legislators merely trot along in its wake, writing up and codifying what has already happened.' So run the slogans of the contemporary mood. We can see how the rejection of Stalinism leads easily into this frame of mind. It is less obvious perhaps how much the moral attitude of the political empiricist has in common with that of the Stalinist. First of all, for both human agency is essentially ineffective. History occurs, whether theory can grasp it or not, independently of human will and desire. For both, a favourite charge is Utopianism, the accusation of trying to extend the sphere of human initiative in ways beyond those which history will allow for. And both too often have an enormous faith in the 'levers' of social engineering: the empiricist in an *ad hoc* way, the Stalinist systematically. One result of this is that the rejection of Stalinism by the empiricist is for the most part based only on the charge that Stalinist means do not as a matter of fact produce the requisite ends; the means–ends model of morality survives unscathed.

What I am contending in this final part of the first stage of my argument is that the moral helplessness of the ex-Stalinist critic of Communism is deepened by his lack of any general theory; that this lack of theory reflects an identification of theory with Stalinism; and that once again his new attitudes have far too much in common with his old. And the only point of the analysis so far is to enable us to formulate with more precision the question of whether there can be an alternative to the barren opposition of moral individualism and amoral Stalinism.

II

The idea of the translation of the ideal into the real is profound. Very important for history.   (V. I. Lenin)

The moral critic of Stalinism, as I have tried to depict him, largely is what he is because he sees no other possibility. He envisages only two moral alternatives. Stalinism on the one hand and his own new position on the other. It is therefore only a first step to argue that his new position is a frail one. What has to be done positively is to show that there is a third moral position. And any attempt to do this will have to satisfy a number of different requirements. If it is to avoid the defects of a purely empirical approach, it will have to provide us with the insights of a general theory without falling into the dogmatic ossifications of Stalinism. If it is to avoid the arbitrariness of liberal morality, it is going to have to provide us with some conception of a basis for our moral standards. If it is going to perform either of the preceding tasks successfully, it is going to have to produce arguments, not just assertions; and it is very important to remember that although in the first section of this essay I may have shown, or tried to show, that the position of the ex-Stalinist moral critic of Communism is more fragile, more ineffective and more liable to self-deception than is often supposed, I have not provided the arguments which would be necessary to exhibit it as mistaken. In order to do this I want in the next stages of the argument to work backwards through the themes touched on in the first section.

This makes my first task vindication of the possibility of a general theory of society. And this is nothing other than the task of replacing a misconceived but prevalent view of what Marxism is by a more correct view. The misconceived view is the one contained in the quotation from Sartre, and what I want to fasten on in it is its conception of the present age, the age of the transition to socialism. It is notorious that Marx himself says very little about the details of the transition. The Stalinist interpretation of the transition is however quite clear. For the Stalinist Marxism is in essence the thesis that a given level of technology and form of production as a basis produces a given form of social life and consciousness. What Stalin did in Russia was to provide the necessary basis on which the superstructure of socialism must arise. The transition from capitalism to socialism must therefore take the form of a manipulation of the economic and industrial arrangements of society and this will have as its effect the creation of a socialist consciousness among the mass of mankind. Because this transition is an exemplification of the general laws governing social development, its form and nature are essentially predictable and inevitable. Side by side with this doctrine of the transition is a doctrine as to the predictable and inevitable collapse of capitalism. And it is noteworthy that when Hanson, for example, asserts that the ethic of

Marxism is essentially futurist he does so on the grounds that this is the age of 'immiseration' and that all we can do, if we are Marxists, is contrive the shortest path out of it. About all this I want to make a number of separate, but connected points.

(1)   Stalinism is, as it were, a meta-Marxism. That is, it not only asserts certain Marxist doctrines, but it is itself a doctrine as to what sort of doctrines these are. And under Stalinism the title 'scientific socialism' is accorded to Marxism on the basis of a view which takes physics to be the paradigm case of a science, or worse still elementary mechanics. Engels in a famous remark compared Marx's achievement to that of Darwin. And the theory of evolution seems to me to provide a far more illuminating parallel to historical materialism than does Newtonian mechanics. Here two points can be stressed. One is that the evolution of species was established as a general truth long before it was possible to say anything of the genetic mechanisms which play such a key role in evolutionary explanation. And the thesis of historical materialism can equally be established in a way that leaves open all sorts of questions about how at a particular epoch basis and superstructure were in fact related. A second point is that the fact that the past history of species not only can but must be viewed in terms of evolution does not entail that the future history of species is predictable. For we do not necessarily know how to extrapolate from past to future. Someone may ask how if we are not concerned with predictability here the theory can ever be verified. The answer is to be found by reading *The Origin of Species*. Darwin states his own thesis with remarkable brevity. He then takes hard case after hard case and shows how in fact all can be fitted into the evolutionary picture. How many hard cases does he need to dispose of before his case is established? Clearly there is no simple answer; but at a certain point conviction becomes overwhelming. Equally historical materialism is established by showing the amount of history that is made intelligible by it; and once again there is no hard and fast rule as to the point at which such a view becomes plausible. Moreover there is the same distinction to be drawn between our ability to see the laws of development in the past and our inability to extrapolate into the future. Inability to extrapolate? Isn't Marxism most importantly a matter of prediction, a matter of what comes next in history? To answer this we must pass on to a new point.

(2)   The predictability which Stalinism offered rested on its conception of a mechanical relation between basis and superstructure. But as Marx depicts it the relation between basis and superstructure is fundamentally not only not mechanical, it is not even causal. What may be misleading here is Marx's Hegelian vocabulary. Marx certainly talks of the basis 'determining' the superstructure and of a 'correspondence' between them. But the reader of Hegel's *Logic* will realise that what Marx envisages is something to be understood in terms of the way in which the nature of

the concept of a given class, for example, may determine the concept of membership of that class. What the economic basis, the mode of production, does is to provide a framework within which superstructure arises, a set of relations around which the human relations can entwine themselves, a kernel of human relationship from which all else grows. The economic basis of a society is not its tools, but the people co-operating using these particular tools in the manner necessary to their use, and the superstructure consists of the social consciousness moulded by and the shape of this co-operation. To understand this is to repudiate the end–means morality; for there is no question of creating the economic base as a means to the socialist superstructure. Creating the basis, you create the superstructure. There are not two activities but one.

Moreover it is no use treating the doctrine that the basis determines the superstructure as a general formula in the way Stalinism has done. For the difference between one form of society and another is not just a difference in basis, and a corresponding difference in superstructure, but a difference also in the way basis is related to superstructure. And the crucial character of the transition to socialism is not that it is a change in the economic base but that it is a revolutionary change in the relation of superstructure to base. That liberation which Marx describes as the ending of prehistory and the beginning of history is a freeing of our relationships from the kind of determination and constraint hitherto exercised upon them. It is therefore absolutely necessary to grasp the nature of this determination correctly.

What may have misled here is the fact that particular features of the basis of any given society are always causally related to what may be counted as features of the superstructure. But this is not to say that the basis as such is causally related to the superstructure as such.

(3)   The question of predictability often takes the form it does for the Stalinist, because Marxist economic theses are detached from Marx's general view. And predictions about the transition to socialism are tied to predictions about immiseration, underconsumption and the business cycle which seem to stand or fall as verifications of immutable laws governing our economic development. Here I want to say only that our stock picture of Marx's economics needs a lot of revision. I have mentioned the role of 'immiseration' in Hanson's argument. It is worth remembering that Marx did not think capitalist crisis an automatic outcome of underconsumption; and those like Hanson who see 'immiseration' as summarising a Marxist view need to be reminded that in volume 2 of *Capital* Marx wrote that 'crises are precisely always preceded by a period in which wages rise generally and the working class actually get a larger share of the annual product intended for consumption.' So far as I can see, Marx's explanation of capitalist crisis is not a matter of underconsumption, but of a falling return on profit which leads the capitalist to lower his investment. And this explanation, like the explanation of

proletarian reaction to such crisis, rests on his view of what has happened to human nature under capitalism. That is, Marx's economics make sense only if related to his general view of human nature. Marx's view of human nature is not a pious addendum to his economic analysis.

(4)   Socialism cannot be impersonally manipulated into existence, or imposed on those whose consciousness resists, precisely because socialism is the victory of consciousness over its previous enslavement by economic and political activity. All other forms of society have been suffered by men; socialism is to be lived by them. And this is where the threads in the previous points come together. Marx inherits from Hegel a conception of the 'human essence'. Human life at any given moment is not a realisation of this essence because human life is always limited in ways characteristic of the basis of a given form of society. In particular, human freedom is always so limited. But in our age we have reached the point where this can change, where human possibility can be realised in a quite new way. But we cannot see the realisation of this possibility as the predictable outcome of laws governing human development independently of human wills and aspirations. For the next stage is to be characterised precisely as the age in which human wills and aspirations take charge and are no longer subservient to economic necessity and to the law-bound inevitability of the past. But Marxists surely say, not that this might happen, but that it will? If they say this, they are no longer predicting. They are re-affirming Marx's belief that human potentiality is such that men will take this new step, and this affirmation is of a different order from predicting. For the Marxist view of history can be written up in the end as the story of how the human ideal was after many vicissitudes translated into the human reality. And at this point we can perhaps begin to establish the connection of all this with the previous argument about the moral critic of Communism.

The moral critic rejected Stalinism because it represented the historical process as automatic and as morally sovereign. And for moral values incapsulated wholly in history he substituted moral values wholly detached from history. To this he added a thorough distaste for general theorising. But if we bring out as central to Marxism the kind of points which I have suggested, may not this suggest a third alternative to the moral critic, a theory which treats what emerges in history as providing us with a basis for our standards, without making the historical process morally sovereign or its progress automatic? In order to ask this question properly we ought to re-examine some of the traditional questions about human nature and morality. What is the relation between what I am, what I can be, what I want to be and what I ought to be? These are the topics to which we must next turn, so that we shall be able to see the questions to which Marx's conception of human nature sought to be an answer.

Part 2

III

'Men make their own history, but . . .' This phrase echoes through the Marxist classics. The political aim of Marxists is to liquidate that 'but'. Their theoretical aim is to understand it. In order to understand it we must first be clear what it is for men to make their own history, for men to act and not just to suffer. So the concept of human action is central to our enquiry. What is it to understand any given piece of behaviour as a human action? Consider the following example. If my head nods, it may be a sign of assent to a question or it may be a nervous tick. To explain the nod as a way of saying 'Yes' to a question is to give it a role in the context of human action. To explain the nod as a nervous tick is to assert that the nod was not an action but something that happened to me. To understand the nod as a nervous tick we turn to the neurophysiologist for a causal explanation. To understand it as a sign of assent is to move in a different direction. It is to ask for a statement of the purpose that my saying 'Yes' served; it is to ask for reasons, not for causes, and it is to ask for reasons which point to a recognisable want or need served by my action. This reference to purpose is important. When social anthropologists come across some unintelligible mode of behaviour, obedience to a primitive taboo, for example, they look for some as yet unnoticed purpose, some want or need to which such obedience ministers; and if they find none they look for some past want or need which the practice once served, even though now it is nothing but a useless survival. That is to say, we make both individual deeds and social practices intelligible as human actions by showing how they connect with characteristically human desires, needs and the like. Where we cannot do this, we treat the unintelligible piece of behaviour as a symptom, a survival or superstition.

One of the root mistakes of the liberal belief in the autonomy of morality now stands out. The believer in the autonomy of morality attempts to treat his fundamental moral principles as without any basis. They are his because he has chosen them. They can have no further vindication. And that is to say among other things that neither moral utterance nor moral action can be vindicated by reference to desires or needs. The 'ought' of morality is utterly divorced from the 'is' of desire. This divorce is most strikingly presented in the position taken by Kant that it is a defining characteristic of moral actions that they shall not be performed 'from inclination'. It is repeated in contemporary terms by those writers who deny that one moral judgment can be based on anything except another more fundamental moral judgment, on the grounds that no 'is' can entail an 'ought' and that entailment is the only logically respectable relationship between statements. And this position does not need to be attacked any further for my present purposes, for it is obvious that to represent morality in this light is to make it unintelligible as a form of human action. It is to make our moral judgments appear like primitive taboos, imperatives which we just happen to utter. It is to turn 'ought' into a kind of nervous cough with which we accompany what we hope will be the more impressive of our injunctions.

At this point it is worth recalling one way of reconnecting morality and desire, namely that produced by the shock effect on eighteenth-century moralists of travellers' tales from Polynesia. A rationalist like Diderot is able to contrast powerfully the simple moral code of the Polynesians, which expresses and satisfies desire, with the complex moral code of Europe, which represses and distorts it. But this contrast may be used to support a simple hedonism, belief in which is as destructive of moral understanding as is belief in moral autonomy. It is no use saying simply 'Do as you want', for at first sight we want many and conflicting things. We need a morality which orders our desires and yet expresses them. The myth of the natural man who spontaneously obeys desire is only comprehensible as the myth of a society where desire appears utterly cut off from morality. How did this divorce occur?

The short and obvious answer would perhaps run like this. Morality expresses the more permanent and long-run of human desires. But for most human history, such desires rarely achieve fulfilment. And so the objects of desire disappear from consciousness. And the rules survive, as a primitive taboo survives. Only the rules still have point, but men have forgotten what their point is. And then as the possibility of the abolition of class society and the possibility of new forms of human community appear, the objects of desire come back into the moral picture. Men recall to consciousness the lost purpose of their moral rules. And if at this point they insist on treating the rules as purposeless and autonomous they contribute only to the frustration of morality. Thus the history of morality is the history of men ceasing to see moral rules as the repression of desire and as something that men have made and accepted for themselves and coming to see them instead either as an alien, eternal, disembodied yet objective law, which constrains and represses, or as an entirely arbitrary subjective choice.

Hegel in his early anti-theological writings thinks of the Jewish law written on stone tablets as the archetype of the objectification of morality, and such objectification is for him symptomatic of human alienation. We can see why. Men objectify moral rules, have to objectify them, when the desires which they repress are too painful or too dangerous for men to know them as their own. (The resemblance between what Hegel says about society and what Freud says about the individual hardly needs remarking on.) They appear instead as the voice of the other, the non-human, the divine; or they just appear. Belief in the autonomy of morality expresses this alienation at the level of philosophy.

One way of writing the history of morality would be this: to see it as the coming together of three strands which have been held apart in class-society. The first of these is the history of moral codes, meaning by this not so much the history of which rules commend themselves in each society as the history of how different societies have conceived of the nature of moral rules. If I suggest in outline the type of thing that I mean it will obviously be no more than a caricature. But even caricatures have their uses.

For the Greeks the connection between the moral life and the pursuit of what men want is always preserved, even if sometimes very tenuously. The desires which the moral life is alleged to satisfy are sometimes a little curious, as for example Aristotle's conception of doing philosophy as the supreme fulfilment of human aspiration. But desire is always kept in the picture. So it is too in the Bible. What God offers is something that will satisfy all our desires. (The commandment that we love our neighbours as ourselves both presupposes and sanctions a high degree of self-love.) And desire remains at the heart of morality in the Middle Ages. It is true that now morality becomes a matter of divine commandments, but the God who commands is the God who created our human nature and His commandments are in consequence desired to be such as will fulfil his purpose of blessedness for that nature. So that in Thomist ethics an Aristotelian view of desire and a Christian view of the moral law are synthesised, even if somewhat unsatisfactorily. But the Protestant reformation changes this. First, because human beings are totally corrupt their nature cannot be a function of true morality. And next because as totally depraved beings, indeed even perhaps as simple finite beings, we cannot judge God. So we obey God's commandments not because they and He are good, but simply because they are his. The moral law becomes a connection of divine fiats, so far as we are concerned totally arbitrary, for they are unconnected with anything we may want or desire. At this stage two other considerations suggest themselves. The first is that if the moral rules have force, they surely do so whether God commands them or not. The second is that perhaps there is no God. 'Do this, because it will bring you happiness'; 'Do this because God enjoins it as the way to happiness'; 'Do this because God enjoins it'; 'Do this.' These are the four stages in the development of autonomous morality. At each stage our moral concepts are silently redefined so that it soon appears self-evident that they must be used in the way that they are used.

The second thread in the history of morality is the history of human attitudes to human desire. For as morality becomes thought of as objective and eternal, so desire becomes something anarchic and amoral. Diderot and his friends could appeal to the 'natural man', his wants uncontaminated by the evils of society, and suppose that desire could be recalled to its central place in the moral life by such an appeal. But in class society desire itself is remoulded, not merely suppressed. Seeking to find an outlet it legitimates itself by becoming respectable. Men try to want what the ruling ethos says that they want. They never succeed, because desire is spontaneous or it is not desire. 'A man's self is a law unto itself,' wrote D. H. Lawrence, 'not unto *himself*, mind you.' And again, 'The only thing man has to trust to in coming to himself is his desire and his impulse. But both desire and impulse tend to fall into mechanical automatism: to fall from spontaneous reality into dead or material reality.' But when social life takes on dead, acceptable, mechanical forms, desire reappears as the negative, as the outlaw. The counterpart of Diderot's myth of the happy Polynesia is the reality of 'Rameau's Nephew', a work which stimulated both Hegel and Marx. This is a dialogue between Diderot himself, the voice of the man who accepts the forms and norms of society, and Rameau, who represents the suppressed desires, the hidden anarchic consciousness. Freud saw in this dialogue an anticipation of his own contrast between conscious and unconscious mental life. But in the dialogue Diderot goes far beyond any individual psychology: here the voice of desire is not the voice of happy Polynesian society, but something become purely individual, the voice that can live only by hypocrisy and an extreme care for self-interest. One remembers Engels' comment on a remark by Hegel:

> 'One believes one is saying something great,' Hegel remarks, if one says that 'man is naturally good'. But one forgets that one says something far greater when one says 'man is naturally evil'. With Hegel evil is the form in which the motive force of historical development presents itself. This contains the two-fold meaning that, on the one hand, each new advance necessarily appears as a sacrilege against things hallowed, as a rebellion against conditions, though old and moribund, yet sanctified by custom; and that, on the other hand, it is precisely the wicked passions of men – greed and lust for power – which, since the emergence of class antagonisms, serve as levers of historical development.

Desire becomes recognisable only as something individualist, which tends, as in Hobbes, to the war of all against all, and morality, when it is related to desire, becomes at best an uneasy truce or peace between warring desires, embodied in a social contract. So that even desire conceived as selfish is never conceived of as more than partly satisfied. And desire as a driving force is stripped of all these qualities which unite men. Nietzsche's superman is pure dehumanised desire despising the values of those who accept the autonomy of morality and 'transvaluing' them. Figures such as Nietzsche's are the reflection in a romanticising consciousness of an entirely non-fictional capitalist type. E. M. Forster in *Howard's End* makes Helen Schlegel say,

> 'Perhaps the little thing that says "I" is missing out of the middle of their heads, and then it's a waste of time to blame them. There's a nightmare of a theory that says a special race is being born which will rule the rest of us in the future just because it lacks the little thing that says "I". There are two kinds of people – our kind, who live straight from the middle of their heads, and the other kind who can't because their heads have no middle. They can't say "I". They *aren't* in fact . . .

Pierpont Morgan has never said "I" in his life. No superman can say "I want" because "I want" must lead to the question "Who am I?" and so to Pity and to Justice. He only says "want" – "Want Europe", if he's Napoleon: "want wives" if he's Bluebeard; "want Botticelli" if he's Pierpont Morgan. Never "I" and if you could pierce through him, you'd find panic and emptiness in the middle.'

The peculiar contribution of the Marxist critic here is the understanding that the 'I' can only be put back into 'I want' if the 'we' is put back into 'we want'. What Forster calls the non-existence of those who say 'want', what Lawrence calls their 'mechanical automatism', these are the outcome of a type of society in which paradoxically it is both true that individuals are isolated from each other and that their individuality is lost to them as the system demands an increasing identification of them with itself. How to regain the 'I' by asserting 'we'?

The fundamental answer to this is the whole Marxist theory of class-struggle. To have set the problem properly I ought to have set those changes in the moral consciousness about which I have written in their real, material context. The rift between our conception of morality and our conception of desire will never be overcome until the rift between morality and desire is overcome in action. But since we are already on the margin of the transition that will heal that breach, we can see in outline at any rate how the two may come together in consciousness. At this point the crucial concept for Marxists is their concept of human nature, a concept which has to be at the centre of any discussion of moral theory. For it is in terms of this concept alone that morality and desire can come together once more. How this is so can be seen if beside the sketchy histories of morality and desire I have given, I place an equally sketchy account of the emergence of this concept.

One can begin with the Bible. In the Bible the dealings of individual men with God are all parts of the dealings of Man with God. Man appears like a character in a morality play, passing from his first nature as Adam (the Hebrew word for 'man') to his second nature as Christ (the 'last Adam', as St Paul calls him). But the unity of human nature is something perceived only at rare moments and in symbolic form; original sin has broken it. So there is no necessary drive within Christianity to incarnate human unity. (This is not to say that some Christians have not looked for such an incarnation. The difficulty is that all the formulations of the Christian religion are politically double-edged. 'All men are equal before God and God wills them to be at one' can either be interpreted to mean that inequality and disunity are a scandal that Christians ought to strive to abolish, or they can be interpreted to mean that it is only before God that men are equal, and only God that can make them at one, so that a merely human equality and unity are neither desirable nor possible. I do not doubt that the original Gospel commands imply the former interpretation; but any Christian who wants to can always rely on the second. As most do.)

In the eighteenth century God becomes a deistic ghost in progressive thought. But the conception of Man remains central. Only whereas the religious conception of Man was ideal in the sense of being a representation of what was believed to be ultimate human destiny, the eighteenth-century conception is ideal in the sense of being concerned with what is human only in an abstract and formal way. Human rights are inalienable and eternal; only it is compatible with their possession that men should suffer poverty and exploitation. Man in the Bible has a cosmic history; Man in the eighteenth century has a rational nature whose history is the slow emergence of Reason into Enlightenment or as often a history in which Reason passes again into darkness (Gibbon); it is only with Hegel that Man begins to possess and with Marx that Man achieves a real history. The point of the word 'real' here is that in Hegel and Marx the history of Man becomes one with the history of men; with empiricist historiography the history of men becomes all the history that there is and the final outcome is Sidney Webb's view that there can only be the history of this or that particular institution, but that there can be no such thing as history as such. This is to say that in Hegel and Marx the history of man is seen as the history of men discovering and making a common shared humanity. For Hegel the subject of this history is Spirit. And individual human lives appear only as finite fragments of the Absolute. For Marx the emergence of human nature is something to be comprehended only in terms of the history of class-struggle. Each age reveals a development of human potentiality which is specific to that form of social life and which is specifically limited by the class-structure of that society. This development of possibility reaches a crisis under capitalism. For men have up to that age lived at their best in a way that allowed them glimpses of their own nature as something far richer than what they themselves lived out. Under capitalism the growth of production makes it possible for man to reappropriate his own nature, for actual human beings to realise the richness of human possibility. But not only the growth of production is necessary. The experience of human equality and unity that is bred in industrial working-class life is equally a precondition of overcoming men's alienation from this and from themselves. And only from the standpoint of that life and its possibilities can we see each previous stage of history as a particular form of approximation to a climax which it is now possible to approach directly.

How does this conception of human nature close the gap between morality and desire? I have given a one-sided and partial view of Marx's approach to history; I now have to give an equally one-sided and partial account of how this view of history bears upon morality. Capitalism provides a form of life in which men rediscover desire in a number of ways. They discover above all that what they want most is what they want in common with others; and more than this that a sharing of human life is not just a means to the accomplishment of what they desire, but that certain ways of sharing human life are indeed what they most desire.

'When Communist workers meet, they have as first aim theory, propaganda and so on. But they take for their own at the same time and by this token a new need, the need for society, and what seems a means has become an end.' So Marx. One meets the anarchic individualist desires which a competitive society breeds in us by a rediscovery of the deeper desire to share what is common in humanity, to be divided neither from them nor from oneself, to be a man. And in this discovery moral rules reappear as having point. For their content can now be seen as important in correcting our short-term selfishness, and thus helping to release desire. Moral rules and what we fundamentally want no longer stand in a sharp contrast.

To discover what we share with others, to rediscover common desire, is to acquire a new moral standpoint. One cannot, of course, make this discovery by introspection whether systematic or random. Whether one makes it at all will depend on whether capitalism places men in a position in which such deep dissatisfaction is born that only a realistic answer to the question 'What do I really want?' can be given. The history of all false consciousness is a history of evasions of this question. And this question can only be answered by a discovery that 'I want' and 'we want' coincide; I discover both what I want and how to achieve it as I discover with whom I share my wants, as I discover, that is, the class to whom I am bound. In a class-divided society, my desires draw me to this or that class. And because the rediscovery of moral rules as having their point in the fulfilment of desire is this sort of discovery, one sees how Marx's contention that all morality is class morality has to be taken. But what content has *our* morality?

The viewpoint we have to meet is the view shared by both the Stalinist and the moral critic of Stalinism, that the only Marxist criterion in moral action is the test of how far the proposed action will take us along the road to socialism. But we have already seen that for a Marxist who realizes that the progress to socialism is not automatic, that the transition is a transition to freedom and not one that can be calculated, there can be in this sense no predetermined 'road to socialism'. Means and ends interpenetrate not just in some moral ideal, but in history itself. Yet this is still only to say what a Marxist morality is not. What is it?

IV

As against the Stalinist it is an assertion of moral absolutes; as against the liberal critic of Stalinism it is an assertion of desire and of history. To begin with the contrast with the liberal. The liberal sees himself as choosing his values. The Marxist sees himself as discovering them. He discovers them as he rediscovers fundamental human desire; this is a discovery he can only make in company with others. The ideal of human solidarity, expressed in the working-class movement, only has point because of the fact of human solidarity which comes to light in the discovery of what we want. So the Marxist never speaks morally just for himself. He speaks in the name of a whole historical development, in the name of a human nature which is violated by exploitation and its accompanying evils. The man who cuts himself off from other people (and this has no content unless we realise that the vast mass of other people is the working class) says at first 'I want' and then just 'want'. His 'I ought' is the most tremulous of moral utterances. For it represents nothing but his own choice. So the liberal moral critic of Stalinism isolates himself, makes his utterance unintelligible and has no defence against the patterns of conformism which his society seeks at every point to enforce upon him.

To speak for human possibility as it emerges, to speak for our shared desires, this is to speak for an absolute. There are things you can do which deny your common humanity with others so that they isolate you as effectively as if you were a liberal. It is for this reason that the Marxist condemns the H-Bomb. Anyone who would use this has contracted out of common humanity. So with the denial of racial equality, so with the rigged trial. The condemnation of Imre Nagy was an act which cut off its authors from humanity. Because in denying the rights and desires of others you deny that they and you share desires and rights in exactly the same way. You only possess either in so far as you have them in common with others. And thus Communist morality is by no means futurist. I think of Dzerzhinsky in gaol, volunteering for the most servile tasks in order to show that labour dishonours no man no matter of what degree of culture. I think of all those Communists who died; what made the moral stuff of their actions was not that it contributed to some future state of society. They may not have contributed at all. What was at the heart of what they did was an embodiment of a human nature of which Communism will be the great release.

The argument at this point, as indeed perhaps throughout this paper, has been so compressed that I may be in some danger of replacing precision by rhetoric. What is it in fact, it may be asked, that leads us as socialists to view with equal contempt those who failed to protest at Nagy's murder and those who jump to protest at the late Cuban trials? The answer to this could only begin from a detailed account of what Nagy did and what happened in Cuba. But to give such an account would be to see, for example, that Nagy abided by and his executioners fought against certain principles and values. The values in question may be only partly expressed in human nature to date, but the attempt to give them full embodiment in human life is that which alone can give meaning to the history of morality. That we take up this point of view is not, as I have already argued, simply the fruit of our own choice. We discover rather than choose where we stand as men with particular aspirations at a particular point in history. What the Stalinist fails to see is that although choice is not the sole basis of socialist affirmation, nevertheless as socialists we confront issues which cannot be understood in terms of the so-called 'objective' laws. It is not that Stalinists take a different view of the moral issues which I have raised in this article. It is that within their framework of thought such issues cannot even arise.

The concept of human nature is therefore what binds together the Marxist view of history and Communist morality. What it teaches is in part that the liberal moral critic is the one person who has no right to criticise Stalinism. The separation of morality from history, from desire discovered through the discovery of that common human nature which history shows as emerging, leaves morality without any basis. But this is not a logical necessity for morality, as the liberal would have it. For we can depict a moral alternative which is not without any basis. The liberal critic may speak against Stalinism; but he speaks for no one but himself and his choices. We saw the fragility of his position at the outset; we can now see why it is fragile. Furthermore we can now see more clearly what the liberal critic and the Stalinist have in common.

The liberal critic accepts the autonomy of ethics; the Stalinist looks to a crude utilitarianism. The liberal accepts the divorce of morality and desire, but chooses morality; the Stalinist accepts the divorce and chooses desire, renaming it morality. But this desire that he chooses is not the desire to be fundamentally at one with mankind. It is desire as it is, random and anarchic, seeking power and immediate pleasure only too often. So one finds under Stalinism the moral belief in an ultimate justifying end, combined with immediate power-seeking. The two do not go as ill together as they seem to at first sight. Both the autonomy of ethics and utilitarianism are aspects of the consciousness of capitalism; both are forms of alienation rather than moral guides. And to see how even the Stalinist perpetuates a class consciousness is to become aware of how liable one may oneself be to be putting forward merely a set of self-justifying attitudes.

For at the end of these notes I am aware only of how little has been achieved in them. Of one thing I am sure: that they are an attempt to find expression at a theoretical level for a moral vision that is being reborn today among socialists, most of whom are not theoreticians. Even if my analysis is wholly mistaken, the historical power of that vision is untouched. That, and not any amount of analysis, is what will lead us out of the moral wilderness.

PART II

Combining Social Science with Moral Theory

'Social Science Methodology as the Ideology of Bureaucratic Authority'

Charles Perrow has remarked of conflict in organizations that 'The matter has been little studied beyond anecdotal or descriptive case studies' (*Complex Organizations*, p. 159). What we find in the literature in fact is a curious discrepancy between theoretical writing on organizations which all too rarely recognizes the fact of conflict except as a marginal phenomenon, and some descriptive studies which have identified conflict as widespread not only in industrial and political situations, but also in such institutions as hospitals and universities. The very ubiquity of conflict suggests that it cannot be merely a marginal phenomenon; yet the writers on theory use schemes of interpretation which insistently relegate it to that category. I want to suggest in this paper a perspective from which this discrepancy becomes intelligible by arguing that the social life of formal organizations is simultaneously ridden with conflicts and sustained by devices which enable participants not to recognize this fact. I want to argue further that the kind of theoretical writing which Perrow criticizes is itself in part an ideological expression of that same organizational life which the theorists are attempting to describe. One key element in this ideology of organizations turns out, so I shall argue, to be the conventional methodology of the social sciences. One key function of this ideology is to sustain bureaucratic authority. A necessary preliminary is to begin by providing a better understanding of the notion of conflict. To this task therefore I turn first.

I Three types of conflict and the concept of ideology

Perrow in the passage already cited considers the type of conflict which arises in the competition of different groups within a formal organization for such goods as security, power, and autonomy. The examples he gives include sales and production departments in firms, doctors, nurses and administrators in hospitals, and faculty and administration in universities. Of such conflicts, he writes, 'To reduce, contain or use these conflicts is the job of the administrator' (Perrow, p. 159). Clearly administrators do generally succeed in such tasks and equally clearly this is one reason why theorists are able to see conflict as secondary and marginal in the life of organizations. But why are administrators able to succeed as easily as they do? Because, so I want to suggest, the participants in these conflicts themselves already share a view of organizations according to which conflict is secondary and marginal and act in accordance with that view. Consider, in order to point a contrast, a very different type of conflict, that involved in war.

What does a military strategist of genius – as against one of mere talent – a Napoleon or a Lee, a Liddell Hart or a Guderian, do? He makes himself and his effects as unpredictable as possible. By innovating in tactics, in organization, and in weapons' technology and use, he disrupts what has hitherto been taken to be the necessary structural order of a war or a battle. In so doing he treats the *de facto* regularities which have been found to hold in past wars and battles in a quite different way than do the lecturers at the Staff colleges of the nations whom the military geniuses defeat. The Staff colleges of such nations are often the unhappy heirs of some earlier genius. The Prussian General Staff codified the practice of Frederick the Great into a series of rules which they treated as the natural laws of war; Napoleon understood their codification, constituted himself a counter-example to their law-like generalizations and defeated them at Jena and Auerstadt. In 1861 the Union generals all knew what Napoleon would have done; they too believed themselves the possessors of the natural laws of war. Lee, who knew that they knew what Napoleon would have done, constituted himself a counter-example to their generalizations and defeated them.

Military history thus makes it clear that one very good way to defeat another nation would be to make sure that it used a certain set of textbooks in its military academies. By contriving that your opponents understood their actions, your actions and regularities embodied in military transactions between the two parties in one particular way, by inducing them to categorize what occurs on battlefields in one way rather than another, you would have made them available as future victims on the battlefield. In fact defeated nations, when they are defeated at the hands of the textbooks, are so defeated by reason of their own contrivances and not by those of the enemy. But it is clear that victorious generals have sometimes adopted the right textbook: Guderian's reading of Liddell Hart is a striking case in point. Hence there is a battle of textbooks, a battle of understanding and of concepts before there is a battle of military force, and one of the best ways to win the latter is to have won the former first.

There is an important parallel between this truth about military conflict and an unnoticed truth about conflict in organizations. Those engaged in conflict within organizations normally understand those conflicts in much the same terms as Perrow describes them. They see themselves as having interests which lead them to want or to try to secure a greater share than their competitors of such goods as power, security, autonomy – and money (curiously unmentioned by Perrow). But in understanding their conflicts in this way they have already accepted some one particular way of understanding their situation, some one particular way of identifying interests, some one particular concept of reward or of power; and it may well be the case that by accepting this particular way of understanding their situation they have rendered themselves manageable and to this extent defeatable by others. They have already been defeated in the conflict of understanding and concepts as a preliminary to being defeated in a conflict of interests.

Take one key example, that of industrial work and its rewards. The dominant way of understanding such work under capitalism – and not only in America – is that whereby workers, management and investors all share in the distribution of what is jointly earned, in order that each gets as much as possible, and what matters is that as much as possible be produced. All three groups therefore have a common interest to which their particular interest ought to be subordinated. On this view men are primarily consumers and they work in order to be able to consume. On this view so long as each group recognizes the common interest it is rational for the others to do so; only when the other groups have selfishly relinquished that interest is it rational to be selfish oneself. So normal is this view among us that it seems natural too. But from another perspective it is precisely unnatural.

On this rival view, what is essentially human is rational activity, and consumption exists to serve activity and not to be served by it. We ought to eat in order to work, not vice versa. The classical expression of this thought is Aristotle's, but all artists, most professors and some socialists believe it too. Only sentimentalists believe that work ought or can be always interesting, but in an order where work serves consumption it is bound to be always uninteresting. On the first view my fundamental interest as a member of one group is in how large a share of the product of work I consume; on the second view I can have *no* fundamental interest in the continuance of an order that represents work, interest and rewards in the way that the first view does. It is clear that if the first view is universally or even just very widely held, the concept of interest employed will be such that conflicts over interests will be local, manageable and, if the managers are sufficiently adroit, marginal; but if the second view were ever to be held by even a substantial minority of workers, then conflict between them and the managing and investing classes would be endemic, central and possibly interminable. But the managing and owning classes do not have to fight this particular battle over interest and privilege as fiercely as they might otherwise, because they have already for the most part won the battle over how interest and privilege are to be conceptualized and understood.

Or consider another closely related example. Modern liberal politics is dominated by a conception of the political process as one of bargaining between interests. Political morality consists in the observance of certain legally enforceable restrictions upon conduct; morality in general is relegated to private life. There is largely lacking any conception of political life as being the pursuit of a common good which transcends all partial interests and which can be realized by the individual only through his participation in political life. There cannot be, for our dominant effective notion of the common good is merely that of an artifact compounded out of individual and partial interests as a result of the bargaining process. Aristotle's *Politics* precisely insofar as it is a successful conceptualization of the Greek city-state fails to comprehend our mode of comprehension of politics and therefore our politics.

Yet matters are more complex than I have hitherto suggested. Human nature being what it is, you may turn your gaze insistently away from Aristotelianism, as the modern bourgeois world does, but perhaps you can never rid yourself of its categories of interpretation entirely. In both the examples which I cited, certain non-Aristotelian modes of understanding and classification have prevailed. Politics, morality, law, economics and justice are all categories understood in a particular way. (In the modern world's understanding, for example, the notion of *a just price* makes no sense; justice belongs in one realm and the price mechanism in another.) Concepts such as interest, power, liberty (see C. B. Macpherson's analysis in *Democratic Theory: Essays in Retrieval*) are understood in highly specific ways. (Notice incidentally that the concepts of interest and competition between rival groups presupposed in Perrow's analysis are the counterpart to my economic and political example.) But questions which cannot be intelligently asked within the dominant conceptual scheme still get asked. The relationship of the good citizen to the good man is an essentially Aristotelian question; and when so understood it is a question about the structure of community, about the distribution of certain dispositions (virtues) in a systematic way within the entire community. This is the question which haunted the Watergate inquiries; but because the conventional idiom would not allow it to be asked, moralizing took the place of inquiry. Instead of looking for corruption in the structure of community (or lack of it), it was looked for in the heart of Richard Nixon. (Not that it could not be found there.)

What I am suggesting is that unresolved conceptual conflicts partially determine the form of some overt conflicts; that it may be that the ubiquity of that conflict which organization theorists take to be marginal stems from the deeper unrecognized conflict in modes of understanding. Between the three types of conflict which have been identified – the first being those competitive conflicts between different interests within socially established organizations in good working order which Perrow acknowledges, the second being military conflict, and the third being those conflicts of conceptualization and understanding on which I am laying emphasis – the resemblances are as important as the differences. The second and the third resemble each other and differ from the first in that they are 'unmanageable' and they characteristically end in victory for one party, defeat for the other. But in the case of the third type both victory and defeat are usually tacit and unrecognized. Indeed part of what makes victory victory and defeat defeat consists, in this type of case, in their being unrecognized.

It is scarcely odd then that this type of conflict has largely gone unrecognized by social theory. With that lack of recognition has customarily gone a lack of recognition of the importance to be attached to certain other features of social reality, all of which tend to make that reality unmanageable and therefore such that if and when they do appear on the scene, they are apt to be treated by the manager and by his social scientific advisors as ghosts to be exorcised. The first is a feature of the relationship of understanding and interpretation of social reality to that reality, a relationship in at least one crucial point very different from that of the understanding of nature to physical reality.

If widespread brain lesions resulted in the loss of all our beliefs about atoms and molecules so that not a trace of such concepts remained in our thought or our language or was embodied in our practice, there would still be atoms and molecules, just as there are now, and nothing that is now true in particle theory would then be false. If similar lesions resulted in the loss of all our beliefs about representative government so that not a trace of that concept remained in thought or language or was embodied in practice, there would be no such thing as representative government any longer. Beliefs about the concepts of physical realities are always secondary to those realities; the physical world does not require us to have any particular beliefs about it or concepts of it, for it to exist. But with social reality it is quite otherwise. Social practices, institutions and organizations are partially constituted by the beliefs and concepts of those who participate in, have transactions with and attitudes towards them. Why do I say only 'partially'? Because it is of course the belief-informed and concept-informed *activities* that *are* practices, institutions and organizations, and activities have other important relevant characteristics. But mere behavior by itself, abstracted from beliefs and concepts, is meaningless; confronted with uninterpreted or uninterpretable behavior we are forced into the position of the protagonists of Kafka's novels.

In any type of practice or institution of any complexity, the modes of interpretation that constitute the practice will not always be entirely coherent internally nor consistent with one another: the patients' understanding of the doctor–patient relationship and the doctors' understanding of that relationship, which together give form to their material transactions, are notably not necessarily at one. To borrow a useful metaphor, although one which can also be misleading, their relationship embodies or may embody *an argument* about sickness, health, expertise, drugs and many other topics. Each attempts to win this argument in part by casting the other into a role which fits the dramatic forms suited to their own side of the argument. As with the doctor–patient relationship, so with the parent–child, the ruler–ruled, the professor–student and so on.

These forms of tension and argument manifest themselves at the level of vocabulary in the essentially contestable character of the concepts which are deployed in such arguments. Examples of essentially contestable concepts include those of art, politics, party, education, disease, natural science. It is of the essence of such concepts that actual or potential debate arises over their application. What counts as a central case exemplifying the concept and what as a marginal case are always open to question. Hence in this area certain key generalizations remain debatable too. If such concepts as those of marriage, tragedy, and education are essentially contestable – as they are – then what are and what are not genuine counter-examples to generalizations about marriage, tragedy, and education will be debatable in a way in which the question of what are or are not genuine counter-examples to generalizations about aminoacids, men over six feet tall, or lugworms, is undebatable. Moreover there is no way of understanding the subject matters to which such concepts apply without employing them. What objectivity requires in the study of such subject matters is an awareness of the contestable and argumentative character of what is going on.

Just because of those characteristics which social practices in general share with arguments of a certain kind – if you like, what I am saying is that arguments of a certain kind are among the paradigmatic social practices – they embody in themselves a certain unpredictability. It is of the nature of debates, arguments, battles and other conflicts that in the centrally important cases their outcome is unpredictable.

Conflict, arguments, contestability, unpredictability; it is striking how much more often these appear in our lives than in our social theories. But there is of course good reason for this. There are historical periods in which these are open and admitted features of social and political life, especially those in which a dramatic move is being made from one fundamental conceptualization of social action to another. Professor W. H. Adkins (*Merit and Responsibility*) has described how the concepts of Greece's heroic age continued side by side and in tension with those of the *polis* in fifth-century Athens. In *Burnt Njal* the concepts of Icelandic paganism strive to retain their hold in a social world already nascently Christian. In such periods rival interpretations of social life manifestly constitute social life. But for many historical episodes this is not so. Rivalry and conflict at the level of conceptualization are more usually latent.

It is a central feature of established social orders that they tend to embody in their social institutions denials of the centrality of conflict, argument, contestability and unpredictability in human life; and it is a central feature of most social theories that they share this characteristic with most social orders. Nor should this parallelism surprise us. On the view that I have taken, social practices are themselves embodied interpretations of social practices. Social theories are unembodied interpretations which attempt to stand in the same relation to society that physical theories stand to nature. There will always be the possibility therefore that instead of mirroring the conflicting interpretations embodied in a practice, instead of achieving the objectivity involved in the acknowledgement of conflict, social theories will, in a way that serves the interests of one of the contending parties, deny by omission the facts of conflict, argument, contestability and unpredictability.

For it is characteristic of the adherents of rival social interpretations embodied in a complex social practice to deny the reality of rivalry in the interest of a claim that there is an incontestable underlying structure; social victory at this deep level is the achievement of inducing those who participate in the practice to agree in conceptualizing their activities in such a way that one of the contestable interpretations no longer appears contestable, but simply how things are – 'the facts'. It is when a social theory serves this form of social practice that it functions as an ideology. Or rather, since the word 'ideology' is available as nobody's property and for everybody's idiosyncratic meaning, that indicates how I am going to apply the word.

Notice three features of the notion of ideology as I am using it. The first is that in order to function as an ideology a theory must express a partial truth. Radically false theories could not so function. We therefore have to be careful about how we make a distinction between science and ideology. A view that is partial may mark progress in science as well as being available for ideological uses. Indeed since all our views in science are subject to a possible need for revision because of their partial character, as well as for other reasons, ideology ceases to be something that we can merely impute to others, exempting ourselves from the charge. Nonetheless, when a view is functioning ideologically, the mode in which it is held is likely to differ from that in which it is held by those who are treating it as part of science. For it is likely to be held in ways that put it *in practice*, although not necessarily in principle, beyond refutation.

Secondly, to call a view ideological says nothing about the motives or the intentions of those who advance it. Thus this account of ideology is not reductionist in the way that some theories of ideology have been. The proponents of such theories claimed that certain thinkers *merely* reflected the social order in their theorizing; but the present claim is that any such reflection is a function of theories, if they are ideological, *over and above* whatever other characteristics those theories may possess. Notice also that my account is incompatible with any basis–superstructure analysis of social orders.

Thirdly and perhaps most importantly, not only is my use of the concept of ideology different from the uses both of Mannheim and of Marx, it differs also from that of those modern political scientists, such as Robert Lane, who have sought to include ideology in their accounts as one more discrete empirical variable. The reason for this is clear. When we have reached the level at which we are engaged in handling social life as a collection of discrete empirical variables, then all the work of interpretation and conceptualization is already behind us. We are already dealing with a fully interpreted world. One conceptualization rather than another is already presupposed. In the world thus understood, the beliefs held by individuals or by groups of individuals may well function as just one more variable factor. But the beliefs, the interpretations, which constitute the ordering of the world to be investigated, which make the available range of variables what it is, these underlying constitutive beliefs, concepts and interpretations will have disappeared from view. With them all too often there will also have disappeared from view argument, conflict, contestability and unpredictability as fundamental phenomena.

There will of course in the constituted investigated world be interpretations, arguments, conflicts and failures in prediction. But these will be understood *within* a context of regularity and order. They will be secondary phenomena. The notion of order will indeed be *regulative* for this kind of investigation and various concepts of system and structure will be the ideals to which empirical theory seeks to conform. In so seeking, indeed in its very acceptance of the constituted world as its starting point, empirical theory, both political and social, will indeed be ideological in just the sense that I have described.

Ideology then has two characteristic effects: it works to conceal the features of particular conflicts, of particular contestable concepts and situations, of particular unpredictabilities; and it does this by working to conceal conflict, contestability and unpredictability as such. Ideology is the mask worn both by particular dominant orders and by order itself. But it is also the mask worn by those critics of social orders who equally with its conservative defenders wish to deny any ultimacy to conflict, contestability and unpredictability. Ideology therefore can be a phenomenon of the Left as well as of the Right.

II

I have already suggested that the characteristic procedures sanctioned by the methodology of empirical social science may be ideological. Yet this suggestion is perhaps a little premature for we need first to recognize that the very existence of methodology as a subject in the social science curriculum is a suspicious circumstance. What is it actually doing in that curriculum? Some writers have understood its task, whether approvingly or disapprovingly, as being that of informing social inquiry with the norms and methods of the natural sciences. But we ought to note at once that neither physicists nor chemists nor biologists study anything called 'methodology'. So that the very inclusion in our curriculum of such a subject itself differentiates our practices from those of natural scientists. I have sometimes therefore been tempted to think of it as essentially a histrionic subject: *how to act the part of a natural scientist on the stage of the social sciences* with the more technical parts of the discipline functioning as do greasepaint, false beards and costumes in the theater. But of course actors in the theater always know that they are actors and so do their audience; whereas methodologists and their audience at least do not recognize their performances as dramatic. What then is actually going on? At least three things.

One might be described as the equivalent of the helpful practical hints that you find at the beginning of some cookbooks. Advice on how different ways of wording questions in your survey will elicit different answers from your respondents is an example. Natural scientists have to learn how to see through a microscope and cooks have to learn how to judge the age of an egg. But neither cooks nor natural scientists elevate the acquiring of useful knacks to the status of a subject in their curriculum.

A second set of activities that go under the label 'methodology' do indeed belong to a discipline in its own right: applied mathematics and statistics. The last thing that I want to deny is the essential part played by statistics and other branches of mathematics in all inquiry (I myself would be quite prepared to make the passing of examinations in statistics, calculus and computing science a prerequisite for graduate study in *any* social science and perhaps in the humanities as well). But it is important to understand what statistics can and cannot do for you. Its genuine power includes an ability to perform two central tasks for the social scientist; it can provide, under certain assumptions, a measure of how far an association between two sets of items is *not* random; and it can in providing such a measure provide evidence that warrants the *elimination* of certain hypotheses from consideration. Note that both abilities are *negative* and only negative.

The crucial truth that is often ignored when an insufficiently puritanical and ascetic view of the power of statistics is taken, is that *from no set of purely statistical premises can any conclusion of a causal kind be validly derived.* This holds even when, as with path analysis, we are able to give a temporal ordering to our variables. And it holds too if we reword it so that it runs: No set of purely statistical premises is adequate evidence for any genuine causal conclusion. This must be the case, for given any correlation between any two sets of items, no matter how strong – it may be perfect, if you wish – the truth of the statement which asserts that correlation is equally compatible with the truth of any one out of an infinite set of statements which relate those items causally, and the truth of any one member of that set entails the falsity of all the others. Thus there is a logical gap between all statistical statements and all causal statements; a social scientist who offers statistical evidence for the truth of any genuine causal statement has performed the logical feat of selecting from an infinite set of statements consistent with that evidence just one. The social science journals are full of evidence that the vast majority of social scientists feel able to perform this logical and heuristic feat without ever telling us how they do it. How do they do it? We are fortunate in possessing at least one authoritative type of account in the conventional writings on methodology. I follow Herbert A. Simon's version ('Causation', pp. 352–4).

Simon of course acknowledges the truth that from statistical premises alone causal conclusions cannot be validly derived in at least two places in his argument. He says this explicitly in distinguishing spurious from genuine correlations (Simon, p. 354); and he has earlier allowed that when we have expressed the relationship between variables in a set of algebraic equations, we have not thereby unambiguously provided a device for genuine causal ordering: 'The causal ordering would be altered, of course, if before solving the equations the system is modified by taking linear combinations of them. This process is algebraically admissible . . .' (Simon, p. 353). The general form of Simon's solution to these is the general form, explicit or assumed, given by a number of writers. 'Since the causal orderings among variables can be determined only within the context of a scientific theory – a complete structure – it is only within such a context that spurious correlation can be distinguished from genuine correlation' (Simon, p. 354). What is 'a scientific theory – a complete structure', according to Simon? It turns out to be a body of causal knowledge concerning a number of the relevant variables. But this of course at once involves us in circularity. We can only acquire the simpler kinds of causal knowledge if we *already* possess a more sophisticated kind. This cannot be right. Technical sophistication has ended in mystification. What Simon has in fact reproduced with admirable clarity is an account of how in well-ordered, well-established, natural sciences, where we do already possess the requisite structures of theory, certain causal inferences are made. But this cannot be how they are made at the theoretical, empirical levels at which social scientific investigation moves. So how do social scientists in fact move from statistical premises to causal conclusions?

What provides them with a bridge, so I want to suggest, are not the sophistications of technique, but the presuppositions which must be accepted prior to the application of such technique. Conventional methodology, I am suggesting, already incorporates a highly particular and partial view of the social world, and in inducing the social scientist to adopt this view the types of connections available for his or her study are greatly reduced in number. Behavior is abstracted from the realm of conflicting meanings, which can then be reintroduced afterwards in suitable reduced form as a separate variable or set of variables. The world that *is* allowed to appear to view is one that conforms to five canons.

First it must be composed of discrete, independently identifiable variables. This is essential for the application of statistical methods. Secondly these variables must be identifiable in an evaluatively neutral non-contestable way. This is essentially for the social scientist to be able to identify which are and which are not the true members of a given population in an undebatable way. Thirdly the conceptualization of the subject matter studied is a task for the social scientist in which what governs his conceptualization is not a relationship to the rival conceptualizations of the society which is being studied, but his own convenience. The doctrine of operational definitions is the crudest version of this canon and embodies a characteristic misrepresentation of the practices of natural science. (On this point see Hilary Putnam, 'A Philosopher Looks at Quantum Mechanics'.) Fourthly the goal is the construction of law-like generalizations; the model here is not natural science, but a particular philosophical view of natural science exemplified in such writers as Herbert Feigl and C. G. Hempel. (Very often social scientists insist that their own generalizations are probabilistic, when the difficulties in identifying genuine law-like generalizations in the social sciences are brought to their notice. But this claim is ambiguous. If they mean that they are concerned *merely* with statistically significant relationships, then they are clearly not doing science at all; but if they are claiming that they either do or aspire to provide genuine law-like probabilistic generalizations – of the kind that occur in statistical mechanics, for example – then it needs to be pointed out that not only is their truth more difficult to establish than that of non-probabilistic law-like generalizations, but also – as we noted earlier – that from statistical premises alone no genuine law-like probabilistic generalizations can ever be derived or even importantly confirmed any more than can non-probabilistic ones. Thus restriction to probabilistic conclusions would not alter the nature of the methodological enterprise.)

Fifthly the type of generalization sought is of such a kind that it will afford a lever for producing predictable change in social structures; the relationship of cause to effect and of causal knowledge to causes is such that knowledge is taken to be productive of manipulative ability. This is of course the link between textbook methodology and social-scientific expertise as a commodity available to government and to private corporations.

These canons select certain features of social reality for attention and omit others. They simplify both the world and the selection of hypotheses. They allow for conflict and for ideology only within contexts of defined regularity, that is, for conflict insofar as it is manageable, and for ideology insofar as it is someone else's and not shared by oneself. Inability to manage conflict or to cope with ideology at this level will always be diagnosable as a symptom of lack of manipulative ability, and that in turn as a lack of social scientific knowledge. This has one splendid implication for the funding of social scientific research: for if the application of our present social scientific knowledge is successful, then of course we are warranted in asking for further funding, but if its application is unsuccessful, then this too is precisely a sign that further funding and further research is necessary. Failure vindicates the project as surely as success does; and, given the actual record of applied social science, how prudent this is! But this kind of irrefutability by failure, is of course one of the characteristic marks of ideology.

Methodology then functions so as to communicate one very particular vision of the social world and one that obscures from view the fundamental levels of conceptualization, conflict, contestability, and unpredictability as they constitute and operate in that world. It thus has one of the two centrally important effects of ideology. Does it have the other? Does it, that is, not only conceal these features of the social world in general but does it conceal them in the interests of one highly specific view of social reality held by individuals with specific social characteristics, so that it more particularly works to conceal conceptualizations, conflicts, contestabilities and unpredictabilities of some one particular character? I shall argue that it does, that social scientific methodology functions as one of the ideologies of bureaucratic authority. But to argue this I shall first have to elucidate the character of that authority.

III   Methodology and the ideology of bureaucratic authority

Molecules do not read chemistry books; but managers do read books on organization theory. Such books therefore, whatever the intentions of their authors, never merely describe; they provide models for future behavior, and if they become sufficiently successful texts in influential business schools, some original descriptive inadequacies may gradually disappear as organizational behavior conforms more closely to the books which managers read. Unfortunately the effects of their own books are not among the phenomena so far studied by organization theorists. But when we find that widely differing schools of organization theory agree on certain key points, we are perhaps entitled to treat this as a clue to the more general ideology of managers. Among these points two seem to be of salient importance; they concern control and – not surprisingly – conflict.

Some theorists lay emphasis upon the motives of those over whom authority is exerted (Likert); some lay emphasis upon the premises from which subordinates argue (March, Simon); some assert and some ignore the importance of informal groupings within organizations. But in each case motives, premises or informal groupings are seen as *means* which a successful manager may employ to achieve *ends* which he himself, if he is sufficiently high in the hierarchy, has selected. The kind of knowledge which a manager has to have is causal, expressible in generalizations, and must provide him with an essentially manipulative ability. Noting this fact we can begin to understand an almost ritualized process in recent writing on organization theory in which those who begin by repudiating Weber tend to end by reinstating something very like the Weberian view of bureaucratic authority. It is easy to understand both phases of this ritual dance, for it is easy to see that the actual behavior of managers and administrators often does not conform closely to Weber's description of the wielding of bureaucratic authority. Anthony Downs (*Inside Bureaucracy*), I. M. Destler (*Presidents, Bureaucrats and Foreign Policy*) and a number of others have made that very clear. So that an initial repudiation of Weber becomes a stock part of the descriptive task. Yet the same evidence shows that when managers are put to the task of *justifying* their authority and their behavior in authority what is striking is the way in which it is to a large degree that in which they deviate from Weber's account that they feel called upon to explain and to justify. Hence the more *ideal* either the theorist's or the manager's description of management, the more Weberian. And it is the ideal which operates at the level of justification and which determines the forms of justification. Charles Perrow (*Complex Organizations*, p. 148) points out this combination of an explicit repudiation of Weber with an unconscious return to Weber in the case of March and Simon; theirs is far from the only case.

Suppose then that we sketch the elements of the ideal of bureaucratic authority; what we find corresponds strikingly to the canons which defined the world view of methodology. First the bureaucrat has to deal in discrete items which can be given an established and unique classification. Anyone and only those who satisfy criteria one to five qualify for welfare; cases of types three to seven must be dealt with by officers of at least grade four; actions involving expenditures of between n and m dollars must be reported under such-and-such headings. Thus the bureaucratic world is composed of discrete variables. Secondly the classificatory scheme which gives rise to, which in an important sense creates those variables, must itself be treated as non-contestable. The scheme has to be accepted independently of the evaluative viewpoint of particular individuals or social groups. Thirdly it is the bureaucrat who is free to create the classificatory scheme; it is he who, so to speak, operationalizes his concepts so that items will be handleable by him in his way.

We thus find that the first three methodological canons which I sketched all have their mirror image in bureaucratic practice. Or rather not so much in actual practice as in that idealized picture of actual practice in terms of which bureaucratic authority holds others and itself responsible. So also are the fourth and fifth canons mirrored in the same way. The relations between already classified items has to be ordered in such a way that the bureaucrat's rules correspond to a set of causal generalizations which warrant predictions: doing A will in fact produce consequences B and C. And these causal generalizations must not only warrant predictions, they must be translatable into recipes for producing effects; they must be levers for effective manipulation.

To justify is precisely to show that one possesses the kind of knowledge that will enable one to perform such manipulations at the appropriate level of the organization. Failure to justify authority will be either failure to impose the relevant classificatory order on the relevant material or to have elaborated the relevant rules and generalizations which will afford prediction, or to have failed to manipulate successfully in order to achieve the goals of the organization.

Two objections might be raised to this account of bureaucratic authority. The first is that, to use André L. Delbecq's terminology ('The Management of Decision-Making within the Firm', pp. 329–31), I have spoken only of that authority exhibited in what he calls routine decision-making, and have ignored what he calls creative decision-making and negotiated decision-making. To this my reply would be that success in the latter two is largely, even if not entirely, measured by the extent to which what formerly belonged in the areas of creativity (the innovative solution of hitherto unsolved problems) or negotiation (bargaining with labor unions, for example) is transferred to the area of routine activity and decision-making (the problem is solved and a formula for future procedure adopted, the strike is settled and a method for avoiding future disputes is laid down).

A second type of objection may be thought more crucial. Egon Bittner has argued ('The Concept of Organization', pp. 239–55) that what the theory of organization embodies are concepts which seem clear-cut, but are not. That of efficiency is perhaps the most notable example. What counts as bureaucratic effectiveness is open to interpretation in a way that Weber himself did not entirely understand. If Bittner is right – and I think that he is – an apparent clarity at certain points, both in organization theory and in administrative practice, is a fictitious clarity, and it might well seem that my account does not recognize this. But what matters for my argument is *the form of justification of bureaucratic authority* as that is employed both prospectively and retrospectively, both practically and theoretically. If key terms employed in the course of that justification are themselves interestingly opaque, that may be important in other respects – indeed it is – but it does not affect the substance of my present argument.

What I am claiming then is that the canons of bureaucratic authority and those of conventional social scientific methodology are mutually reinforcing. Both mask fundamental conflict; and both are liable to make conflict a more marginal phenomenon than it is, or rather than it would otherwise be. By representing conflict as marginal and manageable by administration, both do indeed make it more manageable. We can indeed see the methodology of the social sciences as ideological in its particular as well as in its more general effects. It is important to recall at this point my thesis that a view can only be effectively ideological in function if it is partially true. There is a corresponding truth that a view can only be effectively ideological if up to a certain point it does open up limited possibilities for social control or social change. But the words to be underlined are 'partial' and 'limited'. It is the success of ideology that blinds us, not its failures; and it is precisely by them that we must refuse to be deceived. Hence when Johan Galtung (*Theory and Methods of Social*

Research, p. 1) attempts to disarm philosophical criticism of conventional social scientific methodology as a product of 'oversophistication' by asserting of methodology that it 'works', he misses the point. It works all too well.

IV   Postscript

My argument requires one additional point to be made if its import is not to be misunderstood. It moved from conflict to ideology and from ideology to methodology and from thence to bureaucratic authority. Its structure is such that so far conflict must appear to be the basic concept and consequently I may seem to be endorsing a Heraclitean view of social life in which conflict, rivalry and strife are the fundamental features of the social universe. To avoid this misleading appearance another concept would have had to be introduced, one whose absence seriously injures the present account, but one the introduction of which would have seriously complicated the presentation of my argument. The concept needed is that of a social tradition. Weber of course originally introduced the concept of bureaucratic authority precisely in order to contrast it with that of traditional authority. But his account of tradition was so inadequate that the point of the contrast was partly lost.

The most important social conflicts occur within traditions as well as between them. Such conflicts are conflicts between the various incommensurable goods which men within a particular tradition may pursue. A viable tradition is one which holds together conflicting social, political and even metaphysical claims in a creative way. The activities which inform a tradition are always rationally underdetermined; that is, we can specify no set of rules, no set of rational procedures, which are either necessary or sufficient to guide the activity informing the tradition as it proceeds. The complex of institutions in fifth-century Athens, those in medieval kingships, Christianity or Islam, and indeed natural science, are all examples of traditions in the sense intended. It is when traditions begin to break down that modern bureaucratic organizations characteristically arise. Traditional societies have always had formal organizations, but those in authority within those organizations always had to justify themselves against appeals to the authority of the tradition which the organization served. The Pope has never been able to avoid appeals against his own judgments to the doctrines of the Christian religion; physics itself is always a source of objections to members of the scientific hierarchy. But of course traditions cannot exist without embodying and re-embodying themselves in organizational forms, and organizations always do breed managers. Nonetheless, at most what the managers can control is the organization and not the tradition. Hence conflict in traditional societies survives all attempts at conflict management. The relation of tragic drama to the politics of the assembly in Athenian political life, the quarrel between royal law and church law in twelfth-century Europe, and the debates between the new and the old astronomy in the seventeenth century are paradigmatic examples. Hence also the much greater danger from ideology in modern formal organizations where traditions are always endangered.

The recognition of tradition therefore is a necessary key to understanding the relation of conflict, ideology and organization in political life. Unhappily that recognition has been fatally hindered by two facts. The first is the way in which only conservative writers on politics – a Burke or a Michael Oakeshott – have tended to take tradition seriously. The second is the fact that a prerequisite for understanding the role of tradition – and therefore the role of conflict – is a training in depth in philosophy and in history, just those subjects so often excluded from the political science curriculum in the name of the behavioralist revolution. What that revolution replaced them with was of course the study of methodology. Insofar as that study was simply the study of statistics and applied mathematics, who could but applaud its introduction? *The American Voter* will stand, if not perhaps forever, at least for a very long time as its memorial. But it still remains true that graduate students in political science for the most part know very little more mathematics than they did before. What the introduction of the study of methodology actually did was to drive out those very inquiries which could have revealed its ideological function. By its place in the curriculum, methodology has achieved yet another ideological dimension.

'The Claims of *After Virtue*'

After Virtue was a book that arose out of prolonged reflection on the inadequacies of my own earlier work. Two distinct types of question had informed that work. One concerned how the history of philosophical ethics should be written and what its relationship was to the history of the moralities embodied in the life of the societies inhabited by the philosophers. The other was directed towards elucidating the nature of those intellectual enquiries whose subject-matter is constituted by human actions and passions. The first type of concern was expressed in *A Short History of Ethics*, the second in *The Unconscious*. Both were partly motivated by my increasing recognition of the gross inadequacies of Marxism in both these areas. Both were expressed and related to each other and to that recognition in a book of essays *Against the Self-Images of the Age*, a book whose largely negative and none too systematic character expressed the nature of the conclusions which I had reached by 1971.

Even then however I recognised that those negative and unsystematic conclusions presupposed a set of positive affirmations about the moral and social history of the cultural and social order which we inhabit and that these affirmations in turn were bound to express some particular moral and social stance of a positive kind. But it took me the almost ten years in which I wrote *After Virtue* to discover what these affirmations were. *After Virtue* makes seven central claims.

(1)   It is a distinctive feature of the social and cultural order that we inhabit that disagreements over central moral issues are peculiarly unsettlable. Debates concerned with the value of human life such as those over abortion and euthanasia, or about distributive justice and property rights, or about war and peace degenerate into confrontations of assertion and counter-assertion, because the protagonists of rival positions invoke incommensurable forms of moral assertion against each other. So, for example, in debates over abortion conceptions of individual property rights which were originally at home in the social philosophies of Adam Smith and Locke are used to defend a pregnant woman's rights to do what she will with her own body, conceptions of what justice requires in

the treatment of innocent life whose original context was the medieval understanding of what biblical divine law prescribes are advanced to forbid the doing of harm to a human foetus and utilitarian views are deployed against both. Detached from the theoretical and social contexts in terms of which these conceptions were originally elaborated and rationally defended, the assertions of each of these rival positions in this and other debates have characteristically and generally become no more than expressions of attitude and feeling. The use of moral discourse in our culture has become what some positivistically inclined moral philosophers took all moral discourse to be. From them I borrow the expression 'emotivist' to describe our moral condition.

(2) What brought this state of affairs about? One centrally important cause, it is argued in *After Virtue*, was the failure of what I called 'the Enlightenment project'. The thinkers of the Enlightenment set out to replace what they took to be discredited traditional and superstitious forms of morality by a kind of secular morality that would be entitled to secure the assent of any rational person. So in Scotland, England, France and Germany alike philosophers as different as Hume, Bentham, Diderot and Kant tried to formulate moral principles to which no adequately reflective rational person could refuse allegiance. The attempt failed. What it bequeathed to its cultural heirs were a set of mutually antagonistic moral stances, each claiming to have achieved this kind of rational justification, but each also disputing this claim on the part of its rivals. Hence the continuing clash between various types of Kantian moral philosopher and various types of utilitarian in a series of inconclusive engagements. It was natural that one conclusion drawn from this failure to settle moral disputes rationally was that reason was impotent in this area; hence not only American and British emotivism, but also Kierkegaard's philosophical progeny.

(3) Another consequence of these unsettled and unsettlable debates was the releasing into the culture at large of a set of moral concepts which derive from their philosophical ancestry an appearance of rational determinateness and justification which they do not in fact possess. So that appeal to them appears to make an objectively reason-supported claim whereas in fact such appeals lack rational backing and can be put to the service of a variety of rival and antagonistic purposes. Because they disguise the purposes which they serve, they are useful fictions. The most important members of this class are the concept of human rights and that of utility or welfare.

Insofar as a moral culture is emotivist the relationship between individuals will be manipulative. The manipulative mode is accorded social respect by modernity through the prestige which the concept of managerial effectiveness enjoys. And this too functions as a moral fiction, a fiction because its application presupposes the availability of a set of social scientific laws, knowledge of which will enable managers to control social reality; but we do not in fact know of any such laws. The thinkers of the Enlightenment who taught us to search for them once again misled us. Social reality has a kind of unpredictability which the Weberian managerial ethos cannot acknowledge without revealing how much of the claims of modern private and public bureaucracy rests on deception and self-deception.

(4)   The philosopher who understood best that the Enlightenment project had failed decisively and that contemporary moral assertions had characteristically become a set of masks for unavowed purposes was Nietzsche. Nietzsche however generalised this insight into an overall account of the genealogy of morals. And in so doing he raised two questions. Is his history a true history? And is there perhaps a mistake lying at the root of the failure of the Enlightenment project which Nietzsche failed to understand? That mistake, so I suggest in *After Virtue*, lay in the rejection of Aristotle's ethics and politics which immediately preceded and to some degree made necessary the Enlightenment project. And I go on to argue that Aristotle and Nietzsche represent the only two compelling alternatives in contemporary moral theory.

(5)   Chapters 10 to 14 of *After Virtue* provide an interpretative history of changing conceptions of the virtues from the archaic Greek society depicted in the Homeric poems to the European Middle Ages. This history is intended both to provide a challenge to Nietzsche's genealogical account and to provide the materials for identifying a core concept of the virtues, an identification which requires an account in terms of three distinct stages in the elaboration of an adequate conception of the virtues. The virtues are first of all those qualities without which human beings cannot achieve the goods internal to practices. By a 'practice' I mean 'any coherent and complex form of socially established cooperative human activity through which goods internal to that form of activity are realised in the course of trying to achieve those standards of excellence which are appropriate to, and partially definitive of, that form of activity, with the result that human powers to achieve excellence, and human conceptions of the ends and goods involved, are systematically extended' (below, p. 83). Such types of activity as farming and fishing, the pursuit of the sciences and the arts, and the playing of games such as football and chess are practices. Politics, as Aristotle understood it, and as it was sometimes embodied in institutional life in the ancient and medieval worlds was a practice. Modern politics is not.

This characterisation of the virtues in terms of practices is necessary, but not sufficient for an adequate specification. Virtues are also to be understood as qualities required to achieve the goods which furnish individual human lives with their *telos*. And I argue that the unifying form of an individual human life, without which such lives could not have a *telos*, derives from its possessing some kind of narrative structure. Individual human lives however are only able to have the structures that they do because they are embedded within social traditions. And the third stage in specifying the nature of the virtues is that which explains why they also have to be understood as qualities required to sustain ongoing social traditions in good order.

(6)   It was a failure in the later European Middle Ages to sustain the ongoing tradition of the virtues, understood in both an Aristotelian and a Christian way, that led to the sixteenth- and seventeenth-century rejections of Aristotelian ethics and politics and so opened up the possibility of the Enlightenment project. During the period in which a traditional understanding of the virtues was no longer possible, but in which the Enlightenment project had yet to collapse, there was a revival of certain originally Stoic notions of virtue (as a singular noun), influential both in social life and in philosophical theory, especially in Kant's rendering. But we now live in an aftermath where neither the virtues nor virtue can be central to the general moral culture. We live after virtue in a period of unresolvable disputes and dilemmas, both within contemporary moral philosophy and within morality itself.

(7)   I argue at various points in the book that although the rejection of Aristotelian ethics and politics in the historical circumstances engendered in and after the later Middle Ages is intelligible, it has never yet been shown to be warranted. And I conclude that when moral Aristotelianism is rightly understood, it cannot be undermined by the kind of critique that Nietzsche successfully directed against both Kant and the utilitarians. I therefore conclude that Aristotle is vindicated against Nietzsche and moreover that only a history of ethical theory and practice written from an Aristotelian rather than a Nietzschean standpoint enables us to comprehend the nature of the moral condition of modernity.

After Virtue: A Study in Moral Theory (extracts)

Chapter 3
Emotivism: Social Content and Social Context

A moral philosophy – and emotivism is no exception – characteristically presupposes a sociology. For every moral philosophy offers explicitly or implicitly at least a partial conceptual analysis of the relationship of an agent to his or her reasons, motives, intentions and actions, and in so doing generally presupposes some claim that these concepts are embodied or at least can be in the real social world. Even Kant, who sometimes seems to restrict moral agency to the inner realm of the noumenal, implies otherwise in his writings on law, history and politics. Thus it would generally be a decisive refutation of a moral philosophy to show that moral agency on its own account of the matter could never be socially embodied; and it also follows that we have not yet fully understood the claims of any moral philosophy until we have spelled out what its social embodiment would be. Some moral philosophers in the past, perhaps most, have understood this spelling out as itself one part of the task of moral philosophy. So, it scarcely needs to be said, Plato and Aristotle, so indeed also Hume and Adam Smith; but at least since Moore the dominant narrow conception of moral philosophy has ensured that the moral philosophers could ignore this task; as notably do the philosophical proponents of emotivism. We therefore must perform it for them.

What is the key to the social content of emotivism? It is the fact that emotivism entails the obliteration of any genuine distinction between manipulative and non-manipulative social relations. Consider the contrast between, for example, Kantian ethics and emotivism on this point. For Kant – and a parallel point could be made about many earlier moral philosophers – the difference between a human relationship uninformed by morality and one so informed is precisely the difference between one in which each person treats the other primarily as a means to his or her ends and one in which each treats the other as an end. To treat someone else as an end is to offer them what I take to be good reasons for acting in one way rather than another, but to leave it to them to evaluate those reasons. It is to be unwilling to influence another except by reasons which that other he or she judges to be good. It is to appeal to impersonal criteria of the validity of which each rational agent must be his or her own judge. By contrast, to treat someone else as a means is to seek to make him or her an instrument of my purposes by adducing whatever influences or considerations will in fact be effective on this or that occasion. The generalizations of the sociology and psychology of persuasion are what I shall need to guide me, not the standards of a normative rationality.

If emotivism is true, this distinction is illusory. For evaluative utterance can in the end have no point or use but the expression of my own feelings or attitudes and the transformation of the feelings and attitudes of others. I cannot genuinely appeal to impersonal criteria, for there are no impersonal criteria. I may think that I so appeal and others may think that I so appeal, but these thoughts will always be mistakes. The sole reality of distinctively moral discourse is the attempt of one will to align the attitudes, feelings, preference and choices of another with its own. Others are always means, never ends.

[. . . .]

If we are to understand fully the social context of that obliteration of the distinction between manipulative and non-manipulative social relationships which emotivism entails, we ought to consider some [. . .] social contexts [. . .]

One which is obviously important is that provided by the life of organizations, of those bureaucratic structures which, whether in the form of private corporations or of government agencies, define the working tasks of so many of our contemporaries. [. . . .] The organization is characteristically engaged in a competitive struggle for scarce resources to put to the service of its predetermined ends. It is therefore a central responsibility of managers to direct and redirect their organizations' available resources, both human and non-human, as effectively as possible toward those ends. Every bureaucratic organization embodies some explicit or implicit definition of costs and benefits from which the criteria of effectiveness are derived. Bureaucratic rationality is the rationality of matching means to ends economically and efficiently.

This familiar – perhaps by now we may be tempted to think overfamiliar – thought we owe originally of course to Max Weber. And it at once becomes relevant that Weber's thought embodies just those dichotomies which emotivism embodies, and obliterates just those distinctions to which emotivism has to be blind. Questions of ends are questions of values, and on values reason is silent; conflict between rival values cannot be rationally settled. Instead one must simply choose – between parties, classes, nations, causes, ideals. *Entscheidung* plays the part in Weber's thought that choice of principles plays in that of Hare or Sartre. 'Values', says Raymond Aron in his exposition of Weber's view, 'are created by human decisions . . .' and again he ascribes to Weber the view that 'each man's conscience is irrefutable' and that values rest on 'a choice whose justification is purely subjective' (*Main Currents in Sociological Thought*, pp. 211, 216, 198). It is not surprising that Weber's understanding of values was indebted chiefly to Nietzsche and that Donald G. MacRae in his book on Weber calls him an existentialist; for while he holds that an agent may be more or less rational in acting consistently with his values, the choice of any one particular evaluative stance or commitment can be no more rational than that of any other. All faiths and all evaluations are equally non-rational; all are subjective directions given to sentiment and feeling. Weber is then, in the broader sense in which I have understood the term, an emotivist and his portrait of a bureaucratic authority is an emotivist portrait. The consequence of Weber's emotivism is that in his thought the contrast between power and authority, although paid lip-service to, is effectively obliterated as a special instance of the disappearance of the contrast between manipulative and non-manipulative social relations. Weber of course took himself to be distinguishing power from authority, precisely because authority serves ends, serves faiths. But, as Philip Rieff has acutely noted, 'Weber's ends, the *causes* there to be served, are means of acting; they cannot escape service to power' (*Fellow Teachers*, p. 22). For on Weber's view no type of authority can appeal to rational criteria to vindicate itself except that type of bureaucratic authority which appeals precisely to its own *effectiveness*. And what this appeal reveals is that bureaucratic authority is nothing other than successful power.

[. . . .]

Chapter 5

Why the Enlightenment Project of Justifying Morality Had to Fail

So far I have presented the failure of the project of justifying morality merely as the failure of a succession of particular arguments; and if that were all that there was to the matter, it might appear that the trouble was merely that Kierkegaard, Kant, Diderot, Hume, Smith and their other contemporaries were not adroit enough in constructing arguments, so that an appropriate strategy would be to wait until some more powerful mind applied itself to the problems. And just this has been the strategy of the academic philosophical world, even though many professional philosophers might be a little embarrassed to admit it. But suppose in fact, what is eminently plausible, that the failure of the eighteenth- and nineteenth-century project was of quite another kind. Suppose that the arguments of Kierkegaard, Kant, Diderot, Hume, Smith and the like fail because of certain shared characteristics deriving from their highly specific shared historical background. Suppose that we cannot understand them as contributors to a timeless debate about morality, but only as the inheritors of a very specific and particular scheme of moral beliefs, a scheme whose internal incoherence ensured the failure of the common philosophical project from the outset.

Consider certain beliefs shared by all the contributors to the project. All of them [. . .] agree to a surprising degree on the content and character of the precepts which constitute genuine morality. Marriage and the family are *au fond* as unquestioned by Diderot's rationalist *philosophe* as they are by Kierkegaard's Judge Wilhelm; promise-keeping and justice are as inviolable for Hume as they are for Kant. Whence did they inherit these shared beliefs? Obviously from their shared Christian past compared with which the divergences between Kant's and Kierkegaard's Lutheran, Hume's Presbyterian and Diderot's Jansenist-influenced Catholic background are relatively unimportant.

At the same time as they agree largely on the character of morality, they agree also upon what a rational justification of morality would have to be. Its key premises would characterize some feature or features of human nature; and the rules of morality would then be explained and justified as being those rules which a being possessing just such a human nature could be expected to accept. For Diderot and Hume the relevant features of human nature are characteristics of the passions; for Kant the relevant feature of human nature is the universal and categorical character of certain rules of reason. (Kant of course denies that morality is 'based on human nature', but what he means by 'human nature' is merely the physiological non-rational side of man.) Kierkegaard no longer attempts to *justify* morality at all; but his account has precisely the same structure as that which is shared by the accounts of Kant, Hume and Diderot, except that where they appeal to characteristics of the passions or of reason, he invokes what he takes to be characteristics of fundamental decision-making.

Thus all these writers share in the project of constructing valid arguments which will move from premises concerning human nature as they understand it to be to conclusions about the authority of moral rules and precepts. I want to argue that any project of this form was bound to fail, because of an ineradicable discrepancy between their shared conception of moral rules and precepts on the one hand and what was shared – despite much larger divergences – in their conception of human nature on the other. Both conceptions have a history and their relationship can only be made intelligible in the light of that history.

Consider first the general form of the moral scheme which was the historical ancestor of both conceptions, the moral scheme which in a variety of diverse forms and with numerous rivals came for long periods to dominate the European Middle Ages from the twelfth century onwards, a scheme which included both classical and theistic elements. Its basic structure is that which Aristotle analyzed in the *Nicomachean Ethics*. Within that teleological scheme there is a fundamental contrast between man-as-he-happens-to-be and man-as-he-could-be-if-he-realized-his-essential-nature. Ethics is the science which is to enable men to understand how they make the transition from the former state to the latter. Ethics therefore in this view presupposes some account of potentiality and act, some account of the essence of man as a rational animal and above all some account of the human *telos*. The precepts which enjoin the various virtues and prohibit the vices which are their counterparts instruct us how to move from potentiality to act, how to realize our true nature and to reach our true end. To defy them will be to be frustrated and incomplete, to fail to achieve that good of rational happiness which it is peculiarly ours as a species to pursue. The desires and emotions which we possess are to be put in order and educated by the use of such precepts and by the cultivation of those habits of action which the study of ethics prescribes; reason instructs us both as to what our true end is and as to how to reach it. We thus have a threefold scheme in which human-nature-as-it-happens-to-be (human nature in its untutored state) is initially discrepant and discordant with the precepts of ethics and needs to be transformed by the instruction of practical reason and experience into human-nature-as-it-could-be-if-it-realized-its-*telos*. Each of the three elements of the scheme – the conception of untutored human nature, the conception of the precepts of rational ethics and the conception of human-nature-as-it-could-be-if-it-realized-its-*telos* – requires reference to the other two if its status and function are to be intelligible.

This scheme is complicated and added to, but not essentially altered, when it is placed within a framework of theistic beliefs, whether Christian, as with Aquinas, or Jewish with Maimonides, or Islamic with Ibn Roschd. The precepts of ethics now have to be understood not only as teleological injunctions, but also as expressions of a divinely ordained law. The table of virtues and vices has to be amended and added to and a concept of sin is added to the Aristotelian concept of error. The law of God requires a new kind of respect and awe. The true end of man can no longer be completely achieved in this world, but only in another. Yet the threefold structure of untutored human-nature-as-it-happens-to-be, human-nature-as-it-could-be-if-it-realized-its-*telos* and the precepts of rational ethics as the means for the transition from one to the other remains central to the theistic understanding of evaluative thought and judgment.

[. . . .]

Although each of the [Enlightenment] writers we have been concerned with attempted in his positive arguments to base morality on human nature, each in his negative arguments [against the others] moved toward a more and more unrestricted version of the claim that no valid argument can move from entirely factual premises to any moral or evaluative conclusion – to a principle, that is, which once it is accepted, constitutes an epitaph to their entire project. Hume still expresses this claim in the form of a doubt rather than of a positive assertion. He remarks that in 'every system of morality, which I have hitherto met with' authors make a transition from statements about God or human nature to moral judgments: 'instead of the usual copulations of propositions, *is*, and *is not*, I met with no proposition that is not connected with an *ought*, or an *ought not*' (*A Treatise of Human Nature*, III.i.1). And he then goes on to demand 'that a reason should be given, for what seems altogether inconceivable, how this new relation can be a deduction from others, which are entirely different from it'. The same general principle, no longer expressed as a question, but as an assertion, appears in Kant's insistence that the injunctions of the moral law cannot be derived from any set of statements about human happiness or about the will of God and then yet again in Kierkegaard's account of the ethical. What is the significance of this general claim?

Some later moral philosophers have gone so far as to describe the thesis that from a set of factual premises no moral conclusion validly follows as 'a truth of logic', understanding it as derivable from a more general principle which some medieval logicians formulated as the claim that in a valid argument nothing can appear in the conclusion which was not already in the premises. And, such philosophers have suggested, in an argument in which any attempt is made to derive a moral or evaluative conclusion from factual premises something which is not in the premises, namely the moral or evaluative element, will appear in the conclusion. Hence any such argument must fail. Yet in fact the alleged unrestrictedly general logical principle on which everything is being made to depend is bogus – and the scholastic tag applies only to Aristotelian syllogisms. There *are* several types of valid argument in which some element may appear in a conclusion which is not present in the premises. A. N. Prior's counter-example to this alleged principle illustrates its breakdown adequately; from the premise 'He is a sea-captain', the conclusion may be validly inferred that 'He ought to do whatever a sea-captain ought to do'. This counter-example not only shows that there is no general principle of the type alleged; but it itself shows what is at least a grammatical truth – an 'is' premise *can* on occasion entail an 'ought' conclusion.

Adherents of the 'no "ought" from "is" view' could however easily meet part of the difficulty raised by Prior's example by reformulating their own position. What they intended to claim they might and would presumably say, is that no conclusion with substantial evaluative and moral content – and the conclusion in Prior's example certainly does lack any such content – can be derived from factual premises. Yet the problem would remain for them as to why now anyone would accept their claim. For they have conceded that it cannot be derived from any unrestrictedly general logical principle. Yet their claim may still have substance, but a substance that derives from a particular, and in the eighteenth century new, conception of moral rules and judgments. It may, that is, assert a principle whose validity derives not from some general logical principle, but from the meaning of the key terms employed. Suppose that during the seventeenth and eighteenth centuries the meaning and implications of the key terms used in moral utterance had changed their character; it could then turn out to be the case that what had once been valid inferences from or to some particular moral premise or conclusion would no longer be valid inferences from or to what *seemed* to be the same factual premise or moral conclusion. For what in some sense were the same expressions, the same sentences, would now bear a different meaning. But do we in fact have any evidence for such a change of meaning? To answer this question it is helpful to consider another type of counter-example to the 'No "ought" conclusions from "is" premises' thesis. From such factual premises as 'This watch is grossly inaccurate and irregular in time-keeping' and 'This watch is too heavy to carry about comfortably', the evaluative conclusion validly follows that 'This is a bad watch'. From such factual premises as 'He gets a better yield for this crop per acre than any farmer in the district', 'He has the most effective programme of soil renewal yet known' and 'His dairy herd wins all the first prizes at the agricultural shows', the evaluative conclusion validly follows that 'He is a good farmer'.

Both of these arguments are valid because of the special character of the concepts of a watch and of a farmer. Such concepts are functional concepts; that is to say, we define both 'watch' and 'farmer' in terms of the purpose or function which a watch or a farmer are characteristically expected to serve. It follows that the concept of a watch cannot be defined independently of the concept of a good watch nor the concept of a farmer independently of that of a good farmer; and that the criterion of something's being a watch and the criterion of something's being a good watch – and so also for 'farmer' and for all other functional concepts – are not independent of each other. Now clearly both sets of criteria – as is evidenced by the examples given in the last paragraph – are factual. Hence any argument which moves from premises which assert that the appropriate criteria are satisfied to a conclusion which asserts that 'That is a good such-and-such', where 'such-and-such' picks out an item specified by a functional concept, will be a valid argument which moves from factual premises to an evaluative conclusion. Thus we may safely assert that, if some amended version of the 'No "ought" conclusion from "is" premises' principle is to hold good, it must exclude arguments involving functional concepts from its scope. But this suggests strongly that those who have insisted that *all* moral arguments fall within the scope of such a principle may have been doing so because they took it for granted that *no* moral arguments involve functional concepts. Yet moral arguments within the classical, Aristotelian tradition – whether in its Greek or its medieval versions – involve at least one central functional concept, the concept of *man* understood as having an essential nature and an essential purpose or function; and it is when and only when the classical tradition in its integrity has been substantially rejected that moral arguments change their character so that they fall within the scope of some version of the 'No "ought" conclusion from "is" premises' principle. That is to say, 'man' stands to 'good man' as 'watch' stands to 'good watch' or 'farmer' to 'good farmer' within the classical tradition. Aristotle takes it as a starting-point for ethical enquiry that the relationship of 'man' to 'living well' is analogous to that of 'harpist' to 'playing the harp well' (*Nicomachean Ethics*, 1095a16). But the use of 'man' as a functional concept is far older than Aristotle and it does not initially derive from Aristotle's metaphysical biology. It is rooted in the forms of social life to which the theorists of the classical tradition give expression. For according to that tradition to be a man is to fill a set of roles each of which has its own point and purpose: member of a family, citizen, soldier, philosopher, servant of God. It is only when man is thought of as an individual prior to and apart from all roles that 'man' ceases to be a functional concept.

For this to be so, other key moral terms must also have partially at least changed their meaning. The entailment relations between certain types of sentence must have changed. Thus it is not just that moral conclusions cannot be justified in the way that they once were; but the loss of the possibility of such justification signals a correlative change in the meaning of moral idioms. So the 'No "ought" conclusion from "is" premises' principle becomes an inescapable truth for philosophers whose culture possesses only the impoverished moral vocabulary which results from the episodes I have recounted. That it was taken to be a timeless logical truth was a sign of a deep lack of historical consciousness which then informed and even now infects too much of moral philosophy. For its initial proclamation was itself a crucial historical event. It signals both a final break with the classical tradition and the decisive breakdown of the eighteenth-century project of justifying morality in the context of the inherited, but already incoherent, fragments left behind from tradition.

But it is not only that moral concepts and arguments at this point in history radically change their character so that they become recognizably the immediate ancestors of the unsettlable, interminable arguments of our own culture. It is also the case that moral *judgments* change their import and meaning. Within the Aristotelian tradition to call x good (where x may be among other things a person or an animal or a policy or a state of affairs) is to say that it is the kind of x which someone would choose who wanted an x for the purpose for which x's are characteristically wanted. To call a watch good is to say that it is the kind of watch which someone would choose who wanted a watch to keep time accurately (rather than, say, to throw at the cat). The presupposition of this use of 'good' is that every type of item which it is appropriate to call good or bad – including persons and actions – has, as a matter of fact, some given specific purpose or function. To call something good therefore is also to make a factual statement. To call a particular action just or right is to say that it is what a good man would do in such a situation; hence this type of statement too is factual. Within this tradition moral and evaluative statements can be called true or false in precisely the way in which all other factual statements can be so called. But once the notion of essential human purposes or functions disappears from morality, it begins to appear implausible to treat moral judgments as factual statements.

Moreover the secularization of morality by the Enlightenment had put in question the status of moral judgments as ostensible reports of divine law. Even Kant, who still understands moral judgments as expressions of a universal law, even if it be a law which each rational agent utters to himself, does not treat moral judgments as reports of what the law requires or commands, but as themselves imperatives. And imperatives are not susceptible of truth or falsity.

Up to the present in everyday discourse the habit of speaking of moral judgments as true or false persists; but the question of what it is in virtue of which a particular moral judgment is true or false has come to lack any clear answer. That this should be so is perfectly intelligible if the historical hypothesis which I have sketched is true: that moral judgments are linguistic survivals from the practices of classical theism which have lost the context provided by these practices. In that context moral judgments were at once hypothetical and categorical in form. They were hypothetical insofar as they expressed a judgment as to what conduct would be teleologically appropriate for a human being: 'You ought to do so-and-so, if and since your *telos* is such-and-such' or perhaps 'You ought to do so-and-so, if you do not want your essential desires to be frustrated'. They were categorical insofar as they reported the contents of the universal law commanded by God: 'You ought to do so-and-so: that is what God's law enjoins.' But take away from them that in virtue of which they were hypothetical *and* that in virtue of which they were categorical and what are they? Moral judgments lose any clear status and the sentences which express them in a parallel way lose any undebatable meaning. Such sentences become available as forms of expression for an emotivist self which lacking the guidance of the context in which they were originally at home has lost its linguistic as well as its practical way in the world.

[. . . .]

Chapter 14

The Nature of the Virtues

[. . . .]

The question can therefore now be posed directly: are we or are we not able to disentangle from these rival and various claims a unitary core concept of the virtues of which we can give a more compelling account than any of the other accounts so far? I am going to argue that we can in fact discover such a core concept and that it turns out to provide the tradition of which I have written the history with its conceptual unity. It will indeed enable us to distinguish in a clear way those beliefs about the virtues which genuinely belong to the tradition from those which do not. Unsurprisingly perhaps it is a complex concept, different parts of which derive from different stages in the development of the tradition. Thus the concept itself in some sense embodies the history of which it is the outcome.

One of the features of the concept of a virtue which has emerged with some clarity from the argument so far is that it always requires for its application the acceptance for some prior account of certain features of social and moral life in terms of which it has to be defined and explained. So in the Homeric account the concept of a virtue is secondary to that of *a social role*, in Aristotle's account it is secondary to that of *the good life for man* conceived as the *telos* of human action and in Franklin's much later account it is secondary to that of utility. What is it in the account which I am about to give which provides in a similar way the necessary background against which the concept of a virtue has to be made intelligible? It is in answering this question that the complex, historical, multi-layered character of the core concept of virtue becomes clear. For there are no less than three stages in the logical development of the concept which have to be identified in order, if the core conception of a virtue is to be understood, and each of these stages has its own conceptual background. The first stage requires a background account of what I shall call a practice, the second an account of what I have already characterized as the narrative order of a single human life and the third an account a good deal fuller than I have given up to now of what constitutes a moral tradition. Each later stage presupposes the earlier, but not *vice versa*. Each earlier stage is both modified by and reinterpreted in the light of, but also provides an essential constituent of each later stage. The progress in the development of the concept is closely related to, although it does not recapitulate in any straightforward way, the history of the tradition of which it forms the core.

In the Homeric account of the virtues – and in heroic societies more generally – the exercise of a virtue exhibits qualities which are required for sustaining a social role and for exhibiting excellence in some well-marked area of social practice: to excel is to excel at war or in the games, as Achilles does, in sustaining a household, as Penelope does, in giving counsel in the assembly, as Nestor does, in the telling of a tale, as Homer himself does. When Aristotle speaks of excellence in human activity he sometimes, though not always, refers to some well-defined type of human practice: flute-playing, or war, or geometry. I am going to suggest that this notion of a particular type of practice as providing the arena in which the virtues are exhibited and in terms of which they are to receive their primary, if incomplete, definition is crucial to the whole enterprise of identifying a core concept of the virtues. I hasten to add two *caveats* however.

The first is to point out that my argument will not in any way imply that virtues are *only* exercised in the course of what I am calling practices. The second is to warn that I shall be using the word 'practice' in a specially defined way which does not completely agree with current ordinary usage, including my own previous use of that word. What am I going to mean by it?

By a 'practice' I am going to mean any coherent and complex form of socially established cooperative human activity through which goods internal to that form of activity are realized in the course of trying to achieve those standards of excellence which are appropriate to, and partially definitive of, that form of activity, with the result that human powers to achieve excellence, and human conceptions of the ends and goods involved, are systematically extended. Tic-tac-toe is not an example of a practice in this sense, nor is throwing a football with skill; but the game of football is, and so is chess. Bricklaying is not a practice; architecture is. Planting turnips is not a practice; farming is. So are the enquiries of physics, chemistry and biology, and so is the work of the historian, and so are painting and music. In the ancient and medieval worlds the creation and sustaining of human communities – of households, cities, nations – is generally taken to be a practice in the sense in which I have defined it. Thus the range of practices is wide: arts, sciences, games, politics in the Aristotelian sense, the making and sustaining of family life, all fall under the concept. But the question of the precise range of practices is not at this stage of the first importance. Instead let me explain some of the key terms involved in my definition, beginning with the notion of goods internal to a practice.

Consider the example of a highly intelligent seven-year-old child whom I wish to teach to play chess, although the child has no particular desire to learn the game. The child does however have a very strong desire for candy and little chance of obtaining it. I therefore tell the child that if the child will play chess with me once a week I will give the child 50 cents worth of candy; moreover I tell the child that I will always play in such a way that it will be difficult, but not impossible, for the child to win and that, if the child wins, the child will receive an extra 50 cents worth of candy. Thus motivated the child plays and plays to win. Notice however that, so long as it is the candy alone which provides the child with a good reason for playing chess, the child has no reason not to cheat and every reason to cheat, provided he or she can do so successfully. But, so we may hope, there will come a time when the child will find in those goods specific to chess, in the achievement of a certain highly particular kind of analytical skill, strategic imagination and competitive intensity, a new set of reasons, reasons now not just for winning on a particular occasion, but for trying to excel in whatever way the game of chess demands. Now if the child cheats, he or she will be defeating not me, but himself or herself.

There are thus two kinds of good possibly to be gained by playing chess. On the one hand there are those goods externally and contingently attached to chess-playing and to other practices by the accidents of social circumstance – in the case of the imaginary child candy, in the case of real adults such goods as prestige, status and money. There are always alternative ways for achieving such goods, and their achievement is never to be had *only* by engaging in some particular kind of practice. On the other hand there are the goods internal to the practice of chess which cannot be had in any way but by playing chess or some other game of that specific kind. We call them internal for two reasons: first, as I have already suggested, because we can only specify them in terms of chess or some other game of that specific kind and by means of examples from such games (otherwise the meagerness of our vocabulary for speaking of such goods forces us into such devices as my own resort to writing of 'a certain highly particular kind of'); and secondly because they can only be identified and recognized by the experience of participating in the practice in question. Those who lack the relevant experience are incompetent thereby as judges of internal goods.

This is clearly the case with all the major examples of practices: consider for example – even if briefly and inadequately – the practice of portrait painting as it developed in Western Europe from the late Middle Ages to the eighteenth century. The successful portrait painter is able to achieve many goods which are in the sense just defined external to the practice of portrait painting – fame, wealth, social status, even a measure of power and influence at courts upon occasion. But those external goods are not to be confused with the goods which are internal to the practice. The internal goods are those which result from an extended attempt to show how Wittgenstein's dictum 'The human body is the best picture of the human soul' (*Philosophical Investigations*, p. 178e) might be made to become true by teaching us to '*regard* . . . the picture on our wall as the object itself (the man, landscape, and so on) depicted there' (p. 205e) in a quite new way. What is misleading about Wittgenstein's dictum as it stands is its neglect of the truth in George Orwell's thesis 'At fifty everyone has the face he deserves'. What painters from Giotto to Rembrandt learnt to show was how the face at any age may be revealed as the face that the subject of a portrait deserves.

Originally in medieval paintings of the saints the face was an icon; the question of a resemblance between the depicted face of Christ or St Peter and the face that Jesus or Peter actually possessed at some particular age did not even arise. The antithesis to this iconography was the relative naturalism of certain fifteenth-century Flemish and German painting. The heavy eyelids, the coifed hair, the lines around the mouth undeniably represent some particular woman, either actual or envisaged. Resemblance has usurped the iconic relationship. But with Rembrandt there is, so to speak, synthesis: the naturalistic portrait is now rendered as an icon, but an icon of a new and hitherto inconceivable kind. Similarly in a very different kind of sequence mythological faces in a certain kind of seventeenth-century French painting become aristocratic faces in the eighteenth century. Within each of these sequences at least two different kinds of good internal to the painting of human faces and bodies are achieved.

There is first of all the excellence of the products, both the excellence in performance by the painters and that of each portrait itself. This excellence – the very verb 'excel' suggests it – has to be understood historically. The sequences of development find their point and purpose in a progress towards and beyond a variety of types and modes of excellence. There are of course sequences of decline as well as of progress, and progress is rarely to be understood as straightforwardly linear. But it is in participation in the attempts to sustain progress and to respond creatively to problems that the second kind of good internal to the practices of portrait painting is to be found. For what the artist discovers within the pursuit of excellence in portrait painting – and what is true of portrait painting is true of the practice of the fine arts in general – is the good of a certain kind of life. That life may not constitute the whole of life for someone who is a painter by a very long way or it may at least for a period, Gauguin-like, absorb him or her at the expense of almost everything else. But it is the painter's living out of a greater or lesser part of his or her life *as a painter* that is the second kind of good internal to painting. And judgment upon these goods requires at the very least the kind of competence that is only to be acquired either as a painter or as someone willing to learn systematically what the portrait painter has to teach.

A practice involves standards of excellence and obedience to rules as well as the achievement of goods. To enter into a practice is to accept the authority of those standards and the inadequacy of my own performance as judged by them. It is to subject my own attitudes, choices, preferences and tastes to the standards which currently and partially define the practice. Practices of course, as I have just noticed, have a history: games, sciences and arts all have histories. Thus the standards are not themselves immune from criticism, but nonetheless we cannot be initiated into a practice without accepting the authority of the best standards realized so far. If, on starting to listen to music, I do not accept my own incapacity to judge correctly, I will never learn to hear, let alone to appreciate, Bartók's last quartets. If, on starting to play baseball, I do not accept that others know better than I when to throw a fast ball and when not, I will never learn to appreciate good pitching let alone to pitch. In the realm of practices the authority of both goods and standards operates in such a way as to rule out all subjectivist and emotivist analyses of judgment. De gustibus *est* disputandum.

We are now in a position to notice an important difference between what I have called internal and what I have called external goods. It is characteristic of what I have called external goods that when achieved they are always some individual's property and possession. Moreover characteristically they are such that the more someone has of them, the less there is for other people. This is sometimes necessarily the case, as with power and fame, and sometimes the case by reason of contingent circumstance as with money. External goods are therefore characteristically objects of competition in which there must be losers as well as winners. Internal goods are indeed the outcome of competition to excel, but it is characteristic of them that their achievement is a good for the whole community who participate in the practice. So when Turner transformed the seascape in painting or W. G. Grace advanced the art of batting in cricket in a quite new way their achievement enriched the whole relevant community.

But what does all or any of this have to do with the concept of the virtues? It turns out that we are now in a position to formulate a first, even if partial and tentative definition of a virtue: *A virtue is an acquired human quality the possession and exercise of which tends to enable us to achieve those goods which are internal to practices and the lack of which effectively prevents us from achieving any such goods.*

[. . . .]

To situate the virtues any further within practices it is necessary now to clarify a little further the nature of a practice by drawing two important contrasts. The discussion so far I hope makes it clear that a practice, in the sense intended, is never just a set of technical skills, even when directed towards some unified purpose and even if the exercise of those skills can on occasion be valued or enjoyed for their own sake. What is distinctive in a practice is in part the way in which conceptions of the relevant goods and ends which the technical skills serve – and every practice does require the exercise of technical skills – are transformed and enriched by these extensions of human powers and by that regard for its own internal goods which are partially definitive of each particular practice or type of practice. Practices never have a goal or goals fixed for all time – painting has no such goal nor has physics – but the goals themselves are transmuted by the history of the activity. It therefore turns out not to be accidental that every practice has its own history and a history which is more and other than that of the improvement of the relevant technical skills. This historical dimension is crucial in relation to the virtues.

To enter into a practice is to enter into a relationship not only with its contemporary practitioners, but also with those who have preceded us in the practice, particularly those whose achievements extended the reach of the practice to its present point. It is thus the achievement, and *a fortiori* the authority, of a tradition which I then confront and from which I have to learn. And for this learning and the relationship to the past which it embodies the virtues of justice, courage and truthfulness are prerequisite in precisely the same way and for precisely the same reasons as they are in sustaining present relationships within practices.

It is not only of course with sets of technical skills that practices ought to be contrasted. Practices must not be confused with institutions. Chess, physics and medicine are practices; chess clubs, laboratories, universities and hospitals are institutions. Institutions are characteristically and necessarily concerned with what I have called external goods. They are involved in acquiring money and other material goods; they are structured in terms of power and status, and they distribute money, power and status as rewards. Nor could they do otherwise if they are to sustain not only themselves, but also the practices of which they are the bearers. For no practices can survive for any length of time unsustained by institutions. Indeed so intimate is the relationship of practices to institutions – and consequently of the goods external to the goods internal to the practices in question – that institutions and practices characteristically form a single causal order in which the ideals and the creativity of the practice are always vulnerable to the acquisitiveness of the institution, in which the cooperative care for common goods of the practice is always vulnerable to the competitiveness of the institution. In this context the essential function of the virtues is clear. Without them, without justice, courage and truthfulness, practices could not resist the corrupting power of institutions.

Yet if institutions do have corrupting power, the making and sustaining of forms of human community – and therefore of institutions – itself has all the characteristics of a practice, and moreover of a practice which stands in a peculiarly close relationship to the exercise of the virtues in two important ways. The exercise of the virtues is itself apt to require a highly determinate attitude to social and political issues; and it is always within some particular community with its own specific institutional forms that we learn or fail to learn to exercise the virtues. There is of course a crucial difference between the way in which the relationship between moral character and political community is envisaged from the standpoint of liberal individualist modernity and the way in which that relationship was envisaged from the standpoint of the type of ancient and medieval tradition of the virtues which I have sketched. For liberal individualism a community is simply an arena in which individuals each pursue their own self-chosen conception of the good life, and political institutions exist to provide that degree of order which makes such self-determined activity possible. Government and law are, or ought to be, neutral between rival conceptions of the good life for man, and hence, although it is the task of government to promote law-abidingness, it is on the liberal view no part of the legitimate function of government to inculcate any one moral outlook.

By contrast, on the particular ancient and medieval view which I have sketched, political community not only requires the exercise of the virtues for its own sustenance, but it is one of the tasks of parental authority to make children grow up so as to be virtuous adults. The classical statement of this analogy is by Socrates in the *Crito*. It does not of course follow from an acceptance of the Socratic view of political community and political authority that we ought to assign to the modern state the moral function which Socrates assigned to the city and its laws. Indeed the power of the liberal individualist standpoint partly derives from the evident fact that the modern state is indeed totally unfitted to act as moral educator of any community. But the history of how the modern state emerged is of course itself a moral history. If my account of the complex relationship of virtues to practices and to institutions is correct, it follows that we shall be unable to write a true history of practices and institutions unless that history is also one of the virtues and vices. For the ability of a practice to retain its integrity will depend on the way in which the virtues can be and are exercised in sustaining the institutional forms which are the social bearers of the practice. The integrity of a practice causally requires the exercise of the virtues by at least some of the individuals who embody it in their activities; and conversely the corruption of institutions is always in part at least an effect of the vices.

The virtues are of course themselves in turn fostered by certain types of social institution and endangered by others. Thomas Jefferson thought that only in a society of small farmers could the virtues flourish; and Adam Ferguson with a good deal more sophistication saw the institutions of modern commercial society as endangering at least some traditional virtues. It is Ferguson's type of sociology which is the empirical counterpart of the conceptual account of the virtues which I have given, a sociology which aspires to lay bare the empirical, causal connection between virtues, practices and institutions. For this kind of conceptual account has strong empirical implications; it provides an explanatory scheme which can be tested in particular cases. Moreover my thesis has empirical content in another way; it does entail that without the virtues there could be a recognition only of what I have called external goods and not at all of internal goods in the context of practices. And in any society which recognized only external goods, competitiveness would be the dominant and even exclusive feature. We have a brilliant portrait of such a society in Hobbes's account of the state of nature; and Professor Turnbull's report of the fate of the Ik suggests that social reality does in the most horrifying way confirm both my thesis and Hobbes's.

Virtues then stand in a different relationship to external and to internal goods. The possession of the virtues – and not only of their semblance and simulacra – is necessary to achieve the latter; yet the possession of the virtues may perfectly well hinder us in achieving external goods. I need to emphasize at this point that external goods genuinely are goods. Not only are they characteristic objects of human desire, whose allocation is what gives point to the virtues of justice and of generosity, but no one can despise them altogether without a certain hypocrisy. Yet notoriously the cultivation of truthfulness, justice and courage will often, the world being what it contingently is, bar us from being rich or famous or powerful. Thus although we may hope that we can not only achieve the standards of excellence and the internal goods of certain practices by possessing the virtues *and* become rich, famous and powerful, the virtues are always a potential stumbling block to this comfortable ambition. We should therefore expect that, if in a particular society the pursuit of external goods were to become dominant, the concept of the virtues might suffer first attrition and then perhaps something near total effacement, although simulacra might abound.

The time has come to ask the question of how far this partial account of a core conception of the virtues – and I need to emphasize that all that I have offered so far is the first stage of such an account – is faithful to the tradition which I delineated. How far, for example, and in what ways is it Aristotelian? It is – happily – not Aristotelian in two ways in which a good deal of the rest of the tradition also dissents from Aristotle. First, although this account of the virtues is teleological, it does not require any allegiance to Aristotle's metaphysical biology. And secondly, just because of the multiplicity of human practices and the consequent multiplicity of goods in the pursuit of which the virtues may be exercised – goods which will often be contingently incompatible and which will therefore make rival claims upon our allegiance – conflict will not spring solely from flaws in individual character. But it was just on these two matters that Aristotle's account of the virtues seemed most vulnerable; hence if it turns out to be the case that this socially teleological account can support Aristotle's general account of the virtues as well as does his own biologically teleological account, these differences from Aristotle himself may well be regarded as strengthening rather than weakening the case for a generally Aristotelian standpoint.

[. . . .]

Chapter 15

The Virtues, the Unity of a Human Life and the
Concept of a Tradition

[. . . .]

It is now possible to return to the question from which this enquiry
into the nature of human action and identity started: In what does the
unity of an individual life consist? The answer is that its unity is the unity
of a narrative embodied in a single life. To ask 'What is the good for me?'
is to ask how best I might live out that unity and bring it to completion.
To ask 'What is the good for man?' is to ask what all answers to the
former question must have in common. But now it is important to emphasize that it is the systematic asking of these two questions and the
attempt to answer them in deed as well as in word which provide the
moral life with its unity. The unity of a human life is the unity of a
narrative quest. Quests sometimes fail, are frustrated, abandoned or dis-
sipated into distractions; and human lives may in all these ways also fail.
But the only criteria for success or failure in a human life as a whole are
the criteria of success or failure in a narrated or to-be-narrated quest. A
quest for what?

Two key features of the medieval conception of a quest need to be
recalled. The first is that without some at least partly determinate conception of the final *telos* there could not be any beginning to a quest.
Some conception of the good for man is required. Whence is such a
conception to be drawn? Precisely from those questions which led us to
attempt to transcend that limited conception of the virtues which is
available in and through practices. It is in looking for a conception of
the good which will enable us to order other goods, for a conception
of *the* good which will enable us to extend our understanding of the
purpose and content of the virtues, for a conception of *the* good which
will enable us to understand the place of integrity and constancy in life,
that we initially define the kind of life which is a quest for the good. But
secondly it is clear the medieval conception of a quest is not at all that
of a search for something already adequately characterized, as miners
search for gold or geologists for oil. It is in the course of the quest and
only through encountering and coping with the various particular harms,
dangers, temptations and distractions which provide any quest with its
episodes and incidents that the goal of the quest is finally to be understood. A quest is always an education both as to the character of that
which is sought and in self-knowledge.

The virtues therefore are to be understood as those dispositions which
will not only sustain practices and enable us to achieve the goods internal

to practices, but which will also sustain us in the relevant kind of quest for the good, by enabling us to overcome the harms, dangers, temptations and distractions which we encounter, and which will furnish us with increasing self-knowledge and increasing knowledge of the good. The catalogue of the virtues will therefore include the virtues required to sustain the kind of households and the kind of political communities in which men and women can seek for the good together and the virtues necessary for philosophical enquiry about the character of the good. We have then arrived at a provisional conclusion about the good life for man: the good life for man is the life spent in seeking for the good life for man, and the virtues necessary for the seeking are those which will enable us to understand what more and what else the good life for man is. We have also completed the second stage in our account of the virtues, by situating them in relation to the good life for man and not only in relation to practices. But our enquiry requires a third stage.

For I am never able to seek for the good or exercise the virtues only *qua* individual. This is partly because what it is to live the good life concretely varies from circumstance to circumstance even when it is one and the same conception of the good life and one and the same set of virtues which are being embodied in a human life. What the good life is for a fifth-century Athenian general will not be the same as what it was for a medieval nun or a seventeenth-century farmer. But it is not just that different individuals live in different social circumstances; it is also that we all approach our own circumstances as bearers of a particular social identity. I am someone's son or daughter, someone else's cousin or uncle; I am a citizen of this or that city, a member of this or that guild or profession; I belong to this clan, that tribe, this nation. Hence what is good for me has to be the good for one who inhabits these roles. As such, I inherit from the past of my family, my city, my tribe, my nation, a variety of debts, inheritances, rightful expectations and obligations. These constitute the given of my life, my moral starting point. This is in part what gives my life its own moral particularity.

This thought is likely to appear alien and even suprising from the standpoint of modern individualism. From the standpoint of individualism I am what I myself choose to be. I can always, if I wish to, put in question what are taken to be the merely contingent social features of my existence. I may biologically be my father's son; but I cannot be held responsible for what he did unless I choose implicitly or explicitly to assume such responsibility. I may legally be a citizen of a certain country; but I cannot be held responsible for what my country does or has done unless I choose implicitly or explicitly to assume such responsibility. Such individualism is expressed by those modern Americans who deny any responsibility for the effects of slavery upon black Americans, saying 'I never owned any slaves'. It is more subtly the standpoint of those other modern Americans who accept a nicely calculated responsibility for such effects measured precisely by the benefits they themselves as individuals have indirectly received from slavery. In both cases 'being an American' is not in itself taken to be part of the moral identity of the individual. And of course there is nothing peculiar to modern Americans in this attitude: the Englishman who says, '*I* never did any wrong to Ireland; why bring up that old history as though it had something to do with *me?*' or the young German who believes that being born after 1945 means that what Nazis did to Jews has no moral relevance to his relationship to his Jewish contemporaries, exhibit the same attitude, that according to which the self is detachable from its social and historical roles and statuses. And the self so detached is of course a self very much at home in either Sartre's or Goffman's perspective, a self that can have no history. The contrast with the narrative view of the self is clear. For the story of my life is always embedded in the story of those communities from which I derive my identity. I am born with a past; and to try to cut myself off from that past, in the individualist mode, is to deform my present relationships. The possession of an historical identity and the possession of a social identity coincide. Notice that rebellion against my identity is always one possible mode of expressing it.

Notice also that the fact that the self has to find its moral identity in and through its membership in communities such as those of the family, the neighborhood, the city and the tribe does not entail that the self has to accept the moral *limitations* of the particularity of those forms of community. Without those moral particularities to begin from there would never be anywhere to begin; but it is in moving forward from such particularity that the search for the good, for the universal, consists. Yet particularity can never be simply left behind or obliterated. The notion of escaping from it into a realm of entirely universal maxims which belong to man as such, whether in its eighteenth-century Kantian form or in the presentation of some modern analytical moral philosophies, is an illusion and an illusion with painful consequences. When men and women identify what are in fact their partial and particular causes too easily and too completely with the cause of some universal principle, they usually behave worse than they would otherwise do.

What I am, therefore, is in key part what I inherit, a specific past that is present to some degree in my present. I find myself part of a history and that is generally to say, whether I like it or not, whether I recognize it or not, one of the bearers of a tradition. It was important when I characterized the concept of a practice to notice that practices always have histories and that at any given moment what a practice is depends on a mode of understanding it which has been transmitted often through many generations. And thus, insofar as the virtues sustain the relationships required for practices, they have to sustain relationships to the past – and to the future – as well as in the present. But the traditions through which particular practices are transmitted and reshaped never exist in isolation from larger social traditions. What constitutes such traditions?

We are apt to be misled here by the ideological uses to which the concept of a tradition has been put by conservative political theorists. Characteristically such theorists have followed Burke in contrasting tradition with reason and the stability of tradition with conflict. Both contrasts obfuscate. For all reasoning takes place within the context of some traditional mode of thought, transcending through criticism and invention the limitations of what had hitherto been reasoned in that tradition; this is as true of modern physics as of medieval logic. Moreover when a tradition is in good order it is always partially constituted by an argument about the goods the pursuit of which gives to that tradition its particular point and purpose.

So when an institution – a university, say, or a farm, or a hospital – is the bearer of a tradition of practice or practices, its common life will be partly, but in a centrally important way, constituted by a continuous argument as to what a university is and ought to be or what good farming is or what good medicine is. Traditions, when vital, embody continuities of conflict. Indeed when a tradition becomes Burkean, it is always dying or dead.

The individualism of modernity could of course find no use for the notion of tradition within its own conceptual scheme except as an adversary notion; it therefore all too willingly abandoned it to the Burkeans, who, faithful to Burke's own allegiance, tried to combine adherence in politics to a conception of tradition which would vindicate the oligarchical revolution of property of 1688 and adherence in economics to the doctrine and institutions of the free market. The theoretical incoherence of this mismatch did not deprive it of ideological usefulness. But the outcome has been that modern conservatives are for the most part engaged in conserving only older rather than later versions of liberal individualism. Their own core doctrine is as liberal and as individualist as that of self-avowed liberals.

A living tradition then is an historically extended, socially embodied argument, and an argument precisely in part about the goods which constitute that tradition. Within a tradition the pursuit of goods extends through generations, sometimes through many generations. Hence the individual's search for his or her good is generally and characteristically conducted within a context defined by those traditions of which the individual's life is a part, and this is true both of those goods which are internal to practices and of the goods of a single life. Once again the narrative phenomenon of embedding is crucial: the history of a practice in our time is generally and characteristically embedded in and made intelligible in terms of the larger and longer history of the tradition through which the practice in its present form was conveyed to us; the history of each of our own lives is generally and characteristically embedded in and made intelligible in terms of the larger and longer histories of a number of traditions. I have to say 'generally and characteristically' rather than 'always', for traditions decay, disintegrate and disappear. What then sustains and strengthens traditions? What weakens and destroys them?

The answer in key part is: the exercise or the lack of exercise of the relevant virtues. The virtues find their point and purpose not only in sustaining those relationships necessary if the variety of goods internal to practices are to be achieved and not only in sustaining the form of an individual life in which that individual may seek out his or her good as the good of his or her whole life, but also in sustaining those traditions which provide both practices and individual lives with their necessary historical context. Lack of justice, lack of truthfulness, lack of courage, lack of the relevant intellectual virtues – these corrupt traditions, just as they do those institutions and practices which derive their life from the traditions of which they are the contemporary embodiments. To recognize this is of course also to recognize the existence of an additional virtue, one whose importance is perhaps most obvious when it is least present, the virtue of having an adequate sense of the traditions to which one belongs or which confront one. This virtue is not to be confused with any form of conservative antiquarianism; I am not praising those who choose the conventional conservative role of *laudator temporis acti*. It is rather the case that an adequate sense of tradition manifests itself in a grasp of those future possibilities which the past has made available to the present. Living traditions, just because they continue a not-yet-completed narrative, confront a future whose determinate and determinable character, so far as it possesses any, derives from the past.

[. . . .]

I argued earlier that every moral philosophy has some particular sociology as its counterpart. What I have tried to spell out in this chapter is the kind of understanding of social life which the tradition of the virtues requires, a kind of understanding very different from those dominant in the culture of bureaucratic individualism. Within that culture conceptions of the virtues become marginal and the tradition of the virtues remains central only in the lives of social groups whose existence is on the margins of the central culture.

[. . . .]

Chapter 18

After Virtue: Nietzsche *or* Aristotle, Trotsky *and* St Benedict

In Chapter 9 I posed a stark question: Nietzsche *or* Aristotle? The argument which led to the posing of that question had two central premises. The first was that the language – and therefore also to some large degree the practice – of morality today is in a state of grave disorder. That disorder arises from the prevailing cultural power of an idiom in which ill-assorted conceptual fragments from various parts of our past are deployed together in private and public debates which are notable chiefly for the unsettlable character of the controversies thus carried on and the apparent arbitrariness of each of the contending parties.

The second was that ever since belief in Aristotelian teleology was discredited moral philosophers have attempted to provide some alternative rational secular account of the nature and status of morality, but that all these attempts, various and variously impressive as they have been, have in fact failed, a failure perceived most clearly by Nietzsche. Consequently Nietzsche's negative proposal to raze to the ground the structures of inherited moral belief and argument had, whether we have regard to everyday moral belief and argument or look instead to the constructions of moral philosophers, and in spite of its desperate and grandiose quality, a certain plausibility – unless of course the initial rejection of the moral tradition to which Aristotle's teaching about the virtues is central turned out to have been misconceived and mistaken. Unless that tradition could be rationally vindicated, Nietzsche's stance would have a terrible plausibility.

Not that, even so, it would be easy in the contemporary world to be an intelligent Nietzschean. The stock characters acknowledged in the dramas of modern social life embody all too well the concepts and the modes of the moral beliefs and arguments which an Aristotelian and a Nietzschean would have to agree in rejecting. The bureaucratic manager, the consuming aesthete, the therapist, the protester and their numerous kindred occupy almost all the available culturally recognizable roles; the notions of the expertise of the few and of the moral agency of everyone are the presuppositions of the dramas which those characters enact. To cry out that the emperor had no clothes on was at least to pick on one man only to the amusement of everyone else; to declare that almost everyone is dressed in rags is much less likely to be popular. But the Nietzschean would at least have the consolation of being unpopularly *in the right* – unless, that is, the rejection of the Aristotelian tradition turned out to have been mistaken.

The Aristotelian tradition has occupied two distinct places in my argument: first, because I have suggested that a great part of modern morality is intelligible only as a set of fragmented survivals from that tradition, and indeed that the inability of modern moral philosphers to carry through their projects of analysis and justification is closely connected with the fact that the concepts with which they work are a combination of fragmented survivals and implausible modern inventions; but in addition to this the rejection of the Aristotelian tradition was a rejection of a quite distinctive kind of morality in which rules, so predominant in modern conceptions of morality, find their place in a larger scheme in which the virtues have the central place; hence the cogency of the Nietzschean rejection and refutation of modern moralities of rules, whether of a utilitarian or of a Kantian kind, did not necessarily extend to the earlier Aristotelian tradition.

It is one of my most important contentions that against that tradition the Nietzschean polemic is completely unsuccessful. The grounds for saying this can be set out in two different ways. The first I already suggested in Chapter 9; Nietzsche succeeds if all those whom he takes on as antagonists fail. Others may have to succeed by virtue of the rational power of their positive arguments; but if Nietzsche wins, he wins by default.

He does not win. I have sketched in Chapters 14 and 15 the rational case that can be made for a tradition in which the Aristotelian moral and political texts are canonical. For Nietzsche or the Nietzscheans to succeed, that case would have to be rebutted. Why it cannot be so rebutted is best brought out by considering a second way in which the rejection of Nietzsche's claims can be argued. Nietzschean man, the *Übermensch*, the man who transcends, finds his good nowhere in the social world to date, but only in that in himself which dictates his own new law and his own new table of the virtues. Why does he never find any objective good with authority over him in the social world to date? The answer is not difficult: Nietzsche's portrait makes it clear that he who transcends is wanting in respect of both relationships and activities. Consider part of just one note (962) from *The Will to Power*. 'A great man – a man whom nature has constructed and invented in the grand style – what is he? . . . If he cannot lead, he goes alone; then it can happen that he may snarl at some things he meets on the way . . . he wants no 'sympathetic' heart, but servants, tools; in his intercourse with men he is always intent on *making* something out of them. He knows he is incommunicable: he finds it tasteless to be familiar; and when one thinks he is, he usually is not. When not speaking to himself, he wears a mask. He rather lies than tells the truth: it requires more spirit and *will*. There is a solitude within him that is inaccessible to praise or blame, his own justice that is beyond appeal.'

This characterization of 'the great man' is deeply rooted in Nietzsche's contention that the morality of European society since the archaic age in Greece has been nothing but a series of disguises for the will to power and that the claim to objectivity for such morality cannot be rationally sustained. It is because this is so that the great man cannot enter into relationships mediated by appeal to shared standards or virtues or goods; he is his own only authority and his relationships to others have to be exercises of that authority. But we can now see clearly that, if the account of the virtues which I have defended can be sustained, it is the isolation and self-absorption of 'the great man' which thrust upon him the burden of being his own self-sufficient moral authority. For if the conception of a good has to be expounded in terms of such notions as those of a practice, of the narrative unity of a human life and of a moral tradition, then goods, and with them the only grounds for the authority of laws and virtues, can only be discovered by entering into those relationships which constitute communities whose central bond is a shared vision of and understanding of goods. To cut oneself off from shared activity in which one has initially to learn obediently as an apprentice learns, to isolate oneself from the communities which find their point and purpose in such activities, will be to debar oneself from finding any good outside of oneself. It will be to condemn oneself to that moral solipsism which constitutes Nietzschean greatness. Hence we have to conclude not only that Nietzsche does not win the argument by default against the Aristotelian tradition, but also, and perhaps more importantly, that it is from the perspective of that tradition that we can best understand the mistakes at the heart of the Nietzschean position.

The attractiveness of Nietzsche's position lay in its apparent honesty. When I was setting out the case in favor of an amended and restated emotivism, it appeared to be a consequence of accepting the truth of emotivism that an honest man would no longer want to go on using most, at least, of the language of past morality because of its misleading character. And Nietzsche was the only major philosopher who had not flinched from this conclusion. Since moreover the language of modern morality is burdened with pseudo-concepts such as those of utility and of natural rights, it appeared that Nietzsche's resoluteness alone would rescue us from entanglement by such concepts; but it is now clear that the price to be paid for this liberation is entanglement in another set of mistakes. The concept of the Nietzschean 'great man' is also a pseudo-concept, although not always perhaps – unhappily – what I earlier called a fiction. It represents individualism's final attempt to escape from its own consequences. And the Nietzschean stance turns out not to be a mode of escape from or an alternative to the conceptual scheme of liberal individualist modernity, but rather one more representative moment in its internal unfolding. And we may therefore expect liberal individualist societies to breed 'great men' from time to time. Alas!

So it was right to see Nietzsche as in some sense the ultimate antagonist of the Aristotelian tradition. But it now turns out to be the case that in the end the Nietzschean stance is only one more facet of that very moral culture of which Nietzsche took himself to be an implacable critic. It is therefore after all the case that the crucial moral opposition is between liberal individualism in some version or other and the Aristotelian tradition in some version or other.

The differences between the two run very deep. They extend beyond ethics and morality to the understanding of human action, so that rival conceptions of the social sciences, of their limits and their possibilities, are intimately bound up with the antagonistic confrontation of these two alternative ways of viewing the human world. This is why my argument has had to extend to such topics as those of the concept of fact, the limits to predictability in human affairs and the nature of ideology. And it will now, I hope, be clear that in the chapters dealing with those topics I was not merely summing up arguments *against* the social embodiments of liberal individualism, but also laying the basis for arguments in favor of an alternative way of envisaging both the social sciences and society, one with which the Aristotelian tradition can easily be at home.

My own conclusion is very clear. It is that on the one hand we still, in spite of the efforts of three centuries of moral philosophy and one of sociology, lack any coherent rationally defensible statement of a liberal individualist point of view; and that, on the other hand, the Aristotelian tradition can be restated in a way that restores intelligibility and rationality to our moral and social attitudes and commitments. But although I take the weight and direction of both sets of arguments to be rationally compelling, it would be imprudent not to recognize three quite different kinds of objection that will be advanced from three quite different points of view against this conclusion.

Arguments in philosophy rarely take the form of proofs; and the most successful arguments on topics central to philosophy never do. (The ideal of *proof* is a relatively barren one in philosophy.) Consequently those who wish to resist some particular conclusion are equally rarely without any resort. Let me hasten to add immediately that I do not mean to suggest by this that no central issues in philosophy are settlable; on the contrary. We can often establish the truth in areas where no proofs are available. But when an issue *is* settled, it is often because the contending parties – or someone from among them – have stood back from their dispute and asked in a systematic way what the appropriate rational procedures are for settling this particular kind of dispute. It is my own view that the time has come once more when it is imperative to perform this task for moral philosophy; but I do not pretend to have embarked upon it in this present book. My negative and positive evaluations of particular arguments do indeed *presuppose* a systematic, although here unstated, account of rationality.

It is this account – to be given to a subsequent book – which I shall hope to deploy, and will almost certainly need to deploy, against those whose criticism of my central thesis rests chiefly or wholly upon a different and incompatible evaluation of the arguments. A motley party of defenders of liberal individualism – some of them utilitarians, some Kantians, some proudly avowing the cause of liberal individualism as I have defined it, others claiming that it is misinterpretation to associate them with my account of it, all of them disagreeing among themselves – are likely to offer objections of this kind.

A second set of objections will certainly concern my interpretation of what I have called the Aristotelian or classical tradition. For it is clear that the account I have given differs in a variety of ways, some of them quite radical, from other appropriations and interpretations of an Aristotelian moral stance. And here I am disagreeing to some extent at least with some of those philosophers for whom I have the greatest respect and from whom I have learned most (but not nearly enough, their adherents will say): in the immediate past Jacques Maritain, in the present Peter

Geach. Yet if my account of the nature of moral tradition is correct, a tradition is sustained and advanced by its own internal arguments and conflicts. And even if some large parts of my interpretation could not withstand criticism, the demonstration of this would itself strengthen the tradition which I am attempting to sustain and to extend. Hence my attitude to those criticisms which I take to be internal to the moral tradition which I am defending is rather different from my attitude to purely external criticisms. The latter are no less important; but they are important in a different way.

Thirdly there will certainly be a quite different set of critics who will begin by agreeing substantially with what I have to say about liberal individualism, but who will deny not only that the Aristotelian tradition is a viable alternative, but also that it is in terms of an opposition between liberal individualism and that tradition that the problems of modernity ought to be approached. The key intellectual opposition of our age, such critics will declare, is that between liberal individualism and some version of Marxism or neo-Marxism. The most intellectually compelling exponents of this point of view are likely to be those who trace a genealogy of ideas from Kant and Hegel through Marx and claim that by means of Marxism the notion of human autonomy can be rescued from its original individualist formulations and restored within the context of an appeal to a possible form of community in which alienation has been overcome, false consciousness abolished and the values of equality and fraternity realized. My answers to the first two kinds of critic are to some large degree contained, implicity or explicitly, in what I have already written. My answers to the third type of criticism need to be spelled out a little further. They fall into two parts.

The first is that the claim of Marxism to a morally distinctive standpoint is undermined by Marxism's own moral history. In all those crises in which Marxists have had to take explicit moral stances – that over Bernstein's revisionism in German social democracy at the turn of the century or that over Khrushchev's repudiation of Stalin and the Hungarian revolt in 1956, for example – Marxists have always fallen back into relatively straightforward versions of Kantianism or utilitarianism. Nor is this surprising. Secreted within Marxism from the outset is a certain radical individualism. In the first chapter of *Capital* when Marx characterizes what it will be like 'when the practical relations of everyday life offer to man none but perfectly intelligible and reasonable relations', what he pictures is 'a community of free individuals' who have all freely agreed to their common ownership of the means of production and to various norms of production and distribution. This free individual is described by Marx as a socialized Robinson Crusoe; but on what basis he enters into his free association with others Marx does not tell us. At this key point in Marxism there is a lacuna which no later Marxist has adequately supplied. It is unsurprising that abstract moral principle and utility have in fact been the principles of association which Marxists have appealed to, and that in their practice Marxists have exemplified precisely the kind of moral attitude which they condemn in others as ideological.

Secondly, I remarked earlier that as Marxists move towards power they always tend to become Weberians. Here I was of course speaking of Marxists at their best in, say, Yugoslavia or Italy; the barbarous despotism of the collective Tsardom which reigns in Moscow can be taken to be as irrelevant to the question of the moral substance of Marxism as the life of the Borgia pope was to that of the moral substance of Christianity. Nonetheless Marxism has recommended itself precisely as a guide to practice, as a politics of a peculiarly illuminating kind. Yet it is just here that it has been of singularly little help for some time now. Trotsky, in the very last years of his life, facing the question of whether the Soviet Union was in any sense a socialist country, also faced implicitly the question of whether the categories of Marxism could illuminate the future. He himself made everything turn on the outcome of a set of hypothetical predictions about possible future events in the Soviet Union, predictions which were tested only after Trotsky's death. The answer that they returned was clear: Trotsky's own premises entailed that the Soviet Union was not socialist and that the theory which was to have illuminated the path to human liberation had in fact led into darkness.

Marxist socialism is at its core deeply optimistic. For however thoroughgoing its criticism of capitalist and bourgeois institutions may be, it is committed to asserting that within the society constituted by those institutions, all the human and material preconditions of a better future are being accumulated. Yet if the moral impoverishment of advanced capitalism is what so many Marxists agree that it is, whence are these resources for the future to be derived? It is not surprising that at this point Marxism tends to produce its own versions of the *Übermensch*: Lukács's ideal proletarian, Leninism's ideal revolutionary. When Marxism does not become Weberian social democracy or crude tyranny, it tends to become Nietzschean fantasy. One of the most admirable aspects of Trotsky's cold resolution was his refusal of all such fantasies.

A Marxist who took Trotsky's last writings with great seriousness would be forced into a pessimism quite alien to the Marxist tradition, and in becoming a pessimist he would in an important way have ceased to be a Marxist. For he would now see no tolerable alternative set of political and economic structures which could be brought into place to replace the structures of advanced capitalism. This conclusion agrees of course with my own. For I too not only take it that Marxism is exhausted as a *political* tradition, a claim borne out by the almost indefinitely numerous and conflicting range of political allegiances which now carry Marxist banners – this does not at all imply that Marxism is not still one of the richest sources of ideas about modern society – but I believe that this exhaustion is shared by every other political tradition within our culture. This is one of the conclusions to be drawn from the arguments of the preceding chapter. Does it then follow more specifically that the moral tradition which I am defending lacks any contemporary politics of relevance and more generally that my argument commits me and anyone else who accepts it to a generalized social pessimism? Not at all.

It is always dangerous to draw too precise parallels between one historical period and another; and among the most misleading of such parallels are those which have been drawn between our own age in Europe and North America and the epoch in which the Roman empire declined into the Dark Ages. Nonetheless certain parallels there are. A crucial turning point in that earlier history occurred when men and women of good will turned aside from the task of shoring up the Roman *imperium* and ceased to identify the continuation of civility and moral community with the maintenance of that *imperium*. What they set themselves to achieve instead – often not recognizing fully what they were doing – was the construction of new forms of community within which the moral life could be sustained so that both morality and civility might survive the coming ages of barbarism and darkness. If my account of our moral condition is correct, we ought also to conclude that for some time now we too have reached that turning point. What matters at this stage is the construction of local forms of community within which civility and the intellectual and moral life can be sustained through the new dark ages which are already upon us. And if the tradition of the virtues was able to survive the horrors of the last dark ages, we are not entirely without grounds for hope. This time however the barbarians are not waiting beyond the frontiers; they have already been governing us for quite some time. And it is our lack of consciousness of this that constitutes part of our predicament. We are waiting not for a Godot, but for another – doubtless very different – St Benedict.

PART III

Establishing a Tradition of Practical Rationality

'Précis of *Whose Justice?*
Which Rationality?'

Criticisms of philosophical theses may be misdirected, if such theses are not understood as answers to those questions in response to which they were formulated. A writer usually has only him or herself to blame for this kind of misunderstanding. So let me begin by reiterating, and to some extent reformulating, the questions to which *Whose Justice? Which Rationality?* is addressed.

The first is: confronted by two accounts of justice as radically different as Aristotle's and Hume's, how is one to approach the task of deciding rationally between them? For those rival accounts of justice are each framed in terms dictated by, and in some respects not detachable from, an overall system of thought, one which both imposes constraints upon its philosophical parts and also provides standards by appeal to which each philosopher advances a rational justification for his particular account. So whether either of these two accounts of justice stands or falls depends to some significant extent upon whether or not either of the correspondingly rival accounts of the rational justification of action and practice, stated or presupposed, can itself be vindicated.

In the case of Aristotle more is at stake than his account of practical rationality, for that account is itself embedded in his larger scheme of thought. And so also with Hume, more is at stake than his account of the respective roles of the passions and reason in generating evaluative judgments and action, for Hume's epistemology and metaphysics inform *that* account. So that what have to be evaluated are the claims of two rival philosophical *systems*.

Yet what makes it difficult to decide rationally between the rival claims of Aristotle and Hume, perhaps of course discovering in so doing that neither set of claims can be vindicated, is not only the systematic character of the issues involved. It is also and more fundamentally that each of these accounts draws upon the resources of, and is formulated in terms of a conceptual scheme quite alien to, that informing its rival. Where Aristotle's formulations are in terms of *archē, telos, psychē, logos, ergon, praxis, pathos, aretē,* and *polis,* Hume's deploy *impression, idea, passions calm and violent, nature, artifice, virtue, society* and *government.* It is not that there are not a range of shared meanings and references in the uses of these two sets of terms; were it not so, we could not recognize them as rival conceptualizations of one and the same subject-matter. Nonetheless the radical differences between them are such that if the Aristotelian concepts have application in the way and to the degree that Aristotelians have held, then the Humean concepts are thereby precluded by and large from having application, and vice versa. And hence arises the fundamental incompatibility of theories of justice framed in terms of one of those schemes with theories framed in terms of the other.

The problem of deciding between these rival claims can be approached by considering how and why no similar problem arises in deciding between Aristotle's positions and Plato's or between Hume's positions and Hutcheson's. In each of these two cases there is a continuity of enquiry. Aristotle carries forward Plato's project, even in the course of revising and sometimes abandoning Plato's own theses and arguments in order to remedy a range of incoherences and resourcelessnesses, recognizable as such by Plato's own standards. And even when Aristotle revises those standards he does so in the light of considerations to which Plato too would have had to attach weight.

As Aristotle stands to Plato, so Hume stands to Hutcheson; and so indeed does Plato stand to Socrates – and in some measure also to Parmenides – and Hutcheson both to Shaftesbury and to the theses and arguments of Dutch and Scottish seventeenth-century legal theorists, most notably Lord Stair. But it is not just that we have here two very different philosophical successions, in which philosophers at each stage both draw upon and advance beyond their predecessors. It is also that in both cases the philosophical conversation begins from, and from time to time renews an examination of, the beliefs and concepts of the social group within whose shared life the activities of philosophical enquiry are carried on. So that the philosophy both draws upon and contributes to the other activities of that particular cultural and social order, articulating for that cultural and social order its concepts and beliefs in a way which enables those who inhabit that culture to learn both which criticisms of those concepts and beliefs require a rational answer and to what degree such an answer can be provided. The history of philosophy as a form of rational enquiry is in such cultural and social orders embedded in the larger history of culture and society and will be, if too much detached from that history, in certain respects distorted or even unintelligible.

It is important to notice that in some other times and places philosophy has detached itself or has been made to detach itself from the culture at large, becoming an autonomous and specialized activity whose history, or so at least it has commonly seemed to those engaged in such activity, can be written without much reference to the history of anything else. And it is equally important to notice that in those cases in which the history of philosophy is indeed embedded in significant ways in the general history of some social and cultural order, the ways in which philosophical activity is related to other types of activity vary from case to case. So that although one of my claims is that the line of philosophical enquiry which runs from Socrates through Plato to Aristotle is only adequately intelligible in the context of the history of Athens and that the line of philosophical enquiry which runs from Stair through Hutcheson to Hume is only adequately intelligible in the context of the history of Scotland, I am not claiming that the relationship of the philosophy to its social and cultural context was the same in these two cases. It is in part the difference in this relationship, as well as the difference between the contexts and the difference in philosophical modes, which makes the difficulties of deciding rationally between Aristotle's claims and Hume's so intractable. Yet to have understood this is perhaps also to have understood how we may begin to move towards a resolution of those difficulties.

Let us characterize such sequences in the history of philosophy as that which runs from Socrates through Plato to Aristotle and then onwards into Aristotelianism, including the Aristotelianism of Aquinas, and that which runs in one way from Stair and the Scottish seventeenth-century tradition and in another from Shaftesbury through Hutcheson to Hume as *socially embodied traditions of rational enquiry*. Then we shall need to distinguish between what is required to establish the rational superiority of one position to another *within* some particular tradition and what is required to establish the rational superiority of one tradition to another. Hence a second question arises: how are such traditions to be understood?

The materials for an answer to this question are provided in *Whose Justice? Which Rationality?* by a set of narrative histories of the traditions in question. These narratives serve two central purposes: they exhibit how within each tradition accounts of justice and of rationality in action are interrelated as parts of a single overall philosophical theory, and how such accounts develop in response to confrontation with a variety of criticisms and problems arising both from within and from without each particular tradition. Secondly they are used to show the place of conflict within traditions, as well as between traditions, and the different kinds of outcome which such conflict can have in the splitting apart of a tradition, or in the integration of what have hitherto been disparate and even hostile traditions (this is what Aquinas achieved in his synthesis of Aristotelian and Augustinian standpoints), or in the defeat within a tradition of a multiplicity of rival views and even of the tradition itself by a compelling demonstration from premises which those rivals could not deny (this is what Hume achieved in respect of all his immediate predecessors).

These narratives provide examples of what a socially embodied tradition of rational enquiry is; the concept which they exemplify is further elaborated in the course of defending four further theses: that no way of conducting rational enquiry from a standpoint independent of the particularities of any tradition has been discovered and that there is good reason to believe that there is no such way; that the problems of under-standing and representing faithfully the concepts and beliefs of some tradition alien to one's own in a way that makes those concepts and beliefs intelligible within one's own tradition confront difficulties which can in certain contingent circumstances be overcome; that rival traditions have rival conceptions of rationality and of progress in understanding, but that this does not entail relativism or perspectivism; and finally that although these theses are themselves advanced from the standpoint of a particular tradition, that of a Thomist Aristotelianism, they involve a substantive and nonrelativizable conception of truth, and that in this respect as in others there is no inconsistency in making universal claims from the standpoint of a tradition.

Whose Justice? Which Rationality? (extracts)

Chapter 3
The Division of the Post-Homeric Inheritance

To what standards did post-Homeric Greeks, and more especially Athenians, appeal in making judgments about human excellence? It was part of their Homeric inheritance to believe that excellence is to be judged in terms of the standards established within and for some specific form of systematic activity. To be good is to be good at some activity or in the performance of some role situated within such an activity. There are at least seven types of systematic activity in which in the Homeric and post-Homeric worlds such standards of excellence are elaborated and applied. They are: warfare and combat; seamanship; athletic and gymnastic activity; epic, lyric, and dramatic poetry; farming both arable and the management of animals; rhetoric; and the making and sustaining of the communities of kinship and the household and later of the city-state. To this list architecture, sculpture, and painting were to be added, as were the intellectual enquiries of mathematics, philosophy, and theology.

Such types of activity are often interrelated. Qualities of body, mind, and character acquired in one may play a useful or essential part in achieving success in another. Moreover, all of them require the same kind of disciplined apprenticeship in which, because initially we lack important qualities of mind, body, and character necessary both for excellent performance and for informed and accurate judgment about excellence in performance, we have to put ourselves into the hands of those competent to transform us into the kind of people who will be able both to perform well and to judge well. What is it that we have to learn from them?

We have to acquire both in performance and in judgment the ability to make two different kinds of distinction, that between what merely seems good to us here now and what really is good relative to us here now, and that between what is good relative to us here now and what is good or best unqualifiedly. The first distinction is of course one that can only be applied retrospectively. It is a distinction involved in someone's identification at some later stage of his or her own earlier mistakes, either in performance or in judgment. It is a distinction which will inform later judgments upon one's earlier mistakes in a rational, well-grounded way only if one is able to explain what it was about one in an earlier state that led one into error.

The second kind of distinction is that between what is a good – perhaps the best possible – performance for someone at his or her present stage of educational development relative to his or her particular talents and capacities and what would be the best kind of performance which can now be envisaged by those best qualified to judge, the distinction, for example, between excellent apprentice work and a supremely excellent masterpiece. But it is important to note that the kind of judgments which we make invoking this second type of distinction are themselves subject to later judgments invoking the first kind of distinction. What seemed to us at one stage a perfect performance may later be recognized either as imperfect or as less perfect than some later achievement. That is to say, in all these areas there is not only progress in achievement but also progress in our conception and recognition of what the highest perfection is.

The concept of the best, of the perfected, provides each of these forms of activity with the good toward which those who participate in it move. What directs them toward that goal is both the history of successive attempts to transcend the limitations of the best achievement in that particular area so far and the acknowledgment of certain achievements as permanently defining aspects of the perfection toward which that particular form of activity is directed. Those achievements are assigned a canonical status within the practice of each type of activity. Learning what they have to teach is central to apprenticeship in each particular form of activity.

What can never be done is to reduce what has had to be learned in order to excel at such a type of activity to the application of rules. There will of course at any particular stage in the historical development of such a form of activity be a stock of maxims which are used to characterize what is taken at that stage to be the best practice so far. But knowing how to apply these maxims is itself a capacity which cannot be specified by further rules, and the greatest achievements in each area at each stage always exhibit a freedom to violate the present established maxims, so that achievement proceeds both by rule-keeping and by rule-breaking. And there are never any rules to prescribe when it is the one rather than the other that we must do if we are to pursue excellence.

Excellence and winning, it is scarcely necessary to repeat, are not the same. But it is in fact to winning, and only to excellence on the occasions when it does in fact produce victory, that a certain kind of reward is attached, a reward by which, ostensibly at least, excellence is to be honored. Rewards of this kind – let us call them external rewards – are such goods as those of riches, power, status, and prestige, goods which can be and are objects of desire by human beings prior to and independently of any desire for excellence. In societies and cultures, such as that represented in the Homeric poems, in which the pursuit of these latter goods and that of excellence are to some large degree linked together within the dominant social institutions, any incompatibilities between the human qualities required for the pursuit of such goods and the qualities required for the pursuit of excellence are apt to remain latent and unacknowledged. But when social change transforms institutions, so that the systematic pursuit of excellence in some area or areas becomes incompatible with the pursuit of the goods of riches, power, status, and prestige, the differences between the two types of pursuit and between the goods which are their objects become all too clear.

What qualities of body, mind, and character are generally required to achieve such goods as those of riches, power, status, and prestige? They are those which, in the circumstances in which a given person finds him or herself, enable that person both to identify which means will be effective in securing such goods and to be effective in utilizing those means to secure them. Let us call these qualities of body, mind, and character the qualities of effectiveness, and the goods which provide these qualities with their goal and their justification the goods of effectiveness.

It is at once clear that some of the qualities characteristically and generally necessary to achieve excellence and some of the qualities characteristically and generally necessary to achieve the goods of effectiveness are the same: steadfastness of purpose, for example. But it is equally clear that these two sets of qualities also differ in striking ways, so that what is accounted a virtue in the perspective afforded by the goods of effectiveness will often be very different from what is accounted a virtue from the standpoint of the goods of excellence. Consider in this respect what each characteristically makes of justice, temperateness, courage, and friendship.

In relation to both the goods of excellence and the goods of effectiveness a disposition to obey certain rules of justice will be accounted a virtue, but the justification of the rules, the content of the rules, and the nature of the binding force that the rules have for those who accept their authority is different in the two cases, and these differences are rooted in the fundamental contrast between excellence on the one hand and effectiveness on the other, both defined in terms of performance in the *agōn*. One who excels is one who wins under conditions of fairness [. . .] Moreover, someone who is genuinely excellent has to impose the constraints of fairness upon him or herself, if only because to know how to judge oneself or others excellent, which is part of excellence, involves fairness in judging. The same standards have to be applied to performances under the same standard conditions, appropriate allowances have to be made where someone performs under conditions either more difficult or easier than the standard conditions, and the beginner and the advanced performer must be judged in appropriately different ways. These constraints are expressed in formulas used to define justice: each person and each performance has to be accorded what is due to him or her and to it in respect of merit, like cases being judged on equal terms, unlike with the right degree of proportionality.

The content of justice is thus defined in terms of merit and desert. To be wronged is to be the recipient of undeserved harm inflicted intentionally by someone else; to be unlucky by contrast is to be the recipient of harm from nature, by accident. To redress wrong is to restore the order in which the appropriate goods, whatever they are, are distributed according to desert. But at this point a problem arises. If excellence is always the specific excellence of some particular form of activity, then desert in respect of excellence is presumably also correspondingly specific, and there will be a multiplicity of standards of desert, each independent of the others. So the question will arise: How are the goods of honor and those of the external rewards of excellence to be apportioned among different kinds of achievement? How is the desert of the good soldier to be compared to that of the good farmer or the good poet? Failure to provide some standard in terms of which relative achievement and relative desert can be appraised would leave the members of a community without the possibility of any overall shared standard of just apportionment and just recognition. It would deprive them of any standard which could be what any legitimate claimant to the names '*dikē*' and '*dikaiosunē*' has to be, an expression of some unitary order informing and structuring human life. But how could such a standard be provided?

The only form of community which could provide itself with such a standard would be one whose members structured their common life in terms of a form of activity whose specific goal was to integrate within itself, so far as possible, all those other forms of activity practiced by its members and so to create and sustain as its specific goal that form of life within which to the greatest possible degree the goods of each practice could be enjoyed as well as those goods which are the external rewards of excellence. The name given by Greeks to this form of activity was 'politics', and the *polis* was the institution whose concern was, not with this or that particular good, but with human good as such, and not with desert or achievement in respect of particular practices, but with desert and achievement as such. The constitution of each particular *polis* could therefore be understood as the expression of a set of principles about how goods are to be ordered into a way of life. *The* good for human beings would be the form of life that was best for them; to enjoy what is best is to flourish, to be *eudaimōn*; and what both the constitution and the life of a particular polity express is a judgment as to what way of life is best and what human flourishing consists in.

The ordering of goods within a *polis* was not only a matter of ranking goods hierarchically, by understanding some goods to be valued only for their own sake, others as both for their own sake and for the sake of some further good, and others yet again as only to be valued as means to some further good. It was also a matter of identifying the place of each good within the patterns of the normal day and month and year, so that there would be in some cities at least a time of the year when tragic poetry received its due and a time when comedy did so, and also of identifying both which section of the citizens it was whose peculiar good each particular good was, as the good of excellence in military combat was peculiarly the good of the young, and which section of the citizens it was to whose care the achievement of each particular good peculiarly belonged, as the goods of farming to the farmers and the goods of healing to the guild of physicians, the Asclepiadae.

To what rational principles can appeal be made in such an overall ordering of goods, so that that ordering may be rationally justifiable? It is, of course, this question which must be answered by any theory of practical reasoning that aspires to show what it is for the citizen of the *polis qua* citizen – the citizen who acts in accordance with the ordering of goods established in his particular *polis* – to act rationally. And it is evident that only in the light of such a theory could the justice of any particular *polis*, understood in this way, be justified. For the justice of a *polis* on this view, both in its apportionment of goods and in its correction of wrongdoing, is expressed in the actions of its citizens as they in different ways and with different degrees both of devotion and of success pursue the goods of excellence and reason as to what to do in order to achieve such goods.

Yet at once it needs to be remarked that this was only one way in which the justice of the *polis* and the practical rationality of its citizens came to be understood. From another contrasting and antagonistic perspective the justice of the *polis*, both as a quality of individual citizens and as an ordering of the city, was understood as directed not toward the goods of excellence but toward those of effectiveness. To understand this alternative conception of justice adequately, it is necessary as a preliminary to emphasize the complexity of the relationships between the goods of excellence and those of effectiveness.

It would be a large misconception to suppose that allegiance to goods of the one kind necessarily excluded allegiance to the goods of the other. For on the one hand those forms of activity within which alone it is possible to achieve the goods of excellence can only be sustained by being provided with institutionalized settings. And the maintenance of the relevant institutional and organizational forms always requires the acquisition and retention of some degree of power and some degree of wealth. Thus the goods of excellence cannot be systematically cultivated unless some at least of the goods of effectiveness are also pursued. On the other hand it is difficult in most social contexts to pursue the goods of effectiveness without cultivating at least to some degree the goods of excellence, and this for at least two reasons. The achievement of power, wealth, and fame often enough requires as a means the achievement of some kind of genuine excellence. And, moreover, since the goods of effectiveness are those goods which enable their possessor to have or to be, within the limits of contingent possibility, what he or she wants, whenever what someone whose fundamental allegiance is to the goods of effectiveness just happens to want, for whatever reason, to be genuinely excellent in some way, goods of effectiveness will be put to the service of goods of excellence.

It is, however, always possible for a particular individual or social group systematically to subordinate goods of the one kind to goods of the other, and the fundamental conflicts of standpoint in much Greek and especially Athenian life were provided by those who did so. In the actual social orders of city-states not only was recognition accorded to both sets of goods, but it was often enough accorded in a way that left it indeterminate where the fundamental allegiance of those who inhabited that social order lay. So it was, as I have already suggested, with the order portrayed in the Homeric poems; so it was for the most part in Periclean Athens. Only when certain kinds of practical and theoretical issues – those in which different fundamental allegiances in respect of goods require systematically different and incompatible answers to centrally important practical questions – claimed the attention of a particular social group did they either discover for themselves where it was that their own allegiance had already been given or else for the first time clearly give their allegiance to one set of goods rather than the other.

What made this indeterminateness possible was the fact that one and the same institutionalized set of rules and procedures in the administration of justice may over a wide range of cases be equally compatible with the pursuit of either set of goods, while an ambiguous political rhetoric may for long periods leave it quite unclear, to those who utter it as much as to their hearers, that there are any decisive choices between types of good which need to be made. Nonetheless, there are some continually recurring issues which make it difficult to avoid the making of such choices, and these in time reveal the radical character of the difference between a justice defined in terms of the goods of excellence, that is, a justice of desert, and a justice defined in terms of the goods of effectiveness. What is distinctive about the latter kind of justice?

Under the normal conditions of life in human societies each person can only hope to be effective in trying to obtain what he or she wants, whatever it is, if he or she enters into certain kinds of cooperation with others and if this cooperation enables both him or her and those others generally to have rationally well-founded expectations of each other. Thus a rule-governed mode of social life will be required [. . . .]

What the rules of justice will have to prescribe is reciprocity, and what is to be accounted as reciprocity, what is to be exchanged for what, will depend on what each party brings to that bargaining situation of which the rules of justice are the outcome.

[. . . .]

Unsurprisingly [. . .] the question 'Who should rule?' has a very different answer in respect of the goods of effectiveness from that which it has in respect of those of excellence. For the adherents of each have to conceive of the point and purpose of politics and the *polis* in a very different way. Those who subordinate the goods of excellence to those of effectiveness will, if they are consistent, understand politics as that arena in which each citizen seeks to achieve as far as possible what he or she wants within the constraints imposed by the various forms of political order, and the answer to the question 'Who should rule?' will be 'Whoever has both the skills and the interest to maintain or to promote each type of order.' Which type of order someone promotes will of course depend upon his or her own interests. Politics as a theoretical study will from this point of view be primarily concerned with how far rival interests can be promoted and yet also reconciled and contained within a single order. By contrast, for those whose fundamental allegiance lies with the goods of excellence politics as a theoretical study will primarily be concerned with how a regard for justice relevantly conceived can be promoted so as to increase a shared understanding of and allegiance to the goods of the *polis* and only secondarily with conflicts of interest, especially insofar as they may be destructive of movement toward such a shared understanding and allegiance.

[. . . .]

Chapter 8
Aristotle on Practical Rationality

[. . . .]

Aristotle was [. . .] describing a form of practical rational life both different from and in conflict with that at home in the social orders characteristic of modernity. But it may be instructive to consider those contemporary social contexts in which we do still find application for something very like Aristotelian conceptions of practical rationality. A hockey player in the closing seconds of a crucial game has an opportunity to pass to another member of his or her team better placed to score a needed goal. Necessarily, we may say, if he or she has perceived and judged the situation accurately, he or she must immediately pass. What is the force of this 'necessarily' and this 'must'? It exhibits the connection between the good of that person *qua* hockey player and member of that particular team and the action of passing, a connection such that were such a player not to pass, he or she must *either* have falsely denied that passing was for their good *qua* hockey player *or* have been guilty of inconsistency *or* have acted as one not caring for his or her good *qua* hockey player and member of that particular team. That is to say, we recognize the necessity and the immediacy of rational action by someone inhabiting a structured role in a context in which the goods of some systematic form of practice are unambiguously ordered. And in so doing we apply to one part of our social life a conception which Aristotle applies to rational social life as such.

It is thus only within those systematic forms of activity within which goods are unambiguously ordered and within which individuals occupy and move between well-defined roles that the standards of rational action directed toward the good and the best can be embodied. To be a rational individual is to participate in such a form of social life and to conform, so far as is possible, to those standards. It is because and insofar as the *polis* is an arena of systematic activity of just this kind that the *polis* is the locus of rationality. And it was because Aristotle judged that no form of state but the *polis* could integrate the different systematic activities of human beings into an overall form of activity in which the achievement of each kind of good was given its due that he also judged that *only* a *polis* could provide that locus. No practical rationality outside the *polis* is the Aristotelian counterpart to *extra ecclesiam nulla salus*.

There is yet another feature of Aristotle's conception of practical rationality which is equally or even more at odds with dominant modern conceptions. On a characteristically modern view the claims upon particular individuals of some good may be inconsistent with the claims of some other good, thus creating dilemmas for which on occasion there may be no mode of rational resolution. Precisely because Aristotle's logic in practical argument is the same deductive logic employed in theoretical argument, and precisely because there can only be at any one time one right action to perform, the premises of any Aristotelian practical argument must be consistent with all other truths. It cannot be true of someone on Aristotle's view that he or she is required by the claim upon him or her of some good to do such and such and by the claim of some other equal or incommensurable good not to do such and such. The difference between Aristotle and the modern view is perhaps most clearly apparent in the different interpretations of tragedy which each engenders. From the modern standpoint the incompatibility between the demands of one good and those of another can be real, and it is in terms of the reality of such dilemmas that tragedy is to be understood. It *can* therefore be held to be true of someone that he or she should do such and such (because one good requires it) and also that he or she should refrain from doing such and such (because some other good requires such refraining). But if these both can be held to be true, the concept of truth has been transformed: this is not truth as transmitted in valid deductive arguments. It is for this very reason that from Aristotle's point of view the apparent existence of a tragic dilemma must always rest upon one or more misconceptions or misunderstandings. The apparent and tragic conflict of right with right arises from the inadequacies of reason, not from the character of moral reality.

It would then be highly paradoxical if Aristotle's own writings confronted one with just such a dilemma. Yet something very like this has been claimed by some commentators. For, so they assert, in large parts of the *Nicomachean Ethics* Aristotle presents us with a conception of the highest good, of *eudaimonia*, as embodied in the life of civic duty, more especially in the life of the good ruler who is also a good man. But in Book X he argues that the perfect good is a type of theoretical activity in which the mind contemplates the unchanging and eternal aspects of things, an activity in which the mind, in virtue of that within it which is divine, contemplates in a way that reproduces the activity of God. The political life and the life of moral virtue are *eudaimon* only in inferior and secondary ways (*Nicomachean Ethics*, 1177a12–1178b32). So here we have, according to some interpreters, two rival and conflicting views of the supreme good, both urged upon us by Aristotle.

That Aristotle understood there to be a problem about how to relate the life of political virtue to that of contemplative activity is clear. But he also makes it clear that the good life for human beings which constitutes their supreme good has a number of different types of constituent parts and that these parts each find due place within the whole (J. L. Ackrill 'Aristotle on Eudaimonia' is the best and most cogent exposition of Aristotle's view). How these parts find their place within that whole Aristotle discusses in summary fashion at the beginning of Book VII of the *Politics* in passages whose intended relevance to the discussion of contemplative, theoretical activity in Book X of the *Nicomachean Ethics* is made clear by the way in which he repeats and amplifies certain points.

We need, so Aristotle argues in the opening passages of Book VII of the *Politics*, to pursue the external goods of the body in order to engage in those activities in which the soul perfects itself. So the life of moral and political virtue exists for the sake of and must be subordinated to the life of contemplative enquiry. But the latter is impossible for the individual, let alone for any group of individuals, without the former. Hence the two modes of life must be combined in the overall life of the *polis*, which itself has to be understood, in this light, as existing for the sake of that in human beings which links them to the divine. All rational practical activity has as its ultimate final cause the vision, so far as it is open to human beings, of what God sees.

So a story which began in Homer's poems with the justice of Zeus culminates in Aristotle's philosophy in an account of justice and the other virtues as serving a life moved in its activity toward and by the Unmoved Mover. In Book Alpha of the *Metaphysics* Aristotle gives us a history of his predecessors' successive investigations into the subject matter with which he is going to be concerned, presenting the *aporiai*, the difficulties which arise from their disagreements and from the unsolved problems of their enquiries, in such a way as to enable him to present his own system of thought as a more adequate way of dealing with these *aporiai*. The claim on behalf of his own standpoint is that it transcends the limitations of his predecessors. It is a parallel history of the same kind in respect of Aristotle's political and moral thought which I have tried to construct in my earlier chapters, in an attempt to show that the embodiment of the Homeric vision of action and justice in the life of Periclean Athens confronted Athenians, and to some degree Greeks in general, with a series of practical and theoretical *aporiai* successively confronted by Pericles, by Sophocles, by Thucydides, and by Plato. On the view which I am and have been taking, Aristotle's peculiar achievement was first to provide a framework of thought within which both the achievements and the limitations of his predecessors could be identified and evaluated and, second, in so doing, to transcend those limitations.

What Aristotle therefore had to provide the means for explaining was how the partial misconceptions of a Neoptolemus and an Odysseus, as presented by Sophocles, could be corrected – and this he did by providing the standard of the *phronimos* [one who has practical wisdom]; how the actual failures of Greek states, as narrated by Thucydides, could be identified, defined, and explained as defections from a real possibility of the good and the best in the life of the *polis* – and this he did by contrasting justice and *pleonexia* [acquisitiveness]; and how Plato's account of the relationship of justice and rationality to the structure of the *polis* could be both corrected and completed. And if Aristotle's well-founded claim against his predecessors is that he has by the use of dialectical enquiry overcome their limitations, his challenge to those who will subsequently attempt to displace his philosophical theses, either by extending and correcting or by rejecting them, will have to be that they too must situate themselves within the same history of dialectical enquiry and attempt to identify and to overcome his limitations in the same way, but now by standards which are of his setting.

Aristotle's achievement then is wrongly understood if it is supposed that he offered us an account of justice and of practical reasoning which can be shown to be superior to those advanced from other rival, fundamentally different standpoints, ancient or modern, by appeal to some neutral set of standards, equally available to and equally compelling for the rational adherents of every standpoint. As I argued earlier, in laying out the grounds for disagreement and conflict which divide those whose allegiance is to the goods of excellence from those whose allegiance is to the goods of effectiveness, the disagreements between fundamental standpoints are in key part over how to characterize those disagreements. There is at this level no neutral mode of stating the problems, let alone the solutions.

Progress in rationality is achieved only from a point of view. And it is achieved when the adherents of that point of view succeed to some significant degree in elaborating ever more comprehensive and adequate statements of their positions through the dialectical procedure of advanc-

ing objections which identify incoherences, omissions, explanatory failures, and other types of flaw and limitation in earlier statements of them,
of finding the strongest arguments available for supporting those objections, and then of attempting to restate the position so that it is no longer
vulnerable to those specific objections and arguments.

In precisely this way Plato identified the limitations of Socrates' procedure of *elenchus* and consequently of the Socratic treatment of the virtues, and what he consequently achieved in the *Republic* was a restatement
of the Socratic position, enriched in respect both of the concept of *eidos*
and of the theory of dialectic. And similarly, Aristotle, agreeing with
Plato in Plato's self-criticism of the separation of the *eidos* from those
particulars which exemplify it, was able to provide an account of justice
and of practical reasoning – as also of other key philosophical issues –
which enabled him to exhibit what it was for these to be at home in the
institutionalized *polis* in a way that Plato had himself tried but failed to
achieve convincingly in the *Laws*.

[. . . .]

'Practical Rationalities as Forms of Social Structure'

What I am going to portray are three distinct types of relationship in which it is possible for reasoning to stand to action. Each of these types of relationship I shall present as embodied in the social life of some particular culture and moreover as requiring some culture of that type for its embodiment. In so proceeding I shall be at odds with the dominant contemporary philosophical approach to the study of practical reasoning in at least two important ways. Almost all contemporary writers treat different theories of practical reasoning as rival accounts of one and the same timeless and a historical subject-matter. So Aristotle, Hume and such contemporaries as Kenny or Audi are envisaged as advancing mutually exclusive characterizations of structures of reason-giving which for the most part are the same – which, so some have argued, must be the same – in every social order. Against this I shall suggest that rational action is structured very differently in different times and places and that Aristotle's theory, for example, is best understood as, in the first instance at least, a theory which has a subject-matter specific to one important mode of practical reasoning in classical Greece of the fifth and fourth centuries, while Hume's is a theory about what practical rationality consisted in for many people in eighteenth-century Britain. But it is not just that different modes of practical reasoning are specific to certain types of social context. It is also that in respect of each of these social contexts they fulfil two distinct, albeit closely related functions.

Practical reasoning guides and directs action. But to understand the structure of some particular mode of practical reasoning specific to some particular social order is not only to have learned some particular way of guiding and directing action. It is also to have learned how actions are and are not to be interpreted by others inhabiting that same social order. And that is to say, the norms of practical reasoning in any particular social order are among the norms in terms of which the presentation of each of us by him or herself in action is construed by others, so that those others may know how to respond to our actions and to engage in transactions with us. Every mode of practical reasoning is also a mode of social interpretation. For an individual either to be or to appear rational is then for that individual to participate in the norm-governed transactions and relationships of a particular institutionalized social order. Hence 'rational' is not a predicate to be applied to individuals *qua* individuals, but only to individuals *qua* participants in particular social orders embodying particular conceptions of rationality. It is only because and in so far as social orders embody conceptions of what it is to be rational, that individuals are able to evaluate themselves and others as more or less rational.

In this respect social orders resemble such practices as those of farming or mathematics: to be more or less rational *qua* farmer or mathematician is to participate in the norm-governed activities and relationships of farming or mathematics and to be in greater or lesser degree moved by what at that time and place constitute good reasons, acknowledged or to be acknowledged, within the community of farmers or that of mathematicians. And to learn to be rational is to be initiated into and trained in the habits of action and judgement which dispose one to be so moved. So also to be rational as a member of a particular social order is to participate in some particular community in the relevant ways and to be moved by the acknowledged or to be acknowledged good reasons of that particular social order.

Consider first a form of social life in which a variety of practices, of systematic forms of activity, are cultivated and the goods internal to these practices valued and pursued. The relevant types of practice include farming, war, poetry, drama, the pursuit of gymnastics and athletic excellence, architecture, sculpture and painting, mathematics, and theology. Within each of these practices the training of young apprentices is essential to its transmission and to its future growth and flourishing. Such apprentices learn to make two kinds of distinction: between what merely seems good to them and what really is good (a good way to plough a field, for example, or to write an elegy); and between what is good or best for them in their present circumstances and what is good unqualifiedly. They learn to make these distinctions in the course of acquiring habits of action and of judgement which discipline and redirect the initial untrained desires and responses which they brought with them to their apprenticeship. It is in so far as their desires are thus reworked that in the realm of the practice at least they are moved only by those reasons for action which direct them to the goods of the practice. Hence the question of whether or not something is a good reason for action is and comes to be understood as independent of the will or preferences of any particular individual.

When such individuals are set or set themselves some particular task, the reasoning which leads them to act in one way rather than another will fall into two stages. In the first of these they will assess in the light of the best standards of achievement in their particular area of their particular practice what has to be done to move towards or to achieve these standards; they will, that is to say, deliberate what means to adopt in the light of some overall end and the outcome of successful deliberation will be the identification and characterization of some means to that overall end as their proximate end or good. That proximate good will provide them with two kinds of reason for immediate action, one expressing what is good about that good, the other what makes it proximate.

So the individual will argue from an initial premise of the form: Such-and-such a type of action is good, or productive of good, for someone practising this particular craft at this particular level in such-and-such circumstances; and from a secondary premise of the form: Here and now are circumstances of just such a type. The conclusion will be an action falling under the action-description furnished by the major premise. Notice three features of this type of reasoning.

The first is the specificity required of the action-description in the major premise; it has to furnish adequately precise instructions for action. This specificity is the outcome of the deliberative enquiry which preceded and led to the formulation of the premises. It is not necessarily the case that on each occasion on which such a particular initial premise is employed, it is immediately preceded by deliberation; all that is required for rationality is that at some preceding time the relevant deliberation occurred.

Secondly, the conclusion of the reasoning is an action and not the utterance of a decision, or an expression of intention. Indeed such an utterance or expression would be an interruption of the process of practical reasoning. An individual who had reasoned his or her way through the premises to the point of action, but who was distracted by an impulse to do other than what reason dictated, might of course respond to that impulse by affirming a decision to resist the impulse and follow reason; but while the affirmation of such a decision would have a function in relation to the conflict of irrational desire – irrational, that is, in the context of the practice – with reason, it would be functionless as part of the practical reasoning.

It follows of course that, if the conclusion of the reasoning is an action, then that action must be understood as expressive of a statement, a statement of the form, 'This is what is to be done.' And indeed it is precisely because actions can be so construed that we are able to identify inconsistency and consistency relationships between actions and the premises of the reasoning agent.

Thirdly, if an individual *qua* participant in some particular practice has identified, understood and asserted the relevant set of premises which jointly entail the action which any participant in that particular practice who is instructed in the practice to the degree that that particular individual is would have to recognize as rationally required, but yet none the less fails to perform the action in question, then the only explanations left open are *either* that it was not in that individual's power to perform that particular action *or* that that individual had a motive for the moment at least to act otherwise than as a participant in the practice. Necessarily, that is to say, it is true of the individual, *qua* participant in the practice, that if the premises of his or her practical reasoning are asserted as true, the conclusion which is the action follows.

What I have been trying to delineate so far is the pattern of practical rationality *within* discrete practices. What place rational argument has within practices varies from practice to practice; of the practices which I initially listed its place is perhaps largest within the practices of mathematics and theology and smallest within the practice of poetry. But what makes practical rationality possible within each practice, no matter how large or small its place, is the way in which the practice is directed towards the achievement of certain goods, specific to and internal to each particular practice, which provide both activity and enquiry within each practice with their *telos*. It is of course the understanding of this *telos* which provides the practical syllogisms of this kind of rational practice with their ultimate initial premises, premises of the form, 'The good and the best within this practice is such-and-such'. Such premises partially define the constructive tasks of deliberation by providing a terminus for the chain of deductive reasoning which is the product of successful deliberative activity.

It may seem to follow that in those areas of human life which lie outside the sphere of any particular practice, there can be no place for this kind of practical rationality or for these structures of practical reasoning. For outside the sphere of each particular practice it would seem that there would be available no *telos* which could furnish that initial premise so essential for both deliberative and deductive practical reasoning. Suppose however that there were a culture with the following conception of political community: political community exists for the sake of the creation and sustaining of that form of communal life into which the goods of each particular practice may be integrated so that both each individual and the community as a whole may lead a life informed by these goods. This task of integration will have regard to the different ages at which different goods are appropriated: the goods of athletic exercise and of military service, for example, belong to the young, while the contemplation of the divine is achievable only at the culmination of life. It will also have regard to the different opportunities for the achievement of goods offered by different statuses and occupations. This integrative activity of the political community thus has as its aims and end the achievement of a form of life which is the highest good, and that form of life provides a *telos* above and beyond those internal to the practices integrated into that form of life. This *telos* is the *telos* of the practice of making and sustaining this type of political community by participating in it as a citizen; let us call this practice *politics* and let us call such a form of political community a *polis*.

The *polis* will then provide an arena within which practical reasoning can take the same form as it does within other communities of practice. Just as the individual who reasoned within those other practices in the light of the *telos* of each of them reasoned *qua* farmer or *qua* sculptor, and not just as an individual, so reasoning within the *polis* will be conducted by the individual *qua* citizen. Since the *polis* is the form of community concerned with *all* human goods, this does not place the same restriction upon the subject-matter of reasoning of the individual *qua* citizen as would be placed upon it if we were conceiving of the role of citizen in modern terms rather than in those of classical Greece. But at once the question will be raised: did what I have been describing really characterize the life of the fifth- and fourth-century *polis*? For what I have been doing of course is to take the form of practical reasoning described by Aristotle and interpret it as presupposing by its form the structure of what I have called practices as the background required for it to have application; and what Aristotle himself was doing was to offer an interpretation of the practical rationality – and thereby also of course of the practical irrationality – of educated Greeks of his own and the immediately preceding age. So that what I am advancing is an interpretation of an interpretation.

What is clearly true is at least this: that Athenians from Pericles onwards were accustomed to understanding their *polis* as incarnating the good and the best, so far as that had ever been realized, and that the Spartans too understood their way of life as the best for them in their circumstances. Each city is understood both by its own citizens and by others as providing a milieu for the exercise of those virtues which its citizens take to be a means to – either, that is, causally productive of or partially constitutive of – the range of goods which furnish them with a way of life as a *telos*. So Aristotle is able to compare a variety of actual types of constitution of a *polis* with his conception of the best kind of *polis* in a way that warrants the conclusion that cities can be rank-ordered in respect of the degree and kind of goods which are made available to their citizens in a form that provides their lives with point and purpose and their practical arguments with an ultimate initial premise.

What I am claiming then is that the type of practical reasoning of which Aristotle offers us a schematization requires as its context a particular type of social structure embodying a particular, usually implicit, understanding of the forms of human activity and the nature of human excellence. Consider now by contrast a very different type of social order: one in which actions and transactions are understood as both produced by and conducing to either the satisfaction of or the frustration of desires and aversions, passions. The fundamental classification of individuals in such a society will be in terms not of what they do, but of what they consume or enjoy. The fundamental relationships will be defined in terms of who provides what for whom and of who threatens the satisfaction of others by the pursuit of their own satisfaction.

'Magnates', Roy Porter has written about eighteenth-century England, 'were on the horns of a self-created dilemma. Greed urged them to maximize agrarian profit, pride to bask in undisturbed private grandeur –

both alienating the community. The richer they got, the more they cultivated tastes – Palladianism, French fashions, fine manners and connois-
seurship of the arts – which elevated them above their natural right-hand
men, homespun squires and freeholders. . . . And yet popularity was the
kiss of life. Lacking private armies, in the end they had to rule by bluster
and swank. Authority could be upheld only by consent, through tricky
reciprocal negotiations of will and interests, give and take. . . . The fraternizing game, however nauseating, however phoney, had to be played. . . .
So, to cope with self-created rural polarization . . . grandees stage-
managed a more studied theatre of power: conspicuous menace (and
mercy) from the Judge's Bench; exemplary punishment tempered with
silver linings of philanthropy, largesse and selective patronage; a grudg-
ing and calculating display of *noblesse oblige*' (*English Society in the Eighteenth Century*, pp. 79–81).

The key to this type of social order lies in the reciprocal character of
the passions from which behaviour issues. If I am to be accorded so far as
possible what pleases me and to avoid or be protected so far as possible
from what pains me, it can only be in so far as it pleases others that I
should be pleased and it pains those same others that I should be pained,
and this in turn can only be the case if it pleases me that those others
should be pleased and not pained. Let us call that state of mind in which
we experience 'a certain satisfaction in ourselves, on account of some
accomplishment or possession which we enjoy' (Hume, 'A Dissertation
on the Passions', p. 144) *pride* and let us call the corresponding dissatisfaction *humility*. Pride, thus understood, will only be a socially acceptable
passion if to 'the agreeable impression which arises in the mind, when the
view either of our virtue, beauty, riches or power makes us satisfied with
ourselves (Hume, *A Treatise of Human Nature*, III.i.7) there answers in
others a corresponding agreeable impression. What evokes pride in us
must be such as to evoke esteem or even love in others; what causes
humility in us must be an object of dislike or hatred in others. So in such
a society it will be the case that 'Nothing flatters our vanity more than
the talent of pleasing by our wit, good-humour or any other accomplishment; and nothing gives us a more sensible mortification, than a disap-
pointment in any attempt of that kind' ('A Dissertation on the Passions',
p. 167).

What will practical reasoning be in such a social order? Reasoning will
by and of itself provide no cause for action. It is only if and when a piece
of reasoning informs us how some object of desire is to be achieved or
some object of aversion avoided that reason will become practically relevant. The pursuit of rational enquiry will for example be intelligible only
as the product of an antecedent passion of curiosity and only if the
tracking down of the objects of curiosity can be understood to give to
some persons much the same kind of pleasure as the tracking down of the
objects of the hunt affords to its devotees.

Reasoning becomes practical then whenever it intervenes between a passion and the specification of how and in what way and in what form that passion's object is to be achieved. The objects of passions are both highly particular – for example, to eat this pear – and highly general – for example, to uphold the whole system of justice and, thereby, the stability of property. So passions have internal to them a variety of intentional objects of wanting and aversion, expressible by phrases of the form 'that it should be the case that such-and-such'. And the relevant piece of practical reasoning is then of the form: 'Doing A will make it the case that such-and-such.' Such reasoning may of course be and often is extended so that it runs: 'Doing A will first make it the case that so-and-so and doing B will then secondly make it the case that so-and-so else and only then by doing C will it be brought about that such-and-such.' Here reasoning has set before the particular passion a series of actions as a sequence of means to the attainment of its satisfaction rather than a single action. But no matter how extended the reasoning, it must terminate with a statement about how the state of affairs specified by the characterization of the intentional object of the particular passion is to be brought about. The subsequent action itself is no part of the reasoning, nor indeed produced by it. And just as the action is not and cannot be the conclusion of the reasoning, so the passion is not and does not provide the reasoning with its initial premise. In Humean reasoning just as much as in Aristotelian there is no place for a premise of the form: 'I want such-and-such.' Why not?

In the Aristotelian case it was of course because 'I want . . .' or 'it pleases me' can never by itself be a good reason for action. Each of us initially, before we are introduced to the discipline of the education which practices require, takes pleasure and pain in an undiscriminating way in certain objects, states and experiences. What the training of the habits of action and judgement produces is a disciplining, ordering and transformation of the desires, so that the person excellent in this or that practice takes pleasure or pain in a quite different range of objects, states and experiences from what that same person did initially. And so also with the person who is excellent as such. So practical reasoning will only have force and authority for the person whose desires and habits of action and judgement have been adequately educated so that the agent desires to be and only is moved by good reasons, that is reasons directing that agent towards a genuine good. And the soundness of any piece of Aristotelian practical reasoning must always be distinguished from the force and authority which it has for a particular agent. And indeed it is this distinction that allows us to frame the problem of *akrasia*.

Within Humean practical reasoning, by contrast, a piece of reasoning counts as practical only if and in so far as it is the servant of some passion. And although that passion may be expressed by the agent's saying, 'I want such-and-such', that utterance cannot supply a premise for a practical argument for two distinct reasons. First, the 'I want . . .' of such an utterance is not a statement; its function is expressive, in modern terms emotive, not fact-stating. And secondly, it is not the utterance, the expression of the passion, but only the passion itself which moves the agent to action.

When we respond to the actions of others, our interest must always lie therefore in responding to the passions which produced that action. We 'fix our attention on actions, as on external signs. But these actions are still considered as signs; and the ultimate object of our praise and approbation is the motive, that produc'd them' (*A Treatise of Human Nature*, III.ii.1). A socially shared understanding of and set of beliefs about the passions that produce actions, explicit or implicit, is therefore a necessary condition for the existence of a socially shared vocabulary of evaluation, approbation and disapprobation. To be educated into the use of that vocabulary will be to be educated into habits of causal inference, habits the successful exercise of which require a recognition of the place of reasoning as only providing an identification of means to the satisfaction of the given passion. And thus evaluation and approbation take as their subject-matter one quite other than that which is specified for evaluation by someone educated into Aristotelian practical reasoning. In Aristotelian evaluation what we evaluate are actions as exhibiting a capacity for practical judgement, that is, actions as the conclusions of pieces of sound or unsound practical reasoning. To understand an action as produced by a passion, either immediately or through some piece of reasoning about what means will causally produce what ends, is from an Aristotelian standpoint precisely to understand it as nonrational, as exhibiting not an educated capacity for action or judgement, but either the untutored preferences of the young or else incontinence.

So the different types of evaluation and interpretation advanced from an Aristotelian or a Humean standpoint presuppose not only different functions of reasoning in the production of action, but also different ways of understanding oneself and others embodied in quite different forms of social relationship. The person whose norms of practical reasoning in respect of action-guiding and in respect of interpretation are Aristotelian is committed to viewing others either as participating collaborators in the same or a similar practice-based political community or as outsiders, barbarians. The person whose norms of practical reasoning both in respect of action-guiding and in respect of interpretation are Humean is committed to viewing others either as participating in the reciprocal exchanges of love and pride, the 'tricky reciprocal negotiations of will and interests . . . the fraternizing game . . .', as Porter describes it, or instead as persons of deviant and eccentric passions seduced by their enthusiasm into allegiance to false theories, such persons as the seventeenth-century Levellers had been or as the adherents of the abominated monkish virtues were or perhaps as followers of Pascal or of Diogenes the Cynic. It is within social relationships defined so that such outsiders or deviants are excluded from them that each theory has to be institutionalized if its norms are to be effectively interpretive as well as action-guiding.

It is important to note finally about Hume that in some ways we are more liable mistakenly to assimilate his central conceptions and beliefs to our own than we are in the case of Aristotle, most of all perhaps in supposing that when Hume offers us an account of a passion, he must be offering us an account of what we would mean by an emotion. Hence some modern critics of Hume have argued that Hume's account of the passions is simply mistaken, for passions, so they contend, embody or presuppose judgements, while on Hume's account passions are original existences, conjoined in contingent regularity on occasion to judgements, but themselves prior to and antecedent to all judgement. Passions are, on Hume's view, that is, prelinguistic or preconceptual and this is what enables Hume to speak of 'the correspondence of *passions* in men and animals' ('A Dissertation on the Passions', p. 326).

What we, and contemporary critics of this kind, call an emotion, by contrast, is a patterned regularity of dispositional and occurrent feeling, judgement and action. We do so because we have reconceptualized the relations of feelings to actions in the two and a half centuries between Hume and ourselves and the achievement of this reconceptualization was in part a condition, and in part the result, of the work of the great novelists who moved us from the Humean world of the sentiments – sentiments are simple conjunctions of judgement and passion, whether calm or violent – inhabited by the characters of Sterne, Fielding and Henry Mackenzie, through the patterned integration of feeling, judgement and action achieved by the great nineteenth-century novelists, into that even more complex world of emotion about emotion which by making the elements of those patterns into intentional objects disintegrates patterned emotion into moments of consciousness in one way in the work of Joyce, in another in that of Virginia Woolf. And with this change in conceptualization the idiom of the passions, understood as Hume understood them, ceases to be available for the purposes of the reciprocal understanding of and negotiation between different partners in what Porter calls the fraternizing game. Our emotions are not Hume's passions; we and Hume inhabit a different world of feeling, and consequently also of reasoning, just as we and Aristotle inhabit different worlds of reasoning and consequently also of rational and irrational desire.

What I am claiming then is that individuals are able to live lives which embody Aristotelian or Humean practical rationality, so that their actions and projects may be evaluated accordingly by others and by themselves, only in so far as those lives also are at the point of intersection of social relationships of highly specific types, the one type paradigmatically at home in the *polis* of the fifth and fourth centuries, the other in eighteenth-century Britain. This claim is of course one which would have presented no problem to Aristotle himself; for he took the *polis* to be the only locus of human rationality (*Politics*, 1253a30–35). But with Hume it is quite otherwise, although I note this only to put it, for the moment at least, on one side.

Instead I turn to consider a third type of practical rationality, one with its own contemporary philosophical exponents. Since it is in key part through the expositions by Aristotle and by Hume of the theoretical background to their accounts of the place that reasoning has in the production of action that we are able to identify the social contexts presupposed by those accounts, it might seem that philosophical accounts of practical reasoning which supply no such account will have freed themselves from any entanglement with any specific social context. And contemporary accounts of practical reasoning do characteristically present the agent only from the moment at which he or she moves toward the kind of practical judgement which precedes action by asserting, for example, 'I want to attain such and such an end' (Von Wright), or simply 'I want' (Churchland), or laying it down as a directive, 'Let it be the case that . . .' (Goldman), without this wanting or self-direction being itself presented as the outcome of some essential precedent process or set of occurrences, whether Aristotelian deliberation or Humean passion. We are presented, that is to say, with agents as if detached altogether from any conception of or perception of the good or goods. They are to be understood as practically rational or as failing in practical rationality only in respect of the way in which they argue so as to get their preferences implemented, whatever the grounds for those preferences may be. But of course this is just how persons are in fact presented and how their practical rationality is in fact understood in the public arenas of modern liberal individualist societies, such as our own. Here each person is entitled to express his or her preferences and the institutions which govern and determine public discourse and decision-making are committed to taking no account of how these preferences are arrived at. Public discourse and decision-making exclude any background to preference-formation. All preferences of all individuals are to be weighed in the same balance and accorded the same respect, no matter whose they are or what their grounding.

In saying this it may well seem that I am contradicting an assertion which I made at the outset. For I there asserted that it is not individuals as such who are practically rational in varying degrees, but always individuals *qua* holders of certain social roles specific to certain types of social order. And consistently with this I have since claimed that it is the individual *qua* citizen of a *polis* who is the bearer of Aristotelian rationality and the individual *qua* participant in a quite different type of social order who is the bearer of Humean rationality. But now I am apparently allowing that it is individuals, no matter who they are, who are the bearers of practical reasoning as it is characterized both in contemporary philosophy and in the dominant modes of contemporary society. But there is in fact no inconsistency. For 'the individual' in modern society is the name of a status and a role. 'The individual' is the name of a piece of social fabrication, of a social role created in the sixteenth and seventeenth centuries in order to abstract human beings from certain aspects of their beliefs and circumstances. So it is not human individuals as such, bearing with them the complexities of belief and circumstance, including their allegiance to some theory of the good and their membership in social groups espousing such a theory, who are the agents who appear in modern practical reasoning. It is individuals *qua* individuals of whom I am speaking, individuals viewed by themselves and by others as inhabiting the role of 'the individual'.

The individual *qua* individual reasons from his or her preferences and about this reasoning two facts must be noted. First it has now become possible to use the utterance of 'I want such-and-such' as the assertion of a premise in a practical argument, that is, as the statement of a reason for action and not merely as the expression of a motive for action. What had to happen for this to take place? Wittgenstein drew our attention to the fact that certain types of first-person sentence function in utterances primarily as expressive; so 'I am in pain' functions primarily as a replacement for a groan or perhaps a scream. By contrast the third-person sentence 'He or she is in pain' is a sentence primarily used to make true or false statements. What we need to notice is that we may come to speak about ourselves from an impersonal standpoint using first-person sentences just as we do third-person. So 'I am in pain' can come to be used to make a true or false statement in just the same way as 'He or she is in pain' does, and in so far as it is so used and understood it can no longer function expressively. And so also with 'I want . . .' which instead of expressing a passion and so revealing a motivating cause of action, as it does in a Humean perspective, may come to be used instead to make statements which can function as premises in practical arguments. 'I want . . .' has come to possess the impersonality necessary for a good reason.

When 'I want such-and-such' so functions, it has of course to be conjoined with some premise or premises about how such-and-such is to be attained by action. And the contingent facts stated in these latter premise or premises may be such as to nullify the outcome of what began as a practical argument. For having asserted 'I want such-and-such' in the initial premise of such an argument and then having gone on to assert as a secondary premise that doing so-and-so either is necessary to bring about such-and-such or at least is one way to bring it about, it may turn out that this particular course of action will frustrate some other want felt by the agent. So that we shall need to add as a premise, if the argument is to be genuinely practical, 'And doing so-and-so will not frustrate any other of my relevant preferences'. Hence the following form for the premises of practical reasoning emerges: I want such-and-such; doing so-and-so will enable me to achieve such-and-such; and doing so-and-so will not frustrate any equal or stronger preference. But from a set of premises of this type, what kind of conclusion is to be drawn? Not, it turns out, an action, but a practical judgement of the form 'So I should do so-and-so', a practical judgement which leaves the decision whether or not to satisfy this particular practical judgement in action still to be taken.

Consider the contrast in this respect between Aristotelian and modern practical reasoning. Someone who affirms the premises of an Aristotelian practical syllogism within the context of a practice, knowing what he or she is doing, and who then fails to perform the action which should have been the conclusion of that syllogism, and not because it is not in that person's power to perform it, necessarily lapses into the unintelligibility of blank inconsistency. But someone who affirms the premises of the type of modern practical reasoning which I have delineated and who then fails to act upon the practical judgement which is its conclusion is not therefore to be construed as opaquely unintelligible in the light of his or her preceding reasoning. So Robert Audi has argued in respect of such examples that the reasoning which terminates in a practical judgement is thereby complete, not only whether or not the reasoner acts, but also whether or not the reasoner even decides to act. For not only may the reasoner be weak-willed with respect to the performance of that particular possible action, but it can also be the case that 'as he thinks about how he can do it, he changes his mind' ('A Theory of Practical Reasoning', p. 29). The range of possible intervening considerations which may interpose themselves between practical judgement and action or even between practical judgement and decision is at once too large and too indeterminate for there to be even an appearance of unintelligibility when practical reasoning produces no further outcome.

In what then does rationality on the contemporary view consist? First of all, in the ordering of his or her preferences by each individual, so that the preferences may be ordinally ranked in their presentation in the public realm, and secondly in the maximization of the satisfaction of those preferences in accordance with that ordering. It is the first of these aspects of contemporary rationality that makes the question of how preferences are to be summed, either by individuals or socially, so crucial, and Arrow's theorem and its heirs so relevant in the area of theory. It is the second that makes both the central preoccupations of utilitarianism and its distinctive idiom so ineliminable from contemporary public discourse as well as from moral and political philosophy.

The practical rationality of contemporary liberal, individualist modernity is thus distinctively different from that of either the Humean eighteenth century or the Aristotelian *polis*. It takes its place in a history of rationalities in which it turns out to be as much embedded in a highly specific social context as any other. That history of course still has to be written on a scale and in a way which will provide a genuinely adequate understanding not only of each of these and other episodes, but also of the stages of transformation through which one mode of practical rationality displaces another. But that fuller history does not have to be written for it to be clear that the project necessarily invites two immediate questions.

The first is this: if it is indeed the case that each of these forms of practical rationality has its own conceptual and logical structure, each presupposing one particular type of social relationships and requiring the existence of such social relationships for its embodiment, relationships paradigmatically exemplified in two of the three cases discussed in this article in cultures from a past that is now largely alien to most of us, does it not follow that the study of practical rationalities out of that past can only be of antiquarian interest? How can what belongs to an alien and vanished form of life be in any way practically relevant to us here now? The answer is: it is of course only if and in so far as the relevant type of social relationships are or can be reconstituted that one of these past forms of practical rationality can be re-embodied in some later social world such as our own. The task of living out a life guided by the canons of one of these forms and employing them as canons of interpretation must be, so it emerges from the argument, inseparable from the task of making and sustaining the relevant form of human community. Where a life cannot be structured by integrated practices, the Aristotelian mode of practical rationality must cease to have application; where a life cannot be structured in terms of passion-grounded reciprocities, the Humean mode must become irrelevant. But now it is important to notice that the features of the fifth- and fourth-century *polis* which provided Greeks with the necessary setting for those exercises of rationality which Aristotle was to describe and the features of eighteenth-century Britain which provided Englishmen with the necessary setting for those reciprocal exchanges which Hume was to characterize are in varying degrees recurrent features of social orders, reappearing in widely different cultural modes and suffering dissolution over and over again in the course of widely different occasions of social change. Both Aristotelian hierarchially ordered and integrated practices and Humean systems providing for mutuality in the expression of passions can be and have been socially realized in a number of different historical forms. And the relationship of these institutionalizations of rationality to each other adds a dimension to the conception of practical rationality embodied in each.

Consider some particular embodiment of Aristotelian rationality in social form. It will be characteristic of its politics – and the more Aristotelian it is, the more characteristic it will be – that its political activity will itself be also a form of enquiry, so that established views of what constitutes the good and the best, either unqualifiedly or for the citizens of *that polis* in *their* circumstances, either generally or in this or that particular respect, will from time to time be put in question, perhaps because new relevant theoretical considerations have come to light or perhaps because of changing internal or external circumstances. So the citizens of an Aristotelian *polis* engaged in such enquiry may identify what are from their own Aristotelian point of view a variety of hitherto unsolved problems or unresolved incoherences. They may or may not then be able to reformulate their beliefs about the good and the best and correspondingly to reorder their institutionalized modes of practice, so that some at least of such problems are solved or some of such incoherences resolved. In so far as they can do so, they will have more adequately embodied in their social order the standards of practical rationality, understood as they understand them.

So different stages in the social embodiment of Aristotelian practical rationality in some particular society may be evaluated as themselves more or less rational, and so in similar fashion different embodiments of Aristotelian practical rationality in a variety of cultures and societies may also be so evaluated. Hence as a history unfolds in which at later stages the examples of earlier embodiments provide a starting-point for more or less socially organized reflection and inquiry into how to live together rationally, it becomes possible to speak of an Aristotelian social tradition. Notice not only that later embodiments of that tradition need not immediately succeed earlier ones – may indeed be remote from them in time and place – but also that Aristotelian modes of rational practice may be socially embodied in times and places where Aristotle himself receives no acknowledgement. So it is not only in such societies as the Athens of Demetrius of Phaleron or in various Dominican forms of community that we can identify better or worse, more or less rational versions of Aristotelian practical rationality. It is also to be discerned in societies as various as those governed by the Rule of St Benedict and that established by the Eighth Route Army in Yenan.

And just as there is in this way an Aristotelian tradition, so from a Humean standpoint social orders may be evaluated as embodying to greater or lesser degree the kind of negotiated reciprocity which leads to the satisfaction rather than the frustration of the passions. We cannot from such a standpoint, unless we do what Hume would term speaking with the vulgar, speak of social orders as such as more or less reasonable. But we can evaluate them in terms of the reasonableness of the means of social organization, of the institutionalization of the artificial virtues, through which the ends of the passions are accomplished. And we may read Hume's *History of England* as disclosing the increasing extent to which the embodiment of Humean attitudes had taken place in sixteenth-, seventeenth- and eighteenth-century England. So there may be not only a Humean tradition of theoretical and practical inquiry, as there certainly is, but also a tradition of Humean social practice, with its own standards of evaluation internal to it.

Such traditions are thus socially embodied theories. The ways in which transactions are structured in the social orders which are their bearers both presuppose and give expression to claims to truth and rationality. In so characterizing them I invert a thesis advanced by some protagonists of the sociology of knowledge. They assert that we ought to regard ostensibly rational claims as expressions of and determined by antecedently definable social structures and interests. I by contrast am arguing that theoretical standpoints may be presented, argued for, may provide a framework for debate internal to them and the like, not only in the form of the book, the article and the lecture, or dramatically in the dialogue or the play, but in the form of those social dramas which are at one and the same time historical segments of the life of a community and enacted theories. It was an Hegelian mistake to envisage history as the self-realization of the Idea; it was an Hegelian insight to understand history as partially the realization of a series of ideas. But Hegel's mistake protected him from answering a second question which is inescapably posed by this account of the enterprise of understanding practical rationality in terms of socially embodied practical rationalities. Are we not compelled by the nature of this enterprise, let alone by its conclusions, to draw some kind of relativist and perspectival conclusion? For it seems to be a consequence of the argument so far, that we are confronted not only with three different, but with three rival, albeit historically situated modes of rationality. And indeed further inquiry would surely yield other such modes and not only from the history of Western culture, but also from such cultures as those of China and India. Since each mode has its own canons of rationality internal to it, and since none of these modes can claim to exemplify anything that we might be able to conceive of as *practical rationality* as such, that is as providing us with a set of timeless, ahistorical, transcultural norms, or at least of norms which can for most purposes be treated as such, analogously to the way in which we treat the laws of logic, then it seems that it must be the case that there can be no neutral impersonal set of standards by means of which we can judge one mode of practical rationality rationally superior to alternative modes. And this in turn seems to imply that we can adopt, in evaluating actions and transactions as practically rational, any one out of a range of possible perspectives. We can, so it appears, at least in certain circumstances evaluate from an Aristotelian standpoint or a Humean one or that of liberal individualist modernity. But in so doing we can have no grounds for judging one perspective superior to another.

This argument however is in error in two ways. First, it is a crucial and integral aspect of each of these standpoints that it involves a claim to rational hegemony. The adoption of any version of relativism or perspectivism is incompatible with the claims advanced by Aristotle or by Hume or by the protagonists of liberal individualism and indeed with the corresponding claims implicit in the institutionalized forms of the Athenian *polis*, or of eighteenth-century Britain or of contemporary modernity. All cultures are ethnocentric and these no less than any other. The adherent of a perspectivist relativism, who for a moment seemed to be free to inhabit all and any of these standpoints, is in fact excluded from them all.

Secondly, the very same good reasons that there are for historicizing enquiry into practical rationality, for insisting that the concepts and forms of reasoning which are the object of philosophical enquiry are always *somebody's* concepts and form of reasoning, located in some particular social and cultural milieu, and that a failure to characterize them in terms of their historical, social and cultural specificity will always be liable to engender error and illusion, and for also insisting that philosophical theses and theories too have to be historically and socially understood as articulating not, for example, science as such, but *this* science, not morality as such but *this* morality, and so on, these same good reasons are also good reasons for understanding relativism and perspectivism historically, as arising from and giving expression to the standpoint of a particular type of social and cultural situation.

What then is the specific historical and social situation out of which this kind of relativist and perspectivist speaks? It has to be one in which the individual has been able to or has been compelled to free him or herself from any fixed identity which would impose a standpoint; this individual is not and cannot be the individual *qua* citizen of a *polis* or of any of the institutionalized forms of social life that are the heirs of the *polis*, or the individual *qua* participant in a Humean social order, or even the individual *qua* individual of the realm of public discourse of liberal modernity. It can only be an individual whose distinctive identity consists in key part in the ability to escape social identification, by always being able to abstract him or herself from any role whatsoever; it is the individual who is potentially many things, but actually in and for him or herself nothing. And this may well be someone whom it is very difficult to be outside the arenas of philosophical and literary discussion, but in so far as it is possible to be such an individual, he or she will exemplify what I will borrow a phrase from the late A. A. Zhdanov to describe: rootless cosmopolitanism. Such individuals speak, that is to say, from a standpoint dictated by a stage in the dissolution of social traditions at which no form of practical rationality is any longer possible. They appeared in an earlier incarnation in Durkheim's sociology as the marginalized victims of anomie; but in the century since then they have become philosophers.

What does follow from the argument of this paper is not then relativism or perspectivism. But if its argument is sound, it does indeed follow that each of us can only engage in practical rationality itself and in enquiry into practical rationality from some one particular point of view developed within the kind of tradition which has been able to embody itself to the necessary degree in the kind of social relationships, in the forms of community which are necessary for its exemplification. If, as I do, one speaks and writes from within one particular type of Aristotelian tradition, then the characterization of Humean and liberal individualist standpoints is a task which has to be undertaken from the point of view of that tradition, and the type of characterizations which I have provided in this article turn out to be no more than a starting-point for enquiry, for debate and for conflict. This article therefore ends at the very point at which substantive enquiry has to begin.

'Plain Persons and Moral Philosophy: Rules, Virtues and Goods'

What is the relationship between the moral philosopher's judgments about the life of practice and the everyday plain person's moral questions and judgments? Moral philosophers are of course themselves in most of their lives everyday plain persons, but on some views what they do and judge *qua* moral philosopher is very different from what they do and judge *qua* plain person. Some analytic philosophers, for example, have envisaged the relationship between moral philosophy and everyday moral judgments and activity as analogous to that between the philosophy of science and the judgments and activity of the natural scientist or that between the philosophy of law and legal practice. In each such case the philosophy is to be understood as detached second-order commentary upon first-order judgments and activity. But for moral philosophers at work in the Aristotelian Thomistic tradition this is not at all how that relationship is to be conceived.

For, on an Aristotelian view, the questions posed by the moral philosopher and the questions posed by the plain person are to an important degree inseparable. And it is with questions that each begins, for each is engaged in enquiry, the plain person often unsystematically asking: 'What is my good?' and 'What actions will achieve it?' and the moral philosopher systematically enquiring 'What is *the* good for human beings?' and 'What kinds of actions will achieve the good?' Any persistent attempt to answer either of these sets of questions soon leads to asking the other. The moral philosopher has to recognize that any true account of the human good is incomplete and inadequate, unless and until it enables us to understand how particular plain persons, including her or himself, are able to move towards their particular goods. And if I, as a plain person, ask persistently what good it is that is at stake for me here and now in particular situations, I will soon have to ask the further, already philosophical question. 'What in general is the good, for my kind of person with my kind of history in this kind of situation?' and that in turn will lead to a fundamental philosophical question 'What is the good as such for human beings as such?'

A plain person who begins to understand her or his life as an uneven progress towards the achievement of her or his good is thus to some significant extent transformed into a moral philosopher, asking and answering the same questions posed by Aristotle in the *Nicomachean Ethics* and by Aquinas in his commentary on the *Ethics* and elsewhere. Often enough, such a plain person will not recognize how far she or he has been transformed in this direction, but insofar as a plain person fails to recognize her or himself as a moral philosopher, to that extent that plain person is the more likely to be less competent as a moral philosopher than she or he needs to be and is able to be. So the question to which this lecture is addressed is: just how much of a moral philosopher does the plain person need to become?

At once it may be objected that I already seem to be assuming by my references to Aristotle and Aquinas that, insofar as the plain person becomes a moral philosopher, she or he will at least tend towards becoming an Aristotelian. And this may seem to be question-begging. For I am, it may be said, high-handedly usurping the role of the plain person and putting my philosophical words, or rather Aristotle's and Aquinas's philosophical words, into her or his prephilosophical mouth. But surely the plain person must be allowed to speak for her or himself and to become whatever kind of philosopher she or he chooses to be. Yet this at first sight plausible objection is in fact misleading.

Consider the image of the plain person which this objection presents: that of someone who initially is a stranger to all moral philosophies and therefore wholly unequipped with the resources provided by any particular philosophical standpoint. Such a plain person therefore begins from a position of philosophical neutrality, taking her or his first steps in the direction of this or that philosophical standpoint without the guidance of any reasons which presuppose some philosophical commitment. But this is to leave the plain person bereft of philosophically relevant reasoning. The counterpart of the neutrality of the plain person thus conceived is therefore a rationally unguided arbitrariness in that person's initial choice of which philosophical direction to take. And at this point we experience a shock of recognition. For we have met this particular plain person before, not in the street or on the farm, but in the pages of a number of philosophers since Kierkegaard, especially those of the Sartre of the late 1940s. This is a human being constructed by existentialist philosophical theory, disguised as a plain person; this image of the plain person is itself a philosophical artefact.

When I say this, I do not mean to deny that there are and have been real human beings in the condition represented by this image, human beings, that is, lacking the resources to make fundamental choices in any but a criterionless way. But the question is whether this type of human being is not her or himself a social artefact, someone who has undergone a process of social and moral deprivation, not a plain person as such, but someone who somehow or other has been stripped of the ability to understand her or himself aright. So this attempt to replace my apparently question-begging image of the plain person as someone who is from the very beginning on the verge of becoming a Thomistic Aristotelian by a philosophically untainted image of the plain person has failed. And it could not but have failed. For every conception of the plain person is at home in some particular philosophical standpoint and there is no way of thinking realistically about the plain person except as someone who is from the outset potentially a moral philosopher of one distinctive kind rather than another.

The history of philosophy confirms this. Immanuel Kant's plain person, who possesses what Kant calls an 'ordinary rational knowledge of morality', is already a proto-Kantian. Thomas Reid's plain person does not possess mere common sense, but common sense as articulated philosophically by Reid. And when Henry Sidgwick appeals to 'common moral opinion', its deliverances turn out to furnish a very Sidgwickian point of entry into Sidgwickian theory. So we have good reason to believe that attempts to portray the plain person as initially completely innocent of philosophy in her or his attitudes, presuppositions, beliefs and questionings are bound to fail. Let us then recognize instead that the plain person must always be conceived as already somehow or other engaged with philosophy in some determinate way, and that we need to ask what particular philosophical standpoint it is which is already implicit in her or his initial attitudes, presuppositions, beliefs and questionings. Is she or he perhaps a proto-Kantian or a potential follower of Reid? Or do plain persons vary a good deal in their initial philosophical allegiance? I want to answer these questions by defending the following theses: that plain persons are in fact generally and to a significant degree proto-Aristotelians, and that, insofar as they are not, it is from the standpoint of a Thomistic Aristotelianism that we can most adequately explain why they are not, and why they have become whatever it is instead that they are.

Characteristically and generally, individuals come to ask the question, 'What is my good?' in social contexts in which different aspects of human activity combine to make it difficult not at some point to raise that question explicitly, and impossible, whether one raises it explicitly or not, not to presuppose some answer to it by the way in which one comes to live out one's life. The first of these aspects is the goal-directedness which from a relatively early age one discovers in different types of norm-informed activity in which one has become involved. Some goals are biologically given, some are social. But in activities as elementary as those which sustain and preserve one's own life, as universal among human beings as those which arise from kin, familial and household relationships, and as open-ended as those which provide one's first education into productive, practical and theoretical arts, one inescapably discovers oneself as a being in norm-governed direction towards goals which are thereby recognized as goods. These norm-governed directednesses are what Aquinas calls *inclinationes* (*Summa Theologiae*, IaIIae, 94.2) in a passage in which he says that it is in virtue of our relationship to these *inclinationes*, partially defining as they do our nature as human agents, that the precepts of the natural law are so called.

The connection between *inclinationes* and such precepts I take to be as follows. When I discover that my life is, as a matter of biological and social fact, partially ordered by regularities which give expression to these primary tendencies towards particular ends, I have it in my power to make these ends mine in a new and secondary way by self-consciously directing my activities to these ends and, insofar as I have rightly understood my own nature, it will be rational for me to do so. The rules to which I will have to conform, if I am so to direct my activities, are those expressed by the precepts of the natural law. What was mere regularity becomes rule-governedness.

If this is how Aquinas understood matters, then it is not difficult to respond to a charge levelled by T. H. Irwin that Aquinas entangles himself in contradiction in his account of the relationship between the virtues, inclination towards right ends and deliberation ('A Conflict in Aquinas'). Irwin correctly ascribes to Aquinas the theses that what is in our power depends on our deliberative capacities and that ends are fixed nondeliberatively, and Irwin concludes that Aquinas is therefore committed to holding that what our ends are to be is not in our power. But Aquinas also asserts that an inclination towards right ends distinguishes virtue and vice and that to be virtuous rather than vicious is in our power, so that Aquinas is also committed to holding that what our ends are to be must be in our power. Hence, Irwin further concludes that Aquinas is guilty of inconsistency.

What Irwin has failed to distinguish are two distinct ways in which, on Aquinas's view, someone may have an end. We human beings are indeed by our specific nature directed towards certain hierarchically ordered ends, and it is not in our power to have a nature other than that which we have, and so not in our power to have ends other than these. But it is in our power whether or not in our rational decision-making to direct our activities towards the achievements of those ends. It is open to us to move in quite other directions. So, according to Aquinas, in one way our ends are in our power and in another way they are not, and there is no inconsistency in the conclusions to which he is committed. Irwin, however, has done us a service by compelling us to raise the questions: how does the plain person make of the ends which are her or his by nature ends actually and rationally directive of her or his activities? And in what social contexts do plain persons learn how to order ends rightly and to recognize their mistakes when they have failed to do so?

Such learning is generally achieved only through involvement in a type of activity which raises for individuals the question, 'What is my good?' in a manner that is complementary to that in which that question is posed by *inclinationes*, a type of activity characteristic of practices, those cooperative forms of activity whose participants jointly pursue the goods internal to those forms of activity and jointly value excellence in achieving those goods. Such practices are of very different kinds. The activities of members of string quartets, of the crews of fishing fleets, of architects and construction workers jointly engaged in developing good housing, of members of families making and sustaining the familial community, of farmers and of physicists – to name only a few – are all practice-based and practice-structured. It is through initiation into the ordered relationships of some particular practice or practices, through education into the skills and virtues which it or they require, and through an understanding of the relationship of those skills and virtues to the achievement of the goods internal to that practice or those practices that we first find application in everyday life for just such a teleological scheme of understanding as that which Aristotle presents at a very different level of philosophical sophistication in the *Nicomachean Ethics*. It is by our finding application for this scheme in our practical activities, a scheme which provides the directedness of our *inclinationes* with a further rationale, that we first become evidently, even if unwittingly, Aristotelians. It is in doing so that we also acquire a capacity for becoming reflective about norms and goals.

This capacity is expressed in our learning how to apply two closely related distinctions. The first is that between what I would do, if I did what would please me most here and now, and what I would do if, in the light of the best instruction available to me, I were to do what would make me excellent in the pursuit of the goods internal to the particular practice or practices in which I am engaged. Failure in making this first distinction is characteristically a sign of failure in ordering the appetites and passions. A second distinction is that between what it would be to achieve what is good and best unqualifiedly and what is good and best here and now for me, at my stage in the education of my capacities, to do. Failure in making this second distinction is characteristically a sign of failure in evaluating how far I have progressed in ordering my appetites and passions. How to make these distinctions is something that each person has to learn, and what has to be learned always can be mislearned. So that through a process of learning, making mistakes, correcting those mistakes and so moving towards the achievement of excellence, the individual comes to understand her or himself as *in via*, in the middle of a journey. And as she or he also comes to understand how each practice in which she or he is engaged itself has a history in the course of which goals, skills and virtues have been variously identified, misunderstood and reconceived, so she or he comes to understand her or his own history of progress within that particular practice as embedded in the history of the practice. But no individual lives her or his life wholly within the confines of any one practice. She or he always pursues the goods of more than one practice, as well as goods external to all practices, and so cannot escape posing and answering the question, even if only by the way in which she or he lives, of how these goods are to be ordered, of which part each is to play within the structures of a whole life. The recurrent and rival claims of pleasure, of the pursuit of wealth, of power, of honor and prestige to be the ordering principle of human lives will each have to be responded to in turn; and in so responding, an individual will be defining her or his attitudes to those considerations which Aristotle rehearses in Book I of the *Nicomachean Ethics* and which Aquinas reconsiders in the opening questions of the IaIIae of the *Summa Theologiae*, in the course of their extended dialectical arguments on the nature of the supreme good.

Characteristically, the plain person responds to these claims not so much through explicit arguments, although these may always play a part, as by shaping his or her life in one way rather than another. When from time to time, the plain person retrospectively examines what her or his life amounts to as a whole, often enough with a view to choice between alternative futures, characteristically what she or he is in effect asking is, 'To what conception of my overall good have I so far committed myself? And, do I now have reason to put it in question?' The unity of her or his life about which each human being thus enquires is the unity of a dramatic narrative, of a story whose outcome can be success or failure for each protagonist. Were it otherwise, the notion of an overall good for that life, one which provides that life with its standards of success and failure, would lack application. When someone writes the narrative either of her or his own or of someone else's life, its adequacy can be judged by the extent to which it provides answers to such questions as: What did the person whose life has been thus narrated take to be her or his good? Did she or he misconceive that good? What obstacles and frustrations confronted that person and did she or he possess the qualities of mind and character necessary to overcome them? The conception of a *telos* of human life is generally first comprehended in terms of the outcomes of particular narratives about particular lives.

So when we as readers or spectators put such questions to a narrative, we look for the universal in the particular. Both plot and character have significance for us insofar as we can understand them in terms of universal conceptions of the good and of the virtues and vices which transcend, but inform, the particularities of *this* narrative. When however in the examination of our own past lives we proceed from the narrative structure of those lives, as they have been lived so far, to enquiry about what from now on we are now to make of ourselves, we are compelled instead to ask of the universal how it may be particularized, how certain conceptions of *the* good and of the virtues may take on embodied form through our realization of this possibility rather than that, posing these questions in terms of the specificities of the narratives of our lives. In so doing, we characteristically draw upon resources provided by some stock of stories from which we had earlier learned to understand both our own lives and the lives of others in narrative terms, the oral and written literature of whatever particular culture it is that we happen to inhabit.

An ability to put ourselves to the question philosophically thus in key part depends upon the prior possession of some measure of narrative understanding, but this ability transcends the limitations of such understanding. For in stories, as contrasted with theories, we encounter the universal *only* in and through the particular. What we need are stories which provoke us to move beyond stories – although everything then turns upon what direction it is that our movement takes. Narratives which point beyond themselves towards the theories that we in fact need are to be found in many places: in some folk-tales, in Sophoclean and Shakespearean drama, and above all in Dante's *Commedia*, which directs us beyond itself towards the kind of theoretical understanding provided by Aquinas's commentaries on the *Ethics* and *Politics*.

One of the things that we most need to learn, first from narrative and then from theory, is that it is one of the marks of someone who develops bad character that, as it develops, she or he becomes progressively less and less able to understand what it is that she or he has mislearned and how it was that she or he fell into error. Part of the badness of bad character is intellectual blindness on moral questions. It is important therefore at an early stage to possess resources for right judgment and action, which include resources for explaining how we may come to fail and have come to fail and what we have to do to avoid failure. We need, that is, an extended, practically usable answer to the question 'What is my good?' and 'How is it to be achieved?', which will both direct us in present and future action and also evaluate and explain past action.

Such an answer will have to supply not only an account of goods and virtues, but also of rules, and of how goods, virtues and rules relate to one another. It will be an account which will answer not only the plain person's practical questions about how to achieve her or his good, but also the central question of this lecture, that of how much of a moral philosopher the plain person needs to become. For the plain person, so it has turned out, must become at least enough of a moral philosopher to understand her or himself, in all her or his particularities, as exemplifying the universal concepts of a theory which is not only both explanatorily and prescriptively powerful, but which also is able to justify a claim to be superior to such rival theories as may present themselves in one guise or another as claimants for the plain person's allegiance. What kind of theory then does the plain person need?

Let us begin with the place, in such a theory, of fundamental rules, of those precepts of the natural law whose evidentness to the plain person who aspires to direct her or himself towards her or his good in the company of other rational persons it is hard to disguise, even although it has often enough been denied. For, to violate these rules in one's relationships with other persons is bound to deprive one of their cooperation in the achievement of a good about which one still has much to learn from them. In the search for our good, everyone is a potential teacher and has therefore to be treated as one from whom I still may have to learn. So the rules governing my fundamental relationships with others are not affirmed as conclusions from some yet more fundamental set of premises. Allegiance to those rules cannot depend upon the outcome of theorizing. For suppose someone were to deny this and to embark upon the project of cooperating with others in constructing a theory designed to provide them with a rational justification. In order to do so successfully, she or he would first have to enter into cooperative relationships already informed by allegiance to just those rules for which she or he aspired to provide a justification. Hence, allegiance to these particular rules has to precede any set of arguments, any theorizing.

The same rules have another part to play in the plain person's initial education into the moral life. For a first primitive conception of each of the virtues that we need to acquire, if we are to achieve our good, can be articulated only through a set of rules which turn out to be another application of the primary precepts of the natural law. We can only learn what it is to be courageous or temperate or truthful by first learning that certain types of action are always and exceptionlessly such as we must refrain from if we are to exemplify those virtues. The disposition which we need to acquire by habituation in the case of each virtue is of course a disposition not merely to act in certain rule-governed ways, but also to do more than the rules require. What more is required varies with time, place and circumstance. And knowing how to go beyond the rules in order to judge appropriately in particular circumstances is itself impossible without the virtue of *phronēsis*. So the order of learning is such that we first have to learn in certain initial situations what is *always* enjoined or always prohibited, in order that later we may become able to extrapolate in a non-rule-governed way to other types of situations in which what courage or justice or truthfulness, together with prudence, demand is more than conformity to the universal rule. Learning what the virtues require of us in a wide range of different situations is inseparable from learning which, out of the multiplicity of goods, is at stake in any given situation. So we go on to learn more than we initially could learn from the rules, but part of what we then learn is that we can never dispense with the rules. And that this is so is integral to our understanding of goods and of virtues as well as of the rules themselves. Consider how those rules relate to our supreme good.

It has to be of the nature of whatever is genuinely the supreme good that it makes no sense to think of weighing it against other goods. The supreme good is not a good that just happens on some particular occasions, or even on every particular occasion, to outweigh other goods. It must be that it *cannot* be outweighed. Otherwise its status as supreme good would be contingent and therefore very possibly temporary. It would be vulnerable to displacement. Moreover, the rules, observance of which is required if *our* final good is to be achieved – that is, if we are to achieve whatever relationship to the supreme good it is in which our own final good consists – must define what is necessarily true of that relationship.

Those rules, then, cannot be such as to bind us only so long as certain contingent circumstances obtain, that is, conditionally. So that if someone entertained the thought, as many of course have done, that we perhaps ought on some particular occasion, for the sake of achieving what is taken to be some other good only thus obtainable, temporarily to suspend the requirement of obedience to one or more of those rules, if, that is, we treated them as open to exceptions, we would have misconceived both the nature and function of those rules and the nature of the good and of our good. And in so misconceiving them we would have exhibited a defect both in our possession of and in our understanding of one or more of the intellectual and moral virtues. Virtues, rules and goods, so it turns out, have to be understood in their interrelationship or not at all.

Consider as an analogy the relationship of the rules governing activities of enquiry in mathematics or the natural sciences to the goal of those activities, that of attaining truth: for example, the rule that one should be scrupulous in laying out one's theses and putative proofs so that they are maximally vulnerable to objection and refutation. Suppose that someone were to propose that in the interests of obtaining some nonmathematical and nonscientific good, this rules should, from time to time, be suspended. Such a proposal, ignoring as it does the internal relation between truth and ability to withstand refutation, would make no sense, insofar as it was proposed as a rule for mathematicians *qua* mathematicians or scientists *qua* scientists. And a proposal temporarily to suspend the application of the precepts of the natural law, ignoring, as it would, the internal relation between the conception of the supreme good and those precepts, would similarly make no sense insofar as it was proposed as a rule for rational beings *qua* rational beings. Yet on many occasions, such proposals are made with great seriousness. The benefits of violating some requirement of the natural law are compared with the benefits of conformity. And that is to say that some good or set of goods is being weighed against the supreme good, as if in relation to it any question of weighing could arise. How does such a mistake come to be made?

Characteristically, it is the outcome of fragmenting into independent parts the conceptual scheme in terms of which the plain person had at first organized her or his moral understanding. Goods, rules and virtues are as a result of such fragmentation reconceived as isolable from one another, so that the problem is not that of how to articulate a preexisting relationship, but to construct a relationship apparently not yet established between the disparate parts of one's moral scheme. And the difficulty for the plain person in this situation is that once the different elements in her or his moral conceptual scheme have been thus torn apart, each of them thereby assumes a somewhat different character. Rules, conceived apart from virtues and goods, are not the same as rules conceived in dependence upon virtues and goods; and so it is also with virtues apart from rules and goods and goods apart from rules and virtues.

Observe now that in making these theoretical remarks I have already resorted to the narrative mode. I have begun to tell a story, the story of the decline and fall of the plain person. It is a story in four episodes, a story of a failed quest for what proves in the end to be an illusory grail. In the first of these, the protagonist sets out to discover what the final good for beings such as her or himself is and finds that, in asking 'What is my good?' and 'What is the good?' in any way that is well-designed to secure helpful answers, she or he has to define that quest in a way which already presupposes to a significant degree a particular kind of answer to those questions. For those rules and virtues which alone guide one reliably in the earliest stages of fruitful moral enquiry are structured, so that they already presuppose a great deal about the existence and nature of that same good about which one has only begun to enquire.

The circularity in which the protagonist is thereby involved is one which requires of her or him an asceticism or at least a temperateness about certain classes of less than supreme goods, which she or he will only be able to justify fully at some future time in the light later to be afforded by a more adequate conception of the good. Yet should she or he, solicited by a variety of such goods, physical, aesthetic and intellectual, fail in this temperateness, not only will she or he debar her or himself from ever reaching the point at which such rational justification would become possible, but she or he will, in according independent recognition to a multiplicity of more or less immediate goods, have adopted a set of standards of justification very different from that towards an understanding of which she or he had originally been moving. As a result in this second type of episode a radical discrepancy begins to appear between the rules in obedience to which the quest was originally to have been conducted and the multiplicity of goods now envisaged, possibly as rival candidates for the status of supreme good, possibly as by their very multiplicity excluding the notion of a single supreme good. And already any conception of a good that not only is not but could not be outweighed by other goods has disappeared from view.

In a third type of episode this discrepancy is resolved in either of two incompatible ways. *Either*, the authority of rules is made independent of all relationship to goods, so that obedience to rules is valued for its own sake, *or* the rules are reconceived so that they are authoritative only if and insofar as obedience to them is causally effective in attaining what are taken to be goods.

Whichever of these two resolutions is adopted, new problems are engendered. If conformity to moral rules is now to be valued only for its own sake, as Kant, for example, held, then the question inescapably arises of why and how a rational person should be moved to value such conformity. If rules are only a means to the achievement of goods, and a multiplicity of competing goods are acknowledged, as they are by utilitarians, then it will be necessary to decide how to respond on those occasions when the actions necessary for the attainment of some one particular good violate the rule or rules necessary for the attainment of some other good.

During this third type of episode therefore the protagonist of our story discovers not only that she or he must take sides on these issues, but that other similar persons take opposing sides. The protagonist consequently confronts one or more antagonists and becomes involved in intellectual and moral conflict. And this conflict may extend beyond the initial opposition, in which the upholder of rules independent of goods confronted the upholder of rules as nothing more than a means to the achievement of goods, to further questions about what place the virtues are to have in each of these rival schemes and how the problems internal to each scheme are to be resolved. Our protagonist therefore now confronts a variety of antagonists and perhaps her or himself with a divided mind on these divisive issues.

A fourth and final type of episode opens with the protagonist's discovery that the major issues over which conflict has been joined are not rationally resolvable. It is not that each of the contending parties does not have arguments to deploy, but rather that each gives a different weight to different types of consideration, and that there are no rational criteria, shared between the contending parties, to which appeal can be made in deciding what weight should be so given. Fundamental disagreement turns out to be ineliminable. There is more than one way in which our protagonist might respond to this discovery, perhaps by acting out the part of a wholly prephilosophical and now cynical plain person, standing outside and pouring scorn upon all philosophical points of view, or perhaps by becoming a plain person's version of a proto-Nietzschean, one devoted to unmasking a will to power disguised by the proponents of each contending moral standpoint.

I have told this story of the transformations of the plain person only in bare and skeletal outline. But I hope that I have said enough at least to suggest that this story could be told with sufficient detail to explain both how those changing portraits of the plain person which decorate the history of moral philosophy do in fact correspond to social realities – hence the immense plausibility in one time and place of Kant's portrait of the plain person, in another of Reid's, in a third of Sidgwick's, and in a fourth of Sartre's – and how, nonetheless, the plain person is fundamentally a proto-Aristotelian. What is the force of 'fundamentally' here? What it conveys can be expressed in three claims, first that every human being *either* lives out her or his life in a narrative form which is structured in terms of a *telos*, of virtues and of rules in an Aristotelian mode or has disrupted that narrative by committing her or himself to some other way of life, which is best understood as an alternative designed to avoid or escape from an Aristotelian mode of life, so that the lives of those who understand themselves, explicitly or much more probably implicitly, in terms set by Kant or Reid or Sidgwick or Sartre are still informed by this rejected alternative. Secondly, I have told the story of the decline and fall of the plain person as the narrative of a single life. But the story could have been told, and I have told it elsewhere (in *After Virtue*), as a claim about the narrative history of a set of successive periods in Western culture from the sixteenth to the twentieth century. This partial mirroring of the fate of individuals in the history of the larger social order and of the fate of that larger order in the narratives of individual lives testifies to the inseparability of the two stories.

Thirdly, as these first two claims imply, I am also committed to holding that every human being is potentially a fully fledged and not merely a proto-Aristotelian and that the frustration of that potentiality is among his or her morally important characteristics. We should therefore expect to find, within those who have not been allowed to develop, or have not themselves allowed their lives to develop, an Aristotelian form, a crucial and ineliminable tension between that in them which is and that which is not Aristotelian. The standard modern anti-Aristotelian self will be a particular kind of divided self, exhibiting that complexity so characteristic of and so prized by modernity.

We can now say something more not only about how much of a moral philosopher the plain person has to be, but also about what kind of a moral philosopher the plain person has to be and how this may differ from situation to situation. The plain person needs as much of a theory as will enable her or him to identify what the significant alternatives are which now confront her or him, and to understand why and how it was in the past that she or he did or did not make mistakes in acting in one way rather than another. That need may not be met, not only if the plain person is insufficiently a theorist, but also if the theory which is made available to her or him, even if true and adequate *qua* theory, is stated in too much abstraction from the specificities and particularities of her or his historical and autobiographical situation.

This is why we would not meet the practical needs of contemporary plain persons by simply providing them with copies of the *Nicomachean Ethics* and of Aquinas's commentary, nor even of the IaIIae of the *Summa*. What such persons would still lack is a capacity for reading or hearing what is written in such texts as providing answers to their own specific and particular questions. Such texts may be theoretically powerful, but still remain practically idle, for they do no work for us, until and unless we learn how to read them in such a way as to generate specific and particular answers to the practical questions of all of us, moral philosophers and plain persons alike, since in her or his practical life a moral philosopher is just one more type of plain person. But those texts do, if we read them aright, meet us, so to speak, halfway. They are responsive to this kind of practical reading, because their authors' expectations of this kind of reader already inform those texts. The reader still, however, has the work to do of constructing her or his own specific and particular reading of the text at the points at which her or his practical questions and the text intersect. What form do such specific and particular readings take?

A practical reader can only approach a text with the resources for questioning it which are afforded by her or his social context and relationships. Such resources always limit as well as focus our initial questioning and an effective practical text begins by subordinating our questions to its own. It responds to our interrogation by interrogating us. So it is at the outset in the *Nicomachean Ethics*. So it is at the beginning of the IaIIae, a work designed for teachers, confessors and other intermediaries between its text and the readings of the practical reader or hearer. Such a reader is forced back upon questions to which her or his own questioning has to be subordinated and by which it is likely to be transformed.

Consider the sequence of questioning as expounded in the IaIIae and its shadow counterpart in the sequence of questioning of some particular practical reader. Where Aquinas asks what the ultimate end is towards which the activities of any human being *qua* rational person are directed and explains why wealth, honor, pleasure, power, the goods of the body and the goods of the soul cannot be that end, the practical reader will be concerned with these particular pleasures, with that particular opportunity for enriching her or himself, with the attractions of this or that specific type of power, as these present themselves as the ends of possible courses of action. Where Aquinas presents the most powerful arguments against his own conclusions through a wide range of earlier voices, including those of Plato, Aristotle, Cicero, Boethius, and Augustine, the contemporary practical reader cannot but also hear the practical advice of the major voices of her or his own time, those of, say, Diderot, Rousseau and Kant in the eighteenth century or of Hegel and Mill in the nineteenth, often perhaps in vulgarized and diminished form, presented in the conversation of one's neighbors, rather than in philosophical texts, but not necessarily the less powerful for that. Such a reader needs to learn what Aquinas has to teach us in each of his dialectical responses about how to respond to these contending voices. She or he needs to learn through this process of argumentative debate to identify in concrete terms what here and now she or he must do, if she or he is not to confuse the supreme good with some lesser good.

It was precisely at this point and over this question that the protagonist in my earlier story of the decline and fall of the plain person made a large initial mistake, and the practical reader of the IaIIae will be able to avoid this same error only by learning how to arrive, in practice, at those conclusions which Aquinas reaches theoretically, in moving from his answer to Question 5 about where happiness is to be found, through the conclusions of Questions 18–21 about what makes an act good and evil, to Questions 24–48 about the function of the passions in making her or him act well and badly, and on to Questions 49–66 about the habits which have to be developed as virtues, so that her or his passions are ordered and transformed, so that she or he, in consequence, acts well rather than badly, so that she or he, in further consequence, is directed towards her or his true final end. But if such a person moves successfully through this process of practical enquiry, embodying in the dramatic sequences of her or his life a highly particularized counterpart of the ordered sequences of moral teaching presented in the questions and answers of those parts of the IaIIae, she or he is bound to discover the very same circularity that was evident also in the story of the decline and fall of the plain person.

Such a person, that is, will have to recognize that the point in her or his practical enquiry at which recognition of the nature of and the need for the virtues has been achieved could not have been reached if she or he had not already at a much earlier stage possessed and valued those same virtues to some significant, even if less than perfect degree. Unless the activities in which her or his initial questioning was embodied had been in appropriate measure courageous – both patient, when necessary, and daring, when necessary – just in giving what was due to other participants in those activities, temperate in restraining desires, so that a multiplicity of solicitations liable to distract the course of enquiry were put aside for the sake of a good thereby already implicitly judged to be supreme, and always prudent in the ordering of these activities, she or he could not have achieved any adequate understanding of why without courage, justice, temperateness and prudence her or his enquiry was bound to fail. So a reader making her or his way through the IaIIae will learn only later what it was in her or his earlier relationship to the text which enabled her or him to make of the narrative of her or his own life a particularized version of the progress of Aquinas's argument. How the text is read depends, that is to say, in key part on the incipient virtues of the practical reader and what incipient virtues the reader is able to bring to her or his reading depends in turn on the resources on which that reader can draw in and from the particular social context. What kind of resources are these?

In order to answer this question it is worth considering two important objections that may be advanced against my argument so far. The first of these might begin by pointing out that many plain persons have fared very well morally without ever encountering philosophy. With the moral resources afforded by sound, plain, practical teaching, by the cultivation of the virtues and by an instructed conscience, what need is there for philosophy? It may be thought that it is part of the arrogance of an intellectual to project onto plain persons a need for theory. It is however no part of my case that the plain person needs to become anything like a professional theorist. It is central to my argument that the practice of the moral life by plain persons always presupposes the truth of some particular theoretical standpoint and that, when confronted by rival claims to her or his moral allegiance, the plain person's reflective practical choices will implicitly at least be a choice between theoretical standpoints. In our own society common plain persons who have never heard of John Stuart Mill offer as the deliverances of what they take to be their common sense maxims of hedonistic utilitarianism. Other such plain persons, equally ignorant of Kant, will insist on the irrelevance of consequences to the rightness of their actions. A good deal of ordinary conversation and debate bears out the epigram that common sense is a graveyard of past philosophies.

Plain persons then exhibit their allegiances in their actions and in their reasons for action, not in their theorizing. But this does not deprive those allegiances of a philosophical dimension. It might however be objected that those allegiances could never rightly be described as Aristotelian or even proto-Aristotelian. For Aristotle himself took plain persons to be incapable of philosophical reflection. Aristotle's exclusions of not only barbarians, but also women (*Politics*, 1259b21–1260a33) and product-ive workers (*Politics*, 1328b33–1329a2) from the life of citizenship and of the virtues is surely enough to show that he could not have taken plain persons to be proto-Aristotelians. But Aristotle has of course no worthwhile arguments to support these exclusions, and the Thomistic Aristotelianism of a Maritain or a Simon rightly ignored them. And so do I.

What the first of these objections does draw to our attention is the danger to someone holding my position of too easy an assimilation of the theoretical to the practical life and therefore of the preoccupations of the philosopher to those of the plain person. I have, for example, empha-sized how the plain person's moral understanding is of goods, rules and virtues in his or her interrelationships. And the practical need to under-stand these together, although real, is very different from the philoso-pher's need to develop a theoretical understanding of each of these in its own terms. So that often enough, if we are to make what philosophers say relevant to the practical concerns of plain persons, including philoso-phers in their own practical lives, we need first to reorganize and rethink the philosophers' arguments. Some topics which were, for good analyti-cal and didactic reasons, treated separately in Aristotle and Aquinas need in contexts of practice to be treated together. Aristotle considers the acquisition of the virtues in one set of passages and the nature of practi-cal reasoning in another; and Aquinas, in the *Summa*, not only considers these separately, but discusses the character of the natural law in yet a third set of passages. Both provide in their discussions much that sug-gests the importance of the relationships between them. But subsequent teaching about practical reasoning, virtues and natural law has often enforced a separation of topics which has obscured the fact that at the level of practice, especially initial practice, the ability to judge and to act in accordance with the precepts of the natural law, the ability to acquire an increasing set of dispositions to act virtuously, and the ability to judge rightly about goods are all exercised as aspects of one and the same complex ability, the ability to engage in sound practical reasoning. How is this so?

To reason practically, I must always set in front of myself some good which will be specified in the major premise of my practical reasoning and, if my practical reasoning is in any particular instance not to obstruct my attempt to answer the question 'What is my ultimate good?' alternative immediate goods must from the outset be ordered so that no lesser, but more immediate good can be thought to outweigh my ultimate good. My ultimate good, that is to say, will have to be conceived from the outset as a good than which no greater can be pursued by me, in order to ensure the integrity of my practical reasoning.

At the same time, the various relationships into which I will have to enter, in order to achieve the kind of understanding of myself and others without which I will be unable to learn what the human good is, will themselves have to be informed by those virtues and governed by those rules without which the activities of enquiry will be barren. Any ordering of goods which involves my conceiving of my ultimate good as a good than which no greater can be pursued will have to be matched by an ordering of my life in terms of virtues and rules which is consistent with the affirmation of the true nature of the good and the best as the first premise of my practical reasoning. The movement from that first premise to a conclusion which is right action requires from me a correspondingly ordered character and a correspondingly ordered set of social relationships. This connection between what kind of person I have to become in order to achieve a given end and what the character of that given end is is of course not peculiar to this kind of enquiry. It is a connection embodied in the structure and reasoning of all practice-based activity; what the need for it in enquiry by particular human beings designed to answer the questions 'What is my good?' and 'What is *the* good?' confirms is that such enquiry is itself a practice.

So it is not just that, as I said earlier, practices have an Aristotelian structure. It is also that in engaging in the practice of asking seriously and systematically the question 'What is my good?' plain persons engage in a reflective practice with an Aristotelian content as well as an Aristotelian structure, a practice in which both Aristotle and Aquinas preceded them. So it is less surprising than we may have thought that those who first come to a reading of the *Nicomachean Ethics* or Aquinas's commentary or the IaIIae of the *Summa* may already exhibit the cardinal virtues without as yet knowing the reasons for needing them, and it is not after all paradoxical to assert that we must already have those virtues at least to some degree if we are to understand why we need to have them. The *Nicomachean Ethics* and Aquinas's commentary upon it and the IaIIae are texts in which readers are able to discover themselves as characters, or rather to discover types of character which to some significant degree they already exemplify. And they may also discover that what they are now able to learn about themselves in universal terms from such texts, in beginning to comprehend a philosophical theory of the moral life, is what they had already learned in part through practice-informed activities concerning the particularities of their own lives. If their subsequent practice becomes informed and enriched by philosophical theory, they may feel that they have transcended certain limitations of that past learning, limitations rooted in the relative inarticulacy of the merely practical. But they need never disown, indeed they could not without incoherence disown, the first stages of the enacted narrative of their lives. We are thus able to set beside the fable of the decline and fall of the plain person the story of the plain person who does not go astray, or rather who finds the resources for correcting her or his errors as she or he proceeds towards both an understanding of, and the achievement of, her or his good.

Those stories, it needs finally to be remarked, have genuine application to human lives only if and because certain metaphysical as well as moral claims can be sustained within philosophy. For those stories not only draw explicitly and obviously upon concepts and theses having to do with rules, regularities, passions, dispositions and ends, but also, if less obviously, upon rules and concepts having to do with substances, essential and accidental properties, potentiality and act, and form and matter. They involve explanations of what it is for someone to succeed in progressing towards or to fail in progressing towards their ultimate end, and such explanations are of interest only if and insofar as we have good reason to believe that they are *true*. But such explanations will be true if and only if the universe itself is teleologically ordered, and the only type of teleologically ordered universe in which we have good reason to believe is a theistic universe. Hence, the moral progress of the plain person towards her or his ultimate good is always a matter of more than morality. And the enacted narrative of that progress will only become fully intelligible when it is understood not only in terms of metaphysics but in an adequate theological light, when, that is, the particularities of that narrative are understood to embody what is said about sin and about grace in the IaIIae of the *Summa* as well as what is said about law and the virtues. The moral progress of the plain person is always the beginnings of a pilgrim's progress.

PART IV

Challenging Contemporary Philosophy

Whose Justice? Which Rationality? (extracts)

Chapter 11

Aquinas on Practical Rationality and Justice

[. . . .]

To whom was Aquinas addressing himself in his remarks upon war and for that matter in his discussion of justice in general? He was a teacher of teachers and an advisor of advisors. Both the comprehensiveness and the detail of his discussions reflect the range of persons and problems with whom and by whom those teachers and advisors were called upon for tasks requiring moral and political judgment. The Dominican order was, in the person of Aquinas and of others, a teaching presence not only in universities and *studia*, and not only in countless dioceses and parishes, but in the French court and at the papal court, and in the institutions administering law, both ecclesiastical and secular. Aquinas, like Aristotle before him, had the task of instructing some of the participants in the major institutional and political conflicts and divisions of his day, or at least of instructing their instructors.

I have stressed the extent to which his account of justice is at odds with the characteristic attitudes of contemporary liberal modernity. It is important to stress equally the degree to which the standards to which he tried to hold his thirteenth-century contemporaries involved a radical break with the conventional standards of the age and the arguments commonly employed in their justification. Consider in this respect Aquinas's rigorism with respect to truth-telling and lying. We are, on Aquinas's view, required *never* to assert anything except what we believe to be true. We are under no general obligation to tell all that we know; when to speak and when not to speak is a matter of other duties and obligations, of discretion and of the exercise of prudence. But we may never lie, not for profit, nor convenience, nor pleasure, nor to cause pain or trouble. Lying as such is evil, and lying with malice is a mortal sin (*Summa Theologiae*, IIaIIae, 109 and 110).

In the third article of *Quaestio* 110 Aquinas provides six arguments in favor of the view that lying is sometimes permissible, including the argument that a lie as a lesser evil may be used to prevent some greater evil such as killing or being killed. His rejection of these arguments embodies his conviction that the precepts of justice are not means designed to secure some external end, such as political success or worldly security, but are constitutive of those relationships through which and in which we live out that just life whose end is our true and ultimate end. Insofar as I lie I make myself into the sort of unjust person incapable of achieving my ultimate end. And to this immediate considerations must be subordinated. It follows that my responsibility for averting by some other means the greater evil in the face of which I am tempted to lie is all the greater and that even the sacrifice of my own life may be required of me to secure this, if the evil is sufficiently great.

The stock of arguments against this position, which Aquinas rejected, was of course that relied upon by many in contemporary thirteenth-century discussion. Telling those with power and authority that lying is prohibited to them was as unpopular an activity in the thirteenth century as in the twentieth. What, however, twentieth-century political society, unlike its thirteenth-century counterpart, characteristically lacks is the existence in its midst of any influential body of protagonists of an absolute prohibition upon lying, let alone the presentation of that prohibition as part of a body of thought claiming to merit both its intellectual and its moral allegiance.

That latter claim was also of course a presupposition of the comprehensiveness and detail of Aquinas's argumentative treatment of justice. Against contemporary Aristotelians Aquinas was committed to showing that both in what he accepted from Aristotle and in what he amended or dismissed he had genuinely come to terms with Aristotle's arguments. Similarly against contemporary Augustinians he was committed to a treatment of the patristic and Augustinian texts which gave them their due. And most fundamentally he could accept nothing from either which was irreconcilable with scripture.

[. . . .]

I [. . .] argued earlier that Aquinas does not merely supplement Aristotle, but that he shows Aristotle's account of the teleology of human life to be radically defective. That radical defectiveness in understanding turns out in the light of these sections of the *Summa* to be, on Aquinas's view, not only or so much a radical defectiveness in Aristotle's account as a radical defectiveness in that natural human order of which Aristotle gave his account. A strong thesis about the inadequacies and flaws of the natural human order emerges, so that the relationship of Aquinas's Aristotelianism to his allegiance to Augustine appears in a new light. The Augustinian understanding of fallen human nature is used to explain the limitations of Aristotle's arguments, just as the detail of Aristotle often corrects Augustine's generalizations.

What is clear nonetheless is that Aquinas's account is only fully intelligible, let alone defensible, as it emerges from an extended and complex tradition of argument and conflict that included far more than Aristotle and Augustine. The notion of detaching it from that tradition and presenting its claims in terms of some alleged neutral criteria of a rationality, understood in independence of any tradition of practice and theorizing, makes no sense, for it is an account of the criteria of rationality, and of the part played by the virtues in the exercise of rationality, which itself emerges from and is justified in terms of the background of the traditions to which Aquinas made himself the heir.

Aquinas's response to those traditions was very different either from that of his contemporaries or from that of his successors. There is a history, as yet only written in part, of the stages which had set the scene for Aquinas's enterprise. The revival of learning in the eleventh and twelfth centuries had simultaneously generated two different kinds of enterprise. One was the commentary, especially on sacred scripture, out of which were generated a set of theses about the different kinds of meaning and levels of meaning which could be found in a text along with a set of problems about how disagreements were to be resolved where authoritative writers conflicted or appeared to conflict. The first yielded the concept of the *distinctio*; the second, that of the *quaestio*. At the same time scholars were innovating, often drawing upon fragmentary or misunderstood inheritances from the past in logic, in dialectic, and in the understanding of law and of political authority. When the rediscovery of so much material by Aristotle which had been hitherto unavailable, along with his Islamic and Jewish interpreters, and the revival of Augustinian theology provided frameworks within which to try to understand the relationship between these enterprises, it was in the formal organization of the debates and disagreements recorded as *quaestiones disputatae* and *quaestiones quodlibetales*, and in the elaboration of both the theological and the secular *distinctiones* which these involved, that enquiry at last found the means to become simultaneously comprehensive and systematic. The past had provided a set of *auctoritates*, both sacred and secular. The former could be reinterpreted, although not rejected. The latter could only be rejected when there was sufficient reason to reject them. Enquiry, therefore, had to proceed by counterpoising authority to authority, in respect of both theses and arguments.

Many of Aquinas's contemporaries and immediate successors responded either by rejecting some large part of their intellectual inheritance, in the interests of systematic coherence, or by turning to the piecemeal investigation of particular areas and elaborating solutions to particular problems on the basis of some sharply delimited set of perspectives. The former response characterized not only those Augustinians who rejected Aristotle, for fear of accepting Averroism, but also those other pupils of Albertus who developed this or that strand of Albertus's work in neglect of the rest. The latter response is exhibited by those who compartmentalized to greater or lesser degree their enquiries, so that the pursuit of logical studies proceeded in substantial part independently of enquiries in theology, and both in equal independence of writings about ethics and politics, in a way that foreshadows the compartmentalization of later enquiry.

Neither party fully understood the idiosyncrasy of Aquinas's project, that of developing the work of dialectical construction systematically, so as to integrate the whole previous history of enquiry, so far as he was aware of it, into his own. *His* counterposing of authority to authority was designed to exhibit what in each could withstand dialectical testing from every standpoint so far developed, with the aim of identifying both the limitations of each point of view and what in each could not be impugned by even the most rigorous of such tests. Hence the claim implicitly made by Aquinas against any rival out of the past is that the partiality, one-sidedness, and incoherences of that rival's standpoint will have already been overcome in the unfinished system portrayed in the *Summa*, while its strengths and successes will have been incorporated and perhaps reinforced. Against any similar rival from the future the corresponding claim would be that it too could be brought into the dialectical conversation at every relevant point and that the test of Aquinas's standpoint would lie in its ability to identify the limitations and to integrate the strengths and successes of each rival into its overall structure.

It is characteristic of intellectual, as well as of social, history, however, that it is always subject to a variety of unrelated contingencies. And so it was with Aquinas's standpoint, which, except within Roman Catholic theology, generated for the most part one more tradition of defensive commentary rather than an ability to engage with the greatest of its rivals. What effectively happened was that those rivals came to determine the terms of public fifteenth- and sixteenth-century philosophical debate, so that followers of Aquinas were confronted with a dilemma, albeit one which neither they nor their opponents generally recognized. *Either*, that is to say, they refused to accept the terms of contemporary debate and in so doing isolated themselves and were treated as irrelevant, *or* they made the mistake of accepting those terms of debate and on those terms seemed to have been defeated. Aquinas's thirteenth-century achievement had been to insist upon setting the terms for debate and enquiry. It was generally, even if not quite always, the misfortune of his fifteenth- and sixteenth-century heirs either not to perceive the need to do so or to fail in attempting to do so.

When, therefore, Aristotelianism had a dramatic revival of fortune in the universities of the sixteenth century, it was Aristotle without Aquinas who partially dominated the intellectual scene. The *Nicomachean Ethics* and the *Politics* once again became key educational texts. But Aristotle thus revived had to be vindicated in a milieu to which practically and theoretically his concepts came to seem increasingly irrelevant. The type of context of enquiry which the thirteenth-century university had made available and within which the relationship of Aristotle's texts to other texts had been elaborated lacked any adequate counterpart in the sixteenth and seventeenth centuries. In consequence it was not so much the revival of Aristotelianism as its rejection which was to produce new ways of theorizing about practical rationality and justice in an age when new modes of social life made such innovation once again practically important.

[. . . .]

Chapter 18
The Rationality of Traditions

This book has presented an outline narrative history of three traditions of enquiry into what practical rationality is and what justice is, and in addition an acknowledgment of a need for the writing of a narrative history of a fourth tradition, that of liberalism. All four of these traditions are and were more than, and could not but be more than, traditions of intellectual enquiry. In each of them intellectual enquiry was or is part of the elaboration of a mode of social and moral life of which the intellectual enquiry itself was an integral part, and in each of them the forms of that life were embodied with greater or lesser degrees of imperfection in social and political institutions which also draw their life from other sources. So the Aristotelian tradition emerges from the rhetorical and reflective life of the *polis* and the dialectical teaching of the Academy and the Lyceum; so the Augustinian tradition flourished in the houses of religious orders and in the secular communities which provided the environment for such houses both in its earlier, and in its Thomistic, version in universities; so the Scottish blend of Calvinist Augustinianism and renaissance Aristotelianism informed the lives of congregations and kirk sessions, of law courts and universities; and so liberalism, beginning as a repudiation of tradition in the name of abstract, universal principles of reason, turned itself into a politically embodied power, whose inability to bring its debates on the nature and context of those universal principles to a conclusion has had the unintended effect of transforming liberalism into a tradition.

[. . . .]

All the traditions with which we have been concerned agree in according a certain authority to logic both in their theory and in their practice. Were it not so, their adherents would be unable to disagree in the way in which they do. But that upon which they agree is insufficient to resolve those disagreements. It may therefore seem to be the case that we are confronted with the rival and competing claims of a number of traditions to our allegiance in respect of our understanding of practical rationality and justice, among which we can have no good reason to decide in favor of any one rather than of the others. Each has its own standards of reasoning; each provides its own background beliefs. To offer one kind of reason, to appeal to one set of background beliefs, will already be to have assumed the standpoint of one particular tradition. But if we make no such assumption, then we can have no good reason to give more weight to the contentions advanced by one particular tradition than to those advanced by its rivals.

Argument along these lines has been adduced in support of a conclusion that if the only available standards of rationality are those made available by and within traditions, then no issue between contending traditions is rationally decidable. To assert or to conclude this rather than that can be rational relative to the standards of some particular tradition, but not rational as such. There can be no rationality as such. Every set of standards, every tradition incorporating a set of standards, has as much and as little claim to our allegiance as any other. Let us call this the relativist challenge, as contrasted with a second type of challenge, that which we may call perspectivist.

The relativist challenge rests upon a denial that rational debate between and rational choice among rival traditions is possible; the perspectivist challenge puts in question the possibility of making truth-claims from within any one tradition. For if there is a multiplicity of rival traditions, each with its own characteristic modes of rational justification internal to it, then that very fact entails that no one tradition can offer those outside it good reasons for excluding the theses of its rivals. Yet if this is so, no one tradition is entitled to arrogate to itself an exclusive title; no one tradition can deny legitimacy to its rivals. What seemed to require rival traditions so to exclude and so to deny was belief in the logical incompatibility of the theses asserted and denied within rival traditions, a belief which embodied a recognition that if the theses of one such tradition were true, then some at least of the theses asserted by its rivals were false.

The solution, so the perspectivist argues, is to withdraw the ascription of truth and falsity, at least in the sense in which 'true' and 'false' have been understood so far within the practice of such traditions, both from individual theses and from the bodies of systematic belief of which such theses are constitutive parts. Instead of interpreting rival traditions as mutually exclusive and incompatible ways of understanding one and the same world, one and the same subject matter, let us understand them instead as providing very different, complementary perspectives for envisaging the realities about which they speak to us.

The relativist challenge and the perspectivist challenge share some premises and are often presented jointly as parts of a single argument.

Each of them exists in more than one version, and neither of them was originally elaborated in terms of a critique of the claims to truth and rationality of *traditions*. But considered as such, they lose none of their force. Nonetheless I am going to argue that they are fundamentally misconceived and misdirected. Their apparent power derives, so I shall want to suggest, from their inversion of certain central Enlightenment positions concerning truth and rationality. While the thinkers of the Enlightenment insisted upon a particular type of view of truth and rationality, one in which truth is guaranteed by rational method and rational method appeals to principles undeniable by any fully reflective rational person, the protagonists of post-Enlightenment relativism and perspectivism claim that if the Enlightenment conceptions of truth and rationality cannot be sustained, theirs is the only possible alternative.

Post-Enlightenment relativism and perspectivism are thus the negative counterpart of the Enlightenment, its inverted mirror image. Where the Enlightenment invoked the arguments of Kant or Bentham, such post-Enlightenment theorists invoke Nietzsche's attacks upon Kant and Bentham. It is therefore not surprising that what was invisible to the thinkers of the Enlightenment should be equally invisible to those postmodernist relativists and perspectivists who take themselves to be the enemies of the Enlightenment, while in fact being to a large and unacknowledged degree its heirs. What neither was or is able to recognize is the kind of rationality possessed by traditions. In part this was and is because of the enmity to tradition as inherently obscurantist which is and was to be found equally among Kantians and Benthamites, neo-Kantians and later utilitarians, on the one hand, and among Nietzscheans and post-Nietzscheans on the other. But in part the invisibility of the rationality of tradition was due to the lack of expositions, let alone defenses, of that rationality.

Burke was on this matter, as on so many others, an agent of positive harm. For Burke ascribed to traditions in good order, the order as he supposed of following nature, 'wisdom without reflection' (*Reflections on the Revolution in France*, p. 129). So that no place is left for reflection, rational theorizing as a work of and within tradition. And a far more important theorist of tradition has generally been ignored by both Enlightenment and post-Enlightenment theorists, because the particular tradition within which he worked, and from whose point of view he presented his theorizing, was theological. I mean, of course, John Henry Newman, whose account of tradition was itself successively developed in *The Arians of the Fourth Century* and *An Essay on the Development of Christian Doctrine*. But if one is to extend Newman's account from the particular tradition of Catholic Christianity to rational traditions in general, and to do so in a philosophical context very different from any envisaged by Newman, so much qualification and addition is needed that it seems better to proceed independently, having first acknowledged a massive debt.

[. . . .]

The rationality of a tradition-constituted and tradition-constitutive enquiry is in key and essential part a matter of the kind of progress which it makes through a number of well-defined types of stage. Every such form of enquiry begins in and from some condition of pure historical contingency, from the beliefs, institutions, and practices of some particular community which constitute a given. Within such a community authority will have been conferred upon certain texts and certain voices. Bards, priests, prophets, kings, and, on occasion, fools and jesters will all be heard. All such communities are always, to greater or lesser degree, in a state of change. When those educated in the cultures of the societies of imperialist modernity reported that they had discovered certain so-called primitive societies or cultures without change, within which repetition rules rather than transformation, they were deceived in part by their understanding of the claims sometimes made by members of such societies that they are obedient to the dictates of immemorial custom and in part by their own too simple and anachronistic conception of what social and cultural change is.

What takes a given community from a first stage in which the beliefs, utterances, texts, and persons taken to be authoritative are deferred to unquestioningly, or at least without systematic questioning, may be one or more of several types of occurrence. Authoritative texts or utterances may be shown to be susceptible to, by actually receiving, alternative and incompatible interpretations, enjoining perhaps alternative and incompatible courses of action. Incoherences in the established system of beliefs may become evident. Confrontation by new situations, engendering new questions, may reveal within established practices and beliefs a lack of resources for offering or for justifying answers to these new questions. The coming together of two previously separate communities, each with its own well-established institutions, practices, and beliefs, either by migration or by conquest, may open up new alternative possibilities and require more than the existing means of evaluation are able to provide.

[. . . .]

One of the great originating insights of tradition-constituted enquiries is that false beliefs and false judgments represent a failure of the mind, not of its objects. It is mind which stands in need of correction. Those realities which mind encounters reveal themselves as they are, the presented, the manifest, the unhidden. So the most primitive conception of truth is of the manifestness of the objects which present themselves to mind; and it is when mind fails to re-present that manifestness that falsity, the inadequacy of mind to its objects, appears.

This falsity is recognized retrospectively as a past inadequacy when the discrepancy between the beliefs of an earlier stage of a tradition of enquiry are contrasted with the world of things and persons as it has come to be understood at some later stage. So correspondence or the lack of it becomes a feature of a developing complex conception of truth. The relationship of correspondence or of lack of correspondence which holds between the mind and objects is given expression in judgments, but it is not judgments themselves which correspond to objects or indeed to anything else. We may indeed say of a false judgment that things are not as the judgment declares them to be, or of a true judgment that he or she who utters it says that what is is and what is not is not. But there are not two distinguishable items, a judgment on the one hand and that portrayed in the judgment on the other, between which a relationship of correspondence can hold or fail to hold.

The commonest candidate, in modern versions of what is all too often taken to be *the* correspondence theory of truth, for that which corresponds to a judgment in this way is a fact. But facts, like telescopes and wigs for gentlemen, were a seventeenth-century invention. In the sixteenth century and earlier 'fact' in English was usually a rendering of the Latin 'factum', a deed, an action, and sometimes in Scholastic Latin an event or an occasion. It was only in the seventeenth century that 'fact' was first used in the way in which later philosophers such as Russell, Wittgenstein, and Ramsey were to use it. It is of course and always was harmless, philosophically and otherwise, to use the word 'fact' of what a judgment states. What is and was not harmless, but highly misleading, was to conceive of a realm of facts independent of judgment or of any other form of linguistic expression, so that judgments or statements or sentences could be paired off with facts, truth or falsity being the alleged relationship between such paired items. This kind of correspondence theory of truth arrived on the philosophical scene only comparatively recently and has been as conclusively refuted as any theory can be (see, for example, P. F. Strawson, 'Truth'). It is a large error to read it into older formulations concerning truth, such as *adaequatio mentis ad rem*, let alone into that correspondence which I am ascribing to the conception of truth deployed in the early history of the development of traditions.

Those who have reached a certain stage in that development are then able to look back and to identify their own previous intellectual inadequacy or the intellectual inadequacy of their predecessors by comparing what they now judge the world, or at least part of it, to be with what it was then judged to be. To claim truth for one's present mindset and the judgments which are its expression is to claim that this kind of inadequacy, this kind of discrepancy, will never appear in any possible future situation, no matter how searching the enquiry, no matter how much evidence is provided, no matter what developments in rational enquiry may occur. The test for truth in the present, therefore, is always to summon up as many questions and as many objections of the greatest strength possible; what can be justifiably claimed as true is what has sufficiently withstood such dialectical questioning and framing of objections. In what does such sufficiency consist? That too is a question to which answers have to be produced and to which rival and competing answers may well appear. And those answers will compete rationally, just insofar as they are tested dialectically, in order to discover which is the best answer to be proposed so far.

A tradition which reaches this point of development will have become to greater or lesser degree a form of enquiry and will have had to institutionalize and regulate to some extent at least its methods of enquiry. It will have had to recognize intellectual virtues, and questions lie in wait for it about the relationship of such virtues to virtues of character. On these as on other questions conflicts will develop, rival answers will be proposed and accepted or rejected. At some point it may be discovered within some developing tradition that some of the same problems and issues – recognized as the same in the light of the standards internal to this particular tradition – are being debated within some other tradition, and defined areas of agreement and disagreement with such an other tradition may develop. Moreover, conflicts between and within tradition-constituted enquiries will stand in some relationship to those other conflicts which are present in a community which is the bearer of traditions.

There characteristically comes a time in the history of tradition-constituted enquiries when those engaged in them may find occasion or need to frame a theory of their own activities of enquiry. What kind of theory is then developed will of course vary from one tradition to another. Confronted with the multiplicity of uses of 'true', the adherents of one kind of tradition may respond by constructing an analogical account of those uses and of their unity, as Aquinas did, exhibiting in the way in which he went about his task the influence of Aristotle's treatment of the multiplicity of uses of 'good'. By contrast the same multiplicity may evoke an attempt to identify some single, perhaps complex, mark of truth. Descartes, who ought to be understood as a late follower of the Augustinian tradition as well as someone who attempted to refound philosophy *de novo*, did precisely this in appealing to clarity and distinctness as marks of truth. And Hume concluded that he could find no such reliable mark (*A Treatise of Human Nature*, I.iv.7).

Other elements of the theories of rational enquiry so proposed will also vary from tradition to tradition. And it will be in part these differences which result in still further different and rival conclusions concerning the subject matter of substantive enquiries, including topics such as those of justice and of practical rationality. Nonetheless, to some degree, insofar as a tradition of rational enquiry is such, it will tend to recognize what it shares as such with other traditions, and in the development of such traditions common characteristic, if not universal, patterns will appear.

Standard forms of argument will be developed, and requirements for successful dialectical questioning established. The weakest form of argument, but nonetheless that which will prevail in the absence of any other, will be the appeal to the authority of established belief, merely as established. The identification of incoherence within established belief will always provide a reason for enquiring further, but not in itself a conclusive reason for rejecting established belief, until something more adequate because less incoherent has been discovered. At every stage beliefs and judgments will be justified by reference to the beliefs and judgments of the previous stage, and insofar as a tradition has constituted itself as a successful form of enquiry, the claims to truth made within that tradition will always be in some specifiable way less vulnerable to dialectical questioning and objection than were their predecessors.

[. . . .]

We have already noticed that central to a tradition-constituted enquiry at each stage in its development will be its current problematic, that agenda of unsolved problems and unresolved issues by reference to which its success or lack of it in making rational progress toward some further stage of development will be evaluated. At any point it may happen to any tradition-constituted enquiry that by its own standards of progress it ceases to make progress. Its hitherto trusted methods of enquiry have become sterile. Conflicts over rival answers to key questions can no longer be settled rationally. Moreover, it may indeed happen that the use of the methods of enquiry and of the forms of argument, by means of which rational progress had been achieved so far, begins to have the effect of increasingly disclosing new inadequacies, hitherto unrecognized incoherences, and new problems for the solution of which there seem to be insufficient or no resources within the established fabric of belief.

This kind of dissolution of historically founded certitudes is the mark of an epistemological crisis. The solution to a genuine epistemological crisis requires the invention or discovery of new concepts and the framing of some new type or types of theory which meet three highly exacting requirements. First, this in some ways radically new and conceptually enriched scheme, if it is to put an end to epistemological crisis, must furnish a solution to the problems which had previously proved intractable in a systematic and coherent way. Second, it must also provide an explanation of just what it was which rendered the tradition, before it had acquired these new resources, sterile or incoherent or both. And third, these first two tasks must be carried out in a way which exhibits some fundamental continuity of the new conceptual and theoretical structures with the shared beliefs in terms of which the tradition of enquiry had been defined up to this point.

The theses central to the new theoretical and conceptual structures, just because they are significantly richer than and escape the limitations of those theses which were central to the tradition before and as it entered its period of epistemological crisis, will in no way be derivable from those earlier positions. Imaginative conceptual innovation will have had to occur. The justification of the new theses will lie precisely in their ability to achieve what could not have been achieved prior to that innovation. Examples of such successfully creative outcomes to more or less serious epistemological crises, affecting some greater or lesser area of the subject matter with which a particular tradition-constituted enquiry is concerned, are not hard to come by, either in the traditions with whose history I have been concerned here or elsewhere. Newman's own central example was of the way in which in the fourth century the definition of the Catholic doctrine of the Trinity resolved the controversies arising out of competing interpretations of scripture by a use of philosophical and theological concepts whose understanding had itself issued from debates rationally unresolved up to that point. Thus that doctrine provided for the later Augustinian tradition a paradigm of how the three requirements for the resolution of an epistemological crisis could be met. In a very different way Aquinas provided a new and richer conceptual and theoretical framework, without which anyone whose allegiance was given to both the Aristotelian and Augustinian traditions would necessarily have lapsed either into incoherence or, by rejecting one of them, into a sterile onesidedness. And in a different way again, perhaps less successfully, Reid and Stewart attempted to rescue the Scottish tradition from the incoherence with which it was threatened by a combination of Humean epistemological premises with anti-Humean moral and metaphysical conclusions.

In quite other areas of enquiry the same patterns of epistemological crisis are to be found: thus Boltzmann's 1890 derivation of paradoxes from accounts of thermal energy framed in terms of classical mechanics produced an epistemological crisis within physics which was only to be resolved by Bohr's theory of the internal structure of the atom. What this example shows is that an epistemological crisis may only be recognized for what it was in retrospect. It is far from the case that physicists in general understood their discipline to be in crisis between Boltzmann and Bohr. Yet it was, and the power of quantum mechanics lies not only in its freedom from the difficulties and incoherences which came to afflict classical mechanics but also in its ability to furnish an explanation of why the problematic of classical mechanics was bound in the end to engender just such insoluble problems as that discovered by Boltzmann.

To have passed through an epistemological crisis successfully enables the adherents of a tradition of enquiry to rewrite its history in a more insightful way. And such a history of a particular tradition provides not only a way of identifying the continuities in virtue of which that tradition of enquiry has survived and flourished as one and the same tradition, but also of identifying more accurately that structure of justification which underpins whatever claims to truth are made within it, claims which are more and other than claims to warranted assertibility. The concept of warranted assertibility always has application only at some particular time and place in respect of standards then prevailing at some particular stage in the development of a tradition of enquiry, and a claim that such and such is warrantedly assertible always, therefore, has to make implicit or explicit references to such times and places. The concept of truth, however, is timeless. To claim that some thesis is true is not only to claim for all possible times and places that it cannot be shown to fail to correspond to reality in the sense of 'correspond' elucidated earlier but also that the mind which expresses its thought in that thesis is in fact adequate to its object. The implications of this claim made in this way from within a tradition are precisely what enable us to show how the relativist challenge is misconceived.

Every tradition, whether it recognizes the fact or not, confronts the possibility that at some future time it will fall into a state of epistemological crisis, recognizable as such by its own standards of rational justification, which have themselves been vindicated up to that time as the best to emerge from the history of that particular tradition. All attempts to deploy the imaginative and inventive resources which the adherents of the tradition can provide may founder, either merely by doing nothing to remedy the condition of sterility and incoherence into which the enquiry has fallen or by also revealing or creating new problems, and revealing new flaws and new limitations. Time may elapse, and no further resources or solutions emerge.

That particular tradition's claims to truth can at some point in this process no longer be sustained. And this by itself is enough to show that if part of the relativist's thesis is that each tradition, since it provides its own standards of rational justification, must always be vindicated in the light of those standards, then on this at least the relativist is mistaken. But whether the relativist has claimed this or not, a further even more important possibility now becomes clear. For the adherents of a tradition which is now in this state of fundamental and radical crisis may at this point encounter in a new way the claims of some particular rival tradition, perhaps one with which they have for some time coexisted, perhaps one which they are now encountering for the first time. They now come or had already come to understand the beliefs and way of life of this other alien tradition, and to do so they have or have had to learn [. . .] the language of the alien tradition as a new and second first language.

When they have understood the beliefs of the alien tradition, they may find themselves compelled to recognize that within this other tradition it is possible to construct from the concepts and theories peculiar to it what they were unable to provide from their own conceptual and theoretical resources, a cogent and illuminating explanation – cogent and illuminating, that is, by their own standards – of why their own intellectual tradition had been unable to solve its problems or restore its coherence. The standards by which they judge this explanation to be cogent and illuminating will be the very same standards by which they have found their tradition wanting in the face of epistemological crisis. But while this new explanation satisfies two of the requirements for an adequate response to an epistemological crisis within a tradition – insofar as it *both* explains why, given the structures of enquiry within that tradition, the crisis had to happen as it did *and* does not itself suffer from the same defects of incoherence or resourcelessness, the recognition of which had been the initial stage of their crisis – it fails to satisfy the third. Derived as it is from a genuinely alien tradition, the new explanation does not stand in any sort of substantive continuity with the preceding history of the tradition in crisis.

In this kind of situation the rationality of tradition requires an acknowledgment by those who have hitherto inhabited and given their allegiance to the tradition in crisis that the alien tradition is superior in rationality and in respect of its claims to truth to their own. What the explanation afforded from within the alien tradition will have disclosed is a lack of correspondence between the dominant beliefs of their own tradition and the reality disclosed by the most successful explanation, and it may well be the only successful explanation which they have been able to discover. Hence the claim to truth for what have hitherto been their own beliefs has been defeated.

From the fact that rationality, so understood, requires this acknowledgment of defeat in respect of truth, it does not of course follow that there will be actual acknowledgment. When the late medieval physics of nature was defeated in just this way by Galileo and his successors, there were not lacking physicists who continued to deny both the facts of the epistemological crisis which had afflicted impetus theory and Galileo's, and later Newton's success in providing a theory which not only did not suffer from the defects of impetus theory, but which was able to furnish the materials for an explanation of why nature is such that impetus theory could not have avoided the discovery of its own resourcelessness and incoherence, at just the points at which these defects in fact appeared. The physics of Galileo and Newton identified the phenomena of nature in such a way as to reveal the lack of correspondence between what impetus theory asserted about the phenomena of motion and the character which those phenomena had now turned out to possess and, in so doing, deprived impetus theory of warrant for its claim to truth.

It is important to remember at this point that not all epistemological crises are resolved so successfully. Some indeed are not resolved, and their lack of resolution itself defeats the tradition which has issued in such crises, without at the same time vindicating the claims of any other. Thus a tradition can be rationally discredited by and in the light of appeal to its very own standards of rationality in more than one way. These are the possibilities which the relativist challenge has failed to envisage. That challenge relied upon the argument that if each tradition carries within it its own standards of rational justification, then, insofar as traditions of enquiry are genuinely distinct and different from each other, there is no way in which each tradition can enter into rational debate with any other, and no such tradition can therefore vindicate its rational superiority over its rivals. But if this were so, then there could be no good reason to give one's allegiance to the standpoint of any one tradition rather than to that of any other. This argument can now be seen to be unsound. It is first of all untrue, and the preceding argument shows it to be untrue, that traditions, understood as each possessing its own account of and practices of rational justification, therefore cannot defeat or be defeated by other traditions. It is in respect of their adequacy or inadequacy in their responses to epistemological crises that traditions are vindicated or fail to be vindicated. It does of course follow that something like the relativist charge would hold of any self-contained mode of thought which was not developed to the point at which epistemological crises could become a real possibility. But that is not true of the type of tradition of enquiry discussed in this book. So far as they are concerned therefore, the relativist challenge fails.

[. . . .]

The conclusion of the preceding chapter was that it is an illusion to suppose that there is some neutral standing ground, some locus for rationality as such, which can afford rational resources sufficient for enquiry independent of all traditions. Those who have maintained otherwise either have covertly been adopting the standpoint of a tradition and deceiving themselves and perhaps others into supposing that theirs was just such a neutral standing ground or else have simply been in error. The person outside all traditions lacks sufficient rational resources for enquiry and *a fortiori* for enquiry into what tradition is to be rationally preferred. He or she has no adequate relevant means of rational evaluation and hence can come to no well-grounded conclusion, including the conclusion that no tradition can vindicate itself against any other. To be outside all traditions is to be a stranger to enquiry; it is to be in a state of intellectual and moral destitution, a condition from which it is impossible to issue the relativist challenge.

[. . . .]

Perspectivism, . . . like relativism, is a doctrine only possible for those who regard themselves as outsiders, as uncommitted or rather as committed only to acting a succession of temporary parts. From their point of view any conception of truth but the most minimal appears to have been discredited. And from the standpoint afforded by the rationality of tradition-constituted enquiry it is clear that such persons are by their stance excluded from the possession of any concept of truth adequate for systematic rational enquiry. Hence theirs is not so much a conclusion about truth as an exclusion from it and thereby from rational debate.

Nietzsche came to understand this very well. The perspectivist must not engage in dialectical argument with Socrates, for that way would lie what from our point of view would be involvement in a tradition of rational enquiry, and from Nietzsche's point of view subjection to the tyranny of reason. Socrates is not to be argued with; he is to be mocked for his ugliness and his bad manners. Such mockery in response to dialectic is enjoined in the aphoristic paragraphs of *Götzen-Dämmerung*. And the use of aphorism is itself instructive. An aphorism is not an argument. Gilles Deleuze has called it 'a play of forces' (and see more generally 'Pensée nomade'), something by means of which energy is transmitted rather than conclusions reached.

Nietzsche is of course not the only intellectual ancestor of modern perspectivism and perhaps not at all of modern relativism. Durkheim, however, provided a clue to the ancestry of both when he described in the late nineteenth century how the breakdown of traditional forms of social relationship increased the incidence of *anomie*, of normlessness. *Anomie*, as Durkheim characterized it, was a form of deprivation, of a loss of membership in those social institutions and modes in which norms, including the norms of tradition-constituted rationality, are embodied. What Durkheim did not foresee was a time when the same condition of *anomie* would be assigned the status of an achievement by and a reward for a self, which had, by separating itself from the social relationships of traditions, succeeded, so it believed, in emancipating itself. This self-defined success becomes in different versions the freedom from bad faith of the Sartrian individual who rejects determinate social roles, the homelessness of Deleuze's nomadic thinker and the presupposition of Derrida's choice between remaining 'within', although a stranger to, the already constructed social and intellectual edifice, but only in order to deconstruct it from within, or brutally placing oneself outside in a condition of rupture and discontinuity. What Durkheim saw as social pathology is now presented wearing the masks of philosophical pretension.

The most obtrusive feature of this kind of philosophy is its temporariness; dwelling too long in any one place will always threaten to confer upon such philosophy the continuity of enquiry, so that it becomes embodied as one more rational tradition. It turns out to be forms of tradition which present a threat to perspectivism rather than vice versa.

[. . . .]

First Principles, Final Ends and Contemporary Philosophical Issues

I

Nothing is more generally unacceptable in recent philosophy than any conception of a first principle. Standpoints mutually at odds with each other in so many other ways, of analytic or continental or pragmatic provenance, agree in this rejection. And yet the concept of a first principle seems to have been for Aquinas, just as it had been for Aristotle, and before him for Plato, in itself unproblematic. For both Aquinas and Aristotle, of course, difficult questions do arise about such issues as the relationship of subordinate principles to first principles, the nature of our knowledge of first principles and the differences between the first principles of the different sciences. But in their writings debate even about such complex issues seems always to presuppose as not to be put in question, as never yet having been seriously put in question, the very idea of a first principle.

It is then unsurprisingly in the context of philosophical preoccupations and through the medium of philosophical idioms quite alien to those of either Aristotle or Aquinas that the very idea of a first principle has now been radically put in question, preoccupations which it is, therefore, difficult to address directly from a Thomistic standpoint with only the resources afforded by Aquinas and his predecessors. Hence, it seems that, if this central Aristotelian and Thomistic concept is to be effectively defended, in key part it will have to be by drawing upon philosophical resources which are themselves – at least at first sight – as alien to, or almost as alien to, Thomism as are the theses and arguments which have been deployed against it. We inhabit a time in the history of philosophy in which Thomism can only develop adequate responses to the rejections of its central positions in what must seem initially at least to be unThomistic ways.

To acknowledge this is not to suggest that Aquinas's central positions ought to be substantially reworked or revised in some accommodation to the standpoints of those rejections. It is rather that, in order to restate and to defend those positions in something like their original integrity, it is necessary in our time to approach them indirectly through an internal critique of those theses and arguments which have displaced them, a critique dictated by Thomistic ends, but to be carried through in part at least by somewhat unThomistic means.

Yet if such a critique is genuinely to be directed by Thomistic ends it is worth reminding ourselves at the outset just how foreign to contemporary modes and fashions of thought the Aristotelian and Thomistic concept of a first principle is in at least two ways, one concerned with the firstness of first principles, the other with the difference between standard modern uses of the word '*principle*' in English – and its cognates in other contemporary languages – and the meaning given to '*principium*' by Aquinas and to '*archē*' by Aristotle. Let me begin with the latter.

'*Principium*' as a translation of '*archē*' preserves what from a contemporary English-speaking point of view seems like a double meaning. For us a principle is something expressed in language, something which in the form of either a statement or an injunction can function as a premise in arguments. And so it is sometimes for Aquinas who uses '*principium*' of an axiom furnishing a syllogism with a premise (*Commentary on the Posterior Analytics*, I.5) and speaks of a principle as composed of subject and predicate (*Summa Theoloqiae*, Ia.17.3). But Aquinas also uses '*principium*' in speaking of that to which such principles refer, referring to the elements into which composite bodies can be resolved and by reference to which they can be explained as the '*principia*' of those bodies (*Exposition of Boethius's De Trinitate*, V.4). In fact, '*principium*', as used by Aquinas, names simultaneously the principle (in our sense) and that of which the principle speaks, but not in a way that gives to '*principium*' two distinct and discrete meanings, although it can be used with either or both of two distinct references. For when we do indeed have a *principium*, we have to comprehend the principle *and* that of which it speaks in a single act of comprehension; we can only comprehend the principle *as* it refers us to that of which it speaks and we can only comprehend that of which it speaks *as* articulated and formulated in the principle.

The habits of speech required of us to say this go against the contemporary linguistic grain. And certainly sometimes it does no harm to speak of '*principium*' as though our contemporary conception of principle were all that is involved, but we always have to remember that '*principium*', like '*archē*', is a concept which unites what contemporary idiom divides. A concept with a similar structure is that of *aitia* or *causa*. We in the idioms of our contemporary speech distinguish sharply causes from explanations, but cause is always explanation-affording and *aitia qua* explanation is always cause-specifying. In both cases, that of *aitia/causa* and that of *archē/principium* the modern question: 'Are you speaking of what is or of the mind's apprehension though language of what is?' misses and obscures the conceptual point, which is that the application of this type of concept, when sufficiently justified, gives expression to a coincidence of the mind with what is, to a certain kind of achievement in the mind's movement towards its goal. So it is that *causa* and *principium* are to be adequately elucidated only within a scheme of thought in which the mind moves towards its own proper end, its *telos*, an achieved state in which it is informed by an understanding of its own progress towards that end, an understanding completed by an apprehension of first principles. The meaning of these expressions is not independent of the context of theory within which they are employed.

In recognizing this we encounter a familiar truth about radical philosophical disagreements. Theory and idiom are to some significant degree inseparable. Insofar as I try to deny your theory, but continue to use your idiom, it may be that I shall be trapped into presupposing just what I aspire to deny. And correspondingly the more radical the disagreement over theory, the larger the possibility that each party will find itself misrepresented in the idioms of its rivals, idioms which exclude rather than merely lack the conceptual resources necessary for the statement of its position. So it has been to some significant degree with Thomism in its encounter with post-Cartesian philosophies.

This linguistic difficulty is reinforced by the barrier posed by the conviction which I noticed at the outset, one shared both by different, often mutually antagonistic schools of contemporary philosophy and by the culture of modernity at large, that no principle is or can be first as such. To treat a principle as a first principle is always, on this view, to choose to do so for some particular purpose within some particular context. So we in one type of formal system may wish to treat as a derived theorem what in another is treated as an axiom. Justificatory chains of reasoning generally terminate with what members of some particular social group are willing, for the moment at least, to take for granted; this type of agreement is all that is necessary to serve our contemporary justificatory purposes. But it is not just that the firstness of first principles has been relativized to social contexts and individual purposes. It is also that the range of such purposes is taken to be indefinitely various. And what the purposes of each of us are to be is taken to be a matter of our individual temperaments, interests, desires and decisions.

This contemporary universe of discourse thus has no place within it for any conception of fixed ends, of ends to be discovered rather than decided upon or invented, and that is to say that it has no place for the type of *telos* or *finis* which provides the activity of a particular kind of being with a goal to which it must order its purposes or fail to achieve its own specific perfection in its activity. And this exclusion of the concept of *telos/finis*, I shall want to suggest, is closely related to the exclusion of the concept of *archē/principium*. Genuinely first principles, so I shall argue, can have a place only within a universe characterized in terms of certain determinate, fixed and unalterable ends, ends which provide a standard by reference to which our individual purposes, desires, interests and decisions can be evaluated as well or badly directed. For in practical life it is the *telos* which provides the *archē*, the first principle of practical reasoning: 'Deductive arguments concerning what is to be done have an *archē*. Since such and such is the *telos* and the best . . .' (*Nicomachean Ethics*, 1144a32–35), says Aristotle; and Aquinas comments that this reference to the end in the first principle of practical syllogisms has a parallel in the way in which the first principle of theoretical syllogisms are formulated (*Commentary on the Ethics*, VI.10.17). And it could scarcely be otherwise since the *archai/principia* of theory furnish the theoretical intellect with its specific *telos/finis*. *Archē/principium* and *telos/finis*, so it must seem, stand or fall together.

II

Within distinctively modern schemes of thought they are, of course, taken to have fallen quite some time ago. And when Thomists, therefore, find their central theses concerning *archē/principium* and *telos/finis* rejected within contemporary culture at large as well as within philosophy, it may be tempting to proceed by way of an immediate rejection of the rejection, but this temptation must be resisted. For it will turn out that the considerations which in the context of contemporary discourse are taken to either support or presuppose denials of the possibility of there being either first principles or final ends are in fact theses which for the most part a Thomist should have no interest in denying. What he or she must have the strongest interest in denying are the implications which are commonly nowadays supposed to follow from these.

The first of such theses denies that there are or can be what I shall call epistemological first principles, the type of first principle of which the Cartesian cogito, as usually understood, provides a paradigmatic instance. Such a first principle was required to fulfill two functions. On the one hand, it had to warrant an immediate justified certitude on the part of any rational person who uttered it in the appropriate way, perhaps in the appropriate circumstances. It belongs, that is, to the same class of statements as 'I am in pain', 'This is red here now' and 'I am now thinking'. But, on the other hand, it had, either by itself or as a member of a set of such statements, to provide an ultimate warrant for all our claims to knowledge. Only in virtue of their derivation from it could other statements meet the challenge: How do you know *that*? And the importance of being able to answer this question is not just to rebut those who express scepticism. For since on this view knowledge involves justified certainty and justified certainty requires that, if I genuinely know, I also know that I know, then as a rational person I must be able to answer the question 'How do I know?' in respect of each knowledge claim that I make.

Yet, as by now has often enough been pointed out, no statement or set of statements is capable of fulfilling both these functions. The kind of substantive content required for statements which could function as the initial premises in a deductive justification of the sciences, theoretical or practical, precludes the kind of justified immediate certitude required for this kind of epistemological starting-point, and vice versa. Epistemological first principles, thus conceived, are mythological beasts.

Two kinds of reflection may be provoked in a Thomist by these by now commonplace antifoundational arguments. A first concerns the way in which they leave the Aristotelian or Thomistic conception of *archē/ principium* unscathed. For where the protagonists of the type of foundationalist epistemological first principle, which is now for the most part, even if not universally rejected, characterized those principles so that they had to meet two sets of requirements, each of which could in fact only be met by some principle which failed in respect to the other, Aquinas, as a result of having reflected upon both Aristotle and Boethius, distinguished two different types of evidentness belonging to two different kinds of principle (see, for example, *Summa Theologiae*, IaIIae.94.2).

There are, on the one hand, those evident principles, the meaning of whose terms is immediately to be comprehended by every competent language user, such as 'Every whole is greater than its part', principles which are, therefore, undeniable by any such language user. There are, on the other hand, principles which are to be understood as evident only in the context of the conceptual framework of some more or less large-scale theory, principles expressed in judgments known as evident only to those with an intellectual grasp of the theoretical framework in which they are embedded, that is, as Aquinas puts it, to the wise. It is such judgments which are used to state first principles with substantive content, and their function and the requirements which they have to meet are very different from those of the former type of principle. We should, of course, note that even the former type of principle can, in the light of its applications, be understood in greater depth by those who are theoretically sophisticated than it is by the merely competent language user. But with the distinction between what is immediately apprehended, but not substantive in content, and what is substantive in content, but known as evident only through theoretical achievement, the Thomist distinguishes what the protagonist of epistemological first principles misleadingly assimilates and so remains untouched by this thrust at least of contemporary antifoundationalism.

Yet there is an even more fundamental way in which contemporary hostility to epistemological foundationalism misses the point so far as Thomistic first principles are concerned. For if the Thomist is faithful to the intentions of Aristotle and Aquinas, he or she will not be engaged, except perhaps incidentally, in an epistemological enterprise. The refutation of skepticism will appear to him or her as misguided an enterprise as it does to the Wittgensteinian. Generations of neo-Thomists from Kleutgen onwards have, of course, taught us to think otherwise, and textbooks on epistemology have been notable among the standard impedimenta of neo-Thomism. What in part misled their writers was the obvious fact that Aquinas, like Aristotle, furnishes an account of knowledge. What they failed to discern adequately was the difference between the Aristotelian or Thomistic enterprise and the epistemological enterprise. (See Mark Jordan, *Ordering Wisdom*, pp. 118–19.)

The epistemological enterprise is by its nature a first-person project. How can *I*, so the epistemologist enquires, be assured that *my* beliefs, *my* perceptions, *my* judgments connect with reality external to them, so that *I* can have justified certitude regarding their truth and error? A radical skeptic is an epistemologist with entirely negative findings. He or she, like other epistemologists, takes him or herself to speak from within his or her mind of its relationship to what is external to it and perhaps alien to it. But the Thomist, if he or she follows Aristotle and Aquinas, constructs an account both of approaches to and of the achievement of knowledge from a third-person point of view. My mind or rather my soul is only one among many and its own knowledge of my self *qua* soul has to be integrated into a general account of souls and their teleology. Insofar as a given soul moves successfully towards its successive intellectual goals in a teleologically ordered way, it moves towards completing itself by becoming formally identical with the objects of its knowledge, so that it is adequate to those objects, objects that are then no longer external to it, but rather complete it. So the mind in finding application for its concepts refers them beyond itself and themselves to what they conceptualize. Hence the double reference of concepts which we already noticed in the cases of *archē/principium* and *aitia/causa*. The mind, actualized in knowledge, responds to the object as the object is and as it would be, independently of the mind's knowledge of it. The mind knows itself only in the second-order knowledge of its own operations and is known also by others in those operations. But even such knowledge when achieved need not entail certitude of a Cartesian sort.

'It is difficult to discern whether one knows or not,' said Aristotle (*Posterior Analytics*, 76a26). And Aquinas glosses this by saying that 'It is difficult to discern whether we know from appropriate principles, which alone is genuinely scientific knowing, or do not know from appropriate principles' (*Commentary on the Posterior Analytics*, I.18). The contrast with Cartesianism could not be sharper. If, on the view of Aristotle and Aquinas, one genuinely knows at all, then one knows as one would know if one knew in the light of the relevant set of first principles, but one may, nonetheless, genuinely know, without as yet possessing that further knowledge of first principles and of their relationship to this particular piece of knowledge which would finally vindicate one's claim. All knowledge even in the initial stages of enquiry is a partial achievement and completion of the mind, but it nonetheless points beyond itself to a more final achievement in ways that we may not as yet have grasped. Hence, we can know without as yet knowing that we know, while for the Cartesian, as I remarked earlier, if we know, we must know that we know, since for the Cartesian it is always reference backwards to our starting-point that guarantees our knowledge and, hence, it is only through knowing that we know that we know. By contrast, for the Thomist our present knowledge involves reference forward to that knowledge of the *archē/principium* which will, if we achieve it, give us subsequent knowledge of the knowledge that we now have.

In this relationship of what we now know to what we do not as yet know, a relationship in which what we only as yet know potentially is presupposed by what we already know actually, there is to be observed a certain kind of circularity. This is not, of course, the type of circularity the presence of which vitiates a demonstrative argument. It is the circularity of which Aquinas speaks in endorsing Aristotle's view 'that before an induction or syllogism is formed to beget knowledge of a conclusion, that conclusion is somehow known and somehow not known' (*Commentary on the Posterior Analytics*, I.3). The conclusion which is to be the end of our deductively or inductively (Aristotelian *epagōgē*, not Humean induction) reasoned enquiry is somehow already assumed in our starting-point. Were it not so, that particular type of starting-point would not be pointing us towards this particular type of conclusion (*Disputed Questions on Truth*, XI, 1).

Consider an example from the life of practice. Aquinas follows Aristotle in holding that one reason why the young are incapable of adequate reflective moral theorizing is that they have not as yet that experience of actions which would enable them to frame adequate moral and political arguments (*Nicomachean Ethics*, 1095a2–3; *Commentary on the Ethics*, I.3). But not any experience of human actions will provide adequate premises for sound practical reasoning. Only a life whose actions have been directed by and whose passions have been disciplined and transformed by the practice of the moral and intellectual virtues and the social relationships involved in and defined by such practice will provide the kind of experience from which and about which reliable practical inferences and sound theoretical arguments about practice can be derived. But from the outset the practice of those virtues in an adequately and increasingly determinate way already presupposes just those truths about the good and the best for human beings, about the *telos* for human beings, which it is the object of moral and political enquiry to discover. So the only type of moral and political enquiry through which and in which success can be achieved is one in which the end is to some significant degree presupposed in the beginning, in which initial actualities presuppose and give evidence of potentiality for future development.

This ineliminable circularity is not a sign of some flaw in Aristotelian or Thomistic conceptions of enquiry. It is, I suspect, a feature of any large-scale philosophical system which embodies a conception of enquiry, albeit an often unacknowledged feature. And it could only be thought a flaw from a standpoint still haunted by a desire to find some point of origin for enquiry which is entirely innocent of that which can only emerge later from that enquiry. It is this desire – for an origin which is not an origin – which plainly haunts much of the work of Jacques Derrida (see, for example, *Of Grammatology*, p. 65, and the discussion by Peter Dews in chapter 1 of *Logics of Disintegration*) and which thus informs, even if somewhat paradoxically, the second major contemporary philosophical rejection of any substantive conception of first principles, one very different from its analytic antifoundationalist counterpart.

The most obvious difference is, of course, that, whereas the analytic rejection focuses upon epistemological considerations, the deconstructionist rejection formulated by Derrida focuses upon questions of meaning. What set the stage for Derrida's critique of what he took to be a metaphysical and, therefore, obfuscating understanding of meaning was the structuralist thesis, developed out of a particular way of interpreting Saussure, that in the structures of linguistic systems it is relationships of a certain kind which determine the identity and meaning of terms and not vice versa. It is in and through binary relationships of opposition and difference that such identity and meaning are constituted.

The stability of meaning is thus taken to depend upon the character of the oppositions and differences between terms. And a key part of Derrida's deconstructive work was to show that the oppositions between pairs of terms crucial to metaphysics, such counterpart pairs as form/matter, sensible/intelligible, and passive/active, seem to collapse into each other insofar as the meaning and application of each term already presupposes the meaning and applicability of its counterpart, and hence no term provides an independent stable, unchanging point of definition for its counterpart. Insofar as this is so, any stable meaning is dependent upon something not yet said, and since these metaphysical oppositions are in the relevant respects no different from the binary oppositions which on this type of poststructuralist view constitute language-in-use in general, it is a general truth that the meaning of what is uttered is always in a similar way dependent on some further not yet provided ground for meaning, but there is no such ground waiting to be attained, so that stable meaning is never achieved. So a deconstructive denial of first principles emerges from an analysis of meaning, as part of the denial of the possibility of metaphysical grounding for *anything*. But why does Derrida believe that there can be no such ground?

It is here that Derrida is open to more than one reading. For sometimes it seems that it is from the way in which the terms of his metaphysical pairs each presuppose the other, so that neither member of such pairs can provide an independent grounding for the meaning, identity and applicability of the other, that Derrida is arguing to the conclusion that there can be no grounding for metaphysical thought and theory of the kind which he takes it to require. But at other times he seems to move from the denial of the possibility of such a grounding, on occasion referring us to Heidegger and to Nietzsche, towards conclusions about the consequent instability of meaning exemplified in such terms.

Yet in either case what Derrida presents us with is a strange mirror-image inversion of Thomism. For the Thomist has no problem either with the notion that, where such pairs as form and matter or potentiality and act are concerned, each term is and must be partially definable by reference to the other, or with the view that when such terms are applied at some early or intermediate stage in an enquiry the full meaning of what has been said is yet to emerge and will only emerge when the relevant set of first principles is as fully specified as that particular enquiry requires. Terms are applied analogically, in respect both of meaning and of use, and the grounding of meaning and use through analogy is by reference to some ultimate *archē/principium*. So that stability of meaning, on a Thomist view, is tied to a metaphysically conceived ground, just as Derrida asserts, and the denial of that ground, it follows equally for the Thomist and the deconstructionist, could not but issue in systematic instability of meaning. Yet, if the entailments are the same, the direction of the arguments which they inform is, of course, different. So why move in the deconstructive rather than in the Thomistic direction?

To state Derrida's answer to this justly and adequately would require me to go further into the detail of his position than is possible on this occasion. What is possible is to sketch one central relevant deconstructive thesis which may illuminate what is at stake in the disagreement. For Derrida as for deconstructive thought generally, any metaphysically conceived ground, such as an *archē/principium* would supply, would have to function in two incompatible ways. It would have to exist outside of and independently of discourse, since upon it discourse is to be grounded, and it would have to be present in discourse, since it is only as linguistically conceived and presented that it could be referred to. But these are plainly incompatible requirements, the first of which in any case violates Derrida's dictum that there is nothing outside text. (Notice the instructive resemblances between Derrida's denials and Hilary Putnam's attacks on what he calls external or metaphysical realism in, for example, chapter 3 of *Reason, Truth and History*.) So the binary oppositions of meaning cannot be referred beyond themselves to some first principle and meaning must be unstable.

This deconstructive rejection of first principles raises some of the same questions which arise from the analytic antifoundationalist's rejection. To what kind of reasoning is each appealing in justifying and commending their rejection? Is it a kind of reasoning which is itself consistent with those rejections? Or do those rejections themselves destroy any basis for the reasoning which led to them? Consider the impasse into which thought is led by the difficulties involved in two rival types of answers to those questions. On the one hand, it is easy to construe both the analytic antifoundationalist and the deconstructive critic as offering what are taken to be compelling arguments as to the impossibility of grounding either justificatory argument or discourse itself by means of appeal to some set of first principles. But if these arguments have succeeded in respect of cogency, it can surely be only in virtue of their deriving their conclusions from premises which are in some way or other undeniable. Yet the impossibility of such undeniable premises seems to follow from the conclusions of these same arguments. So can those arguments be construed in a way which will avoid self-deconstruction? This is a more than rhetorical question.

On the other hand, if we begin by taking seriously the thought that there are no in principle undeniable premises – whatever the type of principle – for substantive arguments, then the undeniability claimed must be of some other kind. But the most plausible attempts hitherto to elucidate the notion of an undeniability for the premises of deconstructive and antifoundationalist argument, which is not an undeniability in principle, have resulted in some conception of an undeniability rooted in some particular kind of social agreement. Characterizations of the nature of the social agreement involved have differed widely: more than one of the rival views contending in this area appeals to Wittgenstein, others to Kuhn, others again to Foucault.

Disagreement on these issues by a multiplicity of contending parties, grounded in their shared rejection of metaphysical first principles, indeed of first principles as such, is pervasive in its effects and manifestations both within academic philosophy and outside it, both in the literary and social scientific disciplines and in the rhetorical modes of the culture at large. In the latter it appears in the now, it seems, perpetually renewed debates over continually reformulated end-of-ideology theses; the end of ideology is in politics what the refutation of metaphysics is in philosophy. Within academia it appears in the unsettled and, as I shall claim, unsettlable debates which are now carried on between historicists and antihistoricists, realists and antirealists, pragmaticists and antipragmaticists.

It is at this point that the Thomist has to resist the temptation of premature self-congratulation. For, if it is indeed the case, as I have suggested, that the Aristotelian and Thomistic conception of *archē/ principium* survives unscathed both the analytic antifoundationalist and the deconstructive critique of first principles, it would be all too easy to announce victory. Yet this would be a serious mistake. For it is not so much that Thomism has emerged unscathed from two serious philosophical encounters as that no serious philosophical encounter has as yet taken place. The Thomistic conception of a first principle is untouched by contemporary radical critiques in key part because the cultural, linguistic and philosophical distance between it and them is now so great that they are no longer able seriously to envisage the possibility of such a conception. If then serious encounter is to occur, and the Thomistic understanding of the tasks of natural human reason functioning philosophically makes such encounter mandatory, it can only occur insofar as Thomism can speak relevantly of and to those critiques and the debates which arise out of them, even if they cannot speak of it. The question which I am posing, then, is that of what light the Aristotelian and Thomistic conception of *archē/principium* can throw on such critiques and debates. But a necessary preliminary to that question is a more adequate statement of what that conception is and involves.

III

Aquinas introduced his commentary on the *Posterior Analytics* by distinguishing the task of analyzing judgments within a science, with a view to explaining their warrant and the kind of certitude to which we are entitled by that warrant, from the task of giving an account of investigation. In so distinguishing he pointed towards the resolution of a problem about what Aristotle was trying to achieve in the *Posterior Analytics* which has engaged the attention of some modern commentators.

This problem arises from an evident contrast between the account of the structure of scientific understanding and of how it is achieved which is provided in the *Posterior Analytics* and the way in which Aristotle carries out his own scientific enquiries in the *Physics* and in the biological treatises. If, as has often enough been assumed by modern commentators, the *Posterior Analytics* is Aristotle's theory of scientific method, while the *Physics* and the biological treatises are applications of Aristotle's scientific method, then the discrepancy between the former and the latter is obvious and striking. What the first expounds is just not what the second practices. There have indeed been scholars who have, nonetheless, attempted to deny that there is any problem here. But their arguments have not withstood the test of debate, and it would now be generally agreed that, whatever the method or methods of enquiry put to work in the *Physics* and the biological treatises, they are not the methods described in the *Posterior Analytics*. How then is the discrepancy to be explained?

Is it perhaps that Aristotle changed his mind some time after writing the *Posterior Analytics*? Is it, as some scholars have maintained, that the *Posterior Analytics* is an account only of the mathematical sciences? Or is it, as Jonathan Barnes has argued ('Aristotle's Theory of Demonstration'), after decisively refuting this latter suggestion, that the *Posterior Analytics* is not designed to teach us how to acquire knowledge, but rather how to present knowledge already achieved, that is, that the *Posterior Analytics* is a manual for teachers? There is no problem in agreeing with much of what Barnes says in favor of this view, provided that we do not take the criteria of sound scientific demonstration to be upheld primarily or only because of their pedagogical effectiveness. It is rather that we can learn from the *Posterior Analytics* how to present achieved knowledge and understanding to others only because of what it primarily is: an account of what achieved and perfected knowledge is.

Why do I say this? Not only because everything in the text is consistent with this view, but also because Aristotle's system of thought requires just such an account and it is nowhere else supplied. The *Physics* and the biological treatises report scientific enquiries which are still in progress, moving towards, but not yet having reached the *telos* appropriate to, and providing implicit or explicit guidance for, those specific types of activity. Clearly there must, on an Aristotelian view, be such a *telos*. And we need to know what it is, something only to be found, if anywhere, in the *Posterior Analytics*. So my claim is that the *Posterior Analytics* is an account of what it is or would be to possess, to have already achieved, a perfected science, a perfected type of understanding, in which every movement of a mind within the structures of that type of understanding gives expression to the adequacy of that mind to its objects.

Of course, in furnishing an account of what perfected and achieved understanding and knowledge are, Aristotle could not avoid the task of specifying, in part at least, the relationship between prior states of imperfect and partial understanding and that final state. And it was perhaps by attending too exclusively to what he tells us about this relationship and these prior states that earlier commentators were led to misconstrue Aristotle's intentions. But what matters about his discussions of understanding still in the process of formation, still in progress, in the *Posterior Analytics* is the light cast thereby on the way in which the *telos* of perfected understanding is already presupposed in partial understanding, and this is a concern very different from that of the *Physics* or of the biological treatises. So that when Aquinas in the introduction to his commentary distinguished the subject-matter of the *Posterior Analytics* from any concern with the nature of investigation, he correctly directed our attention to the place of the *Posterior Analytics* within Aristotle's works.

The *telos/finis* of any type of systematic activity is, on an Aristotelian and Thomistic view, that end internal to activity of that specific kind, for the sake of which and in the direction of which activity of that kind is carried forward. Many types of activity, of course, are intelligible as human activities only because and insofar as they are embedded in some other type of activity, and some types of such activity may be embedded in any one of a number of other types of intelligible activity. So it is, for example, with tree-felling, which may as an activity be part of and embedded in an architectural project of building a house or a manufacturing project of making fine papers or an ecological project of strengthening a forest as a habitat for certain species. It is these more inclusive and relatively self-sufficient forms of systematic activity which serve distinctive human goods, so that the *telos/finis* of each is to be characterized in terms of some such good. So the *Posterior Analytics* in its account of scientific demonstrative explanations as the *telos/finis* of enquiry furnishes us with an account of what it is to understand, that is, of the distinctive human good to be achieved by enquiry as a distinctive type of activity.

Achieved understanding is the *theoretical* goal of the *practical* activity of enquiry. Neither Aristotle nor Aquinas themselves discuss the theory of the practical activity of theoretically aimed enquiry in a systematic way, although some of Aristotle's discussions in the *Topics* are highly relevant and Aquinas rightly understood the *Topics* as a partial guide to such activity. Moreover, elsewhere in both Aristotle and Aquinas incidental remarks and discussions abound (see especially *Exposition of Boethius's De Trinitate*, VI.1). But to make use of those remarks and discussion we must first say what, on the view taken by Aristotle and Aquinas, achieved understanding is. In so doing we shall find both that Aquinas, while generally endorsing Aristotle, goes beyond Aristotle's theses, and that later discussions of enquiry by non-Aristotelian and non-Thomistic writers can be put to good use in extending the Aristotelian account still further. So that although I shall be going over largely familiar and even overfamiliar ground, it may not always be in an entirely familiar way.

A perfected science is one which enables us to understand the phenomena of which it treats as necessarily being what they are, will be and have been, because of the variety of agencies which have brought it about that form of specific kinds has informed the relevant matter in such a way as to achieve some specific end state. All understanding is thus in terms of the essential properties of specific kinds. What those kinds are, how they are to be characterized, what the end state is to which those individuals which exemplify them move or are moved, those are matters about which – it seems plain from Aristotle's own scientific treatises as well as from modern scientific enquiry – there may well have been changes of view and even radical changes of view in the course of enquiry. The final definition of these matters in a perfected science may be the outcome of a number of reformulations and reclassifications which have come about in the course of enquiry.

The mind which has achieved this perfected understanding in some particular area represents what it understands – the form of understanding and the form of what is understood necessarily coincide in perfected understanding; that is what it is to understand – by a deductive scheme in whose hierarchical structure the different levels of causal explanation are embodied. To give an explanation is to provide a demonstrative argument which captures part of this structure. What causal explanation enables us to distinguish is genuine causality from mere coincidence. The regularities of coincidence are striking features of the universe which we inhabit, but they are not part of the subject-matter of science, for there is no necessity in their being as they are. It follows from this account that in each distinctive form of achieved understanding, each science, there are a set of first principles, *archai/principia*, which provide premises for demonstrative arguments and which specify the ultimate causal agencies, material, formal, efficient and final for that science. It follows also that, insofar as the perfected sciences are themselves hierarchically organized, the most fundamental of sciences will specify that in terms of which everything that can be understood is to be understood. And this, as Aquinas remarks in a number of places, we call God.

There is then an ineliminable theological dimension – theological, that is, in the sense that makes Aristotle's metaphysics a *theologia* – to enquiry conceived in an Aristotelian mode. For enquiry aspires to and is intelligible only in terms of its aspiration to finality, comprehensiveness and unity of explanation and understanding, not only in respect of the distinctive subject-matters of the separate subordinate sciences, but also in respect of those more pervasive and general features of contingent reality, which inform those wholes of which the subject-matter of the subordinate sciences supply the constituent parts – nature and human history. And, as the most radical philosophers of post-Enlightenment modernity from Nietzsche to Richard Rorty have recurrently insisted, in the course of polemics against their less thoroughgoing colleagues, the very idea of a unified, even if complex, ultimate and final true account of the order of things in nature and human history has hidden – and perhaps not so hidden – within it some view of the relationship of contingent beings to some ground beyond contingent being.

What the substantive first principles which provide the initial premises of any perfected science achieve then is a statement of those necessary truths which furnish the relevant set of demonstrative arguments with their first premises, but also exhibit how if something is of a certain kind, it essentially and necessarily has certain properties. The *de re* necessity of essential property possession is represented in and through the analytic form of the judgments which give expression to such principles. (For an overview of disputed questions on this topic and a view at some points different from mine, see chapter 12 of Richard Sorabji, *Necessity, Cause and Blame*.) It is their analyticity which makes it the case that such principles are evident *per se*, but their evidentness is intelligible only in the context of the relevant body of perfected theory within which they function as first principles, and only an understanding of that body of theory will enable someone to grasp their analytic structure.

That first principles expressed as judgments are analytic does not, of course, entail that they are or could be known to be true *a priori*. Their analyticity, the way in which subject-expressions include within their meaning predicates ascribing essential properties to the subject and certain predicates have a meaning such that they necessarily can only belong to that particular type of subject, is characteristically discovered as the outcome of some prolonged process of empirical enquiry. That type of enquiry is one in which, according to Aristotle, there is a transition from attempted specifications of essences by means of prescientific definitions, specifications which require acquaintance with particular instances of the relevant kind (*Posterior Analytics*, 93a21–9), even although a definition by itself will not entail the occurrence of such instances, to the achievement of genuinely scientific definitions in and through which essences are to be comprehended. To arrive at the relevant differentiating causes which are specific to certain types of phenomena thus to be explained, empirical questions have to be asked and answered (*Posterior Analytics*, 87b28–88a17, 89b9–20, 99b14–100b17). But what results from such questioning is not a set of merely *de facto* empirical generalizations, but, insofar as a science is perfected, the specification through analytic definitions of a classificatory scheme in terms of which causes are assigned, causes which explain, in some way that subsequent enquiry cannot improve upon, the ordering of the relevant set of phenomena. So the analyticity of the first principles is not Kantian analyticity, let alone positivist analyticity. The first principles of a particular science are warranted as such if and only if, when conjoined with whatever judgments as to what exists may be required for that particular science, they can provide premises for a theory which transcends in explanatory and understanding-affording power any rival theory which might be advanced as an account of the same subject-matter. And insofar as the judgments which give expression either to the first principles or to the subordinate statements deriving from them, which together constitute such a theory, conform to how the essential features of things are, they are called true. About truth itself Aristotle said very little, but Aquinas has a more extended account.

Truth is a complex property. 'A natural thing, therefore, being constituted between two intellects, is called true with respect to its adequacy to both; with respect to its adequacy to the divine intellect it is called true insofar as it fulfills that to which it was ordered by the divine intellect,' and Aquinas cites Anselm and Augustine and quotes Avicenna. 'But a thing is called true in respect of its adequacy to the human intellect insofar as concerning it a true estimate is generated . . .' and Aquinas quotes Aristotle (*Disputed Questions on Truth*, I, 2). The complexity of Aquinas's view is a consequence of his having integrated into a single account theses both from Aristotle and Islamic commentary upon Aristotle and from Augustine and Anselm. But the integration is what is most important. Different kinds of predication of truth each received their due within a genuinely unified theory of truth, in which the analogical relationship of different kinds of predication becomes clear.

What emerges then from the discussion of the rational justification of particular judgments within a perfected science by Aristotle in the *Posterior Analytics*, followed closely by Aquinas in his *Commentary*, and from the discussion of truth by Aquinas, in which Aristotelian theses are synthesized with Augustinian, is that both truth and rational justification have their place within a single scheme of perfected understanding and that the relationship between them depends upon their respective places within this scheme. But, as I emphasized earlier, what this conception of a perfected science supplies is a characterization of the *telos/finis* internal to and directive of activities of enquiry. What then is the nature of progress in enquiry towards this type of *telos/finis* and how are truth and rational justification to be understood from the standpoint of those still at early or intermediate stages in such a progress?

IV

In the progress towards a perfected science first principles play two distinct roles. Those which are evident to all rational persons do indeed provide standards and direction from the outset, but only when and as conjoined with initial sketches of those first conceptions and principles towards an ultimately adequate formulation of which enquiry is directed. Examples of the former type of first principle, evident to us as to all rational persons, are, of course, the principle of noncontradiction and the first principle of practical rationality, that good is to be pursued and evil avoided, and these are relatively unproblematic. But how are we even to sketch in outline at the outset an adequately directive account of a first principle or set of first principles, about which not only are we as yet in ignorance, but the future discovery of which is the as yet still far from achieved aim of our enquiry?

It is clear that, if we are able to do so, this will be the kind of case noticed earlier in which we shall be somehow or other already relying upon what we are not as yet fully justified in asserting, in order to reach the point at which we are fully justified in asserting it. But how then *are* we to begin? We can begin, just as Aristotle did, only with a type of dialectical argument in which we set out for criticism, and then criticize in turn, each of the established and best reputed beliefs held amongst us as to the fundamental nature of whatever it is about which we are enquiring: for example, as to the nature of motion in physics, or as to the human good in politics and ethics. As rival views are one by one discarded, leaving as their legacy to enquiry either something in them which withstood criticism or that which turned out to be inescapably presupposed by such criticism, so an initial tolerably coherent and direction-affording conception of the relevant first principle or principles may be constructed. The criticism of rival opinions about the human good in a way which leads on to an account of *eudaimonia* as that good in Book I of the *Nicomachean Ethics* is a paradigmatic case.

Yet, as enquiry progresses, even in these initial stages we are compelled to recognize a gap between the strongest conclusions which such types of dialectical argument can provide and the type of judgment which can give expression to a first principle. Argument *to* first principles cannot be demonstrative, for demonstration is *from* first principles. But it also cannot be a matter of dialectic and nothing more, since the strongest conclusions of dialectic remain a matter only of belief, not of knowledge. What more is involved? The answer is an act of the understanding which begins from but goes beyond what dialectic and induction provide, in formulating a judgment as to what is necessarily the case in respect of whatever is informed by some essence, but does so under the constraints imposed by such dialectical and inductive conclusions. Insight, not inference, is involved here, but insight which can then be further vindicated if and insofar as this type of judgment provides just the premises required for causal explanation of the known empirical facts which are the subject-matter of that particular science.

Moreover, the relationship between the different sciences and their hierarchical ordering becomes important at this point. Initially the shared beliefs which provide premises for dialectical arguments cannot but be beliefs prior to any particular science; such are the beliefs criticized and corrected in Book I of the *Nicomachean Ethics*. But once we have a set of ongoing established sciences, the shared set of beliefs to which appeal can be made includes in addition the beliefs presupposed in common by the findings and methods of those sciences. (The book which states the central issues most fully is T. H. Irwin, *Aristotle's First Principles*; I suspect that, if my account were less compressed, it would be more obviously at variance with Irwin's.) And what those sciences presuppose are those judgments and elements of judgments, understanding of which provides the key to Aristotle's metaphysical enterprise, by directing his and our attention beyond the kinds of being treated by the subordinate sciences to being *qua* being.

Aristotle has sometimes been thought to have undergone a radical change of mind between the earlier *Posterior Analytics* and the later *Metaphysics*, not least because in the first he denies that there can be a supreme science, while in the latter he not only affirms there there can be, but provides it. Yet this discrepancy is less striking than at first seems to be the case. For what Aristotle means by what he calls 'the demonstrative sciences' in the *Posterior Analytics* (for example, 76a37, 76b11–12) are such that none of *them* could be a supreme science: each is concerned with a distinct genus and each is demonstrative and any supreme science would have to be neither. So what Aristotle denied in the *Posterior Analytics* is not what he affirmed in the *Metaphysics*, and Aquinas who construed the relevant passages of the *Posterior Analytics* not as a denial of the possibility of a supreme science, but as a specification of its character had understood this very well (*Commentary on the Posterior Analytics*, I.17).

More than this, we can in this light now understand more adequately how dialectic even within the developing subordinate sciences can, by drawing upon those same presuppositions informing all scientific activity, bring us to the point at which the transition can be made from merely dialectical to apodictic and necessary theses. For the goal of such uses of dialectic thus reinforced is not to establish that there are essences – that is presupposed, not proved, by dialectic and its further investigation is a matter for metaphysics – but to direct our attention to how the relevant classifications presupposing essences are to be constructed, by providing grounds for deciding between the claims of rival alternative formulations of apodictic and necessary theses. Such theses cannot, as we have already noticed, *follow from* any dialectic conclusion any more than any law in the natural sciences can follow from the interpretation of any experimental result (and interpreted experimental and observational results often have in modern natural science the status assigned by Aristotle to dialectical conclusions), but they can be vindicated against their immediate rivals by such conclusions, just as formulations of natural scientific laws can be vindicated against rival formulations by experiment or observation.

We have then within any mode of ongoing enquiry a series of stages in the progress towards the *telos* of a perfected science. There will be dialectical conclusions both initially in the first characterizations of the *archē/principium* of that particular science, which provide the earliest formulations of the *telos/finis* of its enquiries, and later on in the arguments which relate empirical phenomena to apodictic theses. There will be provisional formulations of such theses, which in the light of further evidence and argument are displaced by more adequate formulations. And as enquiry progresses the conception of the *telos* of that particular mode of enquiry, of the type of perfected science which it is its peculiar aim to achieve, will itself be revised and enriched.

Such a mode of enquiry will have two features which coexist in a certain tension. On the one hand, progress will often be tortuous, uneven, move enquiry in more than one direction and result in periods of regress and frustration. The outcome may even be large-scale defeat for some whole mode of enquiry. These are the aspects of enquiry not always recognized in adequate measure by either Aristotle or Aquinas and, consequently, their crucial importance to enquiry also needs a kind of recognition by modern Thomists which cannot be derived from our classical texts. Only types of enquiry, we have had to learn from C. S. Pierce and Karl Popper, which are organized so that they *can* be defeated by falsification of their key theses can warrant judgments to which truth can be ascribed. The ways in which such falsification can occur and such defeat become manifest are very various. But in some way or other falsification and defeat must remain possibilities for any mode of enquiry and it is a virtue of any theory, and of the enquiry to which it contributes, that they should be vulnerable in this regard.

Hence, it was in one way a victory and not a defeat for the Aristotelian conception of enquiry when Aristotelian physics proved vulnerable to Galileo's dialectical arguments against it. And it is a mark of all established genuinely Aristotelian modes of enquiry that they too are open to defeat; that is, what had been taken to be adequate formulations of a set of necessary, apodictic judgments, functioning as first principles, may always turn out to be false, in the light afforded by the failure by its own Aristotelian standards of what had been hitherto taken to be a warranted body of theory. And lesser partial failures of this kind are landmarks in the history of every science.

So scientific progress is indeed not a straightforward matter. But, on the other hand, it is a central feature of enquiry, conceived as Aristotle and Aquinas conceived it, that we should nonetheless continue to think in terms of real and rational progress within sciences towards the *telos/*

finis of each particular mode of enquiry. For it is in key part in terms of their relationship to its specific *telos/finis* that the theoretical statements which give expression to what has been achieved in some particular enquiry so far have to be characterized. Their status is a matter of how far and in what way they bring us closer to that deductively organized body of statements which would constitute the articulation in judgments of perfected understanding. But to understand better how this is so, we must first look at the way in which, on an Aristotelian and Thomistic view, enterprises which issue in theoretical achievement are themselves practical enterprises, partially embedded in, and having many of the central characteristics of, other practical enterprises. Or to put the same point in another way, the *Nicomachean Ethics* and the *Politics* – and correspondingly Aquinas's commentaries upon and uses of those works – provide a context in terms of which the activities which resulted in the various types of science described in the *Posterior Analytics*, the *Physics* and the biological treatises – and indeed in the *Metaphysics* and the *Summa Theologiae* – have to be understood.

So when Aristotle distinguishes genuine enquiry, *philosophia*, from dialectic and sophistic (*Metaphysics*, 1004b17–26), he does so by contrasting the *power* of philosophy with that of dialectic, but by contrasting philosophy with sophistic as the project (*prohairesis*) of a different life, that is, as a moral contrast. And Aquinas comments that the philosopher orders both life and actions otherwise than does the practitioner of sophistic (*Commentary on the Metaphysics*, IV.4). So the life of enquiry has to be structured through virtues, both moral and intellectual, as well as through skills. It is more than the exercise of a *technē* or a set of *technai*. But in spelling out how this is so, we have to go beyond what we are explicitly told by either Aristotle or Aquinas.

The central virtue of the active life is the virtue which Aristotle names '*phronēsis*' and Aquinas '*prudentia*'. Three characteristics of that virtue are important for the present discussion. First, it enables its possessor to bring sets of particulars under universal concepts in such a way as to characterize those particulars in relevant relationship to the good at which the agent is aiming. So it is a virtue of right characterization as well as of right action. Secondly, such characterization, like right action, is not achieved by mere rule-following. The application of rules may indeed be and perhaps always is involved in right characterization as in right action, but knowing which rule to apply in which situation and being able to apply that rule relevantly are not themselves rule-governed activities. Knowing how, when, where and in what way to apply rules is one central aspect of *phronēsis/prudentia*. These two characteristics of this virtue are sufficient to show its epistemological importance for enquiry; the lack of this virtue in those who pursue, and who teach others to pursue, enquiry always is in danger of depriving enquiry of the possibility of moving towards its *telos/finis*.

So enquiry involves not only a teleological ordering of the activities of enquiry, but also a teleological ordering of those who engage in it and direct it, at least characteristically and for the most part. And it is here that a third characteristic of *phronēsis/prudentia* as an epistemological virtue becomes important; both Aristotle and Aquinas stress the way in which and the degree to which the possession of that virtue requires the possession of the other moral virtues in some systematic way. In doing so they anticipate something of what was to be said about the moral and social dimensions of the natural sciences in one way by C. S. Peirce and in another by Michael Polanyi.

It is then within a social, moral and intellectual context ordered teleologically towards the end of a perfected science, in which a finally adequate comprehension of first principles has been achieved, that the Aristotelian and Thomistic conceptions of truth and rational justification find their place, and it is in terms of such an ordering that the relationships between them have to be specified. Consider now how they stand to each other, if we draw upon Aquinas's extended account.

The intellect, as we have already noticed, in this account completes and perfects itself in achieving knowledge. Truth is the relationship of the intellect to an object or objects thus known, and in predicating truth of that relationship we presuppose an analogy to the relationship of such objects to that which they were to be, that which they would be if they perfectly exemplified their kind. Rational justification is of two kinds. Within the demonstrations of a perfected science, afforded by finally adequate formulations of first principles, justification proceeds by way of showing of any judgment either that it itself states such a first principle or that it is deducible from such a first principle, often enough from such a first principle conjoined with other premises. For such perfected demonstrations express in the form of a scheme of logically related judgments the thoughts of an intellect adequate to its objects. But when we are engaged in an enquiry which has not yet achieved this perfected end state, that is, in the activities of almost every, perhaps of every science with which we are in fact acquainted, rational justification is of another kind. For in such justification what we are arguing to is a conclusion that such and such a judgment does in fact have a place in what will be the final deductive structure. We are engaged in the dialectical construction of such a structure, and our arguments will be of a variety of kinds designed first to identify the conditions which a judgment which will in fact find a place in the final structure must satisfy, and then to decide whether or not this particular judgment does indeed satisfy those conditions.

That truth which is the adequacy of the intellect to its objects thus provides the *telos/finis* of the activities involved in this second type of rational justification. And the deductively ordered judgments which provide the first type of justification with its subject-matter are called true in virtue of their affording expression to the truth of the intellect in relation to its objects, since insofar as they afford such expression they present to us actually how things are and cannot but be. Each type of predication of truth and each type of activity of rational justification stand in a relationship to others specifiable only in terms of their place within the overall teleological ordering of the intellect's activities of enquiry.

Those activities, it should be noted, involve a variety of types of intentionality. And were we to attempt to specify those intentionalities adequately, we should have to learn not only from what Aquinas says about intentionality, but from Brentano, Husserl and, above all, Edith Stein. But it is important to recognize that a Thomistic account of types of intentionality, while it will be as much at variance with those who wish to eliminate intentionality from its central place in the philosophy of mind as are the phenomenologists, will be an integral part of, and defensible only in terms of, a larger Thomistic account of the mind's activities, relating types of intentionality to types of ascription of truth and of rational justification, in an overall scheme of teleological ordering. And any rational justification of the place assigned to *archai/principia* in that perfected understanding which provides the activities of the mind with its *telos/finis* is likewise inseparable from the rational justification of that scheme of teleological ordering as a whole.

There are, however, two objections which may be advanced against understanding enquiry in this Aristotelian and Thomistic mode. First, it may be said that on the account which I have given no one could ever finally know whether the *telos/finis* of some particular natural science had been achieved or not. For it might well appear that all the conditions for the achievement of a finally perfected science concerning some particular subject-matter had indeed been satisfied, and yet the fact that further investigation may always lead to the revision or rejection of what had previously been taken to be adequate formulations of first principles suggests that we could never be fully entitled to make this assertion.

My response to this objection is not to deny its central contention, but rather to agree with it and deny that it is an objection. The history of science shows both in the case of geometry, which was widely supposed to be a perfected science until the eighteenth century, and in that of physics, supposed to be approaching that state by Lord Kelvin and others in the late nineteenth century, that this is an area in which error is never to be ruled out. And it is important that any philosophical account of enquiry should be confirmed rather than disconfirmed by the relevant episodes in the history of science.

We ought, however, at this point to note one remarkable feature of Aquinas's account of enquiry, one which differentiates it from Aristotle's. Aquinas, like Aristotle, asserted that enquiry moves towards a knowledge of essences, but unlike Aristotle he denies that we ever know essences except through their effects. The proper object of human knowledge is not the essence itself, but the *quidditas* of the existent particular through which we come to understand, so far as we can, the essence of whatever it is (*Disputed Questions on Spiritual Creatures*, II, reply to objections 3 and 7). So our knowledge is of what is, as informed by essence, but this knowledge is what it is only because of the nature of the causal relationship of the existent particular and its quiddity to the intellect (see chapter 8 of Étienne Gilson, *Thomist Realism and the Critique of Knowledge*, especially pp. 202–4). Aquinas's affirmation of realism derives from this type of causal account. And such realism is quite compatible with a variety of misconstruals in their causal inferences by enquirers.

A second objection may appear to have been strengthened by my answer to the first. For I there appealed to the verdict of the history of science, and yet the history of science makes it plain, as do the histories of philosophy, theology and the liberal arts, that the actual course of enquiry in a variety of times and places has proceeded in a variety of heterogeneous ways, many of them not conforming to, and some radically at odds with, this philosophical account of enquiry, which I have tried to derive from Aristotle and Aquinas. But what point can there be, it may be asked, to a philosophical account of enquiry so much at variance with so much of what actually occurs, especially in specifically contemporary forms of intellectual activity?

The answer is that it is in key part by its power or its lack of power to explain a wide range of different types of episode in the history of science, the history of philosophy and elsewhere, including episodes which are from an Aristotelian and Thomistic standpoint deviant, that an account such as the Aristotelian and Thomistic account is to be tested. For if the Aristotelian view, as extended and amended by Aquinas, is correct, then specific types of departure from enquiry so conceived and specific types of denial of its central theses can be expected to have certain equally specific types of consequence. Intellectual failures, resourcelessnesses and incoherences of various kinds will become intelligible, as well as successes. A particular way of writing the history of science, the history of philosophy and intellectual history in general will be the counterpart of a Thomistic conception of rational enquiry, and insofar as that history makes the course of actual enquiry more intelligible than do rival conceptions, the Thomistic conception will have been further vindicated.

The *locus classicus* for a statement of how that history is to be written is the first and second chapters of Book A of the *Metaphysics*, supplemented by Aquinas's commentary. What Aristotle provides is not a narrative, but a scheme for the writing of narratives of that movement which begins from experience and moves through the practices of the arts and sciences to that understanding of *archai* which provides the mind with its terminus. And in succeeding chapters Aristotle writes a series of narratives, some very brief, some more extended, of those among his predecessors who failed or were only in the most limited way successful in their search for *archai*. At the same time Aristotle is providing indirectly a narrative of his own movement through the positions of his predecessors to his achievement of the positions taken in the *Metaphysics*. In doing so he reveals something crucial both about particular enquiries and about philosophical accounts of enquiry.

Of every particular enquiry there is a narrative to be written, and being able to understand that enquiry is inseparable from, implicitly or explicitly, being able to identify and follow that narrative. Correspondingly every philosophical account of enquiry presupposes some account of how the narratives of particular enquiries should be written. And indeed every narrative of some particular enquiry, insofar as it makes the progress of that enquiry intelligible, by exhibiting the course of its victories and its defeats, its frustrations and endurances, its changes of strategy and tactics, presupposes some ordering of causes of the kind that is only provided by an adequate philosophical account of enquiry.

Aquinas in his commentary endorses and amplifies Aristotle. Indeed, where Aristotle had said, referring to the early myths as precursors of science, that the lover of stories is in some way a philosopher, Aquinas says that the philosopher is in some way a lover of stories. And at the very least, if what I have suggested is correct, a philosopher will, in virtue of his or her particular account of enquiry, always be committed to telling the story of enquiry in one way rather than another, providing by the form of narrative which he or she endorses a standard for those narratives in and through which those engaged in particular sciences cannot but try to make intelligible both to themselves and to others what they are doing, in what direction they are moving, how far they have already moved and so on. Thomism, then, like all other specific philosophical accounts of enquiry, has implicit within it its own conception of how narratives of enquiry are to be constructed. Yet to introduce the Thomistic conception of enquiry into contemporary debates about how intellectual history is to be written would, of course, be to put in question some of the underlying assumptions of those debates. For it has generally been taken for granted that those who are committed to understanding scientific and other enquiry in terms of truth-seeking, of modes of rational justification and of a realistic understanding of scientific theorizing must deny that enquiry is constituted as a moral and social project, while those who insist upon the latter view of enquiry have tended to regard realistic and rationalist accounts of science as ideological illusions. But from an Aristotelian standpoint it is only in the context of a particular socially organized and morally informed way of conducting enquiry that the central concepts crucial to a view of enquiry as truth-seeking, engaged in rational justification and realistic in its self-understanding, can intelligibly be put to work.

To have understood this, and why the Thomist is committed to this way of understanding enquiry, is to have reached the point at which Thomism becomes able to enter certain contemporary philosophical debates by explaining, in a way that the protagonists of opposing standpoints within those debates are themselves unable to, how and why the problems posed within those debates are systematically insoluble and the rival positions advanced within them untenable. I do not, of course, mean that those protagonists would be willing or able to accept a Thomistic diagnosis of their predicament. Indeed, given the fundamental assumptions which have conjointly produced their predicament, it is safe to predict that to the vast majority of such protagonists it will seem preferable to remain in almost any predicament than to accept a Thomistic diagnosis. Nonetheless, it is only by its ability to offer just such a diagnosis, and one, as I have suggested, that will involve a prescription for writing intellectual history, that Thomism can reveal its ability to participate in contemporary philosophical conversation. What, then, is it that Thomism has to say on these matters?

V

Consider in a more general way than previously the unresolved disagreements and unsettled conflicts which characterize those contemporary philosophical theses, arguments and attitudes from which issue both the analytic and deconstructive rejection of first principles. Those disagreements and conflicts are, I want to suggest, symptoms of a set of underlying dilemmas concerning concepts whose status has, however, now been put in question in new and more radical ways.

So, for example, truth has been presented by some as no more than an idealization of warranted assertibility and by others as an entirely dispensable concept. Standards of warrant and justification have, as I noticed earlier, been relativized to social contexts, but the philosophers who have so relativized them have themselves been at odds with each other in multifarious ways. The intentionality of the mind's relationship to its objects, whether as understood by Thomists or otherwise, has been dismissed by some as a misleading fiction, while others have treated it as a pragmatically useful concept, but no more.

Debate over these and kindred issues has proceeded on two levels and on both it has been systematically inconclusive, perhaps in spite of, but perhaps because of the shared background beliefs of the protagonists of rival standpoints. At a first level, where debate has been directly about truth, rationality and intentionality, the difficulties advanced against earlier metaphysical conceptions – conceptions dominant from the seventeenth to the nineteenth centuries – have appeared sufficient to render such conceptions suspect and questionable for many different reasons, yet insufficient to render them manifestly untenable in any version, an insufficiency evident in the need to return again and again and again to the task of disposing of them. And so, at a second level, debate has opened up among those committed to rejecting or displacing or replacing such conceptions as to why what they have had to say has proved less conclusive in the arenas of philosophical debate than their protagonists had expected.

At this level too, disagreements are unresolved and rival views remain in contention. It has been argued, for example, that the antimetaphysical case has seemed less cogent than it is, because its protagonists have been insufficiently ruthless in purging their own positions of metaphysical residues. And it has been further asserted that, so long as the polemic against metaphysical conceptions of truth, rationality and intentionality is carried on in a conventional philosophical manner, it is bound to be thus burdened with what it ostensibly rejects, since the modes of conventional philosophy are inextricably tied to such conceptions. So the modes of conventional philosophical discourse must be abandoned. This is why Richard Rorty has tried to find a way of going beyond Davidson and Sellars (see *Contingency, Irony and Solidarity*, pp. 8–9). This is in part why Derrida has had to go beyond Nietzsche and Heidegger.

Yet to follow Rorty and Derrida into entirely new kinds of writing would be to abandon the debate from which the abandonment of debate would derive its point. So there is a constant return to the debate by those who still aspire to discover an idiom, at once apt for negative philosophical purposes in refuting metaphysical opponents, but itself finally disentangled from all and any metaphysical implications. As yet they have failed.

This is a philosophical scene, then, of unsolved problems and unresolved disagreements, and perhaps it is so because these particular problems are in fact insoluble and these particular disagreements in fact unresolvable. Why might this be so? It is perhaps because within contemporary philosophy the concepts which generate these divisions occupy a distinctively anomalous position. They are radically discrepant with the modes of thought characteristic of modernity both within philosophy and outside it, so that it is not surprising that relative to those modes of thought they appear functionless or misleading or both. Yet they keep reappearing and resuming their older functions, most notably perhaps in those narratives of objective achievement in enquiry, by recounting which philosophers make what they take to be the progress of their enquiries, and the activities of debate which are so central to that progress, intelligible to themselves and to others.

Within such narratives at least, narratives of a type which, so I suggested earlier, are essential constituents of philosophical, as of all other enquiry, but which nowadays are characteristically deleted and even denied when the outcomes of such enquiry are presented in the genre of the conference paper or the journal article, there occurs a return of the philosophically repressed, which reinstates for a moment at least ways of understanding truth, rationality and intentionality which it was a principal aim of the philosophical activities recounted in the narrative to eliminate. We may note in passing that it is perhaps only in terms of their relationship to such narratives – narratives which still embody, even if in very different forms, the narrative scheme of Book A of the *Metaphysics* – that most contemporary philosophers are liable to lapse into something like a teleological understanding of their own activities, even if only for short times and on relatively infrequent occasions.

What I have asserted then is that there is a tension between that in contemporary philosophy which renders substantive, metaphysical or quasimetaphysical conceptions of truth, rationality and intentionality not merely questionable, but such as to require total elimination, and that in contemporary philosophy which, even when it is only at the margins of philosophical activity and in largely unacknowledged ways, prevents such total elimination. This thesis is capable of being sustained only insofar as it can be developed as a thesis about contemporary philosophy, elaborated from some standpoint external to the standpoints which dominate and define contemporary philosophy, for only thus can it be itself exempt from the condition which it describes. But from what point of view then can such a thesis be advanced? And, if it is from a point of view genuinely external to that of the kinds of philosophy which it purports to describe, how, if at all, can it be advanced as part of a conversation with the practitioners of those kinds of philosophy?

Ex hypothesi anyone who advances such a thesis must, it would seem, share too little in the way of agreed premises, beliefs about what is problematic and what is unproblematic, and indeed philosophical idiom with those about whose philosophical stances he or she is speaking. The depth of disagreement between the two parties will be such that they will be unable to agree in characterizing what it is about which they disagree. We are debarred, that is to say, from following Aristotle and Aquinas in employing any of those dialectical strategies which rely upon some appeal to what all the contending parties in a dispute have not yet put in question. How then are we to proceed? It is at this point that we have to resort to unThomistic means, or at least to what have hitherto been unThomistic means, in order to achieve Thomistic ends. What means are these?

Although I have identified the thesis which I have propounded about the nature of distinctively contemporary philosophy as one that can only be asserted from some vantage point external to that philosophy, I have up to this point left it, as it were, hanging in the air. I now hope to give it status and substance by suggesting – and in this lecture I shall be able to do no more than suggest – how, by being elaborated from and integrated into an Aristotelian and Thomistic point of view, it might become part of a theory about the predicaments of contemporary philosophy, providing an account of how those predicaments were generated and under what conditions, if any, they can be avoided or left behind.

The provision of such a theory requires the construction of something akin to what Nietzsche called a genealogy. The genealogical narrative has the function of not arguing with, but of disclosing something about the beliefs, presuppositions and activities of some class of persons. Characteristically it explains how they have come to be in some *impasse* and why they cannot recognize or diagnose adequately out of their own conceptual and argumentative resources the nature of their predicament. It provides a subversive history. Nietzsche, of course, used genealogy in an assault upon theological beliefs which Thomists share with other Christians and upon philosophical positions which Aristotelians share with other philosophers, so that to adopt the methods of genealogical narrative is certainly to adopt what have hitherto been unThomistic means. How then may these be put to the service of Thomistic ends?

What I am going to suggest is that the predicaments of contemporary philosophy, whether analytic or deconstructive, are best understood as arising as a long-term consequence of the rejection of Aristotelian and Thomistic teleology at the threshold of the modern world. I noticed earlier that a teleological understanding of enquiry in the mode of Aristotle and Aquinas has as its counterpart a certain type of narrative, one through the construction of which individuals are able to recount to themselves and to others either how they have achieved perfected understanding, or how they have progressed towards such an understanding which they have not yet achieved. But when teleology was rejected, and Aristotelian conceptions of first principles along with it, human beings engaged in enquiry did not stop telling stories of this kind. They could no longer understand their own activities in Aristotelian terms at the level of theory, but for a very long time they proved unable, for whatever reason, to discard that form of narrative which is the counterpart to the theory which they had discarded. It is only within the last hundred years that it has been recognized by those who have finally attempted to purge themselves completely of the last survivals of an Aristotelian conception of enquiry and of its goals that, in order to achieve this, narratives which purport to supply accounts of the movement of some mind or minds towards the achievement of perfected understanding must be treated as acts of retrospective falsification. But even those, such as Sartre, who have embraced this conclusion have themselves been apt to yield to the temptation to construct just such narratives, a sign of the extraordinary difficulties involved in repudiating this type of narrative understanding of the activities of enquiry.

It is not, of course, that such narratives themselves find an explicit place for distinctively Aristotelian, let alone Thomistic conceptions of truth, rationality and intentionality. It is rather that they presuppose standards of truth and rationality independent of the enquirer, founded on something other than social agreement, but rather imposing requirements upon what it is rational to agree to, and directing the enquirer towards the achievement of a good in the light of which the enquirer's progress is to be judged. These presuppositions can be elucidated in a number of different and competing ways, but it is difficult and perhaps impossible to do so without returning to just that type of framework for narrative provided in the early chapters of *Metaphysics* A. It is thus unsurprising that, so long as this type of narrative survives in a culture, so long also Aristotelian and Thomistic conceptions are apt to recur even among those who believe themselves long since liberated from them.

So that one strand in the history of what followed upon the rejection of Aristotelian and Thomistic teleology would be an account of how, under the cover afforded by a certain kind of narrative, some Aristotelian and Thomistic conceptions survived with a kind of underground cultural life. Another and more obvious strand in that same history concerns the way in which in the history of philosophy and the history of science those conceptions were first displaced and marginalized, undergoing radical transformations as a result of this displacement and marginalization, and then even in their new guises were finally rejected. What were the stages in that history?

In the account which I gave of the Aristotelian and Thomistic account of enquiry, framed as it is in terms of first principles, I emphasized the way in which a variety of types of predication of truth and a variety of modes of rational justification all find their place within a single, if complex, teleological framework designed to elucidate the movement of the mind towards its *telos/finis* in perfected understanding, a movement which thereby presupposes a certain kind of intentionality. It is within that framework and in terms of it that not only are the functions of each kind of ascription of truth and each mode of rational justification elucidated, but also the relations between them specified so that what is primary is distinguished from what is secondary or tertiary and the analogical relationships between these made clear. Abstract these conceptions of truth and reality from that teleological framework, and you will thereby deprive them of the only context by reference to which they can be made fully intelligible and rationally defensible.

Yet the widespread rejection of Aristotelian teleology and of a whole family of cognate notions in the sixteenth and seventeenth centuries resulted in just such a deprivation. In consequence, conceptions of truth and rationality became, as it were, free floating. Complex conceptions separated out into their elements. New philosophical and scientific frameworks were introduced into which the older conceptions could be fitted only when appropriately and often radically amended and modified. And naturally enough conceptions which had been at home in Aristotelian and Thomistic teleological contexts in relatively unproblematic ways were now apt to become problematic and questionable.

Truth as a result became in time genuinely predicable only of statements; 'true' predicated of things came to seem a mere manner of speech, of no philosophical interest. New theories of truth had, therefore, to be invented, and they inescapably fell into two classes: *either* statements were true in virtue of correspondence between either them or the sentences which expressed them, on the one hand, and facts – 'fact' in this sense is a seventeenth-century linguistic innovation – on the other, *or* statements were true in virtue of their coherence with other statements. The protagonists of a multiplicity of rival versions of correspondence and coherence theories succeeded in advancing genuinely damaging critiques of their rivals' theories and so prepared the way for a further stage, one in which truth is treated either as a redundant notion or as an idealization of warranted assertibility.

In a parallel way conceptions of rational justification also underwent a series of transformations. With the rejection of a teleological understanding of enquiry, deductive arguments no longer had a place defined by their function, either in demonstrative explanations or in the dialectical constructions of such explanations. Instead they first found a place within a variety of epistemological enterprises, either Cartesian or empiricist, which relied upon a purported identification of just the type of epistemological first principle which I described earlier. When such enterprises foundered, a variety of different and mutually incompatible conceptions of rational justification were elaborated to supply what this kind of foundationalism had failed to provide. The outcome was a *de facto* acknowledgment of the existence of a variety of rival and contending conceptions of rationality, each unable to defeat its rivals, if only because the basic disagreement between the contending parties concerned which standards it is by appeal to which defeat and victory can be justly claimed. In these contests characteristically and generally no reasons can be given for allegiance to any one standpoint rather than to its rivals which does not already presuppose that standpoint. Hence, it has often been concluded that it is the socially established agreement of some particular group to act in accordance with the standards of some one particular contending conception of rational justification which underlies all such appeals to standards, and that such agreement cannot itself be further justified. Where rationalists and empiricists appealed to epistemological first principles, their contemporary heirs identify socially established forms of life or paradigms or epistemes. What began as a rejection of the Aristotelian teleogical framework for enquiry has, in the case of conceptions of truth, progressed through epistemology to eliminative semantics and, in the case of conceptions of rational justification, through epistemology to the sociology of knowledge.

What I am suggesting then is this: that certain strands in the history of subsequent philosophy are best to be understood as consequences of the rejection of any Aristotelian and Thomistic conception of enquiry. To construct the genealogy of contemporary philosophy – or at least of a good deal of contemporary philosophy – in this way would disclose three aspects of such philosophy which are otherwise concealed from view. First, such a genealogical account would enable us to understand how the distinctive problematic of contemporary philosophy was constituted and what its relationship is to the problematics of earlier stages in the history of modern philosophy. The history of philosophy is still too often written as if it were exclusively a matter of theses and arguments. But we ought by now to have learned from R. G. Collingwood that we do not know how to state, let alone to evaluate, such theses and arguments until we know what questions they were designed to answer.

Secondly, once we understand how the questions and issues of contemporary philosophy were generated, we shall also be able to recognize that what are presented from within contemporary philosophy as theses and arguments about *truth as such* and *rationality as such* are in fact theses and arguments about what from an Aristotelian and Thomistic standpoint are degenerated versions of those concepts, open to and rightly subject to the radical critiques which have emerged from debates about them only because they were first abstracted from the only type of context within which they are either fully intelligible or adequately defensible. Hence, in important respects Thomists need have no problem with much of the contemporary critiques; if indeed truth and rationality were what they have for a long time now commonly been taken to be, those critiques would be well-directed. And in understanding this the Thomist has resources for understanding contemporary philosophy which the dominant standpoints within contemporary philosophy cannot themselves provide.

To this, however, it may well be retorted that the protagonists of those standpoints have no good reason to concede that the history of modern philosophy should be construed as I have attempted to construe it, even if they were to grant for argument's sake that the very bare outline sketch which I have provided could in fact be filled in with the appropriate details. Nothing in their own beliefs, it may be said, nothing in the culture which they inhabit gives them the slightest reason to entertain any conception of enquiry as teleologically ordered towards an adequate understanding of an explanation in terms of *archai/principia*. They, therefore, cannot but understand the sixteenth- and seventeenth-century rejections of Aristotelianism, whether Thomistic or otherwise, as part of a progress towards greater enlightenment. And in this perspective the accounts which they have given of truth, rationality and intentionality are to be understood as culminating achievements in a history of such progress. Where the Thomist sees stages in a movement away from adequate conceptions of truth and rationality, stages in a decline, the protagonists of the dominant standpoints in contemporary philosophy, so it will be said, will see stages in an ascent, a movement towards – but the problem is: towards what?

The defender of contemporary philosophy is at this point in something of a dilemma. For if he or she can supply an answer to this last question – and it is not too difficult to think of a number of answers – what he or she will have provided will have been something much too like the kind of narrative account of objective achievement in enquiry whose structure presupposes just that type of teleological ordering of enquiry the rejection of which is central to the whole modern philosophical enterprise. But if he or she cannot supply an answer to this question, then philosophy can no longer be understood to have an intelligible history of achievement, except in respect of the working out of the details of different points of view. It will have become what David Lewis has said that it is: 'Once the menu of well-worked out theories is before us, philosophy is a matter of opinion . . .' (*Philosophical Papers*, pp. x–xi). Yet, the question arises once again about *this* conclusion: is it an achievement to have arrived at it or not? Is it superior in truth or rational warrant to other opinions? To answer either 'Yes' or 'No' to these questions revives the earlier difficulty.

It is no part of my contention that a protagonist of one of the dominant trends in contemporary philosophy will lack the resources to frame a response to this point, adequate in its own terms. It is my contention that such a protagonist will even so lack the resources to explain the peculiar predicaments of contemporary philosophy and to provide an intelligible account of how and why, given its starting-point and its direction of development, to be trapped within these predicaments was inescapable. Thomism enables us to write a type of history of modern and contemporary philosophy which such philosophy cannot provide for itself.

In the course of writing this kind of genealogical history Thomism will be able to open up possibilities of philosophical conversation and debate with standpoints with which it shares remarkably little by way of agreed premises or shared standards of rational justification. It will be able to do so insofar as it can show how an Aristotelian and Thomistic conception of enquiry, in terms of first principles and final ends, can provide us with an understanding and explanation of types of philosophy which themselves reject root and branch the possibility of providing a rational justification for any such conception. But that is, of course, work yet to be done. In this lecture I have not even come near to showing that in fact it can be done. All that I have been able to do is to sketch in bare outline some suggestions for a way of initiating this enterprise in the hope that it may be less barren than attempts to initiate philosophical conversation between Thomists and protagonists of standpoints in contemporary philosophy have proved to be in the past.

Acknowledgement

I am deeply indebted to Mark Jordan and Ralph McInerny for their assistance at various points.

'Moral Relativism, Truth and Justification'

1 To what are the most plausible versions of moral relativism a response?

Often, if not always, moral relativism is a response to the discovery of systematic and apparently ineliminable disagreement between the protagonists of rival moral points of view, each of whom claims rational justification for their own standpoint and none of whom seems able, except by their own standards, to rebut the claims of their rivals. Examples of such systematic moral conflict are not difficult to find.

Consider for example a certain kind of disagreement about marriage and divorce. Kaibara Ekken, an influential seventeenth-century Japanese neo-Confucian, followed Confucian tradition in arguing that sufficient grounds for a husband to divorce a wife include not only that she is sexually unfaithful, but also that she is disobedient to parents-in-law, or barren, or jealous, or has a serious illness, or engages in frequent gossip and slander, or is a thief. What these grounds provide is evidence of an inability to sustain the social role of a wife, as understood by neo-Confucians (See Mary Evelyn Tucker, *Moral and Spiritual Cultivation in Japanese NeoConfucianism*, pp. 116–18). Further justification of these claims would be provided by considering the place of the role of wife and mother within the family, the relationship of the structure of the family to that of the social and political order and the way in which both of these give expression to a cosmic order, recognized in that practice of the virtues in which an understanding of what is appropriate for each role is embodied.

Yet to hold that a woman's being barren or jealous or a gossip provides sufficient grounds for a husband to divorce her is from some other points of view a gross error. So it is notably from the standpoint of that natural law tradition which developed out of Stoicism and Roman law through a series of definitive medieval statements, most notably by Aquinas (on marriage and divorce see the *Commentary on the Sentences*, IV.26.1, IV.39.6), into the arguments and theses about natural law advanced by modern Thomists (see M.B. Crowe, *The Changing Profile of the Natural Law*). Had a follower of Ekken debated with someone whose conception of natural law was derived from Aquinas, disagreements about practical conclusions would have turned out to be reinforced by disagreements about practical premises, and yet further theoretical disagreements about the nature and status of the relevant practical premises.

Certainly some standards of justificatory reasoning and some premises would be, and could not but be, shared by both rival traditions. But the extent of the differences in fundamental theses and concepts in the schemes of rational justification internal to each of these two great traditions is such that no resolution of their basic disagreements seems possible. For it is to a significant extent the standards by which disagreements are to be evaluated and resolved which are themselves the subject of disagreement. The relationship of conscience to reason, as understood by the natural law tradition, provides what is taken to be a knowledge of primary practical precepts of a kind for which the Confucian scheme affords no place. And the Confucian appeal to what are taken to be shared insights into the nature of cosmic order fails to justify what the Confucian takes it to justify, when evaluated from a natural law perspective. So, neither standpoint seems to possess the resources for constructing a rational justification of its own position in terms which would make that justification rationally compelling to the adherents of its rival. There are, so it appears, no standards of justification, neutral between both traditions, available to any person simply *qua* rational person, and sufficient to provide good reasons to decide the questions disputed between the two moral standpoints. And it is not only the disputes between Confucians and natural law theorists which seem to be irresolvable in this way.

Disagreements over marriage and divorce after all extend beyond the quarrel between Confucians and natural law theorists. The utilitarianism elaborated in Britain from the eighteenth to the twentieth century warrants conclusions on these and other matters radically at variance with those of both the Confucian and the natural law theorist. And the justificatory appeal by the utilitarian to an impersonal, consequentialist measurement of costs and benefits involves quite as radical a disagreement with the practical and theoretical premises from which Confucians and natural law theorists argue. The utilitarian shares this with her or his opponents, that the principles which each invokes to resolve fundamental disagreements turn out to be among those principles about which there is fundamental disagreement. Such disagreements therefore appear to be intractable and not susceptible of rational resolution.

It is perhaps then unsurprising that some should have concluded that, where such rival moral standpoints are concerned, all fundamental rational justification can only be internal to, and relative to the standards of, each particular standpoint. From this it is sometimes further and at first sight plausibly inferred that this is an area of judgement in which no claims to truth can be sustained and that a rational person therefore could, at least *qua* rational person, be equally at home within the modes of life informed by the moral schemes of each of these standpoints. But this is a mistake. In fact a relativist who so concluded could be at home in no such standpoint. Why not?

2   What puts the relativist at odds with those about whom she or he writes?

The protagonists of those standpoints which generate large and systematic disagreements, like the members of the moral communities of humankind in general, are never themselves relativists. And consequently they could not consistently allow that the rational justification of their own positions is merely relative to some local scheme of justification. Their claims are of a kind which require unqualified justification. Aristotle articulates their claim in speaking of fourth-century Greeks who 'consider themselves of good breeding and free not only among themselves, but everywhere, but the barbarians of good breeding only where they are at home, taking it that being unqualifiedly of good breeding and free is one thing, being qualifiedly so another' (*Politics*, 1255a33–36). And in twentieth-century Java, according to Clifford Geertz, 'people quite flatly say, "To be human is to be Javanese"' ('The Impact of the Concept of Culture on the Concept of Man', p. 116). Ancient Greeks and modern Javanese are in this respect typical human beings. What then is it about these claims to unqualified moral hegemony, so nearly universal among human cultures, which has escaped the attention of moral relativists? It is the fact that they are claims to *truth*. What is being claimed on behalf of each particular moral stand-point in its conflicts with its rivals is that its distinctive account (whether fully explicit or partially implicit) of the nature, status and content of morality (both of how the concepts of a good, a virtue, a duty and right action are to be correctly understood, and of what in fact are goods or the good, virtues, duties and types of right action) is *true*.

Two aspects of this claim to truth are important to note at the outset. The first is that those who claim truth for the central theses of their own moral standpoint are thereby also committed to a set of theses about rational justification. For they are bound to hold that the arguments advanced in support of rival and incompatible sets of theses are unsound, not that they merely fail relative to this or that set of standards, but that either their premises are false or their inferences invalid. But insofar as the claim to truth also involves this further claim, it commits those who uphold it to a non-relativist conception of rational justification, to a belief that there must be somehow or other adequate standards of rational justification, which are not the standards internal to this or that standpoint, but are the standards of rational justification as such.

Secondly, just because this is so, making a claim to truth opens up the possibility that the claim may fail, and that the outcome of an enquiry initially designed to vindicate that claim may result instead in a conclusion that the central moral theses of those who initiated the enquiry are false. One might have concluded from the account of the fundamental disagreements between rival standpoints which relativists have taken to warrant their conclusions that, just because the standards to which the partisans of each appeal are to a significant degree internal to each standpoint, any possibility of something that could be recognized as a refutation of one's own standpoint by that of another was precluded. Since each contending party recognizes only judgements by its own standards, each seemed to be assured of judgements only in its favour, at least on central issues. But when one notices that the claim made by each contending party is a claim to truth, this inference is put in question.

Notice that what I am questioning here is not the initial description of the relationships between the contending parties and their modes of rational justification which misled the relativist. It may be that this description will have to be modified or corrected at certain points. But in substance it does seem to capture crucial features of fundamental moral disagreement, including the extent to which the standards to which the adherents of each standpoint make their ultimate appeal are indeed internal to each standpoint, something that explains the *de facto* ineliminability of fundamental disagreement between persons of different standpoints, often from different cultures, all of whom appear equally capable of rational judgement.

Yet if what impressed itself upon the relativist's attention is important, so equally is what escaped the relativist's notice, the claim to truth. It is these two taken together which constitute the problem with which I shall be concerned in this paper. Is it possible to bring into coherent relationship, and, if so, how, a recognition that all rational justification of particular moral standpoints is, to the extent that I have suggested, internal to those standpoints, and an elucidation of the claim to truth universally or almost universally advanced – implicitly or explicitly – by the protagonists of each of those standpoints, a claim which involves appeal to rational justification *as such*, that is, to some mode of justification which transcends the limitations of particular standpoints? To answer this question we have to begin by enquiring what conception of truth it is with which we have to be concerned.

3   How does the conception of truth presupposed in fundamental moral debates relate to rational justification?

It is already obvious that the understanding of truth involved cannot be one which equates truth with what is rationally justified in terms of the scheme of each particular standpoint. For it is precisely and only because the claim to truth involves more and other than the claim to such justification that a problem is posed. It is perhaps less obvious, but as important, that the understanding of truth involved cannot be one which equates truth with rational justification in any way. No one of course has ever claimed that 'true' means the same as 'rationally justified' – but a succession of pragmatist thinkers have held 'that truth comes to no more than idealized rational acceptability' or that 'truth is to be identified with idealized justification.' (See for these formulations Hilary Putnam, *Realism with a Human Face*, pp. 41, 115. Putnam has since reformulated his view in *Representation and Reality*, saying that his intention was to suggest only 'that truth and rational justification are *interdependent* notions', p. 115.) There are three reasons for rejecting any such identification.

The first is that the notion of idealization invoked has never been given adequate content. Actual rational justifications are characteristically advanced by particular persons at particular stages of particular enquiries, while truth is timeless. And the later discovery that an assertion made by someone at some earlier stage of enquiry is false is not at all the discovery that that person was not justified in making it. So that the conceptual distance between ascriptions of truth and actual justificatory practice, whether in the natural sciences or elsewhere, is very great. And those who, like Putnam in his earlier writings, have equated truth with idealized rational justification have always recognized this. But what they have not done is to supply an account of idealization which will provide what their thesis needs. For the only type of rational justification which could be equated with the relevant conception of truth would be one whereby the ideal rational justifications in question were such that we could not say of anyone, real or imagined, that her or his assertions were in this ideal way rationally justified, but not true. That could hold only of some type of rational justification, claims to which were claims that it would and could never be displaced by some superior mode of rational justification, affording different and incompatible conclusions. It would involve a notion of some type of rational justification whose properties guaranteed its status as the ultimate terminus of enquiry in the relevant area. But how this could be no one has ever explained.

Suppose however that this problem did not arise. A second kind of difficulty would remain. For where fundamental moral disagreements of the type which I have described are in question, each contending standpoint has internal to it its own scheme and mode of rational justification, one which of course shares some important features with its rivals, but at key points appeals to principles and to modes of grounding principles which are specific to it and inadmissible from the standpoints of its rivals. And to the degree that this is so, what constitutes an idealization of rational justification will also be specific and idiosyncratic to the standpoint of that particular tradition. Thus an idealization of a neo-Confucian appeal to those principles of natural order which structure the cosmos, the social order more generally and the familial order in particular would be very different from an ideally satisfactory account in Thomistic Aristotelian terms of the epistemology of natural law, conscience and practical reasoning and both will differ from what any utilitarian would take to be ideal rationality.

If the response to this is that ideal rational justification must be conceived as standpoint-independent, then once again the conceptual distance between the actualities of rational justification and the proposed idealization is too great for us to be able to understand what kind of idealization could be constructed that would be adequate. And a third consideration suggests that perhaps we should not be surprised by this. For the project of assimilating truth to rational justification, let alone that of liquidating truth into warranted acceptability, has the unfortunate effect of distorting our understanding not only of truth, but also of rational justification. Rational justifications are characteristically advanced in the context of what are or could become systematic enquiries. It is when and only when the truth about some subject-matter is at issue that there is point or purpose in advancing and evaluating them. And it is when the truth about that subject-matter has been achieved that the relevant set of rational justification has served its purpose.

Practices of rational justification are thus devised and are only fully intelligible as parts of all those human activities which aim at truth: questioning, doubting, formulating hypotheses, confirming, disconfirming and so on. This is why attempts to give an account of truth as no more than rational acceptability or rational justification, idealized or otherwise, are bound to fail. And when the activities, in the course of which rational justifications of one sort or another are invoked, disallowed, amended and the like, are systematically organized in the form of extended and long-term enquiry, as they are in the practices of the sciences, their goal-directedness towards what is more and other than any particular form of rational justification is all the more evident.

Aristotle said that 'Truth is the *telos* of a theoretical enquiry' (*Metaphysics*, 993b20–21) and the activities which afford rational justification are incomplete until truth is attained. What is it to attain truth? The perfected understanding in which enquiry terminates, when some mind is finally adequate to that subject-matter about which it has been enquiring, consists in key part in being able to say how things are, rather than how they seem to be from the particular, partial and limited standpoint of some particular set of perceivers or observers or enquirers. Progress in enquiry consists in transcending the limitations of such particular and partial standpoints in a movement towards truth, so that when we have acquired the ability of judging how in fact it seems or seemed from each limited and partial standpoint, our judgements are no longer distorted by the limitations of those standpoints. And where there is no possibility of thus transcending such limitations, there is no application for the notion of truth.

Successful enquiry terminates then in truth. If we assert that a particular statement is true, we are of course thereby committed to a corresponding claim about its rational justification, namely that any type of rational justification which provides logical support for a denial of that statement must somehow or other be defective. But to explain truth in terms of rational justification will be, if some version of this type of Aristotelian account can be adequately defended, to invert their relationship. What importance does this have for the discussion of moral relativism?

It enables us to identify more precisely what is at issue between on the one hand the protagonists of a variety of fundamental moral standpoints and on the other the proponents of moral relativism. For if it is correct to ascribe to those protagonists a claim, sometimes explicit, sometimes implicit, to the *truth* of the account of goods, rules, virtues, duties and the right which is practically embodied in each particular type of moral practice, and if moreover it is a claim which presupposes just that kind of understanding of truth which I have sketched, then such protagonists are committed, whether they recognize it or not, to defending three theses.

First they are committed to holding that the account of morality which they give does not itself, at least in its central contentions, suffer from the limitations, partialities and one-sidedness of a merely local point of view, while any rival and incompatible account must suffer to some significant extent from such limitations, partialities and one-sidedness. For only if this is the case are they entitled to assert that their account is one of how things are, rather than merely of how they appear to be from some particular standpoint or in one particular perspective. And this assertion is what gives content to the claim that this particular account is true and its rivals false.

Secondly, such protagonists are thereby also committed to holding that, if the scheme and mode of rational justification of some rival moral standpoint supports a conclusion incompatible with any central thesis of their account, then that scheme and mode must be defective in some important way and capable of being replaced by some rationally superior scheme and mode of justification, which would not support any such conclusion.

Thirdly and correspondingly, they are committed to holding that if the scheme and mode of justification to which they at present appeal to support the conclusions which constitute their own account of the moral life were to turn out to be, as a result of further enquiry, incapable of providing the resources for exhibiting its argumentative superiority to such a rival, then it must be capable of being replaced by some scheme and mode of justification which does possess the resources *both* for providing adequate rational support for their account and for exhibiting its rational superiority to any scheme and mode of justification which supports conclusions incompatible with central theses of that account. For otherwise no claim to truth could be sustained.

So there is from the standpoint of every major moral tradition a need to resist any relativist characterization of that standpoint as no more than a local standpoint. What the claim to *truth* denies is, as Nietzsche understood, any version of perspectivism. Conversely the abandonment of claims to truth, even if in the guise of a revision of our conception of truth, so that truth is to be understood as no more than an idealization of rational acceptability or justification, makes it difficult and perhaps impossible to resist perspectivist conclusions, and obviously so in the type of case in which fundamental moral standpoints are in contention. For how any particular moral issue or situation is to be characterized, understood and rationally evaluated – indeed whether any particular situation is to be regarded as posing significant moral issues – will depend, it must seem, upon which particular conceptual scheme it is in terms of which our own moral idiom is framed. Yet if the claims made from the rival and contending points of view are not claims to *truth*, the adherents of the different standpoints in contention will not be able to understand the central claims of their own particular standpoint as logically incompatible with the claims of those rivals.

For consider the form of the fundamental claim made from within each rival standpoint, if it is formulated only in terms of rational justification and acceptability and not in terms of some substantive conception of truth. That claim will be of the form: 'Given that rational justification is what this particular tradition takes it to be, then the nature and status of goods, rules, duties, virtues and rights are such and such, and therefore we ought to live the moral life accordingly.' But a claim of this form advanced from within, say, the Confucian tradition would not contradict a claim of the same form advanced from within either the natural law standpoint or some version of utilitarianism. It is only insofar as the claims of any one such tradition are framed in terms of a conception of truth which is more and other than that of some conception of rational acceptability or justification that rival moral standpoints can be understood as logically incompatible.

If therefore someone who rejected such a conception of truth were to reinterpret the claims made by each of the rival standpoints, so that those claims were no longer to be accounted, in the sense afforded by such a conception, true or false, then that person would indeed be entitled to draw not only perspectivist, but also and in consequence relativist conclusions. So long as the protagonists of such rival standpoints were each understood as claiming truth for their distinctive contentions, the possibility that each or all of them would in the end be rationally defeated remained open. But when that possibility no longer exists, because the rival protagonists are no longer understood as advancing logically incompatible claims, the issues between them can no longer turn on the question of which, if any, is rationally superior to its rivals. And to say this would be to have conceded the substance of relativism.

Whether or not an inference from premises concerning the facts about fundamental disagreements between moral standpoints to a relativist conclusion can or cannot be drawn therefore depends, first upon whether it is in in fact correct, as I have asserted, to ascribe to the adherents of those traditions an implicit, if not an explicit, claim to substantive truth for their accounts of the nature, status and grounds of moral practices and judgement, and secondly upon whether the conception of truth to which appeal is thus made can be rationally sustained.

4   How are acts of assertion, including the assertion of fundamental moral theses, related to truth?

In the case of some well-developed moral standpoints the question of whether the adherents of those standpoints are or are not making a claim to *truth* is easily and uncontroversially answered. For just such a claim has at some stage been made explicit in the course of articulating the systematic structure of the beliefs which inform those standpoints. Both the natural law tradition and utilitarianism provide examples. But how are we to judge in those cases in which, if there is a claim to truth, it is implicit in the accounts advanced by the protagonists of those particular standpoints, but not spelled out or philosophically elucidated or defended? The answer to this question is a matter of how we are to construe the acts of assertion of such protagonists, in advancing their own distinctive answers to evaluative and practical questions, and – a closely related matter – the nature of the arguments by which they support their assertions.

It is a commonplace that truth and assertion are intimately connected. But there are of course ways of understanding that connection which involve an attempt to discredit any substantive conception of truth by interpreting ascriptions of truth as nothing more than expressive endorsements of acts of assertion. Such attempts must, if they are to succeed, understand assertion in some way which makes it expressive of the attitude of whoever utters the assertion so that truth is not a property of what is asserted, let alone a property of a relationship between what is understood by whoever utters the assertion and that which makes what is asserted true. This is not, of course, on the face of it a plausible account of how assertion and the use of truth-predicates are actually understood and employed in any natural language. And some of the most cogent of such attempts therefore are those which are presented not as analyses of how truth-predicates have hitherto been used and understood, but instead as proposals for a radical revision and reinterpretation of some of the uses and presuppositions of expressions in natural languages.

An excellent example of such proposals is Robert Brandom's 'Pragmatism, Phenomenalism, and Truth Talk' which treats pragmatist accounts of truth as an 'innovative rethinking' of how truth and belief are to be understood. At the core of that rethinking are the theses that 'Taking some claim to be true is endorsing it or committing oneself to it' and that 'Endorsing a claim is understood as adopting it as a guide to action . . .' (p. 77). What is it in the discourse of natural languages which resists such rethinking and which therefore for its proponents requires either elimination or reinterpretation? The answer is surely: just those properties of assertion and of the relationship of acts of assertion to the propositions asserted by those acts to which Peter Geach drew our attention in his definitive account of how a variety of misunderstandings of the nature of assertion are to be avoided (Geach, 'Assertion'). What this and subsequent discussions by Geach have made clear is that the notion of assertion cannot be explicated independently of that of truth. It must therefore be the case – this is my inference from Geach's conclusions and he should not of course be held responsible for the use to which I am putting his arguments – that any attempt to give an account of assertion prior to and independent of an account of truth is in the end bound to fail. But without such an account the explanation of truth in terms of assertion is empty. The contemporary neopragmatist reply will presumably be some further expansion of what Brandom says in expounding his thesis that 'Endorsing a claim is understood as adopting it as a guide to action, where this, in turn, is understood in terms of the role the endorsed claim plays in practical inference' (Brandom, pp. 77–9). But the onus here – and one not yet discharged – is upon the neopragmatist to show that what has hitherto been understood as assertion has not been replaced by mere expressions of assertiveness.

What such a replacement could have no genuine counterpart for, I suggest, are those features which connect assertion with valid and sound inference, features already identified in 'Assertion' but whose significance has been further clarified in the later development of examples, by appeal to which Geach has shown (see 'Verdad o Asserción Justificada?') that the interpretation of types of sentences involving logical connectives, in particular disjunctions and conditionals, requires a notion of meaning only to be explained in terms of truth-conditions, an interpretation without which we should not be able to elucidate the difference between unqualified assertion of indicative sentences on the one hand and disjunctive and conditional uses of the same sentences on the other. In showing this Geach has reiterated the importance of what in 'Assertion' he first called 'the' Frege point: 'que uno y el mismo pensamiento puede ser expresado tanto en una sentencia asertórica, como en una mera clausula dentro en una sentencia mas larga' ('that one and the same thought can be expressed both in an assertoric sentence and in a mere clause in a longer sentence': p. 84), adding to Frege's point Aristotle's, that one and the same premise may be asserted or used without assertive commitment in a dialectical argument (*Posterior Analytics*, 72a8–11). It is because in those different types of context the meaning of sentences put to dialectical, disjunctive and conditional uses must be the same as when they are put to assertive uses, while the thought is treated as in one type of context assertible, but in another not, that meaning cannot be understood in terms of assertibility, warranted or otherwise. And it is because it is precisely truth which is transmitted through valid inference from true premises, that the relationship between the meaning of premises and the meaning of conclusions in such arguments, depending as it does on the truth-functional meaning of the logical operators, cannot be understood apart from the truth-conditions of both.

Simon Blackburn has argued against Geach from the standpoint of his own projectivist version of emotivism (*Spreading the Word*, pp. 189–96) that assertive form may in the case of moral and some other types of judgement be interpreted as presenting merely expressive content in a way that takes full account of 'the Frege point'. But this challenge to Geach's thesis is one to which it is both difficult and unnecessary to respond, until a compelling explanation has been provided of what remains so far obscure, namely how on an emotivist or projectivist view the attitudes allegedly evinced or expressed in moral judgements are related to the assertion of sentences of the relevant type. Are those attitudes to be understood as psychological states which can be adequately identified and characterized prior to and independently of such assertions? If so, then the projectivist claim turns out to be an empirical psychological one and is, I believe, false; if not, then such assertions must be characterizable independently of any expressive function, as Geach indeed characterizes them. I have argued elsewhere (*After Virtue*, chapters 2 and 3) that emotivism may on occasion seem to have become plausible, because in a certain kind of social situation types of sentences previously used to express true or false moral judgements may have come to be used for purely expressive purposes. But when they are so used to give expression to sentiments which can only be understood as psychological residues, the meaning of such sentences cannot be explained in terms of their expressive use. Geach's thesis remains the best account of assertion that we possess.

What is the relevance of this to my own overall argument? What Geach's conclusions supply are reasons for holding that we are entitled to ascribe claims to truth to the protagonists of rival moral standpoints, even when such claims have not been explicitly articulated, just because their assertions of their various and incompatible points of view are assertions, and indeed unqualified assertions, and just because the inferences to which they appeal for support are inferences formulated by standard uses of sentences in natural languages. For claims to truth are already present in such acts of assertion and in reliance upon such inferences. *Some* of Geach's arguments in support of this conclusion have been accepted even by some of those who take a radically different view of the present state of debate about truth and justifiability, most notably by Michael Dummett in 'The Source of the Concept of Truth'. For, although Dummett there denies what Geach has urged about disjunctions – and even entertains the possibility that Geach's account is vulnerable to emotivist criticisms – he agrees with Geach about conditionals that 'Although there is indeed a way of understanding conditionals that can be explained in terms of justifiability, rather than of truth, it does not yield even a plausible approximation to the actual use of conditionals in natural language; and that is why it is their use that forces us to form an implicit notion of truth' (p. 9).

A realistic notion of truth and a conception of meaning in terms of truth-conditions are thus 'deeply embedded' in our use of language, but that this is so is nonetheless 'no *defence* of the concept of truth, realistically conceived' (p. 14). For this concept of truth is such that, so Dummett claims, to move beyond the concept of justifiability in the requisite way, in order to acquire it, would require 'a conceptual leap', for which, he says, no justification has ever been made available. The realist about truth has still to show, on Dummett's view, that such a conception of truth does not involve inescapable incoherence, the incoherence involved in holding that over and above satisfying those conditions which specify how justification can be afforded to the use of a sentence by a speaker's exercise of her or his cognitive abilities, an asserted sentence can satisfy a condition which relates to 'some state of affairs obtaining independently of our knowledge' (p. 12).

What Dummett concedes to Geach's arguments – and an adequate statement, let alone critique, of Dummett's positions (see especially *The Logical Basis of Metaphysics*) is far, far beyond the scope of this paper – is perhaps however at least as important as what he denies about realist conceptions of truth. To what Dummett denies one might initially respond by putting in question the metaphor of a 'conceptual leap' with its implications of cognitive inaccessibility. Certainly, as I have already argued, the concept of truth, 'realistically conceived', or at least conceived so that an antirealist interpretation is excluded, cannot be reduced to or constructed out of that of justifiability, any more than the concept of a physical object can be reduced to or constructed out of that of sense-data or the concept of pain reduced to or constructed out of that of bodily expressions of pain. In each such case there have been philosophers prepared to make a reductionist objection, parallel to that advanced by Dummett. But the reductionist appears to her or himself to face the problem of a 'conceptual leap', only because she or he has matters the wrong way round. Bodily expressions of pain have to be already understood in terms of pain, if they are to be understood as expressions of pain and not as something else, and not vice versa, and sense-data equally have to be already understood in terms of physical objects and not vice versa. So too justifiability has to be already understood in terms of truth and not vice versa. There is no conceptual gap waiting to be crossed.

Why this is so I suggested earlier, when I characterized truth as a property of that type of understanding which is the goal and the terminus of systematic rational enquiry concerning any particular subject-matter. We provide rational justifications for the assertion of this or that sentence in the course of moving towards that goal, and the evaluation and re-evaluation of such justifications is in terms of their contribution to the achievement of that goal. It is for this reason, and not at all because truth is definable or needs to be redefined in terms of justifiability, that all claims to truth have implications for justification. For if I assert that 'p' is true, I am thereby committed to holding that, through the history of any set of enquiries concerned to discover whether it is 'p' or '~p' that is true, either '~p' will never be supported by any scheme and mode of rational justification or, if it is so supported, that scheme and mode of rational justification which at some particular stage of enquiry appears to provide support for the conclusion that '~p' will in the longer run be rationally discredited. And in asserting that 'p' is true I am also committed to holding that anyone whose intellect is adequate to the subject-matter about which enquiry is being made would have to acknowledge that 'p'.

Even a preliminary development of this kind of response, whether to Dummett's position or to neo-pragmatist proponents of antirealist positions, such as Brandom, would require an account of truth as *adaequatio intellectus ad rem* which would bring together the issues concerning truth raised in recent philosophical debate and what has now been better understood about Aquinas's discussions (see most recently John F. Wippel, 'Truth in Thomas Aquinas'). What would such a development be designed to achieve? Its primary goal would be to exhibit the relationship between truth as the adequacy of an intellect to its *res* and the truth-conditions of those sentences which express the judgements characteristic of such an intellect. When and insofar as, on Aquinas's type of account, a particular person's intellect is adequate to some particular subject-matter with which it is engaged in its thinking, it is what the objects of that thinking in fact are which makes it the case that that person's thoughts about those objects are what they are – and, in respect of the content of that thought, nothing else. So the activity of the mind in respect of that particular subject-matter is informed by and conformed to what its objects are; the mind has become formally what the object is. This adequacy of the intellect to its objects – and its primary objects are, for example, the actual specimens of sodium or chlorine about which the chemist enquires, or the actual strata about which the geologist enquires, not, as in so many later accounts of mind, ideas or representations of those specimens or strata – is expressed in the making of true judgements about those objects. And true judgements are uses of sentences which satisfy the truth-conditions for those sentences.

It is towards this condition of enquiry that the mind moves in its enquiries, its *telos* provided by its conception of the achievement of just such a relationship of adequacy to *what is*. A mind which has achieved such a relationship will have overcome those limitations of perspective and of cognitive resource which previously restricted it to judgements as to *what seems to be the case* here and now under the limitations of some particular local set of circumstances. And whether and how far those limitations were distorting will only have been recognized when they have been overcome. So, as I remarked earlier, claims to truth, thus conceived, are claims to have transcended the limitations of *any* merely local standpoint. Dummett in a 1972 'Postscript' to his 1959 'Truth' (both reprinted in *Truth and Other Enigmas*), characterized the agreements and the disagreements which ought to be recognized between realists and antirealists about truth, by saying that both ought to agree 'that a statement cannot be true unless it is in principle capable of being known to be true' but that 'the antirealist interprets "capable of being known" to mean "capable of being known *by us*" whereas the realist interprets it to mean "capable of being known by some hypothetical being whose intellectual capacities and powers of observation may exceed our own"' (pp. 23–4). A Thomistic realist would by contrast characterize this difference in terms of an actual or possible progress from a condition in which the mind has not yet freed itself from the limitations of one-sidedness and partiality, towards or to adequacy of understanding. The intellectual capacities and powers of observation of Dummett's 'hypothetical being' have to be understood, on a Thomistic view, as the capacities and powers exercised by an adequate intellect.

How then ought we to envisage the relationship between unqualified claims to truth, on the one hand, which commit those who make them to asserting that this is how things in fact are and, on the other, those qualified claims which through some explicit or implicit parenthetical reservation say no more than this is how things appear to be from some particular local point of view? (On how we are able to move from saying how things seem to be from some particular point of view to saying how they are, see Aristotle, *Eudemian Ethics*, 1235b13–18; on the consequences of not moving beyond saying how they seem to be from some particular point of view see *Metaphysics*, 1062b12–1063a10.) Insofar as we recognize that a claim as to how things seem to be is no more than that, we are already making a claim about what is unqualifiedly the case, namely that this *is* how things seem to be and that from *any* point of view it ought to be recognized that this is how they seem to be from this point of view. And part of knowing how things *are* is being able to say how in consequence they must appear to be from a range of different, limited, local points of view. That is to say, if and when we know how things are, we must be able to explain how things appear to be from such local and partial points of view, in key part by appealing to how they in fact are, and it is only insofar as we have already transcended the limitations of local and partial points of view that we will be entitled to make unqualified assertions about how things must appear to be from such points of view. So it is in part at least by the extent to which they are able to provide such explanations that claims to truth are to be vindicated.

I have argued then that the refutation of moral relativism turns on the further development and rational justification of a conception of truth which is at odds with two major contemporary sets of philosophical theses about truth, both of them involving, but in very different ways, radical revisions of the commitments involved in the standard linguistic uses of the speakers of natural languages. So that for those engaged in these as yet unsettled philosophical controversies there is both much constructive and much critical work to be undertaken. But the adherents of the moral standpoints embodied in the lives of a variety of ongoing moral communities, speaking a variety of natural languages, do not have to wait on the outcome of those controversies in order to decide whether or not to persist in those affirmations and commitments which are bound up with their conception of the truth of what they assert. All that they have to ask is whether any kind of conclusive reason for not so continuing has as yet been offered to them by the adherents of those theories of truth which would, if vindicated, undermine the claims that they make on behalf of their various and contending traditions. And here the force of what has already been said on behalf of the conception of truth to which they are committed, both by writers in the Thomistic tradition in one mode and by Geach in another, suffice to make it evident that nothing remotely like a conclusive reason for not so continuing has yet been advanced.

5   How then can a moral standpoint be rationally vindicated against its rivals?

Yet it may appear that this view of the relationship between truth and rational justification itself raises an insuperable difficulty. I have followed Aristotle in taking truth to be the *telos* of rational enquiry; and rational enquiry so conceived must involve progress towards that *telos* through the replacement of less adequate by more adequate forms of rational justification. So that progress in rational enquiry concerning the nature and status of human goods, duties, virtues and rights would have to exhibit a movement from initial local, partial and one-sided points of view towards a type of understanding – and in the case of the moral life a type of practice – freed in some significant way from the limitations of such partiality and one-sidedness and possessed of the resources which would enable it to explain, in the light of the comprehension thus achieved, just why it is that they appear to be otherwise from the limited perspectives of those local, partial and one-sided standpoints whose limitations have now been transcended. Yet it must seem that, on the account which I initially advanced of the apparently unresolvable fundamental disagreements between major moral standpoints, such progress in rational enquiry concerning the nature of the moral life cannot occur. Why not?

On that account those contending standpoints each have internal to them their own standards of rational justification, and so each, it must seem, is locked into its own mode of rational justification and into the conceptual scheme to which that mode gives expression. But if that is indeed so, then there can surely be no way in which the adherents of each rival standpoint can transcend the limitations of their own local point of view, for the only standards of judgement available to them are the standards of each local standpoint. Yet central to progress in rational enquiry, as I have characterized it, is an ability to transcend such limitations and in so doing to identify and to explain the partiality and the one-sidedness which they impose upon those whose perspective is defined by them. If progress in rational enquiry, so understood, is impossible, then the conception of truth which blocks the inference from the facts about fundamental moral disagreement to the moral relativist's conclusions loses its application, for truth cannot be the *telos* of any type of enquiry condemned for ever to remain locally limited and constrained.

The line of argument which leads to this conclusion is however mistaken. For even in those cases where the facts about fundamental disagreement between moral standpoints are as I have described them, and each of the contending traditions has internal to it its own standards of rational justification, the possibility of transcending the limitations of those standards, as hitherto formulated and understood, through the progress of rational enquiry into the nature of the moral life is not in fact ruled out. One approach to understanding how and why this is so would be to re-examine the history of, for example, the natural law tradition (see Crowe), in which at more than one stage in the development of its own internal enquiries, and of its critical relationships to other traditions, the challenge of transcending the limitations hitherto imposed upon it by its own standards of rational justification has been successfully met. But to understand how this has in fact been possible in such particular cases a more general account of how such limitations can be overcome is needed. There are distinctive characteristics necessary for the development of any enquiry whose starting-point is from within this type of moral position if it is to have any prospect of success in such overcoming.

The first is an acceptance by those engaged in it of the justificatory burden imposed upon anyone who is committed, as they are to a substantive conception of truth. What burden is that? It is the onus upon the adherents of each particular rival tradition of showing, so far as they can, that, if and only if the truth is indeed what they assert that it is, and if and only if it is appropriated rationally in the way that they say that it must be appropriated, can we adequately understand how, in the case of each rival moral standpoint, given the historical, social, psychological and intellectual circumstances in which that standpoint has been theoretically elaborated and embodied in practice, it is intelligible that this is how things should seem to be to the adherents of those other standpoints. How things seem to them from their merely local and therefore limited point of view is to be explained in the light of how things are. But since this onus is equally on the adherents of every standpoint for whose account of morality truth is claimed, different standpoints can be compared in respect of their success in the provision of such explanations, even if to some extent different standards of explanation and intelligibility are invoked from within each contending moral tradition. For the type of understanding yielded by such explanations must, if it is to discharge the justificatory burden, and therefore permit the claim to truth to be sustained, be specific and detailed enough to be open to falsification at a wide variety of points. And that detail and specificity must enable us to understand how the different types of moral disagreement with which we are confronted are generated under different conditions and circumstances. What form would such explanations take?

To answer this question we need to remind ourselves of a central feature of every important moral standpoint. Every standpoint of any theoretical depth that purports to provide an overall account of the moral situation of human beings and of the standards of moral success and failure has internal to it not only its own distinctive theses and arguments, but also its own distinctive problems and difficulties, theoretical or practical or both. And another characteristic necessary for any enquiry which is designed to transcend the limitations of its own standpoint-dependent starting-point is a systematic investigation and elaboration of what is most problematic and poses most difficulty for that particular moral standpoint. It is of course by the degree of ability of its adherents to make progress in solving or partially solving or at least reformulating such problems, first by identifying areas in which either incoherence or resourcelessness threatens, and then by furnishing remedies for these, that a particular standpoint is or is not vindicated by and for those adherents. For we are speaking here of what is or at least ought to be problematic by the standards of that standpoint for whose adherents these issues arise. So for example within utilitarianism the problem of how the happiness of any particular individual is related to the general happiness, a question at once theoretical and practical, was answered initially in one way by Bentham, then in another by Mill, in a formulation designed to supply the defects evident by utilitarianism's own standards in Bentham's response, and then again by Sidgwick in an attempt to correct Mill. And in Japanese Confucianism of the seventeenth and eighteenth centuries we find a continuing and unresolved tension between an evident need to adapt and revise prescriptions for familial relationships to new familial and household arrangements and a continuing requirement that one and the same set of principles should inform both new and older prescriptions. But at a certain point in the history of such attempts to deal with such problems it can become plain that they are not only persistent, but intractable, and irremediably so.

When we find that the adherents of a particular moral standpoint, confronted by this type of persistent and intractable problem, can only avoid resourcelessness at the cost of incoherence, that if enough is said to be practically useful, too much has to be said to remain practically or theoretically consistent, a question is always thereby posed to the adherents of that particular standpoint, whether they recognize it or not, as to the extent to which it is the limitations imposed by their own conceptual and argumentative framework which both generate such incoherences and prevent their resolution. Insofar as it can be established that this is so, by explaining why and how precisely these particular problems must inescapably arise within that particular framework and the obstacles to resolving them be just those obstacles which our diagnosis has enabled us to identify, to that extent the local limitations of that particular stand-point and of its particular established scheme and mode of rational justi-fication will have been transcended. But how could this be achieved?

It would require an ability to put in question the conceptual frame-work of that particular standpoint from within the framework itself by the use of argumentative resources not so far available within that frame-work, but now made so available. It will in the first instance have been only from the standpoint of some other rival moral position that such limitations can have been identified. But how is it possible that someone whose moral beliefs and practice are both informed and limited by the concepts and standards of her or his own particular point of view could have acquired the ability to understand her or his own standpoint from some external and rival vantage point? The answer is that through the exercise of philosophical and moral imagination someone may on occa-sion be able to learn what it would be to think, feel and act from the standpoint of some alternative and rival standpoint, acquiring in so do-ing an ability to understand her or his own tradition in the perspective afforded by that rival. The analogy here is with the ability of an anthro-pologist to learn not only how to inhabit an alternative and very different culture, but also how to view her or his own culture from that alien perspective.

The exercise of this imaginative ability to understand one's own funda-mental moral positions from some external and alien point of view is then yet another characteristic necessary for those engaged in enquiry who, beginning within some one particular moral standpoint, aspire first to identify and then to overcome its limitations. What this ability can on occasion achieve is a discovery that problems and difficulties, incoherencies and resourcelessnesses, in dealing with which over some extended period one's own standpoint has proved sterile, can in fact be understood and explained from some other rival point of view as precisely the types of difficulty and problem which would be engendered by the particular local partialities and one-sidednesses of one's own tradition. If that alternative rival point of view has not proved similarly sterile in relation to its own difficulties and problems, then the enquirer has excellent reasons for treating the alternative rival point of view as more powerful in providing re-sources for moving rationally from a statement of how things seem to be from a particular local point of view to how they in fact are, by revealing what it was that was hitherto limiting in that standpoint which had up till now been her or his own.

So even though all such reasoning has to begin from and initially accept the limitations and constraints of some particular moral stand-point, the resources provided by an adequate conception of truth, by logic and by the exercise of philosophical and moral imagination are on occasion sufficient to enable enquiry to identify and to transcend what in those limitations and constraints hinders enquiry or renders it sterile. But in this progress of rational debate, in which one standpoint may defeat another by providing the resources for understanding and explaining what is or was intractably problematic for that other, some at least of the adherents of a defeated set of positions may remain unable to recognize that defeat. For such adherents will still have all the reasons that they had previously had for invoking the standards of their own particular established scheme and mode of rational justification in support of a denial of rival conclusions. And they may never acquire the ability to understand their own positions from an external standpoint, so that nothing that *they* would have to recognize as a refutation of their own standpoint need have been offered. At most they may only be compelled to acknowledge the intractability of some continuing long-term problems. Insofar as this is the case, the relationship between the two standpoints in conflict will thus have become asymmetrical, and this in two ways. First, one of these two rival moral standpoints will have acquired through the exercise of philosophical and moral imagination the conceptual resources to provide not merely an accurate representation of its rival, but one which captures what by the standards of that rival is intractably problematic, while the continuing adherents of that rival will lack just that type of resource. And secondly it will have provided in its own terms a compelling explanation of why what is thus intractably problematic is so. But the terms in which that explanation is framed may well remain inaccessible to most and perhaps all continuing adherents of that rival standpoint. So on fundamental matters, moral or philosophical, the existence of continuing disagreement, even between highly intelligent people, should not lead us to suppose that there are not adequate resources available for the rational resolution of such disagreement.

Acknowledgement

I am greatly indebted for criticisms of an earlier version of this paper to Marian David, Paul Roth and David Solomon.

PART V

Challenging Contemporary Politics

'The *Theses on Feuerbach*: A Road Not Taken'

When we reread Marx nowadays, that reading has to address two salient and related features of our recent experience. The internal collapse of the Communist state apparatus in so many countries has left behind a variety of groups in those countries struggling to attain or rather to reattain the standpoint of civil society. At the same time the distinctively contemporary social theorizing of our own political culture, theorizing which gives a voice to the now dominant forms of power, either asserts or presupposes that the standpoint of civil society cannot be transcended. What then was and is the standpoint of civil society?

The expression 'civil society' and its cognates in other European languages had first been used to translate Aristotle's '*koinōnia politikē*'. But by the early nineteenth century it had come to be used in a variety of very different ways and Hegel, who learned it from Adam Ferguson, adopted it to name those social, economic and legal relationships into which individuals enter in order to satisfy their needs, forming by so doing 'a system of complete interdependence wherein the livelihood, happiness and legal status of one human being is interwoven with the livelihood, happiness and rights of all' (*Philosophy of Right*, para. 183). The individual from the standpoint of civil society is to be distinguished from and contrasted with the set of social relationships into which she or he has chosen to enter. Those relationships, often understood as contractual, are on the one hand a means to the attainment of each individual's ends and on the other a system so constructed that by entering it each individual becomes a means for the attainment by other individuals of their ends. Among the needs generated by such a system therefore is one for the protection of individuals from being so used by others as a means that their pursuit of their own ends becomes frustrating rather than fulfilling. Hence appeals to moral and legal norms affording such protection have an important function within civil society. The central conceptions informing thought within civil society about human relationships are therefore those of utility, of contract and of individual rights. And the moral philosophy which gives expression to the standpoint of civil society consists of a continuing debate about those concepts and how they are to be applied.

Up to 1844 Marx had engaged in a philosophical debate with Hegel, with the Left Hegelians and with Feuerbach about the nature of civil society, its relationship to the state and to religion, and the inadequacy of the criticism of civil society by its critics so far. The subtitle of *The Holy Family* summarizes his enterprise: 'a Critique of Critical Critique'. In 1845 Marx and Engels together embarked on a new project in the course of first writing and then abandoning the manuscript of *The German Ideology*, that of offering an historical and analytical account of the genesis and dynamic of modern capitalist economies. What were Marx's reasons for thus turning away from philosophical enquiry? When I speak of a turning away from philosophical enquiry I am not of course denying that Marx's later historical and economic analyses are themselves informed by philosophical presuppositions. That would be absurd. But philosophy is no longer the object of his enquiries and the questions which he poses are generally not philosophical questions.

Lucio Colletti has remarked on how few of Marx's later writings advert to this change by giving us 'the reasons, philosophical as well as practical, which had induced Marx to give up philosophy after his break with Hegel and Feuerbach' (Introduction to *Karl Marx: Early Writings*, p. 8), citing the short text to which Engels later gave the title 'Theses on Feuerbach', the *Preface* to *A Contribution to the Critique of Political Economy* published in 1859 and the *Postface* to the second edition of the first volume of *Capital*. But the latter two were written a very considerable time later from what had become Marx's mature standpoint. Only in the first of these do we have a genuinely transitional text.

Colletti's own diagnosis of the change focuses upon Marx's critique of Hegel, in which Marx had worked through Hegel's conceptions of dialectic and of the state to the point at which their empty abstractions and incoherences had led him to reject them. And Colletti understands Marx's next stage as one that had progressed beyond the limitations of those conceptions. I want instead to suggest that the important question is not so much why Marx rejected Hegel and Feuerbach as why, in rejecting them, he rejected philosophy, and moreover that, by rejecting philosophy, at a stage at which his philosophical enquires were still incomplete and were still informed by mistakes inherited from his philosophical predecessors, Marx allowed his later work to be distorted by presuppositions which were in key respects infected by philosophical error.

Marx's *Theses on Feuerbach*, on this view, are in part a successful, but in part an unsuccessful attempt to identify what is involved in transcending the standpoint of civil society. In distinguishing the success from the failure I cannot but presuppose some particular interpretation of the text and there is no interpretation which is not contentious. But I shall bypass the scholarly disputes, because within the space of this paper any adequate treatment of them would be impossible. And in so doing I shall also fail to acknowledge scholarly debts. Informed readers will notice, for example, that I take for granted George L. Kline's thesis ('The Myth of

Marx's Materialism') that Marx did not have a materialist ontology and that the word '*Materiell*' has, in the *Theses on Feuerbach* as elsewhere, to be construed with care; and that I presuppose the truth of Carol Gould's account of Marx's ontology of individuals-in-relation (*Marx's Social Ontology*, chapter 1, especially pp. 30–9) and its Aristotelian antecedents. But they and a number of unacknowledged others cannot be held responsible for an interpretation that I assert rather than argue.

My approach will be to identify and to comment upon six central assertions expressed in Marx's eleven theses. The first of these is that the standpoint of civil society cannot be transcended, and its limitations adequately understood and criticized, by theory alone, that is, by theory divorced from practice, but only by a particular kind of practice, practice informed by a particular kind of theory rooted in that same practice. The philosophers have hitherto tried to understand, but their understanding was not guided by the aim of transforming the social and natural world in the requisite way. The eleventh thesis does not tell philosophers to abandon the attempt to understand; it tells them to direct their tasks of understanding towards the achievement of a particular *telos*. What *telos*?

It is the *telos* of some form of what Marx in the first thesis calls *objective* activity, taking over this expression from Fichte and Hegel. Objective activity is activity in which the end or aim of the activity is such that by making that end their own individuals are able to achieve something of universal worth embodied in some particular form of practice through cooperation with other such individuals. The relationships required by this type of end are such that each individual's achievement is both of *the* end and of what has become her or his own end. Practices whose activity can be thus characterized stand in sharp contrast to the practical life of civil society. It is a contrast which is best expressed in Aristotelian rather than in Hegelian terms.

In activities governed by the norms of civil society there are no ends except those which are understood to be the goals of some particular individual or individuals, dictated by the desires of those individuals, and no goods are recognized except those involved in the satisfaction of the wants and needs of individuals. Because there are many goods which individuals can achieve only by cooperative attention to the goods of others, civil society recognizes as common goods those goods which are pursued in common by individuals. But the only available conception of a common good is one constructed from and reducible to conceptions of the goods pursued by various individuals in their attempts to satisfy their desires.

By contrast the ends of any type of practice involving what Marx calls objective activity are characterizable antecedently to and independently of any characterization of the desires of the particular individuals who happen to engage in it. Individuals discover in the ends of any such practice goods common to all who engage in it, goods internal to and specific to that particular type of practice, which they can make their own only by allowing their participation in the activity to effect a transformation in the desires which they initially brought with them to the activity. Thus in the course of doing whatever has to be done to achieve those goods, they also transform themselves through what is at once a change in their desires and an acquisition of those intellectual and moral virtues and those intellectual, physical and imaginative skills necessary to achieve the goods of that particular practice. So, as Marx puts it in the third thesis, there comes about a 'coincidence of the changing of circumstances and of human activity of self-changing'.

Yet at once it is plain that there are at least two objections to construing Marx in this way. First and most obviously on this construal Marx is presented as if he had made a distinction which is expressed in an Aristotelian vocabulary, a vocabulary which he did not in fact use and some of whose presuppositions he had rejected. The conception of a type of practice teleologically ordered to the achievement of a or the common good may, it will be said, be at home in an Aristotelian or Thomistic perspective, but it is alien to Marx's. To this I respond by agreeing in part: what I have ascribed to Marx is indeed not what Marx said. Nonetheless I am contending that, if Marx had done the work of spelling out in detail the key distinction which the argument of the *Theses on Feuerbach* needs, he would have been compelled to articulate it in something very like Aristotelian terms. Hegel's idiom is just not adequate to the task.

To this a second objection must be that what Marx says is far too compressed and elliptical to support this kind of interpretation. Those interpreters who have elucidated the theses by drawing on Marx's other writings have at least had the evidence of those other writings to offer. To this I reply that, if we understand the theses as on the one hand marking a significant break with what Marx had done hitherto, and on the other pointing in a direction which Marx did not in fact take, then reliance on his other writings may itself be misleading. What we should be looking for is an attempt to articulate, in terms that are not deformed either by the errors of Hegel or by those of Feuerbach, an effective rejection of civil society. So our first question should be: what was it that, on Marx's view, rendered any rejection of civil society in either Hegelian or Feuerbachian terms ineffective?

Marx's rejection of all Hegelianism, and more especially of that of the Left Hegelians, was in important part a rejection of purely theoretical enquiry as an instrument of social change. What the Left Hegelians had characteristically supposed was that to exhibit the incoherences of the principles embodied in the social and political *status quo*, thereby exposing its irrationality, was by itself to have made an important and effective contribution to bringing about its downfall. We should not be harsh in condemning their error. After all we have over a century and a half of experience which they lacked, an experience of modern social orders not merely surviving the exposure of the incoherence of their governing principles, but even in some cases seeming to flourish because of that incoherence. The modern state, for example, behaves part of the time towards those subjected to it as if it were no more than a giant, monopolistic utility company and part of the time as if it were the sacred guardian of all that is most to be valued. In the one capacity it requires us to fill in the appropriate forms in triplicate. In the other it periodically demands that we die for it. This deep incoherence in the modern state is not a secret, but the fact that it is plain for everyone to see of itself does nothing at all to undermine the modern state. And Marx was perhaps the first to recognize how very little the exposure of incoherence generally achieves.

Other aspects of Marx's critique of Hegelian philosophy he shared with and had indeed learned from Feuerbach. By the time that he wrote the theses, he needed to take great care to distinguish his own positions from some of those of the later Feuerbach (on the complexity and subtlety of Feuerbach's development see Marx W. Wartofsky, *Feuerbach*). Feuerbach after all had already written in *Principles of the Philosophy of the Future*, published in 1843, that 'The road taken so far by speculative philosophy from the abstract to the concrete, from the ideal to the real ... will never arrive at true objective reality', but only at a reification of philosophy's abstractions, and that 'The transition from the ideal to the real takes place only in practical philosophy.' This seems to anticipate Marx. How then is Marx's position in the theses to be differentiated?

Marx in the theses makes one of the main heads of his criticism of Feuerbach a charge that Feuerbach's critique of religion had been inadequate. Feuerbach had understood religion as a distorted expression of human sentiment, one in which truths about love were expressed in a disguised form, one in which the true relationships of subject and predicate were inverted. Philosophy was to pierce through this disguise and by setting out the relevant truths in rational form dispel supernaturalist illusions. But Feuerbach then went on to announce what he took to be his discovery that philosophy also by its abstractions generates illusions. Marx's criticism of Feuerbach on religion is therefore perhaps best read as a prologue to Marx's criticism of Feuerbach on philosophy.

Marx's criticism of Feuerbach on religion had two parts. First he complained that Feuerbach, while understanding, in Marx's view correctly, that religion has to be wholly explained in terms of its secular basis, does not then ask what it was in 'the cleavages and self-contradictions' (the fourth thesis) in that basis which had engendered illusion, and how that secular basis would have to be transformed so that it was no longer liable to engender illusion. Secondly Marx contended that Feuerbach had not analysed 'the religious sentiment' adequately as a social product, since Feuerbach's explanation of it terminates at the point at which he analyses it psychologically as a sentiment of individuals, rather than as a mode of expression characteristic of a particular type of social order (the eighth thesis). What matters to Marx here is the particular conception of the individual upon which Feuerbach relies. Feuerbach does not understand about that conception, first that it too is among those conceptions which are defective because abstract, and secondly that it belongs to the conceptual scheme of one particular type of social order.

If we apply Marx's criticisms of Feuerbach's account of religion as distortion to Feuerbach's later account of philosophy as distortion, what then is it that Marx is saying? He is asserting, first that philosophy has its secular basis in a particular type of social order, that informed by the standpoint of civil society, and secondly that, if we suppose that in understanding philosophical enquiry and argument as the activity of individuals, and that by giving an account of the secular basis of that activity as the activity of individuals, we have successfully moved from the abstract to the concrete, then we shall be deceiving ourselves. Marx's use of the notion of abstraction has of course often been criticized. Surely, it has been said, all concepts, all uses of language, involve abstraction, and therefore it cannot be a criticism of any particular concept or conception that it is abstract. But this criticism misses the point, something that has also been often said, but which still bears repeating. In Marx's semitechnical Hegelian usage, to abstract is always to frame a concept in a way which deprives it of the contextual connections in which alone it is at home and therefore to present it as having application independently of the relevant set of contexts. It always in consequence involves conceptual error and misunderstanding. We should perhaps note in passing that Marx's use of this notion of abstraction is often Wittgensteinian rather than Hegelian.

What then is it about the concept of the individual, as deployed by Feuerbach, which renders it abstract, and what is it about that abstraction which enables it to play its part in the thinking and acting characteristic of civil society? An answer to this latter question itself supplies an answer to the former. We already noticed that all transactions in civil society are understood to be between individuals and sets of individuals and that those individuals are only contingently related through their own acts of will to the social circumstances and the social relationships which they happen at any particular moment to inhabit. It may be of course that an individual finds her or himself entangled in certain social relationships without having willed this to be the case. But that she or he continues in them is, except when force or fraud are at work (the force and fraud which the legal and moral protections of civil society are designed to prevent), her or his own doing. Everything that comes about is understood to be either an intended or an unintended consequence of the actions of one or more individuals. The human individual must therefore be viewed in abstraction from her or his social relationships and the human essence must be specifiable by reference only to properties possessed by individuals apart from and in independence of their social relationships.

What is important is to recognize that it is this conception of the individual which is actually embodied not just in the thought, but also in the activities characteristic of civil society. To regard individuals as distinct and apart from their social relationships is a mistake of theory, but not only a theoretical mistake. It is a mistake embodied in institutionalized social life. And it is therefore a mistake which cannot be corrected merely by better theoretical analysis. Better theoretical analysis is of course necessary and in the sixth thesis Marx indicates what kind of theoretical account is required. The human essence is not given by considering the properties of individuals in isolation. 'In its reality it is the ensemble of social relations.' And of course what Marx means by '*the* ensemble' in this aphoristic utterance is not entirely clear. What is clear is that human beings who genuinely understand what they essentially are will have to understand themselves in terms of their actual and potential social relationships and embody that understanding in their actions as well as in their theories.

In civil society however there has to be a contradiction, a cleavage between how human beings really and essentially are and how they understand themselves to be. This 'cleavage and self-contradiction', whereby civil society is a social order in which human beings are generally deprived of a true understanding of themselves and their relationships, is the source of the illusions diagnosed by Feuerbach. Even though these are philosophical illusions, whether about religion or about philosophy itself, they can have no philosophical cure. Here Marx becomes anti-Wittgensteinian. The only remedy for such illusions is an alternative form of practice of just that kind which we have already seen to be incompatible with the standpoint of civil society. Why so?

Civil society is characterized not only by its abstract individualism, but by a particular way of envisaging the relationship between all theory, including social theory, and practice. The adequacy of a theory to its objects is conceived of as a matter of the conformity of 'thought objects' to 'sensuous objects' (the first thesis). On this view we are to correct 'abstract thinking' by our contemplation of the sense-experience afforded by the physical and social world. From the point of view of what Marx calls Feuerbach's 'contemplative materialism' what contemplation of the social world reveals are 'single individuals' and their agglomeration in civil society (the ninth thesis). Theoretical investigation leads to the materialist conclusion that these individuals are what they are because of their circumstances and their upbringing. Human beings are then taken to be a product of causal agencies over which they have had no control.

The social theorist who has arrived at this conclusion has by so doing completed the work of elaborating an adequate theory. Now she or he has to understand her or himself as about to embark on a second distinct task, that of applying this theory in order to effect change. But in so envisaging their task theorists have, characteristically without recognizing it, made the sharpest of distinctions between how they understand themselves and how they understand those who are the subjects of their enquiries. They understand those whose actions and experiences are to be explained by their theory as the wholly determined products of circumstance and upbringing. Their biological and social inheritance makes them what they are, independently of and antecedently to their own reasoning and willing, which are no more than products of that inheritance. By contrast such theorists understand themselves as rational agents, able to and aspiring to embody their intentions in the natural and social world. They understand others in terms of a determinist theory. They understand themselves in terms of a rational voluntarism. Marx put this in the third thesis by saying that 'The materialist doctrine concerning the changing of circumstances and upbringing forgets that circumstances are changed by men and that it is essential to educate the educator himself. This doctrine must, therefore, divide society into two parts, one of which is superior to society.' What do we need to learn from these remarks?

A first lesson concerns the relationship between the autonomy of theory and the social order of civil society. Marx had already identified the autonomy of theoretical enquiry as characteristic of civil society. Now he adds to that as also distinctive of civil society the self-conception of the theorist as an autonomous agent and as therefore in her or his own understanding always a potential legislator for and on behalf of others. Marx here suggests what was misleading in an antithesis which was later to dominate a good deal of discussion of Marxism, that between the view that theoretical enquiries inescapably function within and as part of economic and social formations and the rival view that theoretical enquiries can be autonomous and independent of the social contexts inhabited by theorists. Marx however identifies one particular kind of autonomy and independence of theory as themselves characteristic of and inseparable from a particular type of social order.

Secondly Marx, in asserting that such autonomous social theory cannot but envisage human beings in two incompatible ways, on the one hand as products of objective social and natural circumstances and on the other as rational agents, identified a continuing *aporia* for all modern social theory. It has not been uncommon in this century for social theorists to announce that they have solved the problem thus posed, among them Parsons, Sartre, Habermas and most recently Bourdieu. But various as their solutions are, they have all been solutions from *within* theory. Even Bourdieu, whom Loïc J. D. Wacquant has recently congratulated on 'the inclusion, at the heart of a theory of practice, of a theory of theoretical practice' (Bourdieu and Wacquant, *An Invitation to Reflexive Sociology*, p. 43) relates theory primarily to the practice of the scientific enquirer, that is, of the theorist. But Marx's point, I take it, was that no solution from within theory or even from within the practice of theorists is possible. It is only from the standpoint of social practice of a very different kind, one prior to both enquiry and theory, that a solution will be possible. What kind of practice might that be? It cannot be the kind of practice envisaged by those concerned to reform the institutions of civil society, without however abandoning its basic beliefs. For Marx had identified and found reason to reject the hierarchical structure of that type of reformist theory and practice. Those who without abandoning the standpoint of civil society take themselves to know in advance what needs to be done to effect needed change are those who take themselves to be therefore entitled to manage that change. Others are to be the passive recipients of what they as managers effect. This hierarchical division between managers and managed is thus legitimated by the superior knowledge imputed to themselves by the managing reformers, who have cast themselves in the role of educator. Marx almost certainly had foremost in mind Robert Owen, whom he had described in the Paris manuscripts as the author of 'an abstract philosophical philanthropy'. Owen was to have numerous successors in the subsequent history of socialism, among them both Lenin (at least on occasion) and Beatrice and Sidney Webb.

Notice that in the sixth thesis we once again confront the problem of interpreting what Marx expressed only in compressed and elliptical terms. What is it about the social educator's possession of theory that is taken to legitimate the educator's superior role? It must surely be that the educator takes her or himself not only to know more, but also to know best, that the educator takes her or himself to know what is genuinely good for others, something that they do not themselves know. Hence educators suppose themselves to be entitled to impose upon others *their* conception of the good. Marx contrasts the activity of this type of educator in respect of knowledge of the good with the activity involved in quite another kind of practice, one such that those engaged in it transform themselves and educate themselves through their own self-transformative activity, coming to understand their good as the good internal to that activity. Here again the elucidation of Marx's anti-Hegelian and anti-Feuerbachian thesis has had to be in Aristotelian terms. But this elucidation could scarcely be justified, if it proved impossible to cite any relevant example of just such a form of practice, one which would *both* be entitled to be called 'revolutionary' (the first and third theses) *and* be adequately characterizable only by an Aristotelian reference to the goods internal to it.

We find just such an example in the account given by Edward Thompson in *The Making of the English Working Class* of the communal life of the hand-loom weavers of Lancashire and Yorkshire before and during the greatest prosperity of those weaving communities at the end of the eighteenth and the beginning of the nineteenth century. At its best the hand-loom weaver's way of life sustained his family's independence and his own self-reliance. Honesty and integrity were highly valued and what Thompson calls the 'rhythm of work and leisure' allowed the cultivation of gardens, the learning of arithmetic and geometry, the reading and the composition of poetry. What the hand-loom weavers hoped to, but failed to sustain was 'a community of independent small producers, exchanging their products without the distortions of masters and middlemen' (p. 295). At their best they embodied in their practice a particular conception of human good, of virtues, of duties to each other and of the subordinate place of technical skills in human life, but one which they themselves had no theory to articulate. By so doing they had, to the extent that it was possible, placed themselves outside civil society. And a theory which had successfully articulated their practice and which had been formulated so that its dependence on that practice was evident would have supplied just the kind of example of the relationship of theory to practice which the argument expressed in the theses on Feuerbach so badly needs.

What made the practice of the hand-loom weavers revolutionary? It was the degree to which, in order to sustain their mode of life, they had to reject what those who spoke and acted from the standpoint of civil society regarded as the economic and technological triumphs of the age. So Thompson relates how capitalist progress in the end 'transformed the weavers into confirmed "physical force" Chartists . . .' (p. 302). Marx himself had experience of the militancy of weavers in the insurrection of the Silesian weavers of the Eulengebirge in 1844. But he seems not to have understood the form of life from which that militancy arose, and so later failed to understand that while proletarianization makes it necessary for workers to resist, it also tends to deprive workers of those forms of practice through which they can discover conceptions of a good and of virtues adequate to the moral needs of resistance. Yet in the theses on Feuerbach Marx came very close to formulating just the distinctions which might have enabled him to understand this. But to have expressed those distinctions clearly and to have developed their implications would perhaps have left Marx unable to define his relationship to the large-scale revolutionary changes which he had identified as imminent, tied instead to what he took to be already defeated forms of past life. Marx therefore may have had the alternatives either of rejecting philosophy or else of depriving himself of the possibility of immediate effective participation in great events. And perhaps this is why he rejected philosophy.

Some of Marx's thoughts in the theses do of course reappear in his later writings. But with his rejection of philosophy in 1845 he lost the opportunity to develop those thoughts systematically and to understand their implications for the relationship of theory to practice. In so doing he left behind him unfinished philosophical business and, when, later on, philosophy was revived within Marxism, it was typically either as the dialectical and historical materialism of Plekhanov, which emerged from Engels' misunderstanding of Marx's relationship to Feuerbach, or as the rational voluntarism of the young Lukács, in which Lukács revived strains in Marx's thought whose fullest expression had been in the Paris manuscripts of 1844. But this opposition, between on the one hand the philosophy of Engels and Plekhanov and on the other that of the young Lukács, revived in a new version, or rather in a series of new versions, one of the antitheses already put seriously in question by Marx himself in the theses on Feuerbach. Each party in these subsequent debates had an excellent diagnosis of the errors of its opponents. The partisans of the younger Lukács understood very well that if human beings were the products of circumstance and upbringing, in the terms propounded by Engels and Plekhanov, then the kind of revolutionary agency through which the limitations of circumstance and upbringing could be transcended became unintelligible. The partisans of Engels and Plekhanov understood equally well that if the possibilities of revolutionary agency were what the Lukács of *History and Class Consciousness* and of *Lenin* took them to be, then the nature of the historical determination of social and economic orders became quite unclear. In an early review of the former book Ernst Bloch predicted of the Bolsheviks that 'Some of them will say that Marx had not placed Hegel on his feet so that Lukács can put Marx back on his head' (*Der Neue Merkur*, October 1923–March 1924). Both the Bolsheviks who did so and Lukács himself were in different ways victims of this same misleading metaphor and with it of a philosophical inheritance which prevented both parties from understanding the significance of Marx's theses on Feuerbach.

This failure is peculiarly evident in two aspects of the history of moral philosophy within Marxism. One is the degree to which, when Marxists have been forced into moral debate, they have had to fall back upon the resources already provided by the moral philosophy of civil society, so that the contending parties merely repeat what had been already said earlier and better by the protagonists of that moral philosophy. So Kautsky in one way and Trotsky in another repeated theses of Benthamite utilitarianism, while theorists as different as Bernstein and Guevara echoed Kant. But even more significant is a second aspect of Marxist moral thinking.

From Marx and Engels onwards Marxists have generally supposed that an historical and sociological understanding of moral concepts and precepts as articulated within practices was incompatible with an appeal to objective standards of goodness, rightness and virtue, standards independent of the interests and attitudes of those engaged in such practices. And Marxists of course have not been alone in so supposing. But here once again there is a false antithesis. What the objectivity of moral and other evaluative standards amounts to is to be understood only from within the context of and in terms of the structure of certain types of historically developed practice, in which the initial interests of those engaged in such practices are transformed through their activities into an interest in conforming to the standards of excellence required by those practices, so that the goods internal to them may be achieved. These are types of practice socially marginalized by the self-aggrandizing and self-protective attitudes and activities characteristic of developing capitalism, types of practice alien to the standpoint of civil society. But they are the types of practice within which moral thinking is put to the relevant practical tests and achieves objectivity. It is only in such contexts that the question of 'whether objective truth can be attributed to human thinking' can be answered in respect of moral thought, and this question is not one 'of theory, but is a practical question' (the second thesis), answered by members of fishing crews and farming cooperatives and string quartets, just as by eighteenth-century hand-loom weavers and their medieval and ancient predecessors, only through and by reference to forms of practice which precede the theory that they so badly need. Only in and through such practices can the standpoint of civil society be transcended.

We still therefore need to take serious account of the insights of the theses on Feuerbach, if we are to be able to take a road forward which Marx himself did not take. I have noted how Marx was unable to develop his own insights in the theses. But the important thing now about the errors that resulted is not so much that they were Marx's errors, as that for so many of us they were *our* errors and the defeat of Marxism has been *our* defeat. But Marxism was not defeated, and we were not defeated, by the protagonists of the standpoint of civil society, who now mistakenly congratulate themselves on the collapse of Communist rule in so many states. Marxism was self-defeated and we too, Marxists and ex-Marxists and post-Marxists of various kinds, were the agents of our own defeats, in key part through our inability to learn in time some of the lessons of the theses on Feuerbach. The point is, however, first to understand this and then to start out all over again.

'Politics, Philosophy and the Common Good'

I am grateful to the editors of *Studi Perugini* for their invitation to contribute an introductory essay to this issue. But how should I respond? I have already elsewhere recounted how I found my way into the themes that have preoccupied me (see the interview with Giovanna Borradori and the interview for *Cogito*, below). And to summarize over again theses and arguments from my books would be less than helpful. Philosophy in abbreviated summary is no longer philosophy. How then to proceed?

What may be useful is to confront some misunderstandings of my work, especially those that concern its political implications. Hilary Putnam, for example, has asserted that my point of view is one which, by its attitude to alternative ways of life, tends to immunize institutionalized oppression from criticism (*Renewing Philosophy*, pp. 185–6). And several commentators have mistakenly assimilated my views to those of contemporary communitarianism. One principal aim of this present paper is therefore to dispel such misunderstandings. (For an accurate and perceptive discussion of my political views see Kelvin Knight, 'Revolutionary Aristotelianism'.) But I can only explain the full extent of my differences from communitarianism in the context of a diagnosis of the defects of the dominant politics of contemporary society. To this larger task I therefore turn first.

1 Philosophy and the exclusions of contemporary politics

How should the relationship of philosophy to politics and politics to philosophy be understood? Every complex form of social life embodies some answer to this question and the societies of advanced Western modernity are no exception. A central feature of those societies is the exceptional degree of compartmentalization imposed by their structures, so that the norms governing activities in any one area are specific to that area. As individuals move between home, school, workplace, the activities of leisure, the arenas of politics, bureaucratized encounters with government, and church or synagogue or mosque, they find themselves cast in different roles and required to express different and even sometimes incompatible attitudes. And, to the degree that one is at home in this kind of society, one will have to have acquired, not only the skills necessary for effectiveness in each of one's roles in each area, but an ability to move between areas and to adapt to the norms of different contexts. Someone who, for example, insists upon observing the same ethics of truthful disclosure in every sphere of life, holding her or himself and others accountable for their deceptions in the same way, whether it is a matter of conversation within the family, the pledges of politicians, the presentation of products by advertisers in the marketplace, or the information given to patients by physicians, will acquire a reputation not for integrity, but for social ineptitude. A compartmentalized society imposes a fragmented ethics. (On compartmentalization see further my 'What Has *Not* Happened in Moral Philosophy'.)

Unsurprisingly contemporary philosophical enquiry and contemporary politics both exhibit the marks of this compartmentalization. Each has become a specialized and professionalized area of activity, with its own specific idioms and genres, its own forms of apprenticeship, its own methods of protecting itself from anything that would put the form of its activities seriously in question. Consider how much that philosophers now write is addressed exclusively to other philosophers through the medium of the professional journal or how the teaching of philosophy has increasingly become the teaching of that philosophy that will enable those who receive it to become, if they wish, professional academic philosophers. Philosophical activity involves reflection upon concepts, theses and arguments that are central to the activities, attitudes, choices and conflicts of everyday life. But the outcome of such philosophical reflection cannot any longer play a significant part in reconstituting those activities and attitudes, in directing those choices or resolving those conflicts, just because of the barriers imposed by compartmentalization.

Just as philosophy has thereby been rendered unpolitical, so politics has been rendered unphilosophical. The rhetoric of political life sometimes suggests otherwise, but there is a large gap between that rhetoric and the types of argument that are practically effective in contemporary politics. The modern state is a large, complex and often ramshackle set of interlocking institutions, combining none too coherently the ethos of a public utility company with inflated claims to embody ideals of liberty and justice. Politics is the sphere in which the relationship of the state's subjects to the various facets of the state's activity is organized, so that the activities of those subjects do not in any fundamental way disrupt or subvert that relationship. Voters in liberal democracies are in some sense free to vote for whom and what they choose, but their votes will not be effective unless they are cast for one of those alternatives defined for them by the political elites. Conventional politics sets limits to practical possibility, limits that are characteristically presupposed by its modes of discourse, rather than explicitly articulated. It is therefore important in and to the political sphere that there should not occur extended argumentative debate of a kind that would make issues about these limits explicit and therefore matter for further debate. And one means of achieving this is to proscribe appeals to first principles. So in practice those who appeal in the course of political discussion to the will of God or the natural law or the greatest happiness of the greatest number or the categorical imperative will be heard only as adding rhetorical embellishments to their presentation, not as engaging in serious argument. When on occasion some set of issues from outside politics, as it is now normally understood, issues such as those raised in the United States by the civil rights movement, or by controversies over abortion, seems to make some reference to first principles inescapable, the task of the professionals of political life is to contain and domesticate those issues, so that any political appeal *to* first principles does not become a philosophical debate *about* first principles. And their success in achieving this exemplifies the degree to which politics has been successfully insulated from philosophy and philosophy from politics.

Politically the societies of advanced Western modernity are oligarchies disguised as liberal democracies. The large majority of those who inhabit them are excluded from membership in the elites that determine the range of alternatives between which voters are permitted to choose. And the most fundamental issues are excluded from that range of alternatives. An example of just such an issue is that presented by the threat of the imminent disappearance of the family or household farm and with it of a way of life the history of which has been integral to the history of the virtues from ancient times onwards. Good farming has required for its sustenance, and has in turn sustained, virtues that are central to all human life, and not just to farming.

Of course farming households have often failed to exhibit those virtues and farming societies have sometimes been mean-spirited and oppressive. But good farming has itself provided the standards by which bad farming and bad farmers are to be judged, through the way in which it has at its best fostered virtues of independence, virtues of cooperation in contributing to larger human enterprises and virtues of regard for the relationship of human beings to land that has been entrusted to their care. The destruction of the way of life of the household farm has therefore great significance for all of us and powerful statements of that significance – from Andrew Lytle to Wendell Berry – have not been lacking. Yet these statements have had no effective political impact, and this not because they have been heard within the political arena and then rejected. They have gone politically unheard. Why so?

There are of course issues that do receive recurrent attention within the political arena that are relevant to this final transformation of family farming into multinational agribusiness: taxes, tariffs, farm subsidies, interest rates, bankruptcy laws. What is remarkable is that, although under each of these headings multifarious issues are decided by bureaucrats, or

debated by legislators, or lumped together with others in party programs
for parliamentary elections, there has been nowhere in the entire political
process where the members of modern political societies have been invited to confront systematically the question: 'What do we take the significance of this transformation to be and should we or should we not
acquiesce in this loss of a whole way of life?' Questions about the value of
ways of life, let alone the provision of practically effective answers to
such questions, are excluded from the arenas of political debate and decision-making, even though answers to them are delivered by default, since
among the effects of modern governmental decisions is their impact upon
different ways of life, an impact that promotes some – the way of life
of the fashionably hedonistic consumer, for example – and undermines
others.

So far I have drawn attention to three salient features of the politics of
the modern state: the unphilosophical nature of that politics and with it
the exclusion from politics of philosophical questions concerning politics;
the closely related exclusion from political debate and decision-making of
substantive issues concerning ways of life; and the fact that the activities
of government are such that they are not in their effects neutral between
ways of life, but undermine some and promote others. To these three
features it is important to add a fourth. Political debate, whether in
electoral campaigns, in legislatures or in governmental bureaucracies is
rarely systematic or in any depth. It is not directed by canons of enquiry
or committed to following through the implications of arguments. It is
instead sporadic, apt to be more responsive to immediate concerns than
to the longer term, carried through by those who are both swayed by and
themselves make use of rhetorical modes of self-presentation, and open
to the solicitations of the rich and the powerful. Political debate, that is,
is generally and characteristically the antithesis of serious intellectual enquiry.

This fourth salient feature of contemporary politics marks the frustration of the political hopes of the Enlightenment and especially of Kant.
Enlightenment, on Kant's view, consists in thinking for oneself and not
in thinking as directed by the authority of some other. To achieve independence in one's thinking is to make what Kant called public use of
one's reasoning, that use which the scholar makes before the whole reading public ('An Answer to the Question: What is Enlightenment?'). Foucault
pointed out that the verb that Kant uses here – *räsionieren* – is characteristically used by him to refer to reasoning that pursues the goals internal
to reasoning: truth, theoretical and practical adequacy, and the like. Those
to whom such reasoning is presented are invited to evaluate it not from
the standpoint of this or that interest or purpose, but from the impersonal standpoint of reason as such. And it was Kant's hope that the
modes of thought embodied in scholarly enquiry, publication and debate,
modes which exemplified just such invitations to rational evaluation, would
spread from the arts and sciences to religion and thereafter to the framing

of legislation and the activities of government. But this of course is not
what has happened.

What we have instead in contemporary society are on the one hand a
set of small-scale academic publics – scientific, historical, literary – within
which the rational discourse of enquiry is carried on more or less in
accordance with Kant's ideals, publics however whose discourse has no
practical effect on the conduct of political life, and on the other those
areas of public life in which politically effective decisions are taken and
policies implemented, areas from whose discourse for the most part systematic, rational enquiry is excluded, and in which decisions and policies
emerge from a strange *mélange* of arguments, debating points and the
influence of money and other forms of established power. What is lacking in modern political societies is any type of institutional arena in which
plain persons – neither engaged in academic pursuits nor professionals of
the political life – are able to engage together in systematic reasoned
debate, designed to arrive at a rationally well-founded common mind on
how to answer questions about the relationship of politics to the claims
of rival and alternative ways of life, each with its own conception of the
virtues and of the common good. And it is perhaps in terms of the idiom
of the common good that these issues raised by contemporary politics are
best formulated.

For, if this account of contemporary politics is in outline correct, then
we now inhabit a social order whose institutional heterogeneity and diversity of interests is such that no place is left any longer for a politics of
the common good. What we have instead is a politics from whose agen-
das enquiry concerning the nature of that politics has been excluded, a
politics thereby protected from perceptions of its own exclusions and
limitations. Enquiry into the nature of the common good of political
society has become therefore crucial for understanding contemporary
politics. For until we know how to think about the common good, we
will not know how to evaluate the significance of those exclusions and
limitations.

2   Rival conceptions of the common good

The notion of the common good has been used in so many different
ways and for so many different purposes that some preliminary considerations are in order. First, we may justifiably speak of a common good in
characterizing the ends of a variety of very different types of human
association. The members of a family, the members of a fishing crew and
the members of an investment club, the students, teachers and administrators of a school and the scientists at work in a laboratory all share
aims in such a way that a common good can be identified as the end of
their shared activities. Secondly, among these there are cases in which the
common good of an association is no more than the summing of the

goods pursued by individuals as members of that association, just because the association itself is no more than an instrument employed by those individuals to achieve their individual ends. So it is, for example, with an investment club, by means of which individuals are able to avail themselves of investment opportunities requiring capital sums larger than any one of them possesses. Participation in and support for such associations is therefore rational only so long as and insofar as it provides a more efficient method of achieving their individual ends than would alternative types of activity open to them.

There are also however kinds of association such that the good of the association cannot be constructed out of what were the goods of its individual members, antecedently to and independently of their membership in it. In these cases the good of the whole cannot be arrived at by summing the goods of the parts. Such are those goods not only achieved by means of cooperative activity and shared understanding of their significance, but in key part constituted by cooperative activity and shared understanding of their significance, goods such as the excellence in cooperative activity achieved by fishing crews and by string quartets, by farming households and by teams of research scientists. Excellence in activity is of course often a means to goods other than and beyond that excellence, goods of types as various as the production of food and the making of reputations. But it is central to our understanding of a wide range of practices that excellence in the relevant kinds of activity is recognized as among the goods internal to those practices.

The achievement of excellence in activity characteristically requires the acquisition of skills, but without virtues skills lack the direction that their exercise requires, if excellence is to be achieved. So it is characteristic of such practices that engaging in them provides a practical education into the virtues. And for individuals who are so educated or are in the course of being so educated two questions arise inescapably, questions that may never be explicitly formulated, but which nonetheless receive answers in the way in which individuals live out their lives. For each individual the question arises: what place should the goods of each of the practices in which I am engaged have in my life? The goods of our productive activities in the workplace, the goods of ongoing family life, the goods of musical or athletic or scientific activity, what place should each have in my life, if my life as a whole is to be excellent? Yet any individual who attempts to answer this question pertinaciously must soon discover that it is not a question that she or he can ask and answer by her or himself and for her or himself, apart from those others together with whom she or he is engaged in the activities of practices. So the questions have to be posed: what place should the goods of each of the practices in which *we* are engaged have in *our* common life? What is the best way of life for *our* community?

These questions can only be answered by elaborating a conception of the common good of a kind of community in which each individual's achievement of her or his own good is inseparable both from achieving the shared goods of practices and from contributing to the common good of the community as a whole. According to this conception of the common good the identification of my good, of how it is best for me to direct my life, is inseparable from the identification of the common good of the community, of how it is best for that community to direct its life. Such a form of community is by its nature political, that is to say, it is constituted by a type of practice through which other types of practice are ordered, so that individuals may direct themselves towards what is best for them and for the community.

It is important to observe that, although this type of political society – let us recognize that in it which is Aristotelian by calling it a *polis* – does indeed require a high degree of shared culture by those who participate in it, it is not itself constituted by that shared culture and is very different from those political societies whose essential bonds are the bonds of a shared cultural tradition. A *polis* is at least as different from the political society of a *Volk* as either is from that of a liberal democracy. A *polis* is indeed impossible, unless its citizens share at least one language – they may well share more than one – and unless they also share modes of deliberation, formal and informal, and a large degree of common understanding of practices and institutions. And such a common understanding is generally derived from some particular inherited cultural tradition. But these requirements have to serve the ends of a society in which individuals are always able to put in question through communal deliberation what has hitherto by custom and tradition been taken for granted both about their own good and the good of the community. A *polis* is always, potentially or actually, a society of rational enquiry, of self-scrutiny. The bonds of a *Volk* by contrast are prerational and nonrational. The philosophers of the *Volk* are Herder and Heidegger, not Aristotle.

Enough has now been said for it to be possible to sketch the part that different conceptions of the common good play in different types of political justification. Political justifications are those arguments advanced to show why we, as members of some particular political society, should or should not accept as having legitimate authority over us the commands uttered by someone claiming executive authority over or in that society or the laws uttered by someone or some body claiming legislative authority over or in that society. Consider now the part played by different conceptions of the common good in different types of political justification.

There is, for example, the claim that political authority is justified insofar as it provides a secure social order within which individuals may pursue their own particular ends, whatever they are. Individuals need to cooperate, both in order to pursue their own particular ends effectively and in order to sustain the security of the social order. But all such cooperation is a means to their individual ends. The conception of the common good invoked in this type of justification of political authority is such that the common good is arrived at by summing individual goods. It is a conception at once individualist and minimalist. And justifications which employ it have this important political characteristic: that to the extent that they are believed in a political society, that political society is endangered by them, and this for two reasons.

First, if this is the justification for the acceptance of political authority, then rational individuals will attempt to share fully in the benefits provided by political authority, while making as small a contribution as possible to its costs. It will be rational to be a 'free rider', so long as one can avoid whatever penalties are imposed by political authority for free riding. Secondly, it will correspondingly be contrary to rationality, thus understood, to accept an undue share of the costs of sustaining political authority. But no political authority can be sustained over any extended period of time, unless some of those subject to it are prepared to pay an undue share of those costs and this in the most striking way, since the sustaining of political authority requires that some of those subject to it should be prepared, if necessary, to die for the sake of the security of the political and social order: soldiers, police officers, firefighters.

It follows that no political society can have a reasonable expectation of surviving, let alone flourishing, unless a significant proportion of its members are unconvinced that the only justification for accepting and upholding political society and political authority is individualist and minimalist. Only if they believe that there is some other and stronger type of connection between their own ends and purposes and the flourishing of their political society do they have good reason to be willing, if necessary, to die for the sake of that flourishing. And indeed, only if they believe that there is just such another and stronger type of connection, do they have sufficient reason to resist the temptation to act as 'free riders' on occasions in which they could do so without penalty.

An individualist and minimalist conception of the common good is then too weak to provide adequate justification for the kind of allegiance that a political society must have from its members, if it is to flourish. And any political society whose members hold themselves and one another to account in respect of the rational justification of their actions, including their collective political decision-making, will have to be one in which rational argument can sustain the claim that their practices and institutions exhibit a connection between the goods of individuals and the common good sufficient to afford a justification for their political allegiance. But we must not picture this connection between individual goods and the common good as something that might exist apart from and independently of the rational activity of the members of that society in enquiring and arguing about the nature of their goods. For it is a connection constituted by practically rational activity. Practical rationality is a property of individuals-in-their-social-relationships rather than of individuals-as-such. To be practically rational I must learn what my good is in different types of situation and I can only achieve that through interaction with others in which I learn from those others and they from me. Our primary shared and common good is found in that activity of communal learning through which we together become able to order goods, both in our individual lives and in the political society. Such practical learning is a kind of learning that takes place in and through activity, and in and through reflection upon that activity, in the course of both communal and individual deliberation.

When I speak of practical learning and practical enquiry, I refer to that type of learning and enquiry that takes place in the course of asking and answering practical deliberative questions about some subject matter, whenever there is a serious attempt to answer those questions as adequately as possible and to diagnose and to remedy whatever has been defective in one's past answers. Practical learning and enquiry are therefore features of various kinds of activity. It is found among farmers and fishing crews, in the work of households and in the practice of crafts. What is learned does not have to be formulated explicitly in words, although it may be so formulated. But it cannot take place without some significant transformation of activity. And where deliberation is integral to some type of activity, as it is to any politics of the common good, practical enquiry will be embodied in that type of reflective deliberation to which rational participants in such a politics are committed. Indeed politics will be that practical activity which affords the best opportunity for the exercise of our rational powers, an opportunity afforded only by political societies to whose decision-making widely shared rational deliberation is central, societies which extend practical rationality from the farm and the fishing fleet, the household and the craft workplace, to its political assemblies. It follows that no *Volk* can be such a society. It also follows that, if the political characteristics of advanced Western modernity are as I suggested earlier, and if, as I am now suggesting, claims to political allegiance can be justified only where there is the common good of communal political learning, then modern states cannot advance any justifiable claim to the allegiance of their members, and this because they are the political expression of societies of deformed and fragmented practical rationality, in which politics, far from being an area of activity in and through which other activities are rationally ordered, is itself one more compartmentalized sphere from which there has been excluded the possibility of asking those questions that most need to be asked.

3   Liberalism and communitarianism

Political philosophy in our culture is an academic and not a political activity. There are of course important parallels between the discussions in each sphere. Issues of rights, of utility, of legitimate authority and the like are central to both and in both the same principles are on occasion invoked and attacked. Yet it is only rarely, due to some quite unusual conjunction of circumstances, that something said in political philosophy has any effect on something done in politics. And even when it appears that this has happened, it is always wise to ask whether whatever it was that was done in politics would not have been done anyway, no matter what had been said in political philosophy.

It is therefore one thing to criticize liberalism as a philosophical theory and quite another thing to engage in conflict with contemporary liberal politics. It is true that contemporary liberal politics owes a good deal to past theorizing. For the formative periods of liberalism in the eighteenth and nineteenth centuries were periods in which the relationships of philosophy and politics were other than and closer than they are now. But the actualities of contemporary liberal politics – and I use the word 'liberal' inclusively here, so that it covers the whole spectrum of liberalisms from that of American self-styled conservatives to that of European self-styled social democrats – are not only in crucial respects different from the politics hoped for by the great prophetic theorists of eighteenth- and nineteenth-century liberalism but also at odds with the guiding principles of contemporary liberal theory. It is therefore not at all impossible to elaborate positions that are plainly incompatible with at least some versions of liberal theory, but nonetheless quite at home in the realities of contemporary liberal politics. Just this, I want to suggest, is the case with the theses of the movement that is identified by the name 'communitarianism'.

The principal exponents of communitarianism have defined their own positions by contrast with some central theses advanced by liberal theorists. Where liberal theorists have emphasized rights, communitarians have stressed relationships. Where liberal theorists have appealed to what they take to be universal and impersonal principles, communitarians have argued for the importance of particular ties to particular groups and individuals. And where liberal theorists have characteristically held that it is for each individual to arrive at her or his own conception of her or his good, communitarians have been anxious both to establish the existence of irreducibly social goods and to argue that a failure to achieve such goods will result in a defective social order.

It is easy to frame each of these two positions so that it not only contrasts with, but is set in sharp opposition to the other. And liberal critics of communitarianism have usually presented matters in this way. But there are certainly some versions of liberal theory and some formulations of communitarian positions which are such that the two are not only not in opposition to each other, but neatly complement one another. Communitarianism from this latter point of view is a diagnosis of certain weaknesses in liberalism, not a rejection of it. And consequently it is unsurprising that just as liberal theorists disagree among themselves about their own positions, so too they disagree about the implications of communitarianism. Yet the outcome of these debates at the level of theory may not be of great significance. For at the level of contemporary political actuality the key issues have already been settled. What is it about contemporary politics that makes this so?

Modern states retain the allegiance of those heterogeneous, overlapping and sometimes competing social groups to which their subjects belong by negotiating temporary settlements with those groups, whenever failure to achieve settlement with them would exact too high a price for the state to pay. But, in so doing, those engaged in government and in politics have to adopt a range of varying and sometimes incompatible stances, appealing to different and sometimes incompatible values, here giving market considerations an overriding value, there denying them this weight, here accepting governmental responsibility for this or that aspect of social life, there disowning it, here expressing respect for custom and tradition, there flouting them in the name of modernization. Modern government, that is to say, needs and has a ragbag of assorted values, from which it can select in an *ad hoc* way what will serve its purposes in this or that particular situation with this or that particular group. So it shows different faces and speaks with different and often enough incompatible voices in different types of situation. It is therefore no accident that contemporary politics is a politics of recurrently broken promises or that successful contemporary politicians are so often open to charges of flagrant inconsistency. A willingness to break promises and to shift positions has become, not a liability, but one aspect of what in the social life of modernity is accounted the chief of the virtues, adaptability.

The values defended by liberalism are of course among those indispensable to the governments of advanced modernity. Even those who flout them must pay lipservice to them. But the values of communitarianism are also to be found in the state's ragbag of values and they were there long before the name 'communitarianism' was given to them. So alongside the commitments of modern governments to universal principles that safeguard rights and confer liberties, there are the commitments of the same governments to uphold family ties and the solidarities of a variety of groups. And alongside the commitments of modern governments to extending the scope of market economies, there are a variety of commitments to sustain institutions whose workings are inimical to market relationships. What happens when in some particular situation one set of commitments conflicts with another? The answer is that there is no higher-order set of principles to which appeal can be made to resolve such conflicts. There are instead outcomes determined by shifting coalitions of interest and power within the limits set by and for those elites who determine – although not at all at will – the range of choices confronting governments.

So in the politics of modern government communitarian values coexist, sometimes uneasily, sometimes quite happily, with liberal values and it is only at those extremes of the political spectrum at which consistent adherence to principle entails political impotence that allegiance to liberalism is allowed to entail the rejection of communitarianism or vice versa.

A communitarian politics is at home within the contemporary institutional framework imposed by the state and the market and, just because it is thus at home, its conception of the common good is limited by that framework. Communitarians are apt to place great emphasis on their rejection of any merely individualist conception of the common good. But the communitarian conception of the common good is not at all that of a kind of community of political learning and enquiry participation in which it is necessary for individuals to discover what their individual and common goods are. Indeed in every statement by the protagonists of communitarianism that I have read the precise nature of the communitarian view of the relationship between the community, the common good and individual goods remains elusive. And that it should remain elusive is perhaps a condition of communitarians accommodating themselves, as they have in some cases so notably done, to the realities of contemporary politics.

4   The politics of local community

My arguments so far have resulted largely, if not entirely in negative conclusions. How are we to move beyond these? Any more adequate account of political community and authority will have to begin from a somewhat fuller account of political justification.

Political reflection is a relative latecomer on the human scene. And, when it does emerge, it must inevitably at first be local reflection, reflection upon local political structures, as these have developed through some particular social and cultural tradition, and moreover reflection guided by and limited by the conceptual and argumentative resources of that same tradition. As such reflection develops into philosophy, it continues debates and enquiries that are framed in terms that are in crucial ways specific to its own tradition – consider the differences between Confucian political reflection, the discussions in the *Mahabharata* and the political philosophies of Plato and Aristotle – but the questions that are thus framed in local terms are understood to have universal import and the answers supplied to those questions in local terms give expression to universal claims.

It could not be otherwise. For there is no culture whose inhabitants treat their own norms and their own conceptions of the human good as having merely local significance and local authority. Anthropologists, historians and philosophers may sometimes be relativists, but those about whom they write never are. So that when philosophers come to evaluate those norms and those conceptions, they confront the task of evaluating them as norms for which it is claimed that it would be right and best for all human beings to live by them and as adequate conceptions of the human good, and not of the Greek, or the Indian, or the Chinese good. So local philosophies, each with its own specific conceptual and argumentative resources, its own conception of reason, must pose such questions as: What are *the* norms appropriate for human beings as such? What is the human good? What is reason as such? And these turn out to be political as well as philosophical questions.

For every political and social order embodies and gives expression to an ordering of different human goods and therefore also embodies and gives expression to some particular conception of the human good. Hence when philosophers enquire about goods and the good, and most of all when they enquire about the common good of political society, and about what kind of political society it is in which human beings can best come to an understanding of their good, they necessarily put to the question the political order of their own society.

Correspondingly, when the representatives of the political order claim authority for their legislative, executive and judicial acts, they can now justify their claims only by showing that the exercise of their political authority accords with norms that serve the common good and the human good. There are indeed types of political justification that antedate the rise of philosophy, but the rise of philosophy transforms the nature and standards of political justification, by opening up questions to which political authority must either respond or discredit itself. Among these questions one is central: under what conditions are individuals able to learn about their individual and common goods, so that questions about the justification of political authority can be asked and answered through rational enquiry and debate? What form of social and political life makes this possible?

It will have three sets of characteristics. First, it will be a type of community whose members generally and characteristically recognize that obedience to those standards that Aquinas identified as the precepts of the natural law is necessary, if they are to learn from and with each other what their individual and common goods are (see my 'Natural Law as Subversive: The Case of Aquinas'). In such a society the authority of positive law, promulgated by whatever means the community adopts, will derive from its conformity to the precepts of the natural law and from the acknowledgment of that conformity by plain persons. And plain persons will thereby exhibit their understanding that truthfulness, respect for, patience with and care for the needs of others, and the faithful keeping of promises, are required of us, just because without relationships governed by these norms they will not be able to learn what they most need to learn. But strict observance of these norms of a kind that involves a practical understanding of their point and purpose, rather than a mere fetishism of rules, requires the cultivation and exercise of the virtues of prudence, temperateness, courage and justice. So the life of such a society will embody to some significant extent a shared practical understanding of the relationships between goods, rules and virtues, an understanding that may or may not be articulated at the level of theory, but that will be embodied in and presupposed by the way in which immediate practical questions receive answers in actions.

This type of shared understanding is one familiar to most of us in a variety of local social contexts. We rely on it in many of the everyday enterprises of family and household life, in schools, in neighborhoods, in parishes, on farms, in fishing crews and in other workplaces, and, that is to say, in all those practices and projects in which immediate decision-making has to presuppose rationally justifiable answers to such questions as 'How does my good relate to the good of others engaged in this enterprise?' and 'How does the good to be achieved through this enterprise relate to the other goods of my and their lives?' Where that understanding is absent, is indeed excluded, is in the activities that have come to be labeled 'politics' in the contemporary meaning of that term. So paradoxically the life of so-called politics is now one from which the possibility of rational political justification is excluded, while in many local contexts that possibility remains open. Reflection on why this is so directs our attention to a second set of characteristics that a society must possess, if it is to be one in which individuals are able through practice to learn about their individual and common goods.

Such societies must be small-scale and, so far as possible, as self-sufficient as they need to be to protect themselves from the destructive incursions of the state and the wider market economy. They need to be small-scale, so that, whenever necessary, those who hold political office can be put to the question by the citizens and the citizens put to the question by those who hold political office in the course of extended deliberative debate in which there is widespread participation and from which no one from whom something might be learned is excluded – that is, from which no one is excluded. The aim of this deliberative participation is to arrive at a common mind and the formal constitutional procedures of decision-making will be designed to serve this end. Once again I am not describing something alien to everyday experience. This is a kind of deliberative participation familiar in many local enterprises through which local community is realized. What is less familiar is the claim that these local arenas are now the only places where political community can be constructed, a political community very much at odds with the politics of the nation-state.

Two aspects of the difference between them should be stressed. First, the politics of small-scale local community politics cannot be a separate compartmentalized, specialized area of activity, as it is for the politics of advanced modernity. More generally, the forms of compartmentalization characteristic of advanced modernity are inimical to the flourishing of local community. The activities of local communities will indeed be differentiated into different spheres, those of the family, of the workplace and of the parish, for example. But the relationship between the goods of each set of activities is such that in each much the same virtues are required and in each the same vices are all too apt to be disclosed, so that an individual is not fragmented into her or his separate roles, but is able to succeed or fail in ordering the goods of her or his life into a unified whole and to be judged by others in respect of that success or failure. One and the same set of individuals and groups will encounter each other in the context of a number of very different types of activity, moving between one sphere and another, so that individuals cannot avoid being judged for what they are. And in politics especially individuals show themselves as deserving the confidence of others as holders of political office by the integrity of their own pursuit of both their own good and the common good in a variety of spheres, and especially those of the home and the workplace, as well as in their specifically political abilities. Where adaptability is now the key virtue of the dominant and conventional forms of politics, integrity is the key virtue of the politics of local community.

Once again the difference from the politics of the modern state is striking. For this latter is a politics in which the techniques of self-presentation, the techniques of advertisement in the market place, are characteristically used to project images behind which candidates for public office can conceal aspects of their reality. The candidate has become to some degree a fictional construction, a figure constructed by public relations experts, speech-writers, manipulators of opinion and cosmetic artists, very much as a film star is or used to be. The problem here is not only that of the gap between image and reality. It is that the ambitious candidate tends all too often to become whatever an effective image requires her or him to become.

We have then identified two sets of characteristics that must be possessed by any society in which there is a possibility of rational political justification, and with it of rational politics: first, it must have a large degree of shared understanding of goods, virtues, and rules and, secondly, it must be a relatively small-scale society whose relationships are not deformed by compartmentalization. But there is also a third set of conditions to be satisfied. The deliberative and other social relationships of such a society are systematically violated by some of the most notable effects of large-scale so-called free market economies (see on this the Introduction to the second edition of *Marxism and Christianity*). Such economies are misnamed 'free markets'. They in fact ruthlessly impose market conditions that forcibly deprive many workers of productive work, that condemn parts of the labor force in metropolitan countries and whole societies in less developed areas to irremediable economic deprivation, that enlarge inequalities and divisions of wealth and income, so organizing societies into competing and antagonistic interests. And under such conditions inequality of wealth ensures inequality in access to the sources of both economic and political power.

Genuinely free markets are always local and small-scale markets in whose exchanges producers can choose to participate or not. And societies with genuinely free markets will be societies of small producers – the family farm is very much at home in such societies – in which no one is denied the possibility of the kind of productive work without which they cannot take their place in those relationships through which the common good is realized. Such societies can never of course aspire to achieve the levels of economic and technological development of advanced modernity. But from the standpoint of those who give their allegiance to such societies the price to be paid for limitless development would involve a renunciation of their common good. Indeed the conception of the common good presupposed by large-scale so-called free market economies is necessarily an individualist one, although the 'individuals' are sometimes corporate entities. So that the conflict between the kind of local community that I have been characterizing and the international and national economic order is at the level of practice, as well as that of theory, a conflict between rival conceptions of the common good.

5 A response to some misunderstandings and objections

We are now in a position to understand better what it is that makes some types of social relationship oppressive. Some measure of inequality – it must not be too large – is not necessarily oppressive. And that some people rather than others should exercise power through political office is not necessarily a mark of oppression. What is always oppressive is any form of social relationship that denies to those who participate in it the possibility of the kind of learning from each other about the nature of their common good that can issue in socially transformative action. It is this that makes relationships between slave-owners and slaves oppressive and it is no accident that defenders of slavery from Aristotle to the apologists for slavery in the American South have felt compelled to assert what is plainly false, that their slaves do not possess the capacity for rational learning. And so it is too with certain other forms of oppression. The justification of the oppression of women has characteristically represented them as inferior to men in rationality. The justification of European imperialist annexations of territory has characteristically represented its native inhabitants as lacking the rational powers to develop it.

Although I have not drawn attention to it, the argument that has led us to this point is one that has drawn systematically on the conceptual and argumentative resources of a Thomistic Aristotelianism. But while it is important to notice this, it is also important to notice how much of this account of political community and political justification is at odds with Aristotle himself, and not only because it rejects his exclusions of women and slaves from citizenship. For Aristotle believed falsely that the life of productive labor of a farmer, for example, was incompatible with the political life (*Politics*, 1328b33–1329a2). And here he needs to be corrected, on the basis of his own principles, by drawing upon another tradition, one also stemming from the ancient world, that agrarianism, to which I referred earlier – its charter document is Xenophon's *Oeconomicus* – which has understood that the virtues of the farmer and of the fisherman are the same virtues needed in the politics of small-scale community. And some of the positions for which I have contended in this paper constitute just such a correction. But still more is needed by way of correction, and a philosopher who can provide much of what we need at this point is Marx, Marx himself, that is, rather than those Marxist systems that have been apt to obscure Marx. The questions that we now need to put of Marx's texts are significantly different from those most often posed in the past, whether by those participating in or by those opposed to the movements of social democracy and communism (on this see 'The *Theses on Feuerbach*: A Road Not Taken', above). And they are questions – about the relationship, for example, of the ineradicable defects of the so-called free market economy to the nature of social activity – answers to which are badly needed by any form of Aristotelianism that aspires to contemporary relevance.

It is one of the marks of a community of enquiry and learning that, while it cannot but begin from the standpoint of its own cultural and social tradition, what it is able to learn, in order to sustain itself, includes knowing how to identify its own incoherences and errors and how then to draw upon the resources of other alien and rival traditions in order to correct these. And Hilary Putnam's misinterpretation of the political content of my positions can now be seen to derive not only from failing to understand what they imply about oppression, but also from resolutely ignoring what I have written about the relationships between different and rival traditions of enquiry. Nonetheless there is a much more plausible objection to my positions than Putnam's that is closely related to his.

I have asserted not only that the kind of small-scale political community that deserves our rational allegiance will characteristically have a high degree of shared cultural inheritance, but also that its life will have to be informed by a large measure of agreement not only on its common good, but on human goods in general. And not only liberals may find this alarming. For this may seem at first glance to be a kind of community that could have no room for individuals or groups who do not share the prevailing view of human goods. But this is a mistake, and not only because nothing that I have said precludes the existence within such a political society of individuals and groups who hold and are recognized to hold radically dissenting views on fundamental issues. What will be important to such a society, if it holds the kind of view of the human good and the common good that I have outlined, will be to ask what can be learned from such dissenters. It will therefore be crucial not only to tolerate dissent, but to enter into rational conversation with it and to cultivate as a political virtue not merely a passive tolerance, but an active and enquiring attitude towards radically dissenting views, a virtue notably absent from the dominant politics of the present. This is a lesson to be learned from our own Christian past. For among the worst failures of Christianity has been the inability of Christian societies, except on the rarest of occasions, to listen to and learn from the dissenting Jewish communities in their midst, an inability that has been both a consequence and a cause of the poisonous corruption of Christianity by anti-Semitism.

A very different accusation that has been and will be leveled against my political positions is that I am recommending a politics of Utopian ineffectiveness. It is impossible, so such critics will say, to change anything worth changing in the modern world except by engaging in the conventional politics of the nation-state, since too many of the problems of local communities are inextricably bound up with national and international issues. This objection moves from true premises to a false conclusion. Any worthwhile politics of local community will certainly have to concern itself in a variety of ways with the impact upon it of the nation-state and of national and international markets. It will from time to time need to secure resources from them, but only, so far as is possible, at a price acceptable by the local community. It will from time to time have to concern itself with the conflicts between and within nation-states, sometimes aligning itself with this or that contending party in order to assist in defeating such politically destructive forces as those of imperialism or National Socialism or Stalinist communism. But it will always also have to be wary and antagonistic in all its dealings with the politics of the state and the market economy, wherever possible challenging their protagonists to provide the kind of justification for their authority that they cannot in fact supply. For the state and the market economy are so structured as to subvert and undermine the politics of local community. Between the one politics and the other there can only be continuing conflict.

To this it may be replied in turn that these responses to misinterpretations and objections are much too brief to be convincing to those who advance them. Indeed they are. In this paper all that I have attempted is to state rather than to defend a set of positions, and even so to state them only in outline. Those statements provide, I hope, a starting-point for further debate and enquiry and this in at least three areas. First, the diagnosis of the ills of contemporary politics needs to be extended and deepened. Secondly, it is important to note that the conflict between the politics of local community and the dominant modes of contemporary politics is not only a conflict between rival conceptions of the common good. It is also a conflict between alternative understandings of practical rationality and we need a better philosophical account of what is at stake in this conflict than has hitherto been provided. And finally it is important to examine instructive examples of the politics of local community in a variety of social and cultural contexts, so as to learn better what makes such politics effective or ineffective. There is both philosophical and political work to be done.

PART VI

Reflecting on the Project

An interview with
Giovanna Borradori

Q   Not only are you one of the last European philosophers to have left
    the Old World for the New, but you are also one of the most enig-
    matic, because at the basis of this choice are neither racial nor politi-
    cal considerations. If you had to describe, in a few words, the cultural
    and existential baggage you carried with you on your first crossing,
    what would you include?

A   Long before I was old enough to study philosophy I had the philo-
    sophical good fortune to be educated in two antagonistic systems of
    belief and attitude. On the one hand, my early imagination was en-
    grossed by a Gaelic oral culture of farmers and fishermen, poets and
    storytellers, a culture that was in large part already lost, but to which
    some of the older people I knew still belonged with part of them-
    selves. What mattered in this culture were particular loyalties and ties
    to kinship and land. To be just was to play one's assigned role in the
    life of one's local community. Each person's identity derived from
    the person's place in their community and in the conflicts and argu-
    ments that constituted its ongoing (or by the time of my childhood
    no longer ongoing) history. Its concepts were conveyed through its
    histories. On the other hand, I was taught by other older people that
    learning to speak or to read Gaelic was an idle, antiquarian pastime,
    a waste of time for someone whose education was designed to enable
    him to pass those examinations that are the threshold of bourgeois
    life in the modern world.

Q   What were your perceptions of the 'modern world' during a youth
    spent among these contrasting cultural realities?

A   The modern world was a culture of theories rather than stories. It
    also presented itself as the milieu of what purported to be 'morality'
    as such; its claims upon us were allegedly not those of some particu-
    lar social group, but those of universal rational humanity. So, part of
    my mind was occupied by stories about Saint Columba, Brian Boru,

and Ian Lom, and part by inchoate theoretical ideas, which I did not as yet know derived from the liberalism of Kant and Mill.

Q   Was it philosophy that suggested the way to reconcile these contrasting worlds?

A   Philosophy taught me the importance of not holding contradictory beliefs, partly by reading Plato and partly by coming across the proof, originally discovered by Thomas of Erfurt and then rediscovered by the pragmatist C.I. Lewis, that if you assert a contradiction, you are thereby committed to asserting anything whatsoever. So every contradiction within one's belief is a potential source of disaster. Yet in the same period in which I became aware of the importance of coherence and consistency in belief, the incoherence of my own mind was growing rather than diminishing. My school and undergraduate studies were in Latin and Greek – literature, philosophy, and history – and I became aware of the radical difference not only between classical Greek culture and liberal modernity, but also between the ancient Greeks and Irish tradition.

Q   At that moment of your development, who were your guiding figures?

A   I began to read George Thomson, a professor of Greek first at Galway and then at Birmingham and a member of the Executive Committee of the British Communist Party. He played a part, I believe, in my joining the Communist Party for a short time. In 1941, he published *Aeschylus and Athens*, which came after a history of Greek philosophy up to Plato written in Irish, entitled *Tosnù na Feallsùnachta*, as well as the translation of some Platonic dialogues into Irish. It was through thinking about the problems of translation involved in rendering Greek philosophy into modern languages as different as English and Irish that I had my first inklings of two truths: that different languages as used by different societies may embody different and rival conceptual schemes, and that translation from one such language to some other such language may not always be possible. There are cultures and languages-in-use that one can only inhabit by learning how to live in them as a native does. And there are theories framed in different languages-in-use whose incommensurability arises from their partial untranslatability. These were thoughts that I only developed fully some thirty-five years later in 'Relativism, Power and Philosophy' and in *Whose Justice? Which Rationality?*

Q   From what you say, one might suggest it was a matter of 'hermeneutic glimmers': of intuition about the incommensurability and untranslatability of language, tied to the Continental tradition stretching from German Romanticism to Heidegger and Gadamer.

A   Yes, that's true, though at the time I didn't know much about hermeneutics. The reading that first my undergraduate, and then my graduate studies required of me only accentuated the incoherence of my beliefs. I read Aquinas as well as Aristotle. Sometimes I would find myself thinking about justice in an Aristotelian or Thomistic way, sometimes in a modern liberal way, without recognizing the full extent of my own incoherence. No wonder I found it increasingly difficult to discover adequate rational grounds for the belief in Christianity that I thought I had, and that faith came to look like arbitrariness.

Q   In what sense was Christianity the disruptive element in all your contradictions?

A   For a time, I tried to fence off the area of religious belief and practice from the rest of my life, by treating it as a *sui generis* form of life, with its own standards internal to it, and by blending a particular interpretation of Wittgenstein's notion of a 'form of life' with Karl Barth's theology. But I soon recognized that the claims embodied in the uses of religious language and practice are in crucial ways inseparable from a variety of nonreligious metaphysical, scientific, and moral claims, a conclusion I reached when reading Hans Urs von Balthasar's criticism of Barth. When I came to reject this strange philosophical mixture of a misunderstood Wittgenstein and an all-too-well understood Barth, I mistakenly rejected the Christian religion along with it. But parts of Thomism survived in my thought from those times, together with some more adequate reflections on Wittgenstein.

Q   Your account of your development is saturated with existential inquietude. It is not clear to me how much of this is due to the friction between the ancient Celtic narrative tradition and the modern, Anglo-Saxon utilitarian tradition, and how much to the imposing religious presence.

A, When I look back on my asserted beliefs in that period, I see my thinking as having been a clumsily patched together collection of fragments. And for years this vision was felt as a very disquieting one. Nonetheless, I was able to effect a reconciliation. The history of late nineteenth-century physics and the problems that Maxwell and Boltzman faced when confronted by inconsistencies they could not know how to remove, convinced me that a premature regimentation of one's thought in the interest of total consistency may well lead to the rejection of important truths. However, I do remember my formation as being immersed in a painful state of mind, simultaneously drawn in a number of directions intellectually.

Q   I imagine that this sense of disorientation was further exacerbated by the emergence of Marxism, to which tradition you were connected for a long time.

A   Certainly Marxism added another dimension of complexity. But it also represented a turning point. It was in thinking about Marxism that I began the work of resolving the conflicts in which I was trapped. Even if Marxist characterizations of advanced capitalism are inadequate, the Marxist understanding of liberalism as ideological, as a deceiving and self-deceiving mask for certain social interests, remains compelling. Liberalism in the name of freedom imposes a certain kind of unacknowledged domination, and one which in the long run tends to dissolve traditional human ties and to impoverish social and cultural relationships. Liberalism, while imposing through state power regimes that declare everyone free to pursue whatever they take to be their own good, deprives most people of the possibility of understanding their lives as a quest for the discovery and achievement of the good, especially by the way in which it attempts to discredit those traditional forms of human community within which this project has to be embodied.

Q   The first result of your encounter with Marxism was therefore the refusal and criticism of liberalism in all its versions.

A   Yes, including the liberalism of contemporary American and English conservatives, as well as that of American and European radicals, and even the liberalism of the self-proclaimed liberals. Furthermore, it was Marxism which convinced me that every morality including that of modern liberalism, however universal its claims, is the morality of some particular social group, embodied and lived out in the life and history of that group. Indeed, a morality has no existence except in its actual and possible social embodiments, and what it amounts to is what it does or can amount to in its socially embodied forms. So that to study any morality by first abstracting its principles and then studying these in isolation from the social practice informed by them is necessarily to misunderstand them. Yet this is how almost all modern moral philosophy proceeds.

Q   On this issue you are still, if not a Marxist, a materialist.

A   No. Because if I had gone on being a Marxist this lesson would not have been of much use to me. For Marxism is not just an inadequate, but a largely inept, instrument for social analysis. Most happily for me, when I was a student in London I met the anthropologist Franz Steiner, who pointed me toward ways of understanding moralities that avoided both the reductionism of presenting morality as a mere secondary expression of something else, and the abstractionism that detaches principles from socially embodied practice. Rival forms of such practice are in contention, a contention which is neither only a rational debate between rival principles nor a clash of rival social structures, but always inseparably both.

Q   What is the role of dialogue in this contention? One of the errors of Marxism has often been its tendency to 'canonize' and to dry up forms of social debate.

A   Personally, from the history of Marxism I learned how important it is for any theory to be formulated so that it is maximally open to the possibility of refutation. Only later on I realized that I could have learned the same lesson from a critic of Marxism such as Karl Popper, or from a pragmatist like Charles Peirce. If a standpoint is not able to be shown, by its own standards, to be discordant with reality, it cannot be shown to be concordant either. It becomes a scheme of thought within which those who give it their allegiance become imprisoned and also protected from the realities about which their beliefs were originally formulated.

Q   Until now you have described the development of your thought in a negative key, trying to retrace the theoretical lines from which you have progressively detached yourself. What was the turning point towards the *pars construens* of your identity as a thinker? Your emigration to the United States, perhaps?

A   During the first twenty years of my philosophical career – from 1951 to 1971 when I had just emigrated to the United States – a good deal of what I did and thought was in the style of analytic philosophy. Analytic philosophy's strengths and weaknesses both derive from its exclusive focus on a rigorous treatment of detail, one that results in a piecemeal approach to philosophy, isolable problem by isolable problem. Its literary genres are the professional journal article and the short monograph.

Q   In effect, at least since your book *After Virtue*, you have concentrated on restoring political legitimacy to the so-called great questions. How did these efforts contrast with those of the analytical establishment?

A   What analytic philosophy gains in clarity and rigor, it loses in being unable to provide decisive answers to substantive philosophical questions. It enables us – at least it enabled me – to rule out certain possibilities. But while it can identify, for each alternative view that remains, what commitments one will be making by way of entailments and presuppositions, it is not capable in itself of producing any reason for asserting any one thing over any other. When analytic philosophers do reach substantive conclusions, as they often do, those conclusions only derive in part from analytic philosophy. There is always some other agenda in the background, sometimes concealed, sometimes obvious. In moral philosophy it is usually a liberal political agenda.

Q   Do you believe you have complete control of the 'ideological' net that governs your thought?

A   It was in the latter part of my analytic stage, around the mid-sixties, that I developed a new agenda. I had come to recognize that a second weakness of analytic philosophy was the extent of the divorce between its inquiries and the study of the history of philosophy, and that analytic philosophy, and more especially its moral philosophy, could only itself be adequately understood if placed in historical context and thus understood as the intelligible outcome of extended argument and debate. So I wrote *A Short History of Ethics*, a book from whose errors I learned a lot.

Q   What kinds of errors are you thinking about?

A   First of all, a recurring lack of continuity at certain points in the narrative. There is an account of the development of a distinctively Greek debate about ethics, an account of the development of a very different set of distinctive Christian lines of thought, and an account of the variety of argumentative encounters and rival conclusions that emerged from Enlightenment and post-Enlightenment moral philosophy. But what goes unremarked are the discontinuities at the points of transition from each one of these to the next. The fundamental shifts in central concepts and in basic principles are reported, but they appear as pure facts, unscrutinized and not at all understood.

Q   The error, then, was not having individuated the value of certain discontinuities or epistemological *coupures* in the historical development of moral philosophy – a subject which seems to me to be directly in tune with contemporary debate on both sides of the Atlantic, from Thomas S. Kuhn to Michel Foucault.

A   Up to that point I had at least tried to present each phase in the history of ethics as the expression of the rational moral claims of some specific type of society. In that book I decided to counterpose two forms of moral utterance: on the one hand, the morality of those who use morality to express their membership in some particular type of society; on the other, the morality of those who use it to express their individuality, or social diversity. In a genuine morality it is the rules that have authority, not the individuals. The notion of choosing one's own morality makes no sense. What *does* make sense is the much more radical notion of choosing to displace and overcome morality. So *A Short History of Ethics* should perhaps have ended by giving Nietzsche the final word, instead of leaving him behind two chapters earlier.

Q   I presume you are referring to the mature Nietzsche, author of *Beyond Good and Evil* and hero of the systematic overcoming of any value, the anarchic and individualistic Übermensch.

A   Nietzsche occupies this position insofar as he represents the ultimate answer to the systematic inconclusiveness and irreconcilable disagreements that were the outcome of Enlightenment and post-Enlightenment moral philosophy. The Enlightenment's central project had been to identify a set of moral rules, equally compelling to all rational persons. That project had failed and its heirs were a number of rival standpoints, Kantian, utilitarian, contractualist, and various blends of these, whose disagreements multiplied in such a way that twentieth-century culture has been deprived of any widely shared, rational morality, but has inherited instead an amalgam of fragments from past moral attitudes and theories. From a methodological point of view, it is today clear to me that while I was writing *A Short History of Ethics* I should have taken as a central standpoint what I learned from R. G. Collingwood: that morality is an essentially historical subject matter and that philosophical inquiry, in ethics as elsewhere, is defective insofar as it is not historical.

Q   What do you mean by saying that morality is 'an essentially historical subject matter'? Is it not possible that behind Collingwood and Marx, *lector in fabula*, peeps out Giambattista Vico?

A   Vico reminded us of what the Enlightenment had forgotten, that rational inquiry, whether about morality or about anything else, continues the work of, and remains rooted in, prerational myth and metaphor. Such inquiry does not begin from Cartesian first principles, but from some contingent historical starting point, some occasion that astonishes sufficiently to raise questions, to elicit rival answers and, hence, to lead on to contending argument. Such arguments, when developed systematically through time, become a salient feature of the social relationships they inform and to which they give expression. Prerational cultures of story telling are transformed into rational societies in which the stories are first put into question and then partially developed by theories, which are themselves in turn put to the question.

Q   History would then coincide with pure cultural and narrative tradition. It is difficult to maintain that this argument does not entail a historicist conception of history.

A   To understand some particular philosophical position requires being able to locate it within such a tradition, always in relation to its successors. It is insofar as it transcends the limitations and corrects the mistakes of those predecessors, and insofar as it opens up new possibilities for those successors, that it achieves rational justification. It is insofar as it fails in these tasks that it fails as a philosophical theory. So the best theory, that to which we owe our rational allegiance, in moral philosophy as elsewhere, is always the best theory to be developed so far within the particular tradition in which we find ourselves at work.

Q   However, from this point on it is easy to slide into a form of absolute relativism.

A   It can happen that a tradition of moral thought and practice fails to flourish. Its resources may not be adequate to solve the problems that are crucial to its rational inquiries. Its internal or external conflicts may undermine those agreements which made collaborative debate and inquiry possible. And its dissolution or rejection may leave a society without adequate resources for reconstructing its morality, while making the need for such reconstruction painfully evident.

Q   And is this the case of the European Enlightenment at the end of the eighteenth century?

A   Precisely. In *After Virtue* I argued that the failure of the Enlightenment project is best understood as a sequel to the wrong-headed rejection, in the sixteenth and seventeenth centuries, of what I called 'the tradition of the virtues'. That tradition had its birth first in the transition from older forms of Greek community to the fifth-century Athenian *polis*, and then in the criticism and construction of a theory and practice of the virtues in which Socrates, Plato, and Aristotle are the key names. It is a tradition with a shared core conception of virtues. Virtues are those qualities of mind and character without which the goods internal to such human practices as those of the arts and the sciences and such productive activities as those of farming, fishing, and architecture cannot be achieved. Second, virtues are those qualities without which an individual cannot achieve that life, or-

dered in terms of those goods, which is best for her or him to achieve;
and third, those qualities without which a community cannot flourish, and there can be no adequate conception of overall human good.

Q   From a textual point of view, your stand on the recovery of 'virtues'
as opposed to the universalistic idea of 'a virtue' in the singular, is
anchored in the philosophy of Aristotle.

A   True. This complex conception of virtues received its classical statement from Aristotle in a form that requires not only the justification
of the central theses of his political and moral philosophy, but also
that of the metaphysics which those theses presuppose. This latter
connection between virtue and metaphysics I had not understood
when I wrote *After Virtue*. What I *had* recognized was that the failure
of the Enlightenment project left open two alternatives: to recon-
struct the moral theory and communal practice of Aristotelianism in
whatever version would provide the best theory so far, explaining the
failure of the Enlightenment as part of the aftermath of the breakdown of a tradition; or, instead, to understand the failure of the
Enlightenment as a symptom of the impossibility of discovering any
rational justification for morality as hitherto understood, a sign of
the truth of Nietzsche's diagnosis. So the choice posed by *After Virtue* was: Aristotle or Nietzsche?

Q   Why not Nietzsche?

A   For two reasons. One concerns Nietzsche and the spelling out in
detail of his genealogical project by recent followers such as Michel
Foucault and Gilles Deleuze. What they have quite unintentionally
put in question is the possibility of making that project sufficiently
intelligible in its own terms. The outcome of the unmasking of others
by the genealogist seems to me to have been in the end the self-
unmasking of the genealogists. A second reason for rejecting Nietzsche
is an Aristotelian one. It reflects both a discovery that the narrative
of my own uneven intellectual and moral development could only be
both intelligibly and truthfully written in Aristotelian terms, and a
recognition that in those medieval debates that reconstituted the
Aristotelian tradition in Islamic, Jewish, and Christian milieus,
Aristotelianism as a political and moral philosophy had both progressed by its own standards and withstood external criticism. It
finally emerged in its Thomistic version as a more adequate account
of the human good, of virtues, and of rules, than any other I have
encountered.

Q   Hence you try to reconcile two historically contrasting lines of thought:
on one side, the historicist hypothesis, and on the other, the Aristo-

telian categorical instance. Your version of historicism emphasizes the idea that theories can be elaborated and criticized only in the context of specific historical-cultural traditions. Aristotelianism, in contrast, proceeds on the supposition that things are universally 'based', and it does not start from the historical context of a specific tradition.

A The claims made from within all well-developed traditions of inquiry on behalf of their own best philosophical, moral, and scientific theories are indeed generally claims to truth, claims about what anyone in any tradition must recognize if those claims are to be counted as genuine knowledge. The activities of inquiry themselves presuppose a strong and substantive conception of truth. And even if it is inescapable that the relationship between truth and rationality is problematic, it does not seem to me to be peculiarly a problem for Aristotelianism. One reason why some have thought there is an insuperable difficulty here is that they have understood that if any set of assertions or theory claims truth, then it must be possible to compare the merits of that claim with the merits of rival claims to truth made on behalf of incompatible sets of assertions or theories about the same subject matter. But if there are no neutral standards of rational justification independent of tradition, so that rival theories stemming from different traditions are each evaluated by reference to the standards internal to its own tradition, then it seems impossible to provide the requisite kind of comparison. Such rival theories will be incommensurable. Hence any historicism that relativizes rational justification to the context of particular traditions of inquiry has seemed incompatible with any standpoint, such as that of Aristotelianism, which asserts the truth of its conclusions.

Q And how do you counterattack this apparently flawless argument?

A As I argued in *Whose Justice? Which Rationality?* the mistake is to suppose that if two or more rival bodies of theory have satisfied a condition of being formulated so as to be maximally open to refutation, each by the best standards available within its own tradition, then it is always possible that one of those rivals succeeds by its own standards in meeting all the critical challenges offered to it, while the other or others fail. That they fail by the standards of their own tradition does not make this any less a failure in achieving rational justification. It is in these terms that Aristotelianism failed with respect to key parts of its physics and biology, but succeeded in vindicating itself rationally as metaphysics, as politics and morals and as a theory of inquiry. If this is so, then Aristotelianism has been shown in at least these areas to be not only the best theory so far, but the best theory so far about what makes a particular theory the best one.

At this point, it is rational to proceed in philosophy as an Aristotelian, until and unless reasons are provided for doing otherwise.

Q I think you are the only one on the contemporary philosophical scene, and most of all on this side of the Atlantic, to repropose Aristotelianism as an epistemological perspective. How does it feel to be in this unique position?

A Let's begin with our disagreements. Unlike Davidson, I hold that there are rival and alternative conceptual schemes, in some respect untranslatable into each other, and that alternative and rival conceptions of rationality are at home in different conceptual schemes. Unlike Rorty, I believe that there are strong and substantive conceptions of truth and rational justification – Aristotelian and Thomistic conceptions – that remain unscathed by his critique of epistemological foundationalism. From Gadamer I have learned a great deal about intellectual and moral tradition. I am very close to all in Gadamer that comes from Aristotle; that which comes from Heidegger I reject. I think that Heidegger was not at all in error when he discerned a close relationship between his own views and the philosophical politics of National Socialism. Although Lukács's critique of Heidegger was deformed by the crudities of his conformity to Stalinism, in his central contentions he was right.

Q Then even in this you assume a Marxist voice.

A An Aristotelian critique of contemporary society has to recognize that the costs of economic development are generally paid by those least able to afford them; the benefits are appropriated in a way that has no regard to one's merits. At the same time, large-scale politics has become barren. Attempts to reform the political systems of modernity from within are always transformed into collaborations with them. Attempts to overthrow them always degenerate into terrorism or quasi terrorism. What is not thus barren is the politics involved in constructing and sustaining small-scale local communities, at the level of the family, the neighborhood, the workplace, the parish, the school, or clinic, communities within which the needs of the hungry and the homeless can be met. I am not a communitarian. I do not believe in ideals or forms of community as a nostrum for contemporary social ills. I give my political loyalty to no program.

Q Some critics suspect that your more recent philosophical positions conceal a reassertion of Christianity, that they are a new version of Catholic theology. Is there a basis of truth in all this?

A It is false, both biographically and with respect to the structure of my beliefs. What I now believe philosophically I came to believe very largely before I reacknowledged the truth of Catholic Christianity. And I was only able to respond to the teachings of the Church because I had already learned from Aristotelianism both the nature of the mistakes involved in my earlier rejection of Christianity, and how to understand aright the relation of philosophical argument to theological inquiry. My philosophy, like that of many other Aristotelians, is theistic; but it is as secular in its content as any other.

Q Your training and intellectual growth, as well as your present philosophical views seem to be solidly anchored in a European hinterland, tied to the age-old traditions and values of the Continent. Your love for classicism, your 'hermeneutical' approach to tradition, your experience of the old Celtic oral tradition handed down for hundreds of generations: what do those things have to do with the 'impermeability' and the postmodernism of this country? Has your American naturalization involved a rupture with the past?

A On the contrary, one of the great advantages of North America is that it is a place where different cultures meet and different histories intersect. It is the place where, in perspectives afforded by a variety of European pasts, of African and Asian pasts, and of course of native American ones, the conflicts between tradition and liberal modernity have had to be recognized as inescapable. The issues in moral philosophy that I am most concerned with necessarily have a kind of importance for the cultures of North America that they are not always accorded elsewhere. I have learned a good deal about the importance they have only because of living and working here.

An Interview for *Cogito*

Q   We usually begin with a biographical question, and perhaps this is
    especially appropriate in your case, since *After Virtue* is so concerned
    with ideas of a quest and of a narrative of a life. What would you
    emphasize in your own 'narrative'?

A   Any adequate narrative of my life would have to emphasize a radical
    change in it around 1971. Before then I had had a number of dispa-
    rate and sometimes conflicting sets of concerns and beliefs, and I was
    unable to move decisively towards any resolution either of the prob-
    lems internal to each particular set of concerns or beliefs or of those
    which arose from the tensions between them. Both in political phi-
    losophy and in political practice I had learned, from Marxism, how
    to identify the moral impoverishment and the ideological function of
    liberalism. I had also learned, partly from Marxism and partly from
    non-Marxist sociology and anthropology, that certain older types of
    teleogically ordered community were incompatible with the domi-
    nant economic and social forms of modernity. But I did not as yet
    know how to disengage what I had learned from the erroneous and
    distorting theoretical frameworks, Marxist or Durkheimian, in terms
    of which I had formulated what I had learned. The work which
    issued in *Secularization and Moral Change* had taught me that the
    moral presuppositions of liberal modernity, whether in its theory or
    in its social institutions, are inescapably hostile to Christianity and
    that all attempts to adapt Christianity to liberal modernity are bound
    to fail. But I did not as yet understand either the philosophical pre-
    suppositions of a biblical theism – bound up with the claim that this
    is a teleologically ordered universe – or the resources that the Catho-
    lic church has for sustaining its own form of life in antagonistic
    social environments. Consequently I then believed that the only ver-
    sions of Christianity in which it retained its theological and religious
    integrity, that of Kierkegaard, for example, or Karl Barth, were philo-
    sophically indefensible.
       In philosophy I had had to recognize very early that Frege and

Wittgenstein had transformed our conception of what is problematic. Although I thought that I had already appreciated the truth in Professor Anscombe's remark that investigations prompted by Frege's and Wittgenstein's questions 'are more akin to ancient than to more modern philosophy' (*An Introduction to Wittgenstein's Tractatus*, p. 13), I was only much later beginning to understand the extent to which the inadequacies of my reading of Aristotle, inadequacies brought home to me by subsequent reflection on what I had written about ancient ethics in *A Short History of Ethics*, arose from my failure to bring Aristotle's answers into relationship to modern questions and modern answers to Aristotle's *aporiai*.

Critical reflection on the *Short History* also provided a better focussed view of the difficulties involved in giving a philosophical account of evaluative and normative concepts and judgments which was genuinely informed by an understanding of the range and variety of moral differences between different cultural and social orders, an account which therefore does not confuse the idiosyncratic local moral idioms of modern liberal individualism with '*the*' language of moral evaluation.

The essays collected in *Against the Self-Images of the Age* brought this period to a close. I set out to rethink the problems of ethics in a systematic way, taking seriously for the first time the possibility that the history both of modern morality and of modern moral philosophy could only be written adequately from an Aristotelian point of view. In the same period, after 1971, I had occasion to rethink the problems of rational theology, taking seriously the possibility that the history of modern secularization can only be written adequately from the standpoint of Christian theism, rather than vice versa. It was not until quite some time after I had completed *After Virtue* that these two lines of enquiry finally coincided in a realization that it is from the standpoint of a Thomistic Aristotelianism which is also able to learn from modern philosophy – especially from Frege, Husserl, Wittgenstein and their critics – that the problems of philosophy, and more particularly of moral philosophy, can best be articulated. But already by 1977, when I began to write the final draft of *After Virtue*, I had identified in main outline the framework and central theses of my subsequent enquiries.

So my life as an academic philosopher falls into three parts. The twenty-two years from 1949, when I became a graduate student of philosophy at Manchester University, until 1971 were a period, as it now appears retrospectively, of heterogeneous, badly organized, sometimes fragmented and often frustrating and messy enquiries, from which nonetheless in the end I learned a lot. From 1971, shortly after I emigrated to the United States, until 1977 was an interim period of sometimes painfully self-critical reflection, strengthened by coming to critical terms with such very different perspectives on moral philosophy as those afforded by Davidson in one way and by Gadamer in quite another. From 1977 onwards I have been engaged in a single project to which *After Virtue, Whose Justice? Which Rationality?* and *Three Rival Versions of Moral Enquiry* are central, a project described by one of my colleagues as that of writing *An Interminably Long History of Ethics.*

Q   In fact, have you any plans to write an autobiography?

A   Answering the previous question has already stretched my autobiographical powers to their limit. To write a worthwhile autobiography you need either the wisdom of an Augustine or the shamelessness of a Rousseau or the confidence in one's own self-knowledge of a Collingwood. I fail in all three respects.

Q   *After Virtue* is also very much concerned with the idea of a 'tradition' and you tackled this again in the Gifford Lectures you gave at the University of Edinburgh in 1987–8 [published as *Three Rival Versions of Moral Enquiry*]. Why is it so important?

A   The concept of 'tradition' has at least three different kinds of importance. Concepts are embodied in and draw their lives from forms of social practice. To understand how a particular concept is used it has to be located in terms of the activities and norms of some form of established practice. But any practice of any importance has a history. Practices come to be, are sustained and transformed, and sometimes perish as parts of the histories of particular societies. Within such societies the normative and evaluative modes of judgment and action which inform both activity within practices and attitudes to practices have to be handed on from one generation to another. And one aspect of the social embodiment of concepts is their transmission in this way. So to abstract any type of concept, but notably moral concepts, from the contexts of the traditions which they inform and through which they are transmitted is to risk damaging misunderstandings.

Secondly, a shared ability to ask and answer together such questions as 'What is our common inheritance from our common past?', 'What should we have learned from our shared experience to value in it?' and 'What in it is open to criticism and requires remaking?' is one prerequisite for the kind of social life in which the rational discussion of both ends and means, by its continuing elaboration and reformulation of some conception of a common good, provides an alternative both to the mindless conservatism of hierarchies of established power and to fragmentation through the conflicts of group interests and individual preferences, defined without reference to a common good.

Thirdly, rational enquiry is itself always tradition-dependent. The best established theories – those which it is rational to accept – in contemporary natural science are not worthy of acceptance because they conform to some timeless set of canons for scientific theories, positivist or otherwise. Rather they are worthy of acceptance because of their superiority to their immediate predecessors, in respect of providing resources for the solution of certain types of problem and remedying certain types of incoherence, in the light of some particular conception of what it would be to perfect theory in this or that area. And those predecessors in turn were related, although not in precisely the same ways, to their predecessors, and so on. The vindication of contemporary natural science turns out to be the history of that science, the retrospectively constructed history of a prospectively oriented tradition of enquiry, within which the development of the standards by which incoherence and resourcelessness are judged itself has a history. Of course traditions of rational enquiry may, like other traditions, be disrupted or fail or be displaced in various ways, as I believe the Aristotelian tradition of the virtues was.

Q   In the course of the Gifford Lectures you asked if the modern revival of Thomism had resulted in 'too many Thomisms'. How can we distinguish controversy within a tradition from confusion and disputes not rooted in any tradition?

A   Any tradition depends for its survival on retaining shared beliefs and practices sufficient for identifying common ends and for making and recognizing progress towards achieving those ends. Where there is not agreement in such identification and recognition, there may of course be forms of *ad hoc* cooperation, intellectual, social or whatever, derived from longer or shorter term coincidence of interests, but the necessary conditions for the survival, let alone the flourishing of a tradition will be absent. But when I raised the question 'Too many Thomisms?' about the multiplicity of standpoints within Neo-Thomism, it was not because I believed that in its case these necessary conditions were lacking. What afflicted Neo-Thomism was much more mundane: too many different tasks were imposed upon it in too short a time. So at a very early stage in the Thomistic revival, Thomists were called upon to enter into a variety of philosophical and theological conflicts with different opposing views, while at the same time devising systems of instruction for a number of very different types of institution and student; yet the reappropriation of Aquinas's work was itself still at a relatively early stage. So different and rival perspectives appeared all too soon. And it may be that in order for Thomism to recover adequately from these afflictions it had to go out of fashion for a time, so that what has proved to be a continually deepening scholarly understanding of Aquinas could be dissociated

from a variety of distorting educational tasks and polemical engagements. What has survived as a result of this respite is recognizably a
tradition which is in its own terms flourishing.

Q   Both in *After Virtue* and in the Gifford Lectures one of your main
    complaints about modern secular liberal ethics seems to be that it
    does not constitute a tradition. But in *Whose Justice? Which Ration-
    ality?* you discuss the transformation of liberalism into a 'tradition'.
    Can you clear this up?

A   We need to distinguish the culture of liberal individualist modernity
    at large from liberalism as a changing body of theory, expressing the
    practice of a set of theorists who have handed on, while reformulat-
    ing, the doctrines of liberalism from the eighteenth century to the
    present. There has of course always been a close, if complex, rela-
    tionship between these two, but they are not the same. Earlier liberal
    thinkers were avowed enemies of tradition. In 1865 Sidgwick de-
    clared to Oscar Browning, 'History will have in the future less and
    less influence on Politics in the most advanced countries. Principles
    will soon be everything and tradition nothing, except as regards its
    influence on the form.' This earlier liberal theorizing was the expres-
    sion of modes of social, political and economic practice which in
    what Sidgwick called 'the most advanced countries' often enough
    dissolved tradition and deprived many ordinary people of its possi-
    bilities. But at the same time liberalism as theory embodied itself in a
    continuing and now often dominant tradition of enquiry, and recent
    liberal thinkers have to some degree recognized this. So there is no
    basic incompatibility between the account of the anti-traditional
    character of liberal culture in *After Virtue* and in my Gifford Lectures
    and the account of the development and nature of the liberal intellec-
    tual tradition as a tradition in *Whose Justice? Which Rationality?* But
    I would have done better to make clear the relationship between
    these.

Q   In your work you very much weave philosophy, sociology, history
    and literature together. Indeed, another of your basic complaints
    about modern ethics seems to be that it is so relentlessly abstract, as
    if philosophy can declare its independence from the world and get to
    and from first principles in a realm of pure, universal reason. But if
    there is a liberalism, that you criticize, of this highly rationalist, Kantian
    kind, do you not tend to overlook (like modern 'rationalists') a lib-
    eral tradition in which philosophy, sociology and history are inter-
    woven? As, for example, in the Scottish Enlightenment, or in the
    work of Montesquieu, Tocqueville, Durkheim.

A   The problem with trying to combine a sociological understanding of modernity with liberalism is that what the modern world has realized are the worst fears of the Scottish Enlightenment rather than its best hopes. What we confront in advanced societies is the conjunction of an excluded and dependent cultural proletariat with a set of overlapping élites who control the presentation of political choice, the manipulation of economic organization, the legal structures and the flow of information. Instead of that ever widening educated public of the democratic intellect, who were the intended beneficiaries of those who understood the distinctive merits of the Scottish universities in the eighteenth and nineteenth centuries – George Elder Davie has written their history in *The Democratic Intellect* and *The Crisis of the Democratic Intellect*, two books which should be compulsory reading for every newly appointed university teacher in Britain – we have the mass semiliteracy of television audiences.

Adam Ferguson and Adam Smith both had their apprehensions about the moral effects of modern social and economic modes. Both also thought, however, that there were stronger grounds for optimism than for pessimism. But their pessimism – limited in Smith's case, less limited in Ferguson's – has turned out to be foresight.

Q   You argue that philosophical and ethical enquiry must be within a tradition. Many worry that this is a receipt for relativism, and you devote the last three chapters of *Whose Justice? Which Rationality?* to explaining why it is not. Is it possible for you to sum up here what is so wrong with relativism and why your view of philosophical and ethical inquiry does not lead to it?

A   Those who impute relativism to me have, I suspect, both misunderstood my position and misunderstood relativism. Let me begin with the latter. The mistake in many versions of relativism is to take the argument one or two steps beyond what the relativist needs to make her or his crucial point. That crucial point is that there exist a number of culturally embodied systems of thought and action, each with its own standards of practical reasoning and evaluation. Some of these are such that not only do their adherents arrive at evaluative and normative conclusions which are incompatible with those of the adherents of some other such systems, but their standards of reasoning are such that from the standpoint of each contending party the reasoning of the other must be judged unsound. The relativist then further observes that in relation to some of these rival contending systems the system of thought and action which she or he espouses is in no different a position. It is up to this point that I agree with the relativist. Where then do I disagree?

Relativists universally proceed one stage in the argument beyond this and characteristically two stages. In neither do I accompany them. The first stage is that of supposing that somehow or other these conclusions about the multiplicity of concrete modes of reasoning and of modes of justification for evaluative and normative conclusions provide grounds for putting in question and altering one's view of the justification of one's own reasoning and conclusions. The second is that of supposing that the same considerations should lead to a rejection of the claims of any substantive conception of truth. Neither of these stages in the relativist argument is justified and it is of course only by having pursued the argument to this unwarranted point that the relativist lays her or himself open to those types of self-referential refutation which have so often been deployed against relativism.

Q   There are so many other questions we could ask about your work, whether relatively detailed and concerning, e.g., your interesting idea of a practice, or more general and concerning, e.g., your contribution to the revival of Aristotle and 'virtue ethics'. Can you offer a question of your own and answer it?

A   The question which is perhaps the most important that you could put to me is that of how the concept of a practice must be further developed, if it is to be as philosophically fruitful as I hope that it may be. In *After Virtue* I provided a general characterization of practices and I gestured towards some examples. But a great deal more needs to be said, more particularly in order to throw light on how evaluative concepts and normative concepts have application. Consider how, within the context of at least certain types of practice, shared standards of success and failure make the application of such concepts relatively unproblematic, as, for example, among the crews of a fishing fleet. Their standards of success and failure are set by shared goals: to secure a large enough catch between spring and fall to ensure a reasonable income for the whole year; not to overfish the accessible fishing grounds, so as to deprive themselves of their livelihood; not to lose their lives or their boats or their nets; to be able by doing these things to sustain the lives of their families.

Two kinds of shared achievement provide the goods internal to this type of practice: that which belongs to the attainment of excellence in the cooperative activity of fishing, the excellence or lack of it of each crew member in playing her or his part contributing to the excellence or lack of it of the whole crew, and that which belongs to the excellence attained in sustaining the lives of the households from which the crew members came and to which they return. The range of uses of 'good' and cognate expressions will be intelligible in terms of the structures of activity of the crew and the household. To be good at this or that aspect of the tasks of fishing requires skills whose utility depend on qualities of character and mind in those who use them, qualities which generally and characteristically enable their possessor, by doing what is required of them on the right occasions, to achieve the goods of both crew and household, for the sake of which all else is done. So 'good at', 'good for', the virtue words, the expressions which appraise performance of duty, and 'good for its own sake' are at once socially and semantically ordered. And the next philosophical task is to spell out these related orderings.

When 'good' and its cognates are used intelligibly outside the context of particular practices, it is a presupposition of their use – an Aristotelian presupposition – that human societies as wholes are ordered as practices, wholes of which particular practices, such as fishing or philosophy or cricket, are constituent parts. And here again the ordering of the uses of 'good', as these are socially and semantically structured, is a philosophically urgent task. When by contrast 'good' and its cognates are abstracted from any such context, either theoretically or practically, characteristically in social orders in which practice-based relationships have been marginalized, so that the use of such expressions has to change, they inevitably degenerate into what appear to some as no more than generalized expressions of approval, voicing either what we feel or what we want to feel, and to others as naming peculiar properties, perhaps in virtue of some relationship of supervenience. So philosophical controversies between moral realists and moral antirealists are themselves perhaps symptomatic of a particular type of social condition.

To have understood this, of course, is no more than to have learned how to go back to the beginning in enquiries about good and 'good'.

Q Cogito has a special interest in the development of philosophy teaching in schools. American schools seem, in this matter, to be much further forward than those in the United Kingdom. Do you think there is a strong case to be made for teaching philosophy in schools? How would you state it?

A Introducing philosophy into schools will certainly do no more harm than has been done by introducing sociology or economics or other subjects with which the curriculum has been burdened. But what we need in schools are fewer subjects not more, so that far greater depth can be acquired. And philosophical depth depends in key part on having learned a great deal in other disciplines. What *every* child needs is a lot of history and a lot of mathematics, including both the calculus and statistics, some experimental physics and observational astronomy, a reading knowledge of Greek, sufficient to read Homer or the New Testament, and if English-speaking, a speaking knowledge of a modern language other than English, and great quantities of English literature, especially Shakespeare. Time also has to be there for music and art. Philosophy should only be introduced at the undergraduate level. And then at least one philosophy course and, more adequately two, should be required of every undergraduate. Of course an education of this kind would require a major shift in our resources and priorities, and, if successful, it would produce in our students habits of mind which would unfit them for the contemporary world. But to unfit our students for the contemporary world ought in any case to be one of our educational aims.

Q   When, perhaps in rare moments, you are away from philosophy, which books do you read? Could you tell us of some books that have been/are of importance to you?

A   It is not always as easy as one might think to tell the difference between when in one's reading one is reading philosophy and when one is not. So I leave out the clearly borderline cases, such as Dante, Jane Austen, Dostoievski, Kafka and Borges, including only among books that I have read every twenty years or so: *Redgauntlet*, *Women in Love*, *To the Lighthouse*, among books that I have read more often: *Ulysses*, *Finnegan's Wake*, Flann O'Brien's *At-Swim-Two-Birds*, short stories by Flannery O'Connor, Peter Taylor and Máirtín O'Cadhain: among books without which I might well not have lasted out the last twenty years: Saichi Maruya's *Singular Rebellion*, Randal Jarrell's *Pictures from an Institution*, Robertson Davies's *Rebel Angels*, Patrick McGinley's *Bogmail*; among what I hope still to be reading twenty years from now: *The Táin Bó Cuailnge*, Eileen O'Connell's lament for Art O'Leary, Akhmatova's 'Poem without a Hero', the poetry of George Campbell Hay, Sorley Mac-Lean, Iain Crichton Smith and Mairtín O'Direáin; and of course a perpetual low-life diet of Raymond Chandler, Philip K. Dick, etc., etc., although perhaps reading *them* is still reading philosophy.

Guide to Further Reading

The only notable bibliography of MacIntyre's work is Peter Nicholson's scrupulously edited 'Selected Bibliography of the Publications of Alasdair MacIntyre', in John Horton and Susan Mendus, eds, *After MacIntyre: Critical Perspectives on the Work of Alasdair MacIntyre* (Polity and Notre Dame, 1994), which includes almost everything published until early 1992 that is of continuing importance. *After MacIntyre*, some of the constituent essays of which I refer to below, is, for other reasons also, the most important book yet published on MacIntyre, not the least of those reasons being the incisiveness of MacIntyre's reply to its other contributors.

Thomas D'Andrea's *Alasdair MacIntyre: Tradition, Rationality, and Virtue* (Polity, 1999) is likely to illuminate the relation between MacIntyre's early and recent work, especially regarding its theological aspects. The only other book on MacIntyre in English is Peter McMylor's digressive *Alasdair MacIntyre: Critic of Modernity* (Routledge, 1994), which can be recommended for its discussion of some sociological issues arising from MacIntyre's work up until *After Virtue*. Those who can read Danish will doubtless benefit from Knud Lyngø-Thomsen's brief *MacIntyre's syn på Ideernes Historier* (Forlaget Ciris, 1996). Maria Matteini's *MacIntyre e la Rifondazione dell'Etica* (Città Nuova Editrice, 1995) comprises a synopsis of *After Virtue* and of criticisms of it by others. Her conclusion, that MacIntyre should be more consistent in pursuing a subject-centred ethics of virtue and abandon his sociological and political concerns, draws heavily on the work of Giuseppe Abbà. Abbà's latest essay on MacIntyre, in which he additionally argues that MacIntyre does not adequately appreciate the difference between Aquinas's early and later work, is a contribution to a volume of *Studi Perugini* (no. 3, 1997) devoted to MacIntyre's work. The original English script of MacIntyre's contribution to that volume is printed above as 'Politics, Philosophy and the Common Good'.

Please note the following abbreviations: CUP, for Cambridge University Press; Notre Dame, for University of Notre Dame Press; OUP, for Oxford University (Clarendon) Press; SUNY, for State University of New York Press; *TRVME*, for *Three Rival Versions of Moral Enquiry: Encyclopaedia, Genealogy, and Tradition*; UP, for University Press; *WJWR*, for *Whose Justice? Which Rationality?*

MacIntyre's early work and its critics

MacIntyre's first published work of note was *Marxism: An Interpretation* (SCM Press, 1953), later revised as *Marxism and Christianity* (Duckworth and Schocken Books, 1968; Notre Dame, 1984). The introduction to its latest edition (Duckworth, 1995) summarizes its 'central thesis' that Marxism, as 'a transformation of Hegel's secularized version of Christian theology, has many of the characteristics of a Christian heresy' and is 'a doctrine with the same metaphysical and moral scope as Christianity'. This introduction also casts considerable light on MacIntyre's recent return to Christian orthodoxy and to Marx's critique of capitalism.

Most of MacIntyre's publications over the following few years are now of less interest than are either this first book or 'Notes from the Moral Wilderness'. Responses to the latter by Harry Hanson (reprinted in A. H. Hanson, *Planning and the Politicians and Other Essays*, Routledge, 1969) and Mervyn Jones were published in the *New Reasoner* (no. 9, 1959), E. P. Thompson commending it in 'An Open Letter to Leszek Kolakowski' (in R. Miliband and J. Saville, eds, *The Socialist Register 1973*, Merlin Press, 1974; reprinted in E. P. Thompson, *The Poverty of Theory and Other Essays*, Merlin Press, 1978). Another influential paper, 'Breaking the Chains of Reason', was published in that focal document of the British New Left, E. P. Thompson, ed., *Out of Apathy* (Stevens, 1960). MacIntyre collected most of his other early essays that are of lasting interest, together with some previously unpublished ones, in *Against the Self-Images of the Age: Essays on Ideology and Philosophy* (Duckworth and Schocken Books, 1971; Notre Dame, 1978), a book that remains widely respected for the cogency of its arguments. In the essays in the first half of the book MacIntyre argued that an age that imagines itself as having ended ideology is mistaken and that its main ideologies – liberalism, Christianity, psychoanalysis, Marxism – are incoherent because unaware of their own particularity. In the essays in the second half he argued against doctrines of analytical philosophy.

Also much noticed in the 1960s were MacIntyre's criticisms of Peter Winch's Wittgensteinian and anthropologically informed relativism. MacIntyre's contributions to this debate are 'A Mistake about Causality in Social Science' (in P. Laslett and W. G. Runciman eds, *Philosophy, Politics and Society*, Blackwell, 1962), 'Is Understanding Religion Compatible with Believing?' (in J. Hick, ed., *Faith and the Philosophers*, Macmillan, 1964) and 'The Idea of a Social Science', which is reprinted in *Against the Self-Images of the Age*. Winch's replies are reprinted in his *Ethics and Action* (Routledge, 1972). In addition to the intrinsic value of the arguments articulated, MacIntyre's shifting position is of continuing interest because it evinces how he began to grapple with the problem of relativism. His last shot at Winch is 'The Form of the Good, Tradition and Enquiry' (in R. Gaita, ed., *Value and Understanding*, Routledge,

1990), in which he claims philosophical continuity between Plato and Aristotle in response to Winch's review of *After Virtue* (*Times Higher Education Supplement*, 18 Sept. 1981; Winch reviewed *WJWR* in *Philosophical Investigations*, 15, 1992). MacIntyre has re-engaged Wittgenstein in 'Colors, Culture, and Practices' (*Midwest Studies in Philosophy*, 17, 1992).

MacIntyre authored several books between the late 1950s and his move to the United States in 1970. In his controversial *The Unconscious: A Conceptual Analysis* (Routledge and Humanities Press, 1958; Thoemmes Press, 1997) he defends Freud against some charges while denying that the concept of the unconscious can be explanatory. He edited *Hume's Ethical Writings* (Collier-Macmillan, 1965; Notre Dame, 1979) when still sympathetic to their author. For critical discussions of his attempted co-optation of Hume to his project by means of an interpretation of Hume's *Treatise* that he was later to revoke, see W. D. Hudson, ed., *The Is-Ought Question* (Macmillan 1969) or V. C. Chappell, ed., *Hume: A Collection of Critical Essays* (Doubleday, 1966; Macmillan and Notre Dame, 1968) and, with regard also to MacIntyre's later work, Murray MacBeth, '"Is" and "Ought" in Context' (*Hume Studies*, 17, 1992). MacIntyre also edited *Hegel: A Collection of Critical Essays*, which includes his own well-regarded discussion of Hegel's anti-scientism, 'Hegel on Faces and Skulls' (Doubleday, 1972; Notre Dame, 1976). *A Short History of Ethics* (Macmillan, 1966, and Routledge, 1967; 2nd edn, Routledge, 1997, and Notre Dame, 1998) remains a widely used and cited text because of the perspicacity and historical sensitivity with which it treats all of the major Western ethicists, especially the Greeks, less so the medieval Christians. More intemperate is *Marcuse* (Collins, 1970; as *Herbert Marcuse: An Exposition and a Polemic*, Viking, 1970), MacIntyre's only substantial engagement with the Frankfurt School.

MacIntyre and Antony Flew co-edited the influential *New Essays in Philosophical Theology* (SCM Press, 1955), which applied the methods of analytical philosophy to religion. (MacIntyre subsequently engaged Flew in 'Determinism' in *Mind*, 66, 1957, to which both Flew and M. C. Bradley responded in *Mind*, 68, 1959). The way in which MacIntyre applied those methods in his own contribution, 'Visions', and in *Difficulties in Christian Belief* (SCM Press and Philosophical Library, 1959) points to his subsequent abandonment of Christianity. 'The Logical Status of Religious Belief', his contribution to *Metaphysical Beliefs: Three Essays* (SCM Press, 1957; 2nd edn, SCM Press and Schocken Books, 1970), attracted much critical attention, most notably that of Basil Mitchell in 'The Justification of Religious Belief' (*Philosophical Quarterly*, 11, 1961) and most recently that of Claire Disbrey in *Innovation and Tradition in Religion* (Avebury, 1994). In *Secularization and Moral Change* (OUP, 1967) MacIntyre argued that attempts to combine theology and liberalism are necessarily incoherent. In 'The Debate about God: Victorian Relevance and Contemporary Irrelevance' (his half of A. MacIntyre and P. Ricoeur, *The*

Religious Significance of Atheism, Columbia UP, 1969), he reversed some of the judgments in his 1959 book, proposing that the decline of Christianity was caused by the decline of unquestioning adherence to moral rules which, in turn, was caused by the decline of traditional social practices.

Dorothy Emmet, who had supervised MacIntyre's famous MA dissertation ('The Significance of Moral Judgments', University of Manchester, 1951), later co-edited *Sociological Theory and Philosophical Analysis* with him (Macmillan, 1970). More recently again she has reviewed *WJWR* (*Government and Opposition*, 24, 1989) and written of MacIntyre in *Philosophers and Friends* (Macmillan, 1996). More vivid but less illuminating are the reminiscences of Timothy O'Hagan ('Searching for Ancestors', *Radical Philosophy*, 54, 1990). It is apparent from an interview conducted immediately before MacIntyre's move to the US (reprinted in Bryan Magee, ed., *Modern British Philosophy*, Secker & Warburg, 1971; Paladin, 1973) how far he still had to go in thinking through the problem of relativism. More significant and recent interviews may be found in *Kinesis* (20, 1994, reprinted in 23, 1996, and in a forthcoming book of *Kinesis* interviews) and in *Deutsche Zeitschrift für Philosophie* (44, 1996; first published in Russian).

In the US MacIntyre was at first less prolific than previously, although the development of his arguments about rationality, incommensurability and history can be easily traced. 'The Essential Contestability of Some Social Concepts' (*Ethics*, 84, 1973) was systematic but unoriginal, as was 'Causality and History' (in J. Manninen and R. Tuomela, eds, *Essays on Explanation and Understanding*, Reidel, 1976, with a reply by von Wright) which attacked the Humean conception of science in a way redolent of much anti-positivist polemic from the period. 'Objectivity in Morality and Objectivity in Science' (in H. T. Engelhardt and D. Callahan, eds, *Morals, Science and Sociality*, Hastings Centre, 1978, with a Polanyian response by Marjorie Grene) and the much-reprinted 'Epistemological Crises, Dramatic Narrative and the Philosophy of Science' (*The Monist*, 60, 1977) went considerably further by tackling Kuhn's arguments.

After Virtue

The publication of *After Virtue* in 1981 (Duckworth and Notre Dame) propelled MacIntyre into the thick of academic controversy. *Inquiry* was the first journal to carry a symposium on the book, with MacIntyre responding to Stephen R. L. Clark on Moore, Raimond Gaita on teleology, Onora O'Neill on Kant, (26, 1983; O'Neill's paper is reprinted with a postscript in her *Constructions of Reason*, CUP, 1989) and Marx Wartofsky on Marxism (27, 1984). The debate in English in the German journal *Analyse & Kritik* that is introduced by 'The Claims of *After Virtue*' (reprinted above) has MacIntyre responding ('Rights, Practices and

Marxism', 7, 1985) to critiques by Richard E. Flathman, Alan Gewirth, David Miller, Annette Baier (6, 1984; Baier's contribution is reprinted in her *Postures of the Mind*, Methuen and University of Minnesota Press, 1985, which includes a second essay discussing Aristotle, Hume and MacIntyre), Gerald Doppelt and Kai Nielsen (7, 1985). MacIntyre had already taken issue with Richard Rorty's *Philosophy and the Mirror of Nature* in a symposium in *Analyse & Kritik* (4, 1982; Rorty responded in 6, 1984), in 'Philosophy, "Other" Disciplines and their Histories' (*Soundings*, 65, 1982), and elsewhere. In 'Philosophy: Past Conflict and Future Direction' (*Proceedings and Addresses of the American Philosophical Association*, 61, 1987) he playfully portrays Rorty as emblematic of contemporary philosophy's triviality and political impotence. Rorty's postmodernist bourgeois liberalism is defended against MacIntyre by Nielsen in two essays reprinted in his *After the Demise of the Tradition* (Westview, 1991). Nielsen had previously criticized MacIntyre on other grounds in 'Morality and God' (*Philosophical Quarterly*, 12, 1962) and 'Rationality, Intelligibility and Alasdair MacIntyre's Talk of God' (*Philosophical Forum*, 5, 1974), and still continues to engage with MacIntyre in elaborating his own secular pragmatism.

J. B. Schneewind engaged *After Virtue* in the *Journal of Philosophy* (79, 1982, with MacIntyre's response) and *Midwest Studies in Philosophy* (8, 1983). Benjamin Barber revises his review in his *The Conquest of Politics* (Princeton UP, 1988), Fred R. Dallmayr's is reprinted in his *Critical Encounters* (Notre Dame, 1987), and J. M. Cameron's (*New York Review of Books*, 5 Nov. 1981) is entirely appreciative. Of those critiques that focus upon the weaknesses of MacIntyre's attempt to elaborate a purely social logic for a teleological ethics, the most comprehensive is that by Lyle Downing and Robert Thigpen (*Social Theory and Practice*, 10, 1984). Significant responses to MacIntyre's critique of emotivism are advanced by D. Z. Phillips (*Mind*, 93, 1984), Bruce N. Waller (*Erkenntnis*, 25, 1986) and Nicholas Unwin (*Ratio*, NS, 3, 1990), in addition to some of the reviews that MacIntyre responds to in the 'Postscript to the Second Edition' of *After Virtue*. Also notable from this period of intense philosophical infighting is MacIntyre's critique of Bernard Williams's *Moral Luck*, 'The Magic in the Pronoun "My"' (*Ethics*, 94, 1983), and exchanges in *Synthèse* (53, 1982) over the history of ideas of practical rationality. The latter includes responses by Gerald Dworkin and Harry Frankfurt to 'How Moral Agents Became Ghosts: Or Why the History of Ethics Diverged from that of the Philosophy of Mind', in which MacIntyre criticizes Hume's account of the passions and its influence, and also MacIntyre's response to a paper by Frankfurt. More recently, Arne Johan Vetlesen has contended that MacIntyre misses the significance of emotions for ethics (*Perception, Empathy, and Judgment*, Pennsylvania State UP, 1994).

The only significant confrontation of *After Virtue* with Weber is in Richard Wellen's *Dilemmas in Liberal Democratic Thought since Max Weber* (Peter Lang, 1996). Fredric Jameson's review of *After Virtue* (*So-*

cial Text, 8, 1983) notes the book's proximity to Marxism whereas Peter Sedgwick's review emphasizes MacIntyre's increasing distance from it (in M. Eve and D. Musson, eds, *The Socialist Register 1982*, Merlin Press, 1982). Beginning with Donald N. Levine's review of *After Virtue* (*American Journal of Sociology*, 89, 1983), sociologists have almost uniformly preferred to compare MacIntyre with Durkheim. For some of MacIntyre's own thoughts on Durkheim see 'Positivism, Sociology, and Practical Reasoning: Notes on Durkheim's *Suicide*', (in A. Donagan et al., eds, *Human Nature and Natural Knowledge*, Reidel, 1986). Randolph Feezell expands, slightly, upon MacIntyre's discussion of practices in 'Sport, Character, and Virtue', *Philosophy Today*, 33, 1989). More significantly, John O'Neill develops MacIntyre's juxtaposition of goods internal and external to practices into a distinction between authority internal and external to practices in making an Aristotelian case for green politics (*Ecology, Policy and Politics*, Routledge, 1993). Russell Keat employs MacIntyre's distinction between practices and institutions in arguing for limitations on the scope of markets (*On Market Boundaries and Human Well-Being*, Macmillan, 1998). David Miller demonstrates considerable understanding of the political significance of MacIntyre's idea of practices, most recently in *After MacIntyre*. So too do Elizabeth Frazer and Nicola Lacey, there and elsewhere. Andrew Mason (who writes on incommensurability in *After MacIntyre*) goes further by beginning to tackle the significance of MacIntyre's idea of institutions for his idea of practices in 'MacIntyre on Modernity and How It Has Marginalized the Virtues', in R. Crisp, ed., *How Should One Live?* (OUP, 1996). *How Should One Live?* also includes notable essays by Lawrence Blum, illustrating MacIntyre's idea of the communal underpinnings of virtue, and a liberal feminist critique of MacIntyre's virtue ethics by Susan Moller Okin, which is more incisive but less thoroughgoing than that in her *Justice, Gender, and the Family* (Basic Books, 1989). Okin commends John Exdell's 'Ethics, Ideology, and Feminine Virtue' (in M. Hanen and K. Nielsen, eds, *Science, Morality and Feminist Theory*, *Canadian Journal of Philosophy* supp. vol., 1987) even though this builds upon MacIntyre's idea of practices. Annette C. Baier's *Moral Prejudices* (Harvard UP, 1994) is notable for her ruminations over whether MacIntyre should be granted the status of 'honorary woman' for the anti-Kantianism he shares with Carol Gilligan. Sharon M. Meagher would probably affirm that he should, judging from her 'Histories, Herstories and Moral Traditions' (*Social Theory and Practice*, 16, 1990).

MacIntyre's use of the concept of narrative in *After Virtue* has attracted much attention. Postmodernists now commonly argue that narration plays an important part in all sorts of human reasoning but *After Virtue* was one of the first works in English to articulate this approach. For a perceptive critique of MacIntyre's claims for narrative see Gerald L. Bruns, 'Literature and the Limits of Moral Philosophy' (in L. Toker, ed., *Commitment in Reflection*, Garland, 1994). Tobin Siebers exculpates

MacIntyre from romantic 'Don Quixotism' (*Morals and Stories*, Columbia UP, 1992), while Michael Bell finds more for MacIntyre in Quixotism than romance ('How Primordial Is Narrative?', in C. Nash, ed., *Narrative in Culture*, Routledge, 1990). Less literary and more theological are the critiques of MacIntyre's advocacy of narrative by Paul Nelson (*Narrative and Morality*, Pennsylvania State UP, 1987) and L. Gregory Jones ('Alasdair MacIntyre on Narrative, Community, and the Moral Life', *Modern Theology*, 4, 1987), the latter juxtaposing narrative to friendship within the 'alternative community' of the Church, the former criticizing MacIntyre's narrative ethics as overly involved with an Aristotelian idea of community. Xavier O. Monasterio commends *After Virtue*'s substitution of narrative for epistemology ('On MacIntyre, Rationality and Dramatic Space', *Proceedings of the American Catholic Philosophical Association*, 58, 1984) while Susan Feldman is just one of those who thinks it warrants the familiar charge of relativism ('Objectivity, Pluralism and Relativism', *Southern Journal of Philosophy*, 24, 1986).

The influence of *After Virtue*'s use of narrative continues even though MacIntyre has since moved on, having adopted a robust metaphysics that includes an Augustinian conception of the will and a Thomist conception of truth. He again deployed the concept of narrative in criticizing analytic philosophies of mind and action in 'The Intelligibility of Action' (in J. Margolis et al., eds, *Rationality, Relativism and the Human Sciences*, Martinus Nijhoff, 1986), in which he develops themes from his earlier 'Purpose and Intelligent Action' (*Aristotelian Society Supplement*, 34, 1960) in the light of his developed social theory, and especially in 'Can One Be Unintelligible to Oneself?' (in C. McKnight and M. Stchedroff, eds, *Philosophy in its Variety*, Queen's University of Belfast, 1987). In 'Post-Skinner and Post-Freud: Philosophical Causes of Scientific Disagreements' (in H. T. Engelhardt and A. L. Caplan, eds, *Scientific Controversies*, CUP, 1987) MacIntyre returns to his early critique of the weakness of psychology's philosophical foundations in what is also a critique of the limitations of contemporary philosophy. Further thoughts on selfhood may be found in chapter 9 of *TRVME*, in which MacIntyre criticizes what comes close to being a Nietzschean account of practical rationality, in 'Individual and Social Morality in Japan and the United States: Rival Conceptions of the Self' (*Philosophy East and West*, 40, 1990), and two reviews: 'Persons and Human Beings' (*Arion*, 3rd series, 1, 1991) and 'Miller's Foucault, Foucault's Foucault' (*Salmagundi*, 97, 1993). It is sometimes asserted anachronistically that MacIntyre's arguments rest on little more than an appeal to and an employment of narrative, the most ostentatious of such critics being Louis A. Ruprecht Jr (*Afterwords*, SUNY, 1996). See 'The Claims of *After Virtue*' (above) for MacIntyre's analytical, non-narrative summary of the argument of *After Virtue*.

Among MacIntyre's recent criticisms of modern moral culture are 'Moral Dilemmas' (*Philosophy and Phenomenological Research*, 50 (supplement), 1990), *How to Seem Virtuous without Actually Being So* (Centre for the

Study of Cultural Values, Lancaster University, 1991), 'What Has *Not Happened in Moral Philosophy'* (*Yale Journal of Criticism*, 5, 1992), 'Truthfulness, Lies, and Moral Philosophers: What Can We Learn from Mill and Kant?' (*The Tanner Lectures on Human Values*, 16, 1995), in which he expresses an unprecedented sympathy for Kant, and the introduction that he co-authored with Hans Fink to Knud Ejler Løgstrup's *The Ethical Demand* (Notre Dame, 1997). Other versions of virtue ethics are paraded in Roger Crisp and Michael Slote's reader, which begins quite properly with Elizabeth Anscombe's seminal 'Modern Moral Philosophy' (*Virtue Ethics,* OUP, 1997).

Whose rationality? Which application?

Many of MacIntyre's publications and academic engagements in the 1970s had dealt with issues conventionally considered to lie within the province of applied ethics. Of these, 'Toward a Theory of Medical Fallibility', written with Samuel Gorovitz and reprinted in the *Journal of Medicine and Philosophy* (1, 1976) which thereafter contains a string of responses, and 'How Virtues Become Vices: Medicine and Society', which Gorovitz himself criticized (both in H. T. Engelhardt and S. F. Spicker, eds, *Evaluation and Explanation in the Biomedical Sciences*, Reidel, 1975), together with others about the roles of doctors, patients and the elderly, were to prove among the most controversial. MacIntyre's definitive essay on the subject, entitled (after Prichard) 'Does Applied Ethics Rest on a Mistake?' (*The Monist*, 67, 1984), contends that it is mistaken to think of ethics as something that ought to be theorized in abstraction from practice and then imposed upon practitioners as generalized rules to the exclusion of their own practical judgment. This argument has not prevented many of those working in various well-funded areas of applied ethics from grinding their axes upon *After Virtue*. They usually do so in the eclectic spirit that is engendered by the fragmentary nature of contemporary ethical and academic discourse but that is alien to MacIntyre's Aristotelian project. Abstracting pieces of MacIntyre's argument from the whole has apparently enabled partisans of applied ethics to extend the scope of their subject in a way rationalized by, for example, Donald Scherer ('The Human Quest for the Good Life', *International Journal of Applied Philosophy*, 2, 1984). The most considerable contributions are the few that engage with MacIntyre's substantive arguments (e.g. Edmund B. Lambeth, 'Waiting for a New St Benedict: Alasdair MacIntyre and the Theory and Practice of Journalism', reprinted in *Business and Professional Ethics Journal*, 9, 1990), not the many that borrow whimsically from him. One notably unusual application is that by Ian R. Boyd in 'What are the Clergy For?' (*Theology*, 98, 1995).

The most paradoxical attempts to apply MacIntyre's account of ethics must be those that do so to corporate management (e.g. Iain L. Mangham,

'MacIntyre and the Manager' and commentators in 'Symposium: The Manager and Morality', *Organization*, 2, 1995; Charles M. Horvath, 'Excellence v. Effectiveness', *Business Ethics Quarterly*, 5, 1995), given MacIntyre's affirmative answer to the question posed in 'Corporate Modernity and Moral Judgment: Are They Mutually Exclusive?' (in K. E. Goodpaster and K. M. Sayre, eds, *Ethics and Problems of the 21st Century*, Notre Dame, 1979). Reputedly, when asked why he declined an invitation to address a conference on business ethics, MacIntyre replied that it was for the same reason that he wouldn't attend a conference on astrology. In 'Utilitarianism and Cost-Benefit Analysis: An Essay on the Relevance of Moral Philosophy to Bureaucratic Theory' (in K. M. Sayre, ed., *Values in the Electric Power Industry*, Notre Dame, 1977) he uses arguments about the incommensurability of goods to expose the presuppositions of managerial rationality. Notable defences of managerial rationality against MacIntyre's criticisms are Paul Santilli's 'Moral Fictions and Scientific Management' (*Journal of Business Ethics*, 3, 1984) and Kathryn Balstad Brewer's 'Management as a Practice' (*Journal of Business Ethics*, 16, 1997).

Education is one area where MacIntyre hopes his philosophical arguments may be applied, even if workers now seldom acquire practical wisdom through apprenticeships and, as he notes in 'The Idea of an Educated Public' (in G. Haydon, ed., *Education and Values: The Richard Peters Lectures*, Institute of Education, 1987), university curricula no longer give philosophy the centrality it enjoyed in the Scottish Enlightenment. Kenneth Wain's critique ('MacIntyre and the Idea of an Educated Public',*Studies in Philosophy and Education*, 14, 1995), which draws on those in *Journal of Philosophy of Education* by Walter Feinberg (25, 1991) and Susan Mendus (26, 1992), is the best informed about the development of MacIntyre's arguments about education. John and Patricia White develop a conception of education upon bases provided by *After Virtue* and defend it against rival liberal and Nietzschean views ('Education, Liberalism and Human Good', in D. E. Cooper, ed., *Education, Values and Mind: Essays for R. S. Peters*, Routledge, 1986). That education is a practice in MacIntyre's sense is also argued by Joseph Dunne in *Partnership and the Benefits of Learning* edited by Pádraig Hogan (Educational Studies Association of Ireland, 1995), who elaborates his own historically and philosophically erudite account of Western education in *The Custody and Courtship of Experience* (Columba Press, 1995). Dunne's excellent *Back to the Rough Ground* (Notre Dame, 2nd edn, with a foreword by MacIntyre, 1998) argues against the promotion of technique by contemporary educationalists and explores the idea of practical judgment in Newman, Collingwood, Arendt and, especially, Habermas and Gadamer, before moving on to Aristotle. MacIntyre arrays arguments about the mutual importance of philosophy and of plain persons' practical reasoning, and about academic philosophers' disregard of this importance, in 'Are Philosophical Problems Insoluble? The Relevance of System and

History' (in P. Cook, ed., *Philosophical Imagination and Cultural Memory*, Duke UP, 1993).

The only notable symposium on *Whose Justice? Which Rationality?* (Duckworth and Notre Dame, 1988) was that in *Philosophy and Phenomenological Research* (introduced by the précis reprinted above), in which MacIntyre engaged with Norman O. Dahl on practical rationality, Alicia Juarrero Roque on tradition and, again, Schneewind on tradition and Baier on Hume (51, 1991). The best-known review is by the would-be liberal Aristotelian Martha Nussbaum (*New York Review of Books*, 7 Dec. 1989). Equally spirited but less misleading is Brian Barry's defence of liberalism (*Ethics*, 100, 1989).

Before *WJWR* MacIntyre elaborated what I have called his metatheory in 'The Relationship of Philosophy to its Past' (in R. Rorty et al., eds, *Philosophy in History*, CUP, 1984), which carried on from his 1970s essays on philosophy of science, and in 'Relativism, Power and Philosophy' (*Proceedings and Addresses of the American Philosophical Association*, 59, 1985), in which he first set out his argument about translation, provoking a prescriptivist attack by R. M. Hare in 'A *Reductio Ad Absurdum* of Descriptivism' (in S. G. Shanker, ed., *Philosophy in Britain Today*, SUNY, 1986) and a very different assault by Glenn W. Erickson, who delves into pagan Irish history in making his case for a non-linguistic relativism ('O Som Do Machado No Bosque Sagrado', *Diálogos*, 24, 1989; text in English). David B. Wong, who had already devoted a chapter of *Moral Relativity* (University of California Press, 1984) to *After Virtue* in making his own case for moral relativism, again deals with the subject in reviewing *WJWR* (*Philosophical Books*, 31, 1990), while E. J. Bond presents undergraduates with an ill-conceived account of MacIntyre as a 'sophisticated cultural relativist' (*Ethics and Human Well-Being*, Blackwell, 1996).

Celtic patriotism is evident in 'The Idea of an Educated Public' (see above), 'Poetry as Political Philosophy: Notes on Burke and Yeats' (in V. Bell and L. Lerner, eds, *On Modern Poetry*, Vanderbilt UP, 1988) and *WJWR*. Although MacIntyre's academic life has been lived exclusively in England and the US his work is clearly influenced by his Scottish upbringing. It has been placed in the context of Scotland's remarkable intellectual culture by Craig Beveridge and Ronald Turnbull in *The Eclipse of Scottish Culture* (Polygon, 1989) and *Scotland after Enlightenment* (Polygon, 1997) and by Andrew Lockhart Walker in *The Revival of the Democratic Intellect* (Polygon, 1994). MacIntyre's patriotism is towards a way of life that celebrates practical wisdom and not toward any nation-state. His famous 1984 lecture 'Is Patriotism a Virtue?' (reprinted in e.g. R. Beiner, ed., *Theorizing Citizenship*, SUNY, 1995) has often been misrepresented due to apparent difficulties in acknowledging that he simultaneously endorses liberals' and communitarians' criticisms of each other, which he does in exposing the incoherence in claims for states' legitimacy that depend upon both patriotic identification and procedural impartiality. MacIntyre gives a transcultural rendering of his metatheory in 'Incommensurability, Truth, and the Conversation between Confucians and Aristotelians about the Virtues' (in E. Deutsch, ed., *Culture and Modernity*, University of Hawaii Press, 1991; for a complementary comparison see Lee H. Yearley's *Mencius and Aquinas*, SUNY, 1990) and has taken a number of small opportunities to criticize philosophical imperialism (in numerous reviews, starting with that of Mehta's *Beyond Marxism* in *Political Theory*, 11, 1983, and in encyclopaedia entries), hoping to establish debate with non-Thomistic forms of Aristotelianism and with other philosophical traditions that similarly articulate practical reasoning and pursue truth within other cultures. Even within the West, MacIntyre sides with cultural and other minorities who are excluded, or exclude themselves, from the dominant culture. As the first language of his grandparents was Gaelic, it is likely that a part of his motivation for doing so issues from his own background of cultural oppression.

MacIntyre's most important single work since *WJWR* is *Three Rival Versions of Moral Enquiry* (Duckworth and Notre Dame, 1990), which remains as widely available as the former because it further develops many of the former's arguments and adds ones against Nietzscheanism and modern universities. Also published in 1990 was an important exploration of Thomism and truthfulness, 'The Privatization of Good' (*Review of Politics*, 52, and since reprinted), his inaugural lecture at the University of Notre Dame. As originally published, this lecture is followed by a brief engagement with colleagues at the Catholic university, at which MacIntyre was to stay for only six years until moving with his wife, the historian of philosophy Lynn S. Joy, to Duke University. This move, from something like the sort of partisan institution that he had called for in *TRVME*, does not, though, signal any lesser partisanship on his own part. He has identified the present political implications of Thomism in 'Söphrosunë: How a Virtue Can Become Socially Disruptive' (*Midwest Studies in Philosophy*, 13, 1988) and in his 1994 Agnes Cuming Lectures, one of which has been published as 'Natural Law as Subversive: The Case of Aquinas' (*Journal of Medieval and Early Modern Studies*, 26, 1996). The two best known essays in which MacIntyre has combined faith and reason since his return to Christianity in the early 1980s are 'Which God Ought We to Obey and Why?' (*Faith and Philosophy*, 3, 1986) and 'How Can We Learn What *Veritatis Splendor* Has to Teach?' In the latter MacIntyre applauds Pope John Paul II's rigorous reiteration of the exceptionless negative precepts of the natural law (*The Thomist*, 58, 1994). Those unfamiliar with this encyclical on the moral life may care to consult the text and commentaries in J. Wilkins, ed., *Understanding Veritatis Splendor* (SPCK, 1994). In another essay, 'Hume, Testimony to Miracles, the Order of Nature, and Jansenism' (in J. J. MacIntosh and H. A. Meynell, eds, *Faith, Scepticism and Personal Identity*, University of Calgary Press, 1994), MacIntyre returns to his early concern with the cognitive status of religious claims.

Theological commentary

Much of the best work on MacIntyre has recently been conducted by theologians, especially Thomists. Max L. Stackhouse's 'Alasdair MacIntyre' (*Religious Studies Review*, 18, 1992) provides a concise and insightful survey of MacIntyre's corpus. Alice Ramos suggests in 'Tradition as "Bearer of Reason" in Alasdair MacIntyre's Moral Inquiry' (C. L. Hancock and A. O. Simon, eds, *Freedom, Virtue, and the Common Good*, Notre Dame, 1995) that MacIntyre has long been following a Thomist trajectory. Thomas S. Hibbs has critically reviewed both *WJWR* (*The Modern Schoolman*, 68, 1991) and *TRVME* (*The Thomist*, 57, 1993). Like Hibbs, Michael P. Maxwell Jr's 'A Dialectical Encounter between MacIntyre and Lonergan on the Thomistic Understanding of Rationality' (*International Philosophical Quarterly*, 33, 1993) is concerned with stipulating how a perceived tension between philosophy and theology in MacIntyre's work might be resolved in favour of the latter. The most substantial critique of this type is, unsurprisingly, advanced by a Protestant, Franklin I. Gamwell, whose *The Divine Good* (HarperSan Francisco, 1990; Southern Methodist UP, 1996) attacks the 'empirical' or allegedly secular and social teleology basic to MacIntyre's project. Ronald M. Green compares the 'second-order theorizing' of Gamwell to that of *TRVME* while denying that MacIntyre has any first-order theory ('Recovering Moral Philosophy', *Journal of Religious Ethics*, 23, 1995; see also Gamwell, Barden and Green in 'Recovering Moral Philosophy: An Exchange', 24, 1996). Christopher J. Thompson's 'Benedict, Thomas, or Augustine?' (*The Thomist*, 59, 1995) urges MacIntyre further along the path of Augustine, while John Haldane's question 'MacIntyre's Thomist Revival: What Next?' elicits not an answer but a clarification from MacIntyre in *After MacIntyre*.

Those approaching Aquinas for the first time can benefit from one of several good anthologies and from Ralph McInerny's introductory texts. Daniel Westberg's *Right Practical Reason* (OUP, 1994) and Armand Maurer's Aquinas Lecture, *St Thomas and Historicity* (Marquette UP, 1979), both complement MacIntyre's understanding of Aquinas, an understanding that is criticized by Janet Coleman (in *After MacIntyre*) and Bonnie Kent ('Moral Provincialism', *Religious Studies*, 30, 1994; *Virtues of the Will*, Catholic University of America Press, 1995). MacIntyre's recent work is discussed within the context of the wider revival of Thomism and natural law in Anthony J. Lisska's peculiarly untheological *Aquinas's Theory of Natural Law* (OUP, 1996), reviewed by MacIntyre in *International Philosophical Quarterly* (37, 1997). Anyone who wants to contextualize MacIntyre's virtue ethics theologically should consult *The Christian Case for Virtue Ethics* by Joseph J. Kotva Jr (Georgetown UP, 1996). Briefer surveys are by James F. Keenan ('Virtue Ethics', *Thought*, 67, 1992), Russell Hittinger ('After MacIntyre', *International Philosophical Quarterly*, 29, 1989), whose review of *After Virtue* had already anticipated MacIntyre's move toward Augustinianism (*The New Scholasticism*, 56, 1982), and a number of others in D. W. Hudson and D. W. Moran, eds, *The Future of Thomism* (Notre Dame, 1992). Michael H. Robins, in a comparison that MacIntyre would welcome, detects the same circularity in the ethics of *After Virtue* as in those of Henry B. Veatch ('Veatch and MacIntyre on the Virtues', in R. Porreco, ed., *The Georgetown Symposium on Ethics*, UP of America, 1984). What might still be best described as Catholic personalism is defended against MacIntyre by David Hollenbach ('A Communitarian Reconstruction of Human Rights', in R. B. Douglass and D. Hollenbach, eds, *Catholicism and Liberalism*, CUP, 1994), and MacIntyre is judged similarly unhelpful by Robert P. George in his academic advocacy of natural law against liberal jurisprudence ('Moral Particularism, Thomism, and Traditions', *Review of Metaphysics*, 42, 1989).

Protestant engagements with MacIntyre include criticism of his pessimism by Cornel West ('Alasdair MacIntyre, Liberalism, and Socialism', in B. Grelle and D. A. Krueger, eds, *Christianity and Capitalism*, Center for the Scientific Study of Religion, 1985), who has since become more sympathetic to MacIntyre. In 'Alasdair MacIntyre on Reformation Ethics' (*Journal of Religious Ethics*, 13, 1985) Richard J. Mouw defends the Reformation against MacIntyre's claim, in both *A Short History of Ethics* and *After Virtue*, that it is culpable for the disorder of modern morality. Mouw later accommodates this defence into his impressive exploration of the persistence of Calvinist individualism and divine command ethics as an alternative to emotivism, *The God Who Commands* (Notre Dame, 1990). Fergus Kerr criticizes MacIntyre's Thomist abandonment of the idea of tragic dilemmas ('Moral Theology After MacIntyre', *Studies in Christian Ethics*, 8, 1995). Bruce W. Ballard defends MacIntyre's critique of *Either/Or* against one of Kierkegaard's many defenders ('MacIntyre and the Limits of Kierkegaardian Rationality', *Faith and Philosophy*, 12, 1995). Barry Arnold uses *After Virtue* as the foundation for an idiosyncratically Humean synthesis of psychology with ethics and of sociology with theology in *The Pursuit of Virtue* (Peter Lang, 1989). P. Mark Achtemeier finds affinities between MacIntyre's approach to epistemology and T. F. Torrance's Barthianism ('The Truth of Tradition', *Scottish Journal of Theology*, 47, 1994), a comparison complemented by Eugene F. Rogers Jr's *Thomas Aquinas and Karl Barth* (Notre Dame, 1995). Duncan B. Forrester allies MacIntyre with Barth and liberation theologians in calling upon the Church to opt for the poor (in e.g. *Beliefs, Values and Policies*, OUP, 1989). Raymond Plant directs a similar but attenuated call to the state in *Politics, Theology, and History* (CUP, forthcoming). Robin Gill attenuates MacIntyre's arguments in calling upon churches to opt for an ethics that is both communitarian and pluralist (in e.g. *Moral Communities*, University of Exeter Press, 1992). Whereas Heather O'Reilly-Meacock defends Kantian ideas of justice as grounds for interreligious dialogue ('Kantian Ethics and a Theory of Justice:

Reiman, Kaufman and MacIntyre', *Religious Studies*, 33, 1997), John V. Apczynski uses MacIntyre's account of rationality and rivalry in attacking Hick's liberal conception of such dialogue for being implicitly exclusionary ('John Hick's Theocentrism', *Modern Theology*, 8, 1992). Britain's Chief Rabbi, Jonathan Sacks, engages sympathetically with MacIntyre in enunciating the communitarian virtues of Judaic-liberal tradition (in e.g. *The Politics of Hope*, Cape 1997), as does Muhammad Legenhausen in perspicaciously reviewing *WJWR* and commending it to fellow Islamic opponents of liberalism (*Al-Tawhid*, 14, 1997; text in English).

MacIntyre co-edited *Revisions: Changing Perspectives in Moral Philosophy* (Notre Dame, 1983) with Stanley Hauerwas. This included an introductory essay by MacIntyre and a number of previously published essays with which the editors sympathize. It was published in Revisions: A Series of Books on Ethics which MacIntyre and Hauerwas established and still co-edit. Hauerwas, a Protestant advocate of the particularity of ecclesial community, has often adopted MacIntyre's arguments (not least regarding medical ethics; see above) in his own numerous and influential works, which are surveyed by Arne Rasmusson in *The Church as Polis* (Notre Dame, 1996). Hauerwas's *A Community of Character* is compared to *After Virtue* by both John D. Barbour ('The Virtues in a Pluralistic Context', *Journal of Religion*, 63, 1983) and E. Clinton Gardner (*Justice and Christian Ethics*, CUP, 1995). Hauerwas reviewed *After Virtue* with Paul J. Wadell (*The Thomist*, 46, 1982), who also follows MacIntyre's account of ethics in his own *Friendship and the Moral Life* (Notre Dame, 1989). Hauerwas's most recent and critical engagement with MacIntyre is in *Christians among the Virtues*, co-authored with Charles Pinches (Notre Dame, 1997), in which MacIntyre is criticized for maintaining a pagan, Aristotelian conception of the virtues. This criticism is inspired by John Milbank's uncompromising *Theology and Social Theory* (Blackwell, 1990). Milbank follows MacIntyre in unmasking liberal reason but breaks from MacIntyre in repudiating any form of secular social theory.

Liberal Christians are usually less well disposed to MacIntyre. Ian S. Markham subordinates Thomism to liberal pluralism, constructing his own historicist and postmodernist position out of arguments borrowed from Milbank and Jeffrey Stout, among others ('Faith and Reason', *Religious Studies*, 27, 1991; *Plurality and Christian Ethics*, CUP, 1994). Stout is one of MacIntyre's most penetrating critics, having followed a wide-ranging and sympathetic review of *After Virtue* ('Virtue among the Ruins', *Neue Zeitschrift für Systematische Theologie und Religionsphilosophie*, 26, 1984; MacIntyre responds in the 'Postscript to the Second Edition') with a review of *WJWR* ('Homeward Bound', *Journal of Religion*, 69, 1989) in which he cuttingly turned the polemical tools fashioned by MacIntyre in dissecting Marcuse back upon their author. Stout's first book, *The Flight from Authority* (Notre Dame, 1981, initiating the Revisions series), presents a substantial account of the development of modern Western ethics. Stout here draws on MacIntyre but argues that Jansenism blocks any return to Thomistic ethics and that the Enlightenment finds historical bases, and sufficient justification, in the necessity of toleration evinced by the European wars of religion. Even more influential has been the selective use of MacIntyre's arguments that Stout makes in his well-respected *Ethics after Babel* (James Clarke and Beacon Press, 1988). Stephen E. Fowl uses Stout to combat MacIntyre's anti-liberalism in his incisive 'Could Horace Talk with the Hebrews?' and Peter J. Mehl adopts a Stoutian stance in comparing MacIntyre's account of rationality and tradition with that of Basil Mitchell in 'In the Twilight of Modernity' (both in *Journal of Religious Ethics*, 19, 1991). Conversely, Philip L. Quinn wields *TRVME* in dialectical combat with Stout's eclecticism in 'Religious Ethics after *Ethics after Babel*: MacIntyre's Tradition versus Stout's *Bricolage*', in S. T. Davis, ed., *Philosophy and Theological Discourse* (Macmillan and St Martin's Press, 1997).

Philosophy and Theological Discourse also contains suggestions by Linda Trinkaus Zagzebski and Nancey Murphy as to how MacIntyre's account of practices might inform theology and epistemology. Zagzebski's excellent *Virtues of the Mind* (CUP, 1996) might well be thought to complement what could be described as MacIntyre's own virtue epistemology. Murphy poses MacIntyre as the central figure in a postmodernism of a peculiarly non-relativist and non-Nietzschean kind in *Anglo-American Postmodernity* (Westview, 1997).

Jean Porter is more receptive to both MacIntyre and Aquinas than is Stout, although her judgment about the significance of MacIntyre is similar to his. In *The Recovery of Virtue* (Westminster John Knox Press, 1990; SPCK, 1994) she follows MacIntyre in juxtaposing Aquinas's ethical synthesis to contemporary ethical fragmentation. However, in her second book, *Moral Action and Christian Ethics* (CUP, 1995), she distances herself from MacIntyre's claims about the ethical significance of philosophical rivalry. This is consistent with her argument in 'Openness and Constraint' (*Journal of Religion*, 73, 1993) that MacIntyre is best understood not as a Thomist but as a pragmatist and a liberal.

Political commentary

The most widespread mischaracterization of MacIntyre is that of him as a member of a communitarian movement initiated by Michael Sandel, inspired by Hegel and led by Amitai Etzioni, a characterization that owes much to coincidence of timing and little to understanding of MacIntyre's own impetus and trajectory. The best of several textbook portrayals of MacIntyre as a communitarian is Stephen Mulhall and Adam Swift's *Liberals and Communitarians* (2nd edn, Blackwell, 1996; MacIntyre engages Mulhall in *After MacIntyre*). More superficial and polemical characterizations of MacIntyre as a communitarian cast him not just in the role of nostalgic reactionary (as in Ross Poole's *Morality and Modernity*, Routledge, 1991) but also as a potential totalitarian, then going on to charge 'communitarian critics of liberalism' with guilt by association (Derek L. Phillips, *Looking Backward*, Princeton UP, 1993; David Conway, *Classical Liberalism*, Macmillan and St Martin's Press, 1995; Stephen Holmes, *The Anatomy of Antiliberalism*, Harvard UP, 1993, this last being reviewed by MacIntyre in *Radical Philosophy*, 70, 1995). Of the innumerable survey articles on communitarianism, that which is best informed about MacIntyre, and yet still misleading, is Jeffrey Friedman's 'The Politics of Communitarianism' (*Critical Review*, 8, 1994). Stout compares *After Virtue* to the influential communitarian polemic *Habits of the Heart*, a comparison that Robert N. Bellah commends (both in *Soundings*, 69, 1986, republished as C. H. Reynolds and R. V. Norman, eds, *Community in America*, University of California Press, 1988). The central figure of philosophical communitarianism, Charles Taylor, who returns to the themes of the *New Reasoner* debate in 'Marxism and Socialist Humanism' (in Oxford University Socialist Discussion Group, ed., *Out of Apathy: Voices of the New Left Thirty Years On*, Verso, 1989), has responded to MacIntyre's 'Predictability and Explanation in the Social Sciences' (both in *Philosophic Exchange*, 1, 1972), written an extended appreciation of *After Virtue* (in M. Benedikt and R. Berger, eds, *Kritische Methode und Zukunft der Anthropologie*, Braümuller, 1985; text in English) and enlisted MacIntyre in his own critique of Kantianism (in R. Beiner and W. J. Booth, eds, *Kant and Political Philosophy*, Yale UP, 1993). Engagements between MacIntyre and Taylor have occurred over the latter's *Sources of the Self* (*Philosophy and Phenomenological Research*, 54, 1994) and in *After MacIntyre*, and MacIntyre has since critically reviewed books on and by Taylor (*Philosophical Quarterly*, 46, 1996, and 47, 1997). Communitarians may be among those who admire the intransigence of MacIntyre's Aristotelianism but they do not share the courage of his convictions, opting to strengthen rather than reject the institutions imposing order under capitalism.

Ronald Beiner ably rehearses the communitarian case for liberal practice against liberal theory in *What's the Matter with Liberalism?* (University of California Press, 1992). In doing so he rebuts the defence of liberal neutrality mounted by Charles E. Larmore in *Patterns of Moral Complexity* (CUP, 1987), which at least treats MacIntyre as an Aristotelian rather than a communitarian. Giovanni Giorgini, careful in his nomenclature, judges MacIntyre to be a liberal in 'Crick, Hampshire and MacIntyre, or Does an English Speaking Neo-Aristotelianism Exist?' (*Praxis International*, 9, 1989). Liberals who consider that attack is the best form of defence have recently written books arguing against MacIntyre that Aristotle was himself some sort sort of proto-liberal (Douglas B. Rasmussen and Douglas J. Den Uyl, Stephen G. Salkever, Bernard Yack, Fred D. Miller Jr, and others) or 'strong republican' (Ronald J. Terchek). Earlier, T. H. Irwin made the most authoritative of such claims

('Tradition and Reason in the History of Ethics', *Social Philosophy and Policy*, 7, 1989), perhaps provoking revisions by MacIntyre.

Idealist objections to the Aristotelianism of *After Virtue* were raised in *Ancient Philosophy* (3, 1983, alongside naturalistic objections raised by A. A. Long) by Arthur Madigan, who criticizes MacIntyre's acceptance of tragic conflict. A similarly Platonic engagement with *After Virtue* is J. K. Swindler's 'MacIntyre's Republic' (*The Thomist*, 54, 1990). MacIntyre is compared by Don MacNiven (in James Bradley, ed., *Philosophy after F. H. Bradley*, Thoemmes Press, 1996) to the Hegelian idealist F. H. Bradley, whom MacIntyre has compared with Edmund Pincoffs ('My Station and its Virtues', *Journal of Philosophical Research*, 19, 1994; to close a circle, MacIntyre is compared to Pincoffs by David Braybrooke and, ineptly, by T. K. Seung in *Social Theory and Practice*, 17, 1991). Oakeshottian critiques of MacIntyre's critique of ideology are advanced by D. H. Rashid (in D. J. Manning ed., *The Form of Ideology*, Allen & Unwin, 1980), and by Ian Adams in *The Logic of Political Belief* (Harvester Wheatsheaf, 1989). MacIntyre's critique of Vico's historicized Platonism ('Imaginative Universals and Historical Falsification: A Rejoinder to Professor Verene', *New Vico Studies*, 6, 1988) was answered paradoxically by John D. Schaeffer's attempted Vichian abduction of *WJWR* (*New Vico Studies*, 7, 1989). Gordon Graham has attempted a similar Hegelian abduction of MacIntyre's entire corpus in his contribution to *After MacIntyre* and his *The Shape of the Past* (OUP, 1997). Nevertheless, few go so far as does Ian Shapiro in accusing MacIntyre, a philosophical realist, of 'extreme philosophical idealism' (*Political Criticism*, University of California Press, 1990).

Hans-Georg Gadamer takes issue with *After Virtue* in identifying Aristotelian aspects of Kant and Kierkegaard and in emphasizing the significance of Aristotle's metaphysical grounding of ethics ('Ethos und Ethik', *Philosophische Rundschau*, 32, 1985). MacIntyre had earlier reviewed Gadamer's *Truth and Method* ('Contexts of Interpretation', *Boston University Journal*, 26, 1980) in a way that clarifies his proximity to much in Gadamer's philosophy. Although much in MacIntyre's treatment of tradition resembles Gadamer, MacIntyre's opposition of Aristotelianism to the Enlightenment sets him in opposition to Gadamer's own project and to its conservative implications. Those who would have it that MacIntyre is not only a conservative but a conservative of the increasingly fashionable postmodernist kind suggest that MacIntyre's affinities go beyond Gadamer to Heidegger, even though the latter is someone for whom MacIntyre seldom expresses anything but hostility. The most substantial comparison of MacIntyre and Gadamer is in P. Christopher Smith's Gadamerian *Hermeneutics and Human Finitude* (Fordham UP, 1991) but see also Georgia Warnke's *Justice and Interpretation* (Polity and MIT Press, 1992).

Those who pursue all-inclusive agreement sometimes approach MacIntyre as a challenging test-case. Richard J. Bernstein has been put off neither by MacIntyre's critical review of *Praxis and Action* (*Review of Metaphysics*, 25, 1972) nor by MacIntyre's clarificatory response to his own review of *After Virtue* (Bernstein, 'Nietzsche or Aristotle?', and MacIntyre, 'Bernstein's Distorting Mirrors', both in *Soundings*, 67, 1984; Bernstein's is reprinted in his *Philosophical Profiles*, Polity and University of Pennsylvania Press, 1986). Mark Kingwell's *A Civil Tongue* (Pennsylvania State UP, 1995) is the most notable of several attempts to co-opt a chastened MacIntyre to the Habermasian cause of revitalizing liberal reasoning through a theory of dialogic justice. Habermas engages MacIntyre in *Justification and Application* (Polity and MIT, 1993). Habermas is defended against MacIntyre by William Rehg ('Discourse Ethics and the Communitarian Critique of Neo-Kantianism', *Philosophical Quarterly*, 22, 1990), while others attempt to reconcile the two (John A. Doody, 'Recent Reconstructions of Political Philosophy', *Philosophy Today*, 28, 1984, and 'MacIntyre and Habermas on Practical Reason', *American Catholic Philosophical Quarterly*, 65, 1991; Michael Kelly, 'MacIntyre, Habermas, and Philosophical Ethics', *Philosophical Forum*, 21, 1989; Jon P. Gunnemann, 'Habermas and MacIntyre on Moral Learning', in H. Beckley, ed., *The Annual of the Society of Christian Ethics 1994*, Society of Christian Ethics, 1994; any future comparison should refer to what MacIntyre says about language in 'Truthfulness, Lies, and Moral Philosophers'; see above). Habermas's contrast of system and life-world is redolent of MacIntyre's juxtaposition of institutions to practices, although Habermas refuses to base what he opposes to instrumental rationality in anything more than communication. Even more alien to MacIntyre are Habermas's 'constitutional patriotism' and his Kantian contrast of morality with ethics. Both George R. Lucas Jr ('Agency After Virtue', *International Philosophical Quarterly*, 28, 1988) and Philip J. Ross (*De-privatizing Morality*, Avebury, 1994) attempt the ardous task of absorbing MacIntyre's critique of the Enlightenment Project into some form of neo-Kantianism. In contrast, William M. Sullivan's 'After Foundationalism' (in E. Simpson, ed., *Anti-foundationalism and Practical Reasoning*, Academic Printing & Publishing, 1987) typifies the equally mistaken but once widespread attempt to pose MacIntyre as a leading figure in an anti-cognitivist movement that would now be called postmodern. Jeffrey S. Turner's 'Socrates amidst the Academics?' (*Inquiry*, 34, 1991) and David M. Wagner's 'Alasdair MacIntyre' (in C. Wolfe and J. Hittinger, eds, *Liberalism at the Crossroads*, Rowman & Littlefield, 1994) are more reliable accounts of his project.

The most substantial Nietzschean critique of MacIntyre to date is that made by Dwight Furrow in *Against Theory* (Routledge, 1995). *Différance* is brandished at MacIntyre by William Corlett (*Community without Unity*, Duke UP, 1989) and by Barbara Herrnstein Smith (in D. Cornell et al., eds, *Deconstruction and the Possibility of Justice*, Routledge, 1992), among others. The Nietzschean criticism is basically the same as the pragmatist one advanced by Joseph Margolis (in e.g. *Life without Principles*, Blackwell,

1996), that MacIntyre incoherently attempts to combine a historicist critique of liberal ethics, which allegedly commits him to relativism, with an ahistorical faith in the truth of his own ethics. This line of criticism is also pursued by a couple of essays in *Philosophy and Social Criticism* (Gary Kitchen, 'Alasdair MacIntyre', 23, 1997; Mark Colby, 'Moral Traditions, MacIntyre and Historicist Practical Reason', 21, 1995; see also Colby, 'Narrativity and Ethical Relativism', *European Journal of Philosophy*, 3, 1995), whose editor, David M. Rasmussen, used it as the vehicle for his own singularly hostile review of *After Virtue* (9, 1982). The journal has also carried a more constructive piece by John Cleary ('The Modern Malaise', 10, 1984), a Habermasian indictment of MacIntyre for sharing Foucault's fault of 'total critique' (Roger Paden, 'Post-structuralism and Neo-romanticism or Is MacIntyre a Young Conservative?', 13, 1987) and, most recently, a hermeneutically based agreement with MacIntyre on the relation of tradition to reason (John W. Tate, 'Dead or Alive?', 23, 1997).

MacIntyre's idea of tradition is appropriated by an academically voguish analytical Marxism that does more than most to resist neo-classical economists' liberal conception of practical rationality in Michael Luntley's *The Meaning of Socialism* (Duckworth, 1989; Open Court, 1990). Marx's critique of alienation is related to the Aristotelian tradition in Nicholas Lobkowicz's exegetically excellent *Theory and Practice* (UP of America, 1967) and in many more recent works. Most notable among the latter are some elaborations of an Aristotelian economics: James Bernard Murphy, *The Moral Economy of Labour* (Yale UP, 1993), William J. Booth, *Households* (Cornell UP, 1993), and Scott Meikle, *Aristotle's Economic Thought* (OUP, 1995). MacIntyre's favoured account of the rise of capitalism is Karl Polanyi's classic *The Great Transformation* (still in print with Beacon Press, 1957). Suggestions by MacIntyre for further reading may be found above.

Bibliography

Referenced Works by MacIntyre

Marxism: An Interpretation, 1953, SCM Press.

The Unconscious: A Conceptual Analysis, Routledge & Kegan Paul and Humanities Press, 1958 (Thoemmes Press, 1997).

'On Not Misrepresenting Philosophy', *Universities and Left Review*, 4 (1958).

'The "New Left"', *Labour Review*, 4 (1959).

A Short History of Ethics: A History of Moral Philosophy from the Homeric Age to the Twentieth Century, Macmillan, 1966; Routledge, 1967 (2nd edn, Routledge, 1997; University of Notre Dame Press, 1998).

Secularization and Moral Change: The Riddell Memorial Lectures, Oxford University Press, 1967.

Against the Self-Images of the Age: Essays on Ideology and Philosophy, Duckworth and Schocken Books, 1971 (University of Notre Dame Press, 1978).

'Ideology, Social Science, and Revolution', *Comparative Politics*, 5 (1973).

'Moral Rationality, Tradition, and Aristotle: A Reply to Onora O'Neill, Raimond Gaita, and Stephen R. L. Clark', *Inquiry*, 26 (1983).

After Virtue: A Study in Moral Theory (1981), 2nd edn, University of Notre Dame Press, 1984; Duckworth, 1985.

'Relativism, Power, and Philosophy', in K. Baynes et al., eds, *After Philosophy: End or Transformation?*, MIT Press, 1987.

Whose Justice? Which Rationality?, University of Notre Dame Press and Duckworth, 1988.

Three Rival Versions of Moral Enquiry: Encyclopaedia, Genealogy, and Tradition, University of Notre Dame Press and Duckworth, 1990.

'The Privatization of Good: An Inaugural Lecture', *Review of Politics*, 52 (1990).

'What Has *Not* Happened in Moral Philosophy', *Yale Journal of Criticism*, 5 (1992).

Marxism and Christianity (1968; revision of *Marxism: An Interpretation*, 1953), 2nd edn, Duckworth, 1995.

'Natural Law as Subversive: The Case of Aquinas', *Journal of Medieval and Early Modern Studies*, 26 (1996).

Other Referenced Publications

Ackrill, J. L., 'Aristotle on *Eudaimonia*' (1974), in A. O. Rorty, ed, *Essays on Aristotle's Ethics*, University of California Press, 1980.

Adkins, W. H., *Merit and Responsibility*, Oxford University Press, 1960.

Anscombe, G. E. M., *An Introduction to Wittgenstein's Tractatus*, Hutchinson and Harper & Row, 1959.

Aron, Raymond, *Main Currents in Sociological Thought*, vol. 2, trans. Howard and Weaver, Penguin, 1970.

Audi, Robert, 'A Theory of Practical Reasoning', *American Philosophical Quarterly*, 19 (1982).

Barnes, Jonathan, 'Aristotle's Theory of Demonstration', in J. Barnes et al., eds, *Articles on Aristotle*, vol. 1, Duckworth, 1975.

Bittner, Egon, 'The Concept of Organization', *Social Research*, 32 (1965).

Blackburn, Simon, *Spreading the Word*, Oxford University Press, 1984.

Bourdieu, Pierre and Loïc J. D. Wacquant, *An Invitation to Reflexive Sociology*, Polity Press and Chicago University Press, 1992.

Brandom, Robert, 'Pragmatism, Phenomenalism, and Truth Talk', *Midwest Studies in Philosophy*, 12 (1988).

Burke, Edmund, *Reflections on the Revolution in France*, ed. C. C. O'Brien, Penguin, 1982.

Colletti, Lucio, 'Introduction', trans. Nairn, in *Karl Marx: Early Writings*, ed. Q. Hoare, Penguin and Vintage, 1975.

Crowe, M. B., *The Changing Profile of the Natural Law*, Martinus Nijhoff, 1977.

Davie, George Elder, *The Democratic Intellect*, Edinburgh University Press, 1961.

Davie, George Elder, *The Crisis of the Democratic Intellect*, Polygon Books, 1986.

Delbecq, André L., 'The Management of Decision-Making within the Firm', *Academy of Management Journal*, 10 (1967).

Deleuze, Gilles, 'Pensée nomade', *Nietzsche Aujourd'hui?*, 1 (1973).

Derrida, Jacques, *Of Grammatology*, trans. Spivak, Johns Hopkins University Press, 1976.

Destler, I. M., *Presidents, Bureaucrats and Foreign Policy*, Princeton University Press, 1972.

Dews, Peter, *Logics of Disintegration*, Verso, 1987.

Downs, Anthony, *Inside Bureaucracy*, Little, Brown, 1967.

Dummett, Michael, *Truth and Other Enigmas*, Harvard University Press, 1978.

Dummett, Michael, 'The Source of the Concept of Truth', in G. Boolos, ed., *Meaning and Method: Essays in Honor of Hilary Putnam*, Cambridge University Press, 1990.

Dummett, Michael, *The Logical Basis of Metaphysics*, Harvard University Press, 1991.

Galtung, Johan, *Theory and Methods of Social Research*, Columbia University Press, 1967.

Geach, Peter, 'Assertion', *Philosophical Review*, 74 (1965).

Geach, Peter, ' Verdad o Asserción Justificada?', *Anuario Filosófico*, 15 (1982).

Geertz, Clifford, 'The Impact of the Concept of Culture on the Concept of Man', in J. R. Platt, ed., *New Views of the Nature of Man*, University of Chicago Press, 1965.

Gilson, Étienne, *Thomist Realism and the Critique of Knowledge*, trans. Wauck, Ignatius Press, 1986.

Gould, Carol, *Marx's Social Ontology*, MIT Press, 1978.

Hanson, A. H., 'An Open Letter to Edward Thompson', *New Reasoner*, 2 (1957).

Hume, David, 'A Dissertation on the Passions', in *The Philosophical Works of David Hume*, vol. 4, ed. T. H. Green and T. H. Grose, Longmans, Green, 1882.

Irwin, T. H., *Aristotle's First Principles*, Oxford University Press, 1988.

Irwin, T. H., 'A Conflict in Aquinas', *Review of Metaphysics*, 14 (1990).

Jordan, Mark, *Ordering Wisdom*, University of Notre Dame Press, 1986.

Kline, George L., 'The Myth of Marx's Materialism', *Annals of Scholarship*, 3 (1984).

Knight, Kelvin, 'Revolutionary Aristotelianism', in I. Hampsher-Monk and J. Stanyer, eds, *Contemporary Political Studies 1996*, vol. 2, Political Studies Association of the United Kingdom, 1996.

Lewis, David, *Philosophical Papers*, vol. 1, Oxford University Press, 1983.

Macpherson, C. B., *Democratic Theory: Essays in Retrieval*, Oxford University Press, 1974.

MacRae, Donald G., *Weber*, Collins, 1974.

Newman, John Henry, *The Arians of the Fourth Century*, rev. edn, Longmans, Green, 1871.

Newman, John Henry, *An Essay on the Development of Christian Doctrine*, rev. edn, Longmans, Green, 1878.

Perrow, Charles, *Complex Organizations*, Scott, Foresman, 1972.

Porter, Roy, *English Society in the Eighteenth Century*, Penguin, 1982.

Putnam, Hilary, 'A Philosopher Looks at Quantum Mechanics', in R. G. Colodny, ed., *Beyond the Edge of Certainty*, Prentice Hall, 1965.

Putnam, Hilary, *Reason, Truth and History*, Cambridge University Press, 1981.

Putnam, Hilary, *Representation and Reality*, MIT Press, 1988.

Putnam, Hilary, *Realism with a Human Face*, ed. J. Conant, Harvard University Press, 1990.

Putnam, Hilary, *Renewing Philosophy*, Harvard University Press, 1992.

Rieff, Philip, *Fellow Teachers* (1973), Faber and Faber, 1975.

Rorty, Richard, *Contingency, Irony and Solidarity*, Cambridge University Press, 1989.

Simon, Herbert A., 'Causation', in D. L. Sills, ed., *International Encyclopedia of the Social Sciences*, vol. 2, Macmillan and Free Press, 1968.

Sorabji, Richard, *Necessity, Cause and Blame*, Duckworth and Cornell University Press, 1980.

Strawson, P. F., 'Truth', in *Logico-Linguistic Papers*, Methuen, 1971.

Thompson, E. P., *The Making of the English Working Class*, Victor Gollancz, 1963.

Tucker, Mary Evelyn, *Moral and Spiritual Cultivation in Japanese NeoConfucianism*, State University of New York Press, 1989.

Wartofsky, Marx W., *Feuerbach*, Cambridge University Press, 1977.

Wippel, John F., 'Truth in Thomas Aquinas', parts I and II, *Review of Metaphysics*, 43 (1989–90).

Wittgenstein, Ludwig, *Philosophical Investigations*, ed. G. E. M. Anscombe and R. Rhees, trans. Anscombe, 3rd edn, Blackwell, 1967.

Index